FORTRAN and the
ART of
PC PROGRAMMING

FORTRAN and the
ART of
PC PROGRAMMING

TIM WARD
Harrison-Ward Associates Ltd, UK

and

EDDIE BROMHEAD
Kingston Polytechnic, Kingston upon Thames, UK

JOHN WILEY & SONS
Chichester · New York · Brisbane · Toronto · Singapore

Wiley Editorial Offices

John Wiley & Sons Ltd, Baffins Lane, Chichester,
West Sussex, PO19 1UD, England

John Wiley & Sons, Inc., 605 Third Avenue,
New York, NY 10158–0012, USA

Jacaranda Wiley Ltd, G.P.O. Box 859, Brisbane,
Queensland 4001, Australia

John Wiley & Sons (Canada) Ltd, 22 Worcester Road,
Rexdale, Ontario M9W IL1, Canada

John Wiley & Sons (SEA) Pte Ltd, 37 Jalan Pemimpin #05–04,
Block B, Union Industrial Building, Singapore 2057

Library of Congress Cataloging-in-Publication Data:

Ward, Tim.
 FORTRAN and the art of PC programming / Tim Ward and Eddie Bromhead.
   p.   cm.
 Bibliography: p.
 Includes index
 ISBN 0 471 92253 6
 1. FORTRAN (Computer program language)   2. Microcomputers–
Programming.   I. Bromhead, Eddie.   II. Title.
QA76.73.F25W37   1989
005.13′3—dc20   89-31593
                                                                                CIP

British Library Cataloguing in Publication Data:

Ward, Tim
 FORTRAN and the art of PC programming.
 1. Computer systems. Programming languages : Fortran language
 I. Title   II. Bromhead, Eddie
 005.2′6

 ISBN 0 471 92253 6

Printed and bound in Great Britain by Courier International, Tiptree, Essex

CONTENTS

Disk set with manual

Price £25/$40 (including VAT, postage and packing)

The programs described in this book, together with the two utility libraries and the graphics library described in Chapter 15, plus example programs and manual, are available in source code on a disk set for your IBM PC (and most compatibles). They are written in FORTRAN and assembler code. and the assembler routines will also be supplied as object code libraries. You will need a FORTRAN compiler (the authors used Microsoft FORTRAN); the assembler code libraries will have been assembled using Microsoft's MACRO Assembler.

The disk set and manual are *only* available from the authors at the following address:

Tim Ward
Harrison-Ward Associates Ltd
14 St Georges Road
Farnham
Surrey GU9 8NB
UK
(Tel: (0252) 714055)

Cheques should be made payable to Harrison-Ward Associates Ltd. Don't forget to include your own address!

CHAPTER 1

WHY FORTRAN, WHY PCs?

1.1 WHY FORTRAN?

Traditionally, FORTRAN (FORmula TRANslation) has been *the* language for scientific and engineering software, and has been widely used in other fields. Other computer languages have had vogues, which have passed. These include languages of the same era as FORTRAN, such as ALGOL, which had a far richer syntax, and a better structure. FORTRAN has fended them all off. Even upstart languages of the 1970s and 1980s, such as Pascal and C, are still not used in the main for numeric applications. There are a number of reasons for this. Perhaps the most important is that FORTRAN was developed and supported by the giant computer company International Business Machines (George Backus, IBM, 1956), and so was available on all the most popular computers. Also FORTRAN's relatively primitive syntax, which translates easily and efficiently into the underlying machine language of the host computer, leads to high speed processing, an increasingly important component of any scientific language. Today, over 30 years after FORTRAN was developed, there is a huge investment in FORTRAN code and expertise. This, together with its slow but steady improvement, particularly in the areas in which the language has been traditionally weak—such as character handling—means that FORTRAN will be with us for some time to come. The persistence of FORTRAN has led to the implementation of the language on every mainframe and minicomputer of which we are aware, making FORTRAN source code extremely portable (although implementation specifics sometimes make this less easy than it should be).

Most major analysis systems in the technological arena have been written in FORTRAN because it is so portable and enduring, and because of its built-in mathematical and trigonometrical functionality. Typical of these are large finite element analysis systems. Many widely used systems started life in the mid to late 1960s. The majority of machines available in those days often lacked the memory or processing power of today's microcomputer, and only met the needs of small communities of users who were prepared to suffer a poor turn-round (i.e. slow and unresponsive) batch service, if for no better reason than because they had no choice.

Whether time sharing systems became available to match increases in computer power, or the reverse, FORTRAN users moved away from punched cards and line printer listings (usually in capitals only) to terminal based systems, with much less emphasis on hard copy. Tragically, the user was often faced with very little betterment in the resources made available to him, since multi-user systems require huge amounts of computer resource to be devoted to monitoring all the terminals for the odd keypress, and to scheduling the timeslice for each terminal, and comparatively little of the computer power was available immediately to each user.

1.2 WHY PCs?

The microcomputer, when it first appeared, left many FORTRAN users unimpressed. Often, the 64 kbytes maximum of the CP/M micro, which seemed astronomic in comparison to early 8 or 16 kbyte capacity machines, was still far too small to accommodate the data structures of the average FORTRAN program, and it is noteworthy that those few FORTRAN compilers which made headway in the 8-bit micro world concentrated on the larger, 128 kbyte bank switched machines.

The 16-bit micro changed all that forever. Here was a machine which had (potentially rather than actually at first) the capacity to run almost all applications. And it had processing power to match. Many users found, like the authors, that the combination of that amount of power, built-in graphics, and all for the price of a terminal, an irresistible temptation.

Early experiences were disappointing. The first version of any piece of software, however well tested, normally has a number of 'bugs', not even this knowledge prepared us for the unacceptable quality of the early FORTRAN compilers. This forced many FORTRAN programmers back to BASIC(s!) or to learn assembler or to abandon the microcomputer for ever. The graphics, the potential of which was well illustrated by demonstration software, was frustratingly intractable except to the most persistent computer hobbyist. The computer manuals were unintelligible to all but the person who wrote them (at least, we presume so, but with that degree of impenetrability?), and technical help was by and large non-existent. The only saving grace was that the software which had been developed on the 8-bit microcomputers quickly became available on the 16-bit machines.

Due to their immense potential, microcomputers were produced and bought in large quantities, and good but expensive software became available in increasing quantities. Today our early faith in microcomputers has been amply rewarded. There is almost too large a choice of top quality software some at ludicrously modest prices. Also, as it turned out, the microcomputers were, and still are, remarkably reliable. Even the FORTRAN compilers are now polished professional products with only a few idiosyncrasies reminding us of the earlier versions. Graphics is readily available through such products as GEM (Digital Research) and Windows (Microsoft) to both users and programmers alike, and the Microsoft disk operating system, with GEM or Windows, gives a powerful, and compared to most mainframe computers, accessible and user friendly interface.

Microprocessor power has increased in almost exponential proportions since those early days, with 32-bit processors in microcomputers becoming more affordable, making the distinction between microcomputers and minicomputers almost impossible to define. Part of the reason for this is that the prices of RAM (Random Access Memory) and mass storage devices (Winchester disks) have fallen dramatically. But the main reason is the popularity of the microcomputers themselves, which has allowed mass production with its resulting economies of scale, and at the same time has created a competitive market-place in which there is fierce price competition.

The most popular microcomputers are those which mimic the computers marketed by IBM. Copies abound, with the most notable being manufactured by Compaq, Dell, Tandon, and Amstrad. Although there are a number of Japanese manufacturers of microcomputer parts and whole computers, this is one area of the electronic market that they are yet to dominate. The reason is because the most popular microprocessors are still all made in America.

The only other microcomputers to have a sustained popularity are the Apple Macintosh range. These are built around a 32-bit chip from Motorola, and have an entirely different architecture. The strength of the Macintosh is in its user interface, and application tools for the programmer are not readily available. Although FORTRAN compilers are just beginning to appear on the Macintosh they are still in their infancy, and it is not yet a machine for the FORTRAN programmer.

The IBM microcomputers and compatibles, commonly known under the umbrella term PCs (Personal Computers), coined by IBM for their first microcomputer the IBM PC, use a Disk based Operating System called PC DOS or MS DOS. PC DOS is IBM's proprietary product developed under contract by Microsoft, which with IBM's contract has become one of the three largest software companies in the world. It is worth noting that the other two of these three companies specialize largely in software products for Microsoft's operation system. They are Ashton Tate (dBASE), and the Lotus Corporation (Lotus 1-2-3). MS DOS (Microsoft DOS) was also developed by Microsoft, and is as far as the user is concerned almost identical to PC DOS. Throughout the book we will refer to both these operating systems as DOS unless we wish to distinguish between the two.

As we shall see, DOS has one or two limitations, the most important of which is the restriction on the amount of memory that can be addressed, and the inability to run a number of processes at the same time. These limitations have become increasingly restrictive as the microprocessors have become more powerful. A new operating system was needed, and OS/2 (Operating System 2) is the result. However there are too many DOS users for it to be abandoned altogether, and OS/2 contains many of the familiar DOS commands. Software compatibility is also important, and the new system can emulate DOS. In addition, software is already being developed which will enable applications to be targeted to DOS or OS/2. The latest Microsoft FORTRAN compiler is available as an OS/2 product or a DOS product, with negligible differences in its use under either operating system.

At the time of writing, OS/2 is still in its infancy. This means that it will be some time before the operating system will be fully functional and boast as many applications as DOS—except for those which run under DOS too. Even then, there will still be a vast population of people running DOS on machines which cannot run OS/2. Version 4 of MS DOS has just been released, and so we do not believe that the lessons learnt under DOS will be wasted, rather, to make full use of new systems, additional information will be required, and new techniques will have to be learned.

1.3 WHY, THEN, THIS BOOK?

Purchasers of PCs bought with programming in mind are likely to run through a number of stages in their familiarization with the machine. These are:

- Period of enchantment
- Period of disenchantment
- Period of envy
- Period of utilization

The period of enchantment covers the time in which one unpacks the hardware, boots it up, runs a simple application, begins the process of transferring FORTRAN source (often it is simplest to retype a few small programs initially) to the PC, and then compiles and runs a simple application. Enchantment is still the name of the game when you find that all the FORTRAN code you ever wrote uses up negligible amounts of floppy disk space, and what you thought were quite large programs run easily. That tiny PC really is a useful computer!

The period of disenchantment begins when a fundamental limitation of your FORTRAN compiler comes to light. Or you cannot establish a communications link with the mainframe on which your code is stored. Or a floppy disk fault loses crucial files. Or you forgot that you used some system specific facility like a graphics library on the mainframe, and do not have the equivalent on the PC. Or quite simply you lack the range and quality of peripherals you had grown used to on the mainframe. Hopefully, this book will help you over some of the disenchantments.

The period of envy comes about when you have overcome many of the foregoing problems, and are using the PC in earnest. It is a simple phenomenon, brought on by using other software, not usually written in FORTRAN.

Many PCs offered some bundled software as a sales gimmick. Regardless of how useful it was, it inevitably had a polished appearance. On-line help, properly designed screen layouts, proper use of emboldened, underlined or inverse video text and so on. These had to be simple to program, as the resulting executable files were often small in length, especially compared to the smallest program (even one of the 'Hello World' variety) which could be generated from FORTRAN. It must be possible to program this sort of material, and the purpose of this book is to show how.

Envy is also experienced when reading the microcomputer press. Beware! The microcomputer press is full of tomorrow's products, even if they are available today, in many cases they will not work properly. Do not buy version 1 of *anything*! The astounding success enjoyed by the company Amstrad is founded on giving the customer a product that will be useful at an affordable price—often this is based on yesterday's technology (but manufactured by today's). There is very little innovation here.

The period of utilization comes with experience. Your FORTRAN programs compile and run, applications that you write have friendly user interfaces and exploit the graphical capabilities of your machine, you have mastered the printer and plotter, you fully exploit the power of your microcomputer and peripherals. There are no short cuts to this degree of experience, but with direction a lot of wasted time can be saved. We hope our book will show you the way, and be a companion in the hours of darkness when nothing seems to go right.

The reader of this book is probably a FORTRAN programmer of some years experience, embarking as we did, into unexplored areas with a new PC. He will know that his machine has the power and facilities to do almost everything he needs. He will, however, be frustrated at how unpolished and unprofessional his programs look in comparison to the user interfaces of inexpensive (often free) utilities. This book is an attempt to save him some of the slow learning process which we experienced. The rules are often simple, and with hindsight, glaringly obvious. Once one understands escape codes, for instance, much hitherto impenetrable computer jargon becomes instantly comprehensible (see Chapters 12 and 14). The contents of this book should make it possible for you too to do all (well, most) of these things in FORTRAN.

It was not our aim to convert the micro-wise to the merits of FORTRAN. The best computer language to use is always the one with which you are familiar.

Two things make the Eden of FORTRAN on a PC rather unidyllic. The first of these is the memory organization of the Intel chip family as used in simpler PCs. This poses a considerable challenge to the 'power user' who needs every facility he can lay his hands on, and which he has a right to expect in a megabyte address space. The second is the nonsensical 640 kbytes limit imposed by PC DOS, and hence for reasons of compatibility, on MS DOS. This has led to an industry in overcoming it. Some ideas appear in the book.

1.4 WHAT'S IN THE BOOK?

Each chapter in the book is designed to be self-contained, with a minimum of forward and backward references to other chapters.

Chapter 2 looks at 'Microcomputer Architecture' and the relatively simple 8086 Intel processor. A passing knowledge of how microprocessors compute will help us to understand more about the PC (whether it is based on the 8086 processor or not). It also introduces assembly language programming. FORTRAN programmers do not ordinarily want to write in assembler unless absolutely necessary, but it does give us one of the keys to unlocking the power of the PC. Assembly language routines are surprisingly simple to access from FORTRAN.

Chapter 3 is about the 'Disk Operating System'. All the power of the microcomputer is available through DOS if you know where to look.

In Chapter 4 we turn our attention to 'Programs, Files, and Filenames'. The chapter contains hints on editing and creating our FORTRAN programs, and the names we should give to them; we also consider the files that are created by our FORTRAN programs, and how and where programs and files are stored.

In the early days of microcomputing, FORTRAN compilers tended to be pretty crude, and the environment encountered by the FORTRAN programmer could be very different to the one he was used to on the mainframe computer. Current compilers are much more professionally presented, and less error prone. In Chapter 5 we look at 'Compiling, Linking, and Debugging' on the microcomputer.

A widely held misconception is that microcomputers store numbers to a lower precision than mini or mainframe computers and hence will not give accurate answers. In Chapter 6, 'Precision, Accuracy, and the Right Answer', we put the record straight.

Chapter 7 is about 'Readable and Maintainable Code'. Productivity is greatly enhanced if programs are written so that errors can be quickly spotted.

What about code already written on a mainframe, how can it be transferred to a PC? If code was developed on a PC how can it be sent to other systems? Having moved code or changed compilers what problems will be faced? And what about those old codes written in FORTRAN 66 (FORTRAN IV)? Will FORTRAN 8x have anything new to offer? These and other questions are posed and answered in Chapter 8, 'Code Transfer, and Portable Code'.

In Chapter 9, 'Invoking FORTRAN Programs and Other DOS Interfaces', the execution of the FORTRAN program is discussed, together with how to make use of the operating system commands from inside a FORTRAN program.

One of the differences between most microcomputers and mini and mainframe computers is that they usually have less core memory (RAM). This need not be a problem for all but the largest programs if you get into the habit of 'Using Memory Effectively', the subject of Chapter 10.

In Chapter 11 consideration is given to the problems associated with 'Coping with a Slow Computer' and aspects of code optimization.

One of the joys of FORTRAN programming on the microcomputer comes with the mastery of writing to the screen. In Chapter 12, 'Screen Handling: Text Modes', the ways that text can be manipulated on the screen are discussed; and in Chapter 13, 'Screen Handling: Graphics Modes', the principles involved in graphical output to the screen are considered.

The next problem is to obtain hard copy output of text and graphics. This is a common area of confusion and disappointment: extremely powerful printers can turn out to be next to useless, if your software does not drive them. Chapter 14 is full of tips for the FORTRAN programmer, and if you are yet to buy a printer or plotter, you should read this chapter, 'Printing and Plotting—The Hard Copy Jungle', first.

Storing tried and tested FORTRAN utilities in object code libraries is a must for all serious FORTRAN programmers. Libraries of FORTRAN utilities are also marketed commercially. In Chapter 15, 'FORTRAN Libraries and Utilities', we look at the use of libraries. This chapter also details the libraries of DOS, screen handling and graphics utilities that you will find on the accompanying disk set.

Finally, Chapter 16, 'Choosing a FORTRAN Compiler', takes a brief look at some of the compiler products available to the FORTRAN programmer on the microcomputer.

To accompany this book there is a disk set. It contains all the complete programs that appear in the text, plus screen driver software using ASCII codes, KERMIT the communications product (see Chapter 8), and any other useful assembler or FORTRAN subroutines and libraries that we think might be of use and lie in the public domain.

1.6 WHAT'S *NOT* IN THE BOOK?

This is not a book about FORTRAN programming. There are many good texts on the market, and to add another just for the sake of it would not be a productive use of precious time. In the bibliography, we list a number of such books, and we suggest that, as a serious FORTRAN programmer, you should have more than one of them on your bookshelf.

Nor is this a book about MS DOS, either from the user's or programmer's point of view. There are many books on both of those aspects. Again, we think you will want to have specialist books on these subjects.

Instead, this book is about the in-between area which it is so difficult to find out about. The jargon, for one thing, may well be comprehensible to trained programmers: much of it will certainly·be alien to the FORTRAN user. Not only that, but what information there is tends to be hidden away in the most unlikely corners.

1.7 WHAT YOU NEED

If you are yet to buy microcomputer equipment then this book contains a host of information which will be invaluable when you come to make your choice of PC and peripherals, and we hope it will save you a lot of money too.

To get the most out of this book and its contents, you will need access to a personal computer running MS DOS or PC DOS, a text editor capable of producing text files in 'non-document' or 'system' format, any one of the FORTRAN compilers listed in Chapter 16, and an assembler. We have successfully used WordStar, Microsoft FORTRAN, and the Microsoft Macro Assembler on a variety of machines. We have based our discussion of screen graphics around the graphics primitives and drivers provided in GEM, any GEM application contains the necessary environment and the subroutines in the text or on the accompanying disk will allow you to access these facilities (Digital Research's previous product GSX can also be accessed in the same way). A number of other graphics primitives products with bindings for most FORTRAN compilers exist, and the range of facilities provided does not vary a great deal from product to product. So the general points on graphics will still apply if you have one of these products, or indeed the Microsoft Windows ISV (independent software vendor's) tool-kit.

Hardcopy devices are more of a luxury: any dot matrix printer, an Epson compatible preferably, is on the border of necessity. If buying a plotter, get one which offers compatibility with the Hewlett Packard Graphics Language (HPGL).

Both of us have spent many years using FORTRAN, and over five years with our PCs. The book distils some of this experience. However, we cannot hope to know all there is to know, and in any case, the compilers on offer get more sophisticated and generally better as time goes on. This means that the reader will find errors, out-of-date allusions, and matters of opinion no longer tenable, among the more generally usable material in this book. We hope that our readers will write with their own comments and observations, which we will try to include in future editions of the book.

1.8 ANNOTATED BIBLIOGRAPHY

The FORTRAN programmer probably needs a full bookshelf. Since we do not set out to cover FORTRAN programming from first principles, one of the first books he will require is a text on the language. Depending on the level you start from, the choice is varied. For the beginner, there is plenty of choice, but for the 'expert', looking to improve, the number of books is much smaller. We start with the beginner.

All the books described below cover FORTRAN programming, which we do not in this book. This is by no means a complete list of FORTRAN 77 books on the market nor are these necessarily the best of them. However, we think there are some good books here. When assessing a FORTRAN book look particularly at the example programs presented in the text. Are they complete? Are they varied and interesting? Are there many of them?

The list is alphabetical by author.

FORTRAN 77 Fundamentals and Style
Walter S. Brainerd, Charles H. Goldberg, and, Jonathan L. Gross, 1985, Boyd & Fraser Publishing Company ISBN 0 87835 143 4
A large book aimed at the beginner. We did not find the programming examples very interesting, and we felt that the programming style was inconsistent, presumably depending on who wrote which section. After writing this book, we sympathize!

FORTRAN 77 for Engineers
G. J. Borse, 1985, PWS Publishers ISBN 0 534 04650 9
A nice book well presented, and full of problems from all engineering disciplines. The example programs are well commented. The book is clearly for people who need to use FORTRAN to solve 'real' problems, rather than those who merely wish to learn another language. Recommended.

Interactive FORTRAN 77 a Hands-on Approach
Ian Chivers and Malcolm Clark, 1984, Ellis Horwood Ltd. ISBN 0 85312 775 1
A well-written book from the Imperial College computing department. Has a very good index. Not enough complete program examples for a book offering 'a hands-on approach'!

A Structured Approach to FORTRAN Second Edition
J. Weston Crawley, and Charles E. Miller, 1987, 1983, Prentice Hall
ISBN 0 13 854183 3 025
A full (632 pages) and well-written book. Uses the same two or three programs throughout, developing them to cover the material in each of the chapters. A good reference text.

Structured FORTRAN 77 for Scientists and Engineers Second Edition
D. M. Etter, 1987, The Benjamin/Cummings Publishing Company Inc. ISBN 0 8053 2495 X
A very good reference text with interesting examples. This book is beautifully set out, and obviously a lot of time and thought has been put into the presentation of the material. The only disappointment is the sparsity of comments in the example programs. Recommended.

Problem Solving with FORTRAN 77
Brian D. Hahn, 1987, Edward Arnold Ltd. ISBN 0 7131 3592 1
Quite a nice FORTRAN book. The programming examples presented do not have many comments—although they may not be necessary for understanding the examples, they would encourage good programming habits!

Introduction to FORTRAN 77 and the Personal Computer
Robert H. Hammond, William B. Rogers, and John B. Crittenden, 1987, McGraw-Hill Inc. ISBN 0 07 100469 6
The book doesn't seem to address the problems and limitations of using FORTRAN 77 on the PC. There are few complete programming examples, and these tend to be mathematical and academic. The description of the PC is rudimentary.

FORTRAN 77 for Scientists and Engineers
J.N.P. Hume and R.C. Holt, 1985, Reston Pub. Co. Prentice Hall ISBN 0 8359 2065 8

An excellent book for learning to program. Lots of well-presented programming examples. Not a good reference book–it does not try to cover the complete FORTRAN language so you would need a reference text or your manual handy. Only one quibble, all the example programs are presented in lower case–this is not standard FORTRAN although most compilers probably will not mind! Recommended. (Not to be confused with the book of a similar name by Etter, another book worth looking at!)

Computing for Engineers and Scientists with FORTRAN 77
McCracken, 1984, John Wiley and Sons, Inc. ISBN 0 471 09701 2
A nice well-presented book with interesting example programs. McCracken is the doyen of FORTRAN authors, and most FORTRAN programmers probably owe something to him.

Principals of FORTRAN 77 Programming
Jerold L. Wagener, 1980, John Wiley and Sons, Inc. ISBN 0 471 04474 1
A good book, well-presented, interesting examples. Beware though the author uses shorthand 'do', 'repeat', and 'exit' which allow him to be lazy when presenting examples towards the end of the book, and which mean that these example programs will not work as written.

Now for the FORTRAN programmer who wants to develop his skills. There isn't a lot!

The Elements of FORTRAN style
Kreitzberg and Schneiderman, Harcourt Brace Jovanovich ISBN 0 15 522156 6
This is a small, expensive, and hard-to-obtain paperback which is written entirely in terms of FORTRAN 66. It is readable, and makes a number of contributions to the subject of readable code and efficient code that are still valid today.

Fortran Optimization
Michael Metcalf, 1985, Academic Press ISBN 0 12 492482 4
The book is addressed largely to programmers using large computer systems like those from CDC, Cray Research, and the mainframe side of IBM. It is detailed and thorough, and has much interesting material.

FORTRAN 8x Explained
Michael Metcalf and John Reid, Oxford University Press ISBN 0 19 853751 4
The Committee which decides FORTRAN standards has been hard at it almost since the day they saw FORTRAN 77 off their hands. There is a move afoot to radically change the language, and these authors have written up the draft of the proposed new standard as if it already existed. Many FORTRAN programmers will not recognize what they see, and may not like it even if they do. Well worth a read.

PC Portable FORTRAN
Malcolm W. Clark, Ellis Horwood ISBN 0 7458 0005 X
Apart from the fact that the author appears to have written it on a PC, and nods in the direction of an early version of Microsoft FORTRAN, this book has little to do with PCs. His argument is that portability is promoted by using Subset FORTRAN 77, and so he stresses this. A number of examples from many areas of science are presented in a sometimes amusing fashion.

Another area in which the reader may wish to extend his knowledge is in assembly language. There are many books on this: some good, some less good. A bibliography on the subject of assembly language is given towards the end of Chapter 2.

CHAPTER 2

MICROCOMPUTER ARCHITECTURE

2.1 INTRODUCTION

An IBM PC or compatible microcomputer typically consists of three boxes: a keyboard, a processor box, and a screen. The keyboard and the screen are the direct interface between the user and the computer, and the processor box is responsible for supervising all the data manipulation as well as carrying out all the computation. The processor processes data input from the keyboard and outputs data to the screen. In addition it controls input/output from storage media such as floppy and hard disks, from serial and parallel ports, and from expansion cards fitted to expansion slots. The brain within this control centre is the microprocessor 'chip'. This sits in the centre (metaphorically if not physically) of the primary circuit board affectionately known as the 'mother' board. The mother board will contain a number of processors. These have specific jobs such as the screen, keyboard, and audio controllers which look after the display, the keyboard input, and the sound respectively. There is, however, one dominant general purpose processor which is in overall control. The characteristics of this 'central' processor largely determine the speed, power, and memory capacity of the microcomputer.

The microcomputer is capable of most of the functions provided by a mainframe computer, only limited in comparison by its memory and speed. Indeed, its compactness and convenience, and single user operation, give the microcomputer in real terms a number of advantages over its big brothers. For example, a program may take longer to run on a microcomputer than a mainframe, but the results may be available sooner. There could be a number of reasons for this: the mainframe may have scheduled the program to run at a later time than when it was submitted, or the results needed post-processing on a graphics terminal, and this was being used.

A major disadvantage for the new microcomputer user, particularly, perhaps, the FORTRAN programmer, is that the microcomputer generally does not have the support team that a mainframe user would take for granted. Communications, graphics, printing, and plotting, the details of which could be left safely in the hands of the computer unit, have to be tackled directly by the microcomputer user. There are, of course, commercial products available for all of these tasks, but will they work together? Will they work with a particular FORTRAN compiler? Which product is best? The commercial market can be very confusing and expensive. Some answers to these and other problems will be found in this book.

Control over the microcomputer and its many functions and capabilities is provided by the operating system. Unfortunately FORTRAN in its standard form only allows the programmer to interface with the operating system in a restricted manner through OPEN and CLOSE, and READ and WRITE, statements. What is required is a more direct interface to the operating system.

Some FORTRAN compilers on the PC give the programmer direct access to the operating system, although this is attractive it can lead to non-standard code which may be difficult to maintain. Our preferred route is to access the operating system through calls to assembly language subroutines. This at least keeps the non-standard FORTRAN code in small, well-defined, subroutines which can be rewritten so that they work under any system.

The other rationale for using assembler is speed. The FORTRAN programmer has to rely on the compiler writer for the machine code version of the program, and the compiler writer is hampered by having to allow for the different constructs allowed under the FORTRAN syntax.

Assembler code may be responsible for the power and speed of a complex graphics program, or the flexibility of fully featured communications software, but learning to code these packages is beyond the scope of this book. As FORTRAN programmers, we want to do most of our coding in FORTRAN; we only use assembler code to give us access to operating system facilities (and commercial software) which would otherwise be unavailable to us.

The Intel Corporation are responsible for the 8086/8088/80x86 family of microprocessors which are found in all IBM and IBM compatible microcomputers. As in any family these microprocessors have many characteristics in common. To follow the assembly language examples in this book you will not require a detailed knowledge of how these processors work, but we hope that a brief description of the Intel 8086/8088 processor will help those of you who wish to understand better what is happening when your program runs. We will not attempt to define the mnemonics of the assembler language, or teach formally the principles of assembly programming. There are a number of books devoted to these subjects and some of the better ones are referenced in the bibliography at the end of this chapter.

For those of our readers who would prefer never to program in assembler, may we recommend the disk set which accompanies this book. This contains libraries of assembler subroutines which can be linked to your FORTRAN programs giving access to every operating system function you're ever likely to need. A description of these libraries is given in Chapter 15. You may wish to skip the early sections of this chapter and go directly to Section 2.7 which describes how to call an assembly language subroutine from FORTRAN, and where some examples are presented.

For the rest we start in Section 2.2 by considering what happens when an executable program is loaded into memory. In Section 2.3 some terms are defined and there is a brief reminder of binary and hexadecimal arithmetic. In Sections 2.4, 2.5, and 2.6 we take a closer look at the registers and what they do.

2.2 LOADING AND RUNNING AN EXECUTABLE PROGRAM

When an executable program is run, by typing its name at the operating system prompt, the first task faced by the processor is where in memory to load the program and its data. In the days of the 8-bit microcomputer this was not a problem since it was the responsibility of the programmer to instruct the processor precisely where in memory to place the code and the data. This is also true of command (COM) programs which have to be loaded into low memory, but is no longer true of executable programs. Delaying the decision, until an executable program is run, allows the processor to place a number of programs in memory at the same time. This is feasible with 16- and 32-bit microcomputers because of their larger memory addressing capabilities. Of course it is still possible to address memory directly, and for certain applications (normally where speed is of the essence) this is desirable; however, it can lead to conflicts when two such programs co-reside in memory. Allowing programs to be 'relocatable' has opened up a whole range of possibilities. These include background printing, multi-processing, sophisticated networking, etc.; perhaps the most celebrated example of a co-resident program is 'Sidekick' from Borland International, which provides a whole range of desk accessories to the user at any time at the press of a key combination.

The processor cannot tell whether a particular memory location contains code or data. Once a program is loaded into memory, the programmer still has to tell the processor where the next instruction to be executed is stored and where his data resides. To do this the programmer has to be able to refer to a memory address (called an **offset**) relative to some as yet unknown starting address (called a **segment**).

To handle this memory management, and also the manipulation of data, the processor has a number of storage locations which it has direct, and very fast, access to, these are called **registers**. Some of the registers have specific tasks, for example **segment registers** which contain the memory locations for the start of code and data. Other registers are general purpose registers used for manipulating data, but which may also have specialized tasks. A detailed description of the Intel 8086/8088 processor, its registers, and what they do is given in the following sections.

Once the processor has placed a program in memory, it will consult its **instruction** registers. These point to the next instruction to be executed. Assembly language instructions typically move (MOV) data from random access memory to registers, manipulate the data and then move it back again. Some instructions will cause the segment registers to change, data or code will then be referenced relative to the new segment address until such time as it changes again. To get a feel for the assembly language we suggest you study the assembler subroutines at the end of this chapter and throughout the book.

The processor will continue to execute a program until instructed to return control back to the operating system or another program.

2.3 DEFINITIONS

The term 'bit' is derived from the expression Binary digIT. A binary digit is a number which can only have one of two values, 0 or 1. To obtain a numerical value greater than 1 you need more than one bit, just as with decimal arithmetic to express a number greater than 9 you need more than one decimal digit.

With four bits you can express the numbers between 0 and 15 as follows:

0000 = 0;	0001 = 1;	0010 = 2;	0011 = 3;	0100 = 4;	0101 = 5;
0110 = 6;	0111 = 7;	1000 = 8;	1001 = 9;	1010 = 10;	1011= 11;
1100 = 12;	1101 = 13;	1110 = 14;	1111 = 15		

Notice that the largest number that can be expressed using four bits is 15; and that the maximum number of different combinations is 16. If four bits is used to express both positive and negative numbers then some convention is needed for representing the negative numbers. The usual convention used is two's complement. For four bytes this gives:

0000 = 0;	0001 = 1;	0010 = 2;	0011 = 3;	0100 = 4;	0101 = 5;
0110 = 6;	0111 = 7;				

1111 = −1;	1110 = −2;	1101 = −3;	1100 = −4;	1011 = −5;
1010 = −6;	1001 = −7;	1000 = −8		

The rule for obtaining a number of the opposite sign for any given number is:

1) in the given number change all the 1s to 0s and all the 0s to 1s, then
2) add 1 to the result.

Thus for example:

$$1011 = -5$$

changing the 1s to 0s and 0s to 1s gives

$$0100$$

and adding 1 gives

$$0101 = 5$$

Notice also that very conveniently the leftmost bit is 0 for positive numbers and 1 for negative numbers. This is always true when using two's complement, and the leftmost bit is called the sign bit.

The largest number that can be expressed using 'n' bits is $(2^n) - 1$ (this assumes that only positive numbers are being expressed), and the maximum number of combinations using 'n' bits is 2^n. Thus if 16 bits were used to express numbers, the largest ordinal would be 65 535 and the maximum number of combinations would be 65 536.

The binary system is used with computers because the bit value of 1 or 0 can be regarded as a 'switch' being on or off. Thus a row of switches can be used to represent any binary number up to a maximum (depending on the number of switches) by turning appropriate switches on and off. For four switches in a row the number 6 could be represented by setting the switches:

> off   on   on   off

Binary numbers can be manipulated in all the same ways that decimal numbers are manipulated but it can become rather tedious. In order to alleviate the boredom of using binary arithmetic, programmers tend to use hexadecimal arithmetic. A hexadecimal number can express 16 different values (0–15) using only one digit.

Why use hexadecimal numbers and not decimal numbers? There are two reasons. Firstly the conversion between binary and hexadecimal numbers is in general simpler than binary–decimal conversion. As shown below binary to hexadecimal conversion is never more difficult than converting a four bit binary number to decimals. Secondly hexadecimal numbers are more concise than decimals: Consider the following 16-bit binary number:

> 1010   0110   0111   1000

it has been conveniently set out in groups of four binary digits.

A hexadecimal digit can represent any number between 0 and 15, and four binary digits can represent any number between 0 and 15. So the first step in converting from binary to hexadecimal numbers is to group four binary digits at a time starting from the right. (If you don't have a number of binary digits exactly divisible by four then add 0s to the left of the number until you have. Adding 0 to the left of an unsigned number does not change its value so the binary number 101 is the same as 0101 in unsigned arithmetic. With signed numbers the rule for adding bits to the left is to extend the sign bit to the left. Thus with signed numbers 101 is the same as 1101, 11111101, etc.)

Having grouped the binary digits in fours, convert each set of four into its decimal and hence its hexadecimal equivalent. In hexadecimals the numbers from 10 to 15 have to be expressed using just one digit. To do this the letters A–F are borrowed from the alphabet and used. To return to the example:

> 1000b = 8d = 8h

where b indicates a binary number and d and h represent a decimal and hexadecimal number respectively. Similarly

$$0111b = 7d = 7h; \quad 0110b = 6d = 6h; \quad 1010b = 10d = Ah$$

thus 1010 0110 0111 1000b = A678h. *Note* this is 42616d (*Not* 87610d). You should confirm that this is the correct answer for decimals by converting directly from binary to decimal; we think this will convince you that binary to hexadecimal conversion is easier than binary to decimal.

Similarly

$$1111 \quad 1111 \quad 1111 \quad 1111b = FFFFh = 65535d$$

the largest unsigned number that can be expressed using 16 bits.

A 'byte' is generally defined as 8 bits. (On some unusual minicomputers a byte is defined as 9 bits but this is exceptional.) With 8 bits the maximum unsigned number that can be represented is 255, thus in unsigned numbers a byte can express the range of decimal numbers between 0 and 255, 256 different numbers in all.

The 'word-length' of a microcomputer is defined as the number of bits in the processor registers. These registers may be used for addressing the processor memory (random access memory) directly or they may be used for manipulating data. Typically computers have word lengths of 8 bits, for the most humble micro, 16 bits, 32 bits, or 64 bits for the most powerful mainframe computer (which at the time of writing is the CRAY 2).

For the Intel 8086/8088 processors the registers and the word length are 16 bits. The 8088 is the processor used in the IBM PC and XT microcomputers. Many other DOS PCs use the 8086, which differs from the 8088 in that although both are 16-bit internally, the 8088 talks to the outside world 8 bits at a time, and the 8086 does so in 16-bit units. The Intel 80286/80386 processors have registers and word lengths of 32 bits. (Some minicomputers have a processor with a word length of 36 bits: it is on these minicomputers that a byte is defined as 9 bits because it is convenient if there is an exact number of bytes, 4, in a word.)

A 16-bit microcomputer is usually defined as a microcomputer whose processor has a word length of 16 bits and which in addition has a data bus 16 bits wide. The data bus carries the data from the memory in the processor to the registers and back again. With the 8088 processor the data bus is only 8 bits wide so each transfer of 16-bit data needs two journeys on the bus, a byte at a time. The 8088 processor is not strictly a 16-bit processor.

The 8086 processor has a data bus 16 bits wide (a double-decker bus) thus making most transfers of 16-bit data in one journey. This is the only significant difference between these two processors. The 8086 processor is a true 16-bit processor.

Figure 2.1 gives a schematic diagram of the 8086/8088 processor. It shows how the processor has 14 registers which can be separated into five distinct groups. Each group of registers has a particular role in the movement and the manipulation of data and the execution of commands.

2.4 THE REGISTERS

Each register within each group also has its own specific purpose. In the following paragraphs we will describe briefly each register and its use. For a more detailed description of the 8086/8088 software architecture please refer to the bibliography at the end of this chapter.

The segment registers are used to point to particular locations within the random access memory (commonly known as RAM). This is the memory that can be directly address by the processor, and the maximum amount of RAM for a particular processor is thus limited by the addressing capability of the processor.

The 8086/8088 processor can directly address 2 to the power 20 different locations or 1 048 576 bytes (that is 1 megabyte) of memory. Notice that although the registers are 16 bits long

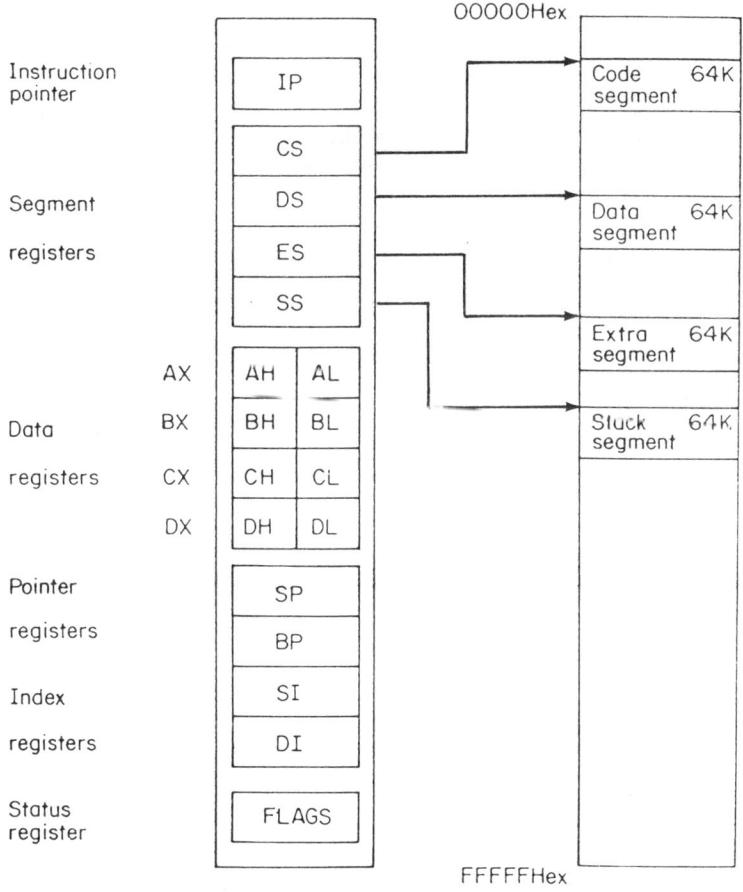

Figure 2.1 Software model of the Intel 8086/8088 processor

(2 bytes) the processor can address a single byte of memory; this is useful because, for example, all the standard characters that are in common use can easily be encoded into 1 byte of information (see the ASCII collating sequence in Appendix 1).

The 8086/8088 processors execute instructions 1 byte at a time, and indeed some instructions are only 1 byte long, so being able to refer to each byte in RAM means that 1 byte instructions can be addressed directly and executed by the processor very quickly.

Another important point to notice is that although the registers are 16 bits long the processor can address 2 to the power 20 bytes in RAM (not 2 to the power 16 as you might expect). This is achieved by combining the contents of two registers to calculate a memory address. A segment register to point to the start of a segment of memory and another register which gives the 'offset' to a particular location within that segment of memory. The contents of the segment registers are multiplied by 16 to obtain the start address of a segment of memory.

So, for example, the **code segment** register when multiplied by 16 points to the start of RAM where the program currently under execution resides.

Similarly the **data segment** register points to the start of RAM where the program data resides, and the **extra segment** register is also used to point to the start of another segment of RAM in which program data resides.

The **stack segment** register points to the start of the **stack segment** in RAM.

We will see later how the **instruction pointer**, the **index** pointers, and the pointer registers are used to point to memory locations within these segments of memory.

Before a program is executed, all the segments will typically be initialized to point to the same area in memory. It is up to the assembler writer or compiler writer to set up the **data** and **extra segments** to point to those areas of RAM where the data has been stored.

The **stack segment** will automatically be set to point to the last memory location in the RAM, although this also may be redirected by the assembler programmer or compiler writer. The **stack segment** is used to store temporary data during execution of a program.

For example when a program calls a subroutine the processor has to know the address of the next instruction which is to be executed after returning to the program from the subroutine. This return address is stored in the **stack segment**. When the RETURN instruction is executed at the end of a subroutine the address of the next instruction from the calling routine is taken ('popped') off the stack into the instruction pointer register.

The stack is also used for passing data from one subroutine to another. In FORTRAN for example the data that is actually passed from one subroutine to another through the argument list is the memory addresses of the arguments. These addresses would typically be placed ('pushed') on the stack by the calling routine and taken ('popped') off the stack by the routine called.

The **pointer** and **index** registers are used to point to specific memory locations within each segment. Since each of these registers are 16 bits long the number of different locations they can point to is 2 to the power 16 (64 kbytes = 64*1024 bytes). This implies that each segment is 64 kbytes long and that only 4*64 kbytes of memory (i.e. since 1 megabyte = 16*64 bytes this is $^1/_4$ of the memory) can be addressed at any one time.

The **instruction pointer** is used exclusively to point to locations within the **code segment** see Figure 2.2. The **instruction pointer** always contains the address of the next instruction to be executed by the processor.

As an example of how registers are used to locate addresses in memory we will use the **code segment** register and the **instruction pointer** register to calculate the address of the next instruction to be executed in a hypothetical situation. We will first use decimal arithmetic then hexadecimal and finally binary arithmetic to calculate the address. Suppose the **code segment** contains the number 19479d and the **instruction pointer** contains the number 42511d. The rule to obtain the memory address is to multiply the segment register by 16 (in this case the **code segment**) and then add the offset (in this case the number in the **instruction pointer** register), so we have:

CS = 19479d   IP = 42721d

Thus the memory address = 19479*16d + 42721d = 354385d
Now in hexadecimal arithmetic:

CS = 4C17h   IP = A6E1h   (Note: 16 decimal = 10 hex.)
4C17h*10h = 4C170h   4C170h + A6E1h = 56851h

Now finally as the processor does it in binary arithmetic:

CS = 0100 1100 0001 0111b   IP = 1010 0110   11100001b

    0100 1100 0001 0111 0000   CS * 16d   (16d=10000b)
+   1010 0110 1110 0001   + IP
=   0101 0110 1000 0101 0001

You should verify that all the answers are correct and the same. The binary sum is certainly the easiest, and can be performed very quickly by the processor. The processor doesn't even need to perform any multiplications, because 16d = 10000b, multiplying the segment register by 16d is just a matter of adding four 0s to the end of the binary number (i.e. shift left four times).

This method of obtaining memory addresses is very versatile, it means that segments can overlap (completely if necessary), be consecutive or be entirely independent, and it allows the programmer to use the memory very efficiently. The start of each segment is always the value of the segment register multiplied by 16d, this means that the starting address of each segment is always a number that ends in 0000b. In computer jargon this is equivalent to saying that a segment always starts on a 16-bit boundary, or 'paragraph boundary'.

Figure 2.2 Memory adressing

The **pointer** registers and **index** registers are used to point to locations within the **data, extra** and **stack segments**.

The **stack pointer** register always points to the top of the stack where the next item of temporary data will be placed.

The **base pointer** register is used to reference addresses within the **stack segment**.

The **index** registers are used to reference addresses within the **data segment** and the **extra segment**, either **index** register can be used with either **data segment**, however, if not instructed otherwise the processor will take the **source index** (SI) register as a pointer within the **data segment**, and the **destination index** (DI) register as a pointer within the **extra segment**.

2.5 THE DATA REGISTERS

The **data** registers consist of the four general purpose registers AX, BX, CX, DX. Each of these 16-bit registers can be divided into two 8-bit registers, i.e. its low byte and its high byte, and each of these can be addressed independently. Thus the AX register can be split into the low byte AL, and the high byte AH. Similarly the other registers can be split into low and high bytes as BL, BH, CL, CH, and DL, DH, respectively. Each register, in either its 16-bit or 8-bit mode can be used in arithmetic or logic operations, such as ADD or XOR.

The registers are used for the temporary storage of frequently used intermediate results in a calculation because they are accessed much faster than memory addresses. In addition each register has a specific role or roles, in particular numerical and character string manipulations. We will describe these roles very briefly:

- The AX register (arithmetic register) is used in conjunction with the DX register in 'word multiply' and 'word divide' operations as well as being used specifically in input/output (I/O) operations.
- The BX register (base register) is used in address calculations to store the base address.
- The CX register (count register) is used as an implied counter by the processor in loop and string operations.

2.6 THE STATUS REGISTER

The status register contains nine 1-bit flags which monitor the consequence of any instruction executed by the processor. Since the status register, like all the other registers, is 16 bits long, 7 of the bits in the status register are unused. The nine flags are divided into two groups.

Group one, the 'condition flags', are:

> the sign flag, the zero flag, the parity flag, the carry flag, the auxiliary carry flag, and the overflow flag

Group two, the 'control flags', are:

> the direction flag, the interrupt enable flag, and the trap flag

As an example of how the condition flags are set we will consider the condition flags after the processor has performed an addition. Suppose the processor were to execute the following sum:

```
      0101   0100   0011   1001
  +   0100   0101   0110   1010
      ─────────────────────────
      1001   1001   1010   0011        the result
```

Having obtained the result the condition flags will be set as follows:

Sign flag = 1   since the leftmost bit (the sign bit) is 1 indicating a negative result when using signed arithmetic

Zero flag = 0   non-zero result (note if the result had been zero the zero flag would be 1–such is life)

Parity flag = 1   indicating an even number of 1s in the result. (This flag is used extensively in communication packages. Characters can be encoded into 7 bits using a system called the ASCII collating sequence. The eighth bit of the byte containing the character can thus be chosen at random. It can be chosen so that the number of bits in the byte add up to an even number—'even parity'. Thus before transmitting a file from one device to another a communications package may ensure that all the characters in the file have even parity. Now after the file has been transmitted it is a simple matter to check whether all the bytes in the file continue to have even parity. If not then something has gone wrong, if even parity is maintained then further checks can be made on the data.)

Carry flag = 0   no carry out of the leftmost bit

Auxiliary = 1
carry flag   indicating a carry out of the first four bits (this flag is used in binary coded decimal arithmetic)

Overflow flag = 1   the addition of two positive numbers has given a negative result; this causes the overflow flag to be set

The condition flags are used as follows:

Direction flag   used by string manipulation instructions to allow the counter in such instructions to be either incremented or decremented after each instruction; if the direction flag is 0, the counter is incremented.

Interrupt enable flag   if this flag is set then a maskable interrupt can be recognized by the processor

(If you are using a computer with a pointing device such as a mouse, then the processor needs to monitor the movement of the mouse. However, if it spent all its time monitoring the mouse then no processing could be performed when the mouse was attached. What happens in practice is that the processor continues to execute instructions in a program until the mouse is moved. When the mouse moves an interrupt request is sent to the processor. If the interrupt enable flag is set then the processor, after finishing the instruction currently being processed, suspends execution of the program while the interrupt is performed i.e. the movement of the mouse is tracked on the screen. The processor then returns to the program under execution until a new interrupt request is received. Under some circumstances it is not desirable for the program to be interrupted in this way, for example if an error has occurred in the program it may be neater to disable interrupts while terminating the program, under these circumstances the interrupt enable flag would be set to 0.)

The trap flag   if this flag is set to 1 then the processor only executes one instruction at a time; this facility is provided for the debugging of programs; it allows the assembler programmer to see the action taken by the processor when one line of assembler program is executed

2.7 CALLING AN ASSEMBLER SUBROUTINE FROM FORTRAN

The primary consideration when calling an assembler subroutine (called a procedure in assembly language) is to determine how the FORTRAN compiler passes its arguments on a subroutine call. If you are using a FORTRAN 77 compiler then the arguments should be passed by memory address. The only parameter that will be passed by value is the one returned on a function call. The assembly language makes no distinction between subroutines and functions, and some routines coded in assembler will work whether called as a subroutine or a function. However the return argument of a function may be a character, an integer or a 4-byte real, or an 8-byte real number, depending on how the function is declared, it could also be logical of course. Each of these may cause subtle differences in the way that the passed arguments are stored. In addition the type of function will need to be declared in each FORTRAN routine from which it is called, otherwise a syntax error may result or worse still a run time bug. For these reasons we always code our assembler routines with the assumption that they will be called as subroutines.

We will assume that a FORTRAN 77 compiler is being used and that the subroutine arguments are passed by memory address. This will normally require 4 bytes to be stored for each argument, 2 bytes for the segment and 2 bytes for the offset. It is necessary to discover where these memory addresses will be stored on entry to the assembler subroutine, and how much 'housekeeping' is done by the compiler. The memory addresses may be pushed onto the stack by the compiler (this method is used by Microsoft FORTRAN) or they may be stored relative to the contents of one of the registers (Ryan MacFarland FORTRAN uses the BX register). What else will the compiler do? Typically it will push the return address which is the next instruction in the calling routine on the stack and not much more. It is then up to the subroutine which is called to ensure that nothing important is overwritten, for example if the **base pointer** is overwritten the return address of the calling subroutine will never be found.

Your compiler might also require that certain names are used for the **code** and **data segments** in your assembler routine and also that you use a specific assembler product. For example the demonstrations on how to interface FORTRAN to assembler given in the Digital Research FORTRAN manual assume that you use the Digital Research Assembler which is subtly different from the Microsoft MACRO Assembler.

We have written our subroutines with the Microsoft FORTRAN compiler in mind, and we have used the Microsoft MACRO Assembler (MASM). This is probably the most common combination of such products that you will come across. Indeed Microsoft's MACRO Assembler is acceptable for most FORTRAN compilers. Also in recognition of the fact that a large number of assembler utilities are written for the Microsoft FORTRAN compiler, Ryan MacFarland supply with their compiler an interface to assembler routines written for Microsoft FORTRAN. Since the IBM FORTRAN compiler is also a version of Ryan MacFarland's FORTRAN compiler, you will appreciate why we have made this choice. For details of the FORTRAN/assembler interface on your compiler you should consult your manuals. With Microsoft FORTRAN, the arguments in a subroutine call are passed by placing the segment and offset of the memory where they are stored on the stack. For a subroutine call the memory address for the last argument in the call will start 6 bytes beyond the stack base pointer (BP+6) (the 6 bytes are used to store the 4- byte return address of the calling subroutine, and the value of the BP pointer which we PUSH onto the stack at the start of the assembler routine), the segment and offset take 2 bytes each so that the memory address for the next argument will start at BP+10, the next at BP+14 and so on. The arguments are pushed from left to right in the argument list, and since the stack grows downwards the last argument will be at BP+6 and the first at BP+ (n−1) ∗4+6, where n is the number of arguments.

For Microsoft FORTRAN the code segment should be called 'CODE' and declared to be part of the 'CGROUP' GROUP. A user defined data segment should be called 'DATA' and declared as part of the 'DGROUP' GROUP. Although stated as such in the Microsoft manual we have found (certainly for v. 4.0 of Microsoft FORTRAN) that these naming conventions can be relaxed.

To illustrate the procedure involved we start with a subroutine that could easily be written in FORTRAN, we would expect the assembler routine to be faster and produce a slightly smaller executable code. The assembler subroutine and FORTRAN subroutine are shown below, in full, as well as a test program which can be used to call either routine. You can make a direct comparison of the sizes of executable code on your machine, the difference in speed will be of the order of clock ticks and so will not be discernible.

The subroutine is passed a character string, the job of the subroutine is to convert any lower case characters in the string into upper case characters. Since the length of the string is not passed through the argument list, we have designed the assembler code to stop processing the string if the NUL character is encountered. We shall code the FORTRAN subroutine in an analogous way.

Here is the FORTRAN routine.

```
        SUBROUTINE CONVLU (STRING)
C-------------------------
C
C       program to convert a character string from lower
C       case to upper case - it mimics the Assembler code
C
C--------------------------------------------------------------
        CHARACTER * (*) STRING
C
        I = 1
  10    CONTINUE
C
C                       is the next character in string  a
C                       null, i.e. char(0)if so we have
C                       finished so return
C
        IF (STRING(I:I) .EQ. CHAR(0)) GO TO 30
C
C                       not a NUL so do we have to convert
C                       the character to upper case? Only
C                       convert if lower case a to z -
C                       otherwise loop to next character in
C                       string
C
        IF (STRING(I:I) .LT. 'a') GO TO 20
        IF (STRING(I:I) .GT. 'z') GO TO 20
C
C                       character is lower case a to z,
C                       so convert to upper case by
C                       subtracting 32 (20 hex) from its
C                       ASCII code
C
```

```
          STRING(I:I) = CHAR(ICHAR(STRING(I:I))-32)
 20       CONTINUE
          I = I + 1
          GO TO 10
C
C                         all done
C
 30       RETURN
          END
```

We might be well advised to use the FORTRAN 77 lexical comparison functions in the two main IF statements, but since DOS collates according to ASCII, so too do all DOS FORTRANs.

Now the same routine in Assembler.

```
          NAME      CONVLU
;
CGROUP   GROUP CODE
;
;
CODE     SEGMENT PUBLIC 'CODE'
         ASSUME  CS:CGROUP
;
PUBLIC  CONVLU
CONVLU  PROC    FAR
;
;    save base pointer we will read this value before
;    returning to calling routine
;
         PUSH    BP
;
;    set base pointer to point to top of stack so that
;    we can use the base pointer to point to the arguments
;    in the call
;
         MOV     BP,SP
;
;    read the address of argument 'string' off the stack
;
         LES     BX,DWORD PTR [BP+6]
;
;    zero SI. SI is like 'I' in the FORTRAN subroutine
;
         XOR     SI,SI
```

```
NEXT:
;
;     start loop by reading next character from memory
;     put it into AL
;
          MOV       AL,BYTE PTR ES:[BX]+[SI]
          CMP       AL,0                  ;is it the NUL character
          JE        FIN                   ;yes, return to caller
;
;     character doesn't need converting if it is
;     not lower case 'a' to lower case 'z',
;     if it doesn't need converting read next
;     character from memory
;
          CMP       AL,"a"                ;is character 'a'
          JL        UP                    ;character less than 'a'
                                          ;so don't convert
          CMP       AL,"z"                ;is character 'z'
          JG        UP                    ;character is greater than
                                          ;'z' so don't convert
          SUB       AL,20H                ;convert to upper case by
                                          ;subtracting 20 hex from
                                          ;ASCII code
;
;     write upper case character back to memory
;
          MOV       BYTE PTR ES:[BX]+[SI],AL
UP:
          INC       SI                    ;increment SI by one
          JMP       NEXT                  ;loop to next character
;
FIN:
;
;     all done
;     pop original value of base pointer from stack
;     and return to caller clearing the 4 bytes for
;     the address of the argument off the stack as we go
;
          POP       BP
          RET       4
;
CONVLU    ENDP
CODE      ENDS
;
          END
```

This procedure takes the address of the start of a character string from the stack (at BP+6), and then checks successive bytes of the character sting. A character is represented in a byte by a number, which number refers to which character is given by the ASCII code (see Appendix 1). The code first checks whether the byte is the NUL character (ASCII 0), a NUL character signifies that the end of the string has been reached. Then it checks if the byte is the character "a" (lower case), notice how if we put "a" in quotes it will be automatically converted to its ASCII code for comparison purposes. If the ASCII code for the byte is less than that for lower case "a" then conversion to upper case is not required so we jump to the next character. Next we check if the byte is the character "z" (lower case). If the ASCII code for the byte is greater than that for lower case "z" then no conversion is required so we jump to the next character. If the byte is neither lower than the ASCII code for lower case "a", or higher than that for lower case "z", then the byte must represent a lower case letter so we need to convert it to upper case. This is done by subtracting 20 hex (32 decimal) from the byte. Upper case letters in the ASCII code are 20 hex less than their lower case equivalents. Having converted the byte to upper case we write it back into the string. When a null byte is encountered control is transferred to the 'FIN' label, where the value of the base pointer is restored to that at the start of the procedure, and we return to the calling routine, jumping over the 4 bytes put on the stack by the calling routine, for the address of the argument, as we go.

To call either version of CONVLU from our FORTRAN program all we need is the statement:

```
    CALL CONVLU (STRING)
```

where 'STRING' has been declared as a character string, and we have ensured that the last character in 'STRING' is the NUL character. For example:

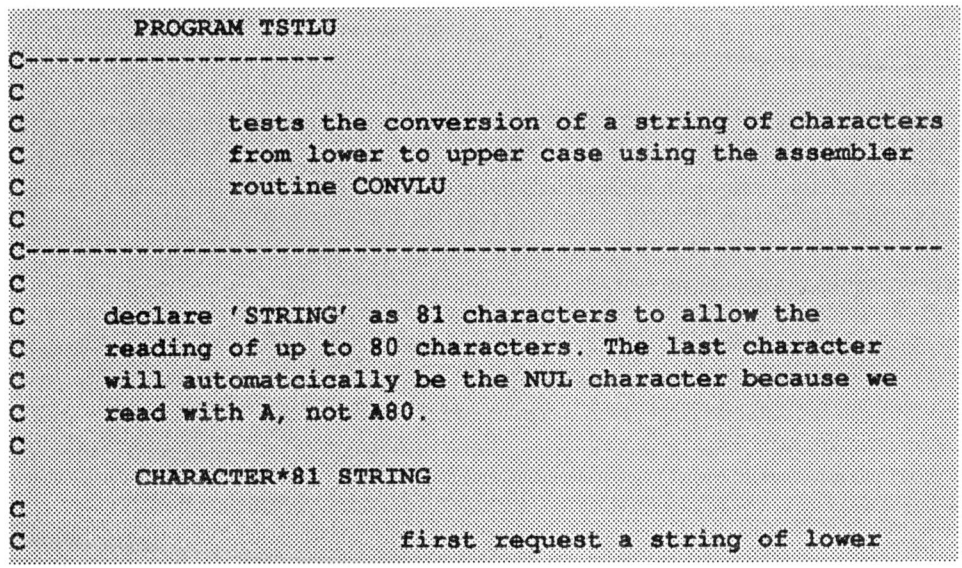

```
      PROGRAM TSTLU
C-----------------------
C
C               tests the conversion of a string of characters
C               from lower to upper case using the assembler
C               routine CONVLU
C
C-------------------------------------------------------------------
C
C     declare 'STRING' as 81 characters to allow the
C     reading of up to 80 characters. The last character
C     will automatcically be the NUL character because we
C     read with A, not A80.
C
      CHARACTER*81 STRING
C
C                   first request a string of lower
```

```
C                              case characters, upper case
C                              letters and symbols will not be
C                              affected
C
        PRINT *, ' Please enter up to 80 lower case',
     1  'characters'
C
        READ(*,100) STRING
 100    FORMAT(A)
C
C                              string has been declared *81
C                              so that the last character is
C                              always a NUL character
C
C                              call the assembler or FORTRAN
C                              routine that does the conversion
C
        CALL CONVLU(STRING)
C
C                              now write out the string
C
        WRITE(*,*) STRING
C
        STOP
        END
```

We don't have to use the name 'STRING'—any valid variable name will do.

You might like to try, as an exercise in assembler programming, changing the assembler procedure to convert from upper case to lower case characters.

The following assembler routine initializes to zero each component of a vector of a given length. The routine expects to find the addresses of three arguments on the stack. The first argument is the vector to be initialized, the second argument is its length, and the third argument is an **integer** variable which will be set to 1 if there is an error. Since the **integer** variable (IERR) is the last argument in the call, its address is the last to be placed on the stack and the Assembler routine expects to find it at BP+6. The length of the vector (N) is also an **integer**: its address will be found at BP+10 on the stack. By default FORTRAN 77 uses four bytes for an **integer**. If the highest two bytes are greater than zero, it is likely that there is an error, since the size of vector would have to be greater than 65 500. The routine checks if these bytes are zero and if not sets IERR to one. Finally the address of the vector is read off the stack at BP+14, a loop is then entered in which each component of the vector is set to zero.

```
        NAME ZERO
;
CGROUP  GROUP CODE
;
CODE    SEGMENT PUBLIC 'CODE'
        ASSUME  CS:CGROUP
;
PUBLIC  ZERO
ZERO    PROC    FAR
;
        PUSH    BP        ;save base pointer
;
        MOV     BP,SP     ;set base pointer to point to top
                          ;of stack
;
;   initialize error flag 'IERR' to zero
;
        LES     BX,DWORD PTR [BP+6]
        XOR     AX,AX                   ;make AX zero
        MOV     WORD PTR ES:[BX],AX
        MOV     WORD PTR ES:[BX+2],AX
;
;   put address of count in ES:BX and then the contents
;   of count in DX:AX. If DX is greater than 0 then
;   size of count is too large so jump to error label
;
        LES     BX,DWORD PTR [BP+10]
        MOV     AX,WORD PTR ES:[BX]
        MOV     DX,WORD PTR ES:[BX+2]
        CMP     DX,0
        JNE     ERROR
;
;   AX contains size of vector
;   put this in CX for loop
;
        MOV     CX,AX
;
;   now load the address of VECTOR in ES:BX
;
        LES     BX,DWORD PTR [BP+14]
        XOR     SI,SI                   ;zero index
NEXT:
;
;   put contents of CX on stack temporarily so that we
;   can loop through inner loop using CX register
```

```
;
         PUSH    CX
;
;        we will zero a word at a time, a REAL or INTEGER is
;        4-bytes or 2 words long, so we need an inner loop
;        of length 2
;
         MOV     CX,2
NEXT1:
         XOR     AX,AX              ;zero AX and store in memory
         MOV     WORD PTR ES:[BX]+[SI],AX
         INC     SI                 ;add 1 to SI
         INC     SI                 ;add 1 to SI
         LOOP    NEXT1              ;loop until CX is 0
;
         POP     CX                 ;get outer loop count off
                                    ;stack
         LOOP    NEXT               ;loop until CX is 0
         JMP     FIN                ;all done
ERROR:
;
;     the size of vector was too large
;     return IERR as 1
;
         LES     BX,DWORD PTR [BP+6]
         MOV     AX,1
         MOV     WORD PTR ES:[BX],AX
FIN:
;
         POP     BP      ;pop base pointer from stack
         RET     12      ;return 4*number of arguments
;
ZERO     ENDP
CODE     ENDS
;
         END
```

A FORTRAN program that calls this assembler procedure is set out below:

```
         PROGRAM TSZERO
C--------------------
C
C        Program to zero a large array
C
C----------------------------------------------------------------
```

```
        DIMENSION XX(10)
C
C                       put some values in XX
C
        XX(1) = 1.0
        XX(2) = 5.345
        XX(3) = -12345.67890
        XX(10) = 1000.9999
C
C                       display the values on screen
C
        WRITE(*,*) XX
C
C                       call assembler routine to zero XX
C
        CALL ZERO(XX,N,IERR)
C
C             if no error occurs display values to screen
C
        IF (IERR.EQ.0)  WRITE(*,*) XX
C
C           now force the error check to activate by setting
C           N to 66010
C
        N = 66010
        CALL ZERO(XX,N,IERR)
C
        IF (IERR.EQ.1) WRITE(*,10)
   10   FORMAT(' When N is set to 66010, an error is',
      1          ' detected in the assembler routine')
C
        STOP
        END
```

2.8 ANNOTATED BIBLIOGRAPHY

For a FORTRAN programmer, assembler programming is not difficult but it can be a bit tedious. Indeed some people find the discipline of writing each instruction explicitly surprisingly easy. The problem is to find a good book with clear instructions and interesting examples. We hope the following bibliography will be helpful in this respect.

Assembler for the IBM PC and PC-XT
Peter Abel, Prentice-Hall ISBN 0 8359 0153 X
A nice book, well presented with lots of well-commented programming examples.

The 8086 Book
Russell Rector and George Alexy, 1980, McGraw-Hill ISBN 0 931988 29 2
A complete reference book of instructions for assembler programming on the 8086/8088 family of processors. It won't teach you how to program in assembler but it is very handy when you are programming.

Microcomputer Systems: The 8086/8088 Family Architecture, Programming, Design
Yu-Chung Liu and Glenn A. Gibson, 1984, Prentice Hall ISBN 0 13 580944 4
A complete reference book for all aspects of the 8086/8088 family of microcomputer systems. Not so good for learning to program in assembler.

IBM PC & XT Assembler Language: A Guide for programmers
Leo J. Scanlon, 1983, Prentice Hall ISBN 0 89303 241 7
A good book to learn assembler programming. Lots of interesting examples.

Assembly language routines for MS-DOS computers
Leo J. Scanlon, TAB books Inc. ISBN 0 8306 0867 2
More good examples from Leo Scanlon.

IBM PC/8088 Assembly Language Programming
Avtar Singh and Walter A. Triebel, 1985, Prentice Hall ISBN 0 13 448358 8
A nice description of the software architecture and the DEBUG program.

All the above books concern the 8086/8088 Assembler; however, this is the place to start even if you have an 80286 or 80386 Intel processor. The instruction sets for these processors are a super set of the 8086/8088 instruction set.

Other publications of interest are:

Microsoft MS-DOS Programmers Reference Manual
Microsoft Corporation
This manual contains all the operating system functions, with some assembler code to show their use.

The Peter Norton Programmer's Guide to the IBM PC
Peter Norton, 1985, Microsoft Press ISBN 0 914845 46 2
Peter Norton is well known for his assembler utilities which sooth the brow of the frustrated PC user who has just deleted all the files off his floppy disk by mistake.

8087 Applications and Programming for the IBM PC, XT and AT
Richard Startz, Brady ISBN 0 89303 485 1
Shows how the 80*87 mathematics coprocessor chip can be directly addressed.

Advanced MS DOS
Ray Duncan, 1986, Microsoft Press ISBN 0 914845 77 2
Details many DOS functions in an interesting and readable style.

CHAPTER 3

DISK OPERATING SYSTEM

3.1 INTRODUCTION

The operating system is our primary interface to the microcomputer. In this chapter we take a closer look at the PC DOS/MS DOS operating system. We also take a brief look at the OS/2 operating system which is set to replace PC DOS and MS DOS on the faster and more powerful microcomputer systems that are currently being built around the 32-bit 80286/80386 Intel microprocessors.

MS DOS and PC DOS are both operating systems that have been developed by Microsoft. The differences between PC DOS and MS DOS are in practice superficial. Those differences that could have been significant have been ignored by most software developers, who recognize that, by restricting their attention to the common facilities offered by both systems, they can maximize their potential market for minimal effort. MS DOS and PC DOS have a lot in common, indeed the only reason why they are different is that IBM insist on having proprietorial products on their machines. Most IBM compatible computers will run both MS DOS and PC DOS quite happily, and most software products will function in an identical manner under both operating system. In what follows we shall consider PC DOS and MS DOS to be variants of the same operating system.

The DOS operating system is the most popular operating system on microcomputers. The reason for this is simple: it is the operating system that was adopted by IBM when it entered the microcomputer market-place. Its pre-eminent position seems likely to be threatened only when the ever-increasing power and memory addressing capabilities of the latest microprocessors lead to users demanding an operating system to match.

DOS was developed for a 16-bit microprocessor chip which could address (theoretically) a maximum memory of one megabyte. It was considered unlikely that anyone would actually want to use as much as this, after all the 8-bit microcomputers which were at that time the standard, would typically be sold with memories of 16 or 32 kbytes. When IBM entered the microcomputer market with the IBM PC and the PC DOS operating system, the standard RAM on offer was 64 kbytes. Soon other microcomputer manufacturers entered the 16-bit market offering systems with the 'almost unlimited memory' of 128 kbytes. The idea, therefore, that people might demand microcomputers with a megabyte of memory was plainly absurd. IBM decided that 640 kbytes was enough for anyone, and so placed the video RAM at 640 kbytes in the memory, thereby effectively rendering unusable any memory left above 640 kbytes.

Some manufacturers were able to implement their versions of MS DOS with the screen memory located at higher addresses than IBM had chosen. Typical of these machines were the Victor 9000/Sirius, and the Apricot. These tended to have more total memory potentially available than did the IBM PC.

However, as the microprocessors became faster and the microcomputers became more powerful, more and more applications which were thought to be mainframe computing tasks were adapted for the microcomputer. Here at last was cheap computing for all—and so what if the microcomputer took all night to run a large program, it was of no inconvenience to anybody else. Often it was significantly faster than anyone expected, and some applications ran just as fast on the micro as on the mainframe that they used before.

Very soon the new processors being developed could address 4 megabytes or more, and the limit of 640 kbytes needed to be breached. A number of techniques for overcoming the 640 kbytes barrier were adopted but there was another feature of the new processors that DOS was unable to exploit. The new processors (80286/80386) could run DOS much faster than the old ones (8086/8088), but this capability was provided by Intel to allow upward compatibility; if exploited to their full the new processors could not only run many times faster in their so-called 'protected' mode, they were also capable of full multi-processing, i.e. the running of several applications simultaneously. It was obvious that the microcomputer users would have to adapt to a new operating system that could fully exploit the power of the processors; OS/2—operating system 2—is Microsoft's new operating system and PS/2–personal system 2–is the IBM version of OS/2 developed jointly by Microsoft and IBM. These operating systems are still not available as we write but will certainly be the forerunner for microcomputing operating systems in the 1990s (if the UNIX supporters do not get their way).

DOS should not be dismissed out of hand, this operating system has many users who will not want to learn a new operating system just yet, and who are quite satisfied with the job that their current microcomputer is performing. There is also a vast pool of software which runs very happily on this operating system and which will need to be adapted to run under OS/2 and PS/2. Moreover the new operating system maintains many of the commands and features found in the DOS operating system.

Although DOS may not be as powerful as the operating systems found on larger computers such as UNIX or VMS, it nevertheless gives us a rich tool-box of commands and utilities for addressing the memory (RAM and disk), addressing the screen and for batch programming.

3.2 PC/MS DOS 1,2,3,... — WHAT THEY DO, THEIR HISTORY

The first mass-produced microcomputers were 8-bit microcomputers, that is they had a word length of 8 bits only. Although not very powerful by today's standard, they were infinitely more powerful than the calculators at that time.

The most popular operating system at that time was CP/M (Central Processor Manager? Control Program for Microprocessors? It is still a mystery what CP/M stands for) written by a company called Digital Research. Popular software included the spreadsheet Visicalc and the word processor WordStar. The database management system dBASEII from Ashton Tate was also developed on 8-bit microcomputers.

However, the majority of people who owned these early microcomputers were keen enthusiasts who mainly through necessity developed their own software. The software development tools were provided, by and large, by the company Microsoft Inc., who developed an industry standard BASIC interpreter and a FORTRAN compiler.

Most 8-bit microcomputers were sold with the CP/M operating system and the Microsoft BASIC interpreter. When the 8086/8088 processor from the Intel corporation was developed it was clear that microcomputers were here to stay. The 8086/8088 processor offered 16-bit registers with the capacity to address one megabyte of memory. The giant computer company IBM was interested. Microsoft was keen to enter the operating system market but they had no product of their own. They decided to buy in a proprietary operating system developed by Seattle Computer Products for their own 8086/8088 based machines. Microsoft made some major changes to it and released it as MS DOS 1.0. IBM adopted this product for its hugely popular IBM PC as well as offering CP/M-86, Digital Research's 16-bit operating system. However, IBM wanted to make the operating system an 'IBM only' product and so Microsoft produced PC DOS 1.0 for IBM.

PC DOS and MS DOS have subtle differences, but for the scope of this book they can be thought of as the same.

Fortunately for Microsoft the major software writers adopted MS DOS (PC DOS) as their favoured operating system, and as this operating system developed IBM abandoned CP/M-86. Despite valiant efforts to regain the high ground, even Digital Research have now conceded that MS DOS is the standard on 16-bit machines, and as long as Microsoft are favoured by IBM their operating systems will remain the industry standard for microcomputers.

In the following paragraphs the development of the DOS operating system with the major new features of each release will be described.

MS DOS 1.0 was the first 16-bit operating system marketed by Microsoft. Its major benefits over the 8-bit CP/M operating system were:

1 an AUTOEXEC.BAT batch file which is executed automatically when the microcomputer is 'rebooted'; this allows the user to predefine a series of commands in a batch file which will be carried out when the system is switched on or reset;

2 an improved structure for the disk directory and improvements in the disk management and allocation; these changes speeded up program loading and allowed much quicker sequential or random record access; in addition files stored on disk were given attributes such as the date the file was created or last changed, its size in bytes, and whether it was a system file or a hidden file;

3 an increased number of operating system commands.

MS DOS 1.0 (PC DOS 1.0) was followed by MS DOS 1.25 (PC DOS 1.1). Most software houses use a common convention when changing version numbers of their software for new releases. The number before the decimal point changes when significant new features are offered in a software product. Changes in the numbers after the decimal point indicate that the new release will address any mistakes or 'software bugs' that were discovered in the previous release and may contain a few minor new features; the product itself though will be very similar to the previous release. Microsoft use this convention for their software products.

The only significant new feature in MS DOS 1.25 was the support of double-sided disks. IBM was the only 'Original Equipment Manufacturer' (OEM) who sold their microcomputers with version 1.0 of DOS included. MS DOS 1.25, however, was taken up by several OEMs including Compaq (who are today probably the most successful manufacturers of IBM compatible microcomputers), Texas Instruments and Victor for the Victor 9000/Sirius 1 microcomputer which was very popular in Europe.

MS DOS 1.0 was released towards the end of 1981, MS DOS 1.25 was released in June 1982 and version 2.0 was first released in March 1983. DOS 2.0 contained many new features and improvements, although great care was taken to ensure that compatibility (where possible) with previous versions was maintained. Perhaps the most significant changes were the introduction of a UNIX-like hierarchical file structure, and support for hard disks.

To illustrate the concept of an hierarchical file structure consider a microcomputer with a hard disk which is used for writing letters; creating, editing and running FORTRAN programs and playing games.

With the larger capacity of hard disks and the potential to store a large number of files on these disk a hierarchical file structure is essential for efficient disk management. Also, with the ability to create directories and subdirectories for files, disk maintenance on a large capacity hard disk is as simple as on a single-sided floppy disk. (The backing up for security purposes of a large capacity hard disk is another matter! This, even with quite sophisticated tools at your disposal, is a task that requires discipline, patience and a large number of formatted floppy disks—or a tape spooler.) Such a hierarchical file structure is as follows:

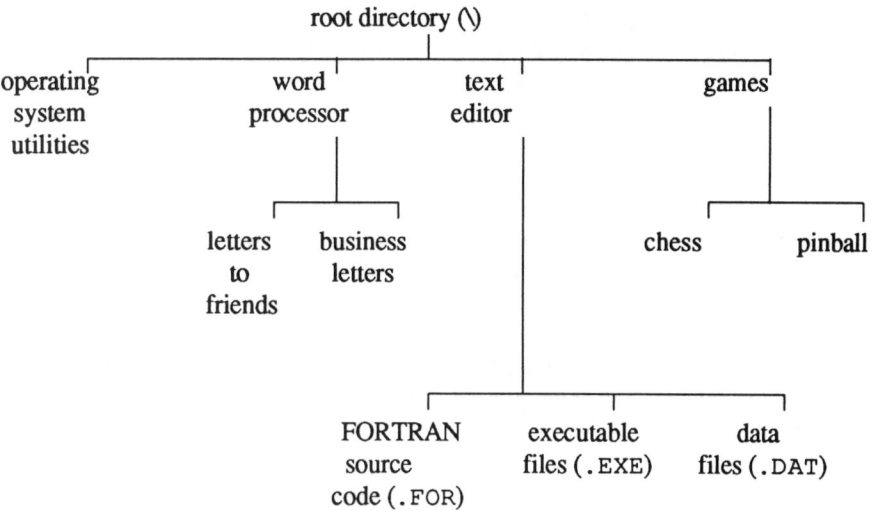

In DOS 1.x, files were referred to using 'File Control Blocks' (FCBs) which contain the file attributes such as size and date created, etc. However, it is not possible to refer to a file in a different directory using an FCB as there is not enough space in the FCB definition to store the pathname of a file. At the time that the FCB was defined, subdirectories did not exist and so files were always in the current directory.

In DOS 2 a new method was developed for file reference (although for compatibility FCBs were retained). Files could now be referenced using file 'handles' (another idea borrowed from UNIX). A file handle is similar in concept to a unit number in FORTRAN. It is a number that is a coded reference to a file path name. Where a handle differs from the FORTRAN unit number is that the handle (a 16-bit number) is allocated by the operating system (not by the programmer).

Other major features introduced in v. 2.0 of the operating system are listed below:

1 more UNIX-like features such as pipes and filters;
2 print spooling, printing as a background process;
3 ANSI display drivers for hardware independent display control;
4 installable device drivers;
5 CONFIG.SYS, a user defined system configurator file that is automatically loaded when the microcomputer is switched on or reset (software packages, particularly those that use graphics, frequently require certain instructions to be included in a CONFIG.SYS file; one of the most common mistakes that people make, when using new software for the first time, is to forget to 'reboot' the operating system after altering the CONFIG.SYS file; if you don't reboot the computer the new CONFIG.SYS file will not be installed and the new software will not work!);
6 international support for modification of currency symbols and date formats;

7 support for shells (another common UNIX concept), that is, user defined command interpreters, principally so that software companies could develop turnkey applications; few DOS applications make use of this facility;

8 control of blocks of memory dynamically from within application programs.

Subsequently, DOS 2.11 was released. DOS 2.11 fixed some bugs and improved international support. DOS 2.25 was then released in October 1985 to improve international support still further and to make compatible many of the system utilities which had been improved in the already released DOS 3.0. DOS 3.0 was released in August 1984, DOS 3.0 contained the software facilities required for Microsoft Networks.

Initially DOS 3.0 was only distributed with file servers as part of a network of microcomputers. This explains to some extent the parallel development of DOS 2.25 and DOS 3.0. All DOS versions 3 can be seen as improved version 2, with the correction of minor bugs, and the inclusion of many useful facilities such as 'external commands', which are operating system facilities implemented as separate programs. Some of these are so useful that they merit use on non-networked computers, and so DOS 3 is now in widespread use.

Since the release of DOS 3.1 (November 1984), with additional support for Microsoft Networks, DOS 3.2 has been released (mid- 1986) and this version of the operating system is distributed as standard at the time of writing. One of the enhancements in DOS 3.2 is that it now supports 3.5 inch floppy disks. This may come as something of a surprise to those users of certain MS DOS PCs which always had 3.5 inch floppy disks, and which may well have run happily under DOS 2.0—they all had significantly modified areas in the operating system, written by the machine manufacturers.

3.3 THE FUTURE...

It was Microsoft's stated intention to develop DOS to become more and more UNIX-like through DOS 4 and DOS 5, although it appears that they have never envisaged DOS becoming a multi-user operating system such as UNIX. This is because UNIX is already available on microcomputers under the name XENIX. XENIX is distributed by Microsoft, and it is UNIX System V compatible. As we write, DOS 4 has in fact been released. It appears to offer useful extensions to DOS 3, but early reviews suggest that it contains bugs.

Microsoft's earlier plans have been shaped too by the arrival of more powerful processors and the success of the graphics icon operating system popularized by the Apple Macintosh microcomputers. Not only that, but the demands of IBM have required Microsoft to develop a new operating system called OS/2. OS/2 is much more sophisticated than DOS, and makes fuller use of the additional memory addressing capacity inherent in 80286 and 80386 processors.

The graphics interface developed by Microsoft—Microsoft Windows—is set to become the industry standard and will work under DOS or OS/2.

Intel 8086 and 8088 processors are incapable of running OS/2, so will Microsoft continue the development of MS DOS for the 3 million or so machines which use these processors? We were in the process of doubting it, for what seemed sensible reasons, when DOS 4 was released. We doubted it because Microsoft appears to make most of its money on operating systems by selling them to OEMs. The operating systems are then sold with the microcomputer as a complete package. Most new microcomputers will be built around the 80286/80386 processors; thus the OEMs will demand the new operating system. People with microcomputers built around the old processors will probably have to make do with existing operating systems. DOS 4 is probably a means of running later versions of Windows on the older machines, or has facilities which allow DOS machines and OS/2 machines to be networked.

3.4 THE STRUCTURE OF DOS

DOS is made up of essentially three distinct parts:

- The Basic Input/Output System or BIOS
- The Disk Operating System kernel
- The command processor 'COMMAND.COM'

The basic input/output system—the BIOS—is the interface between the operating system functions and the hardware—the microcomputer, the keyboard, the monitor, the printer ports, etc. These components and the way they work in relation to the microcomputer depend on the specific architecture of the microcomputer and so the BIOS is provided by the manufacturer of the system.

In the early 1980s, the years of the 16-bit microcomputer revolution, before IBM dominated the market, there were a number of different microcomputer systems available, all of which used the MS DOS operating system. However, these microcomputers were not necessarily compatible. Manufacturers developed unique architectures as they competed to produce the best system. Most of the successful 8-bit microcomputer manufacturers and system designers were involved in the design of the new 16-bit microcomputers. One of the most popular designs in Europe was the Sirius microcomputer (called the Victor 9000 in the US). This microcomputer was designed by Chuck Peddle who had previously worked with Commodore on 8-bit microcomputers. The Sirius 1 was way beyond its time, with a high resolution screen, as well as two serial ports and 600 kbyte single-sided disks and 128 kbyte RAM. Chuck Peddle managed to get 600 kbytes on an ordinary single-sided double-density disk by rotating the disks at variable speeds. This allowed him to take advantage of the larger circumference at the perimeter of the disk. Most microcomputers store the same amount of information at the edge of the disk as they do in the middle which is simple but rather wasteful! The Sirius architecture was very different from other MS DOS machines at that time but it still ran standard MS DOS 1.25 as its operating system. This is because the BIOS written specifically for the Sirius was able to interpret the MS DOS instructions in terms of its architecture. Unfortunately the Sirius did not become the standard microcomputer despite its advanced features. The humble IBM PC with its low resolution screen, one serial port and 360 kbyte (or less) disks and 64 kbyte RAM dominated the microcomputer world because it was made by IBM. In fact the Sirius' non-standard disks was one of the causes of its downfall. Software vendors were slow in installing their software on Sirius disks and without software even the best computers are limited.

The BIOS is responsible for driving the console display and keyboard, the line printer, the auxiliary device (serial port), the clock, and the block devices which transfer data in chunks generally for storage on floppy and hard disks or tape streamers. MS DOS sends input/output request packets for these devices which are interpreted by the BIOS drivers into the correct commands for the various bits of hardware which control the devices. The BIOS is read into RAM when the microcomputer is switched on and the system is initialized. The BIOS is part of a file called IO.SYS in MS DOS and IBMBIO.COM in PC DOS. The BIOS remains in RAM all the time that the microcomputer is on, it is vital because it controls all interaction with the hardware.

The DOS kernel is a proprietary program supplied by Microsoft which provides services such as access to the real time clock, file and record management, memory management, loading and running other programs and input/output to character devices. Programs can access the functions supplied by the DOS kernel by using software interrupts. Microsoft have provided a whole series of useful functions using software interrupts. The most used system interrupts are those provided under software interrupt 21 hexadecimal (usually referred to as 'int 21 facilities'). These are used in various places throughout this book, and are explained as necessary. Whenever a particular concept requires facilities not available in pure FORTRAN, they can often be obtained from DOS via a small assembly language interface function.

The command processor—the program COMMAND.COM provides all the operating system commands available to the user at the DOS prompt. The command processor parses these commands and then causes the commands to be executed. The command processor is also known as the shell since the duties it performs are directly comparable to the shells that are part and parcel of the UNIX operating system.

The command processor can be replaced to give a totally different user interface. This is rarely done. Instead, graphical 'front-end' software such as GEM or Windows is used to shield the user from the details of COMMAND.COM. Other applications have so many facilities that it is possible to use them without ever coming into contact with DOS, except perhaps to wonder what the hieroglyphics are when the computer boots up and loads the application. Accounting software is a typical example.

Most FORTRAN users will change the operating environment very little. They may increase the apparent number of operating system commands by using batch files (operating system 'macros'), and set certain file names to aliases, but that is about all.

The number of batch commands is fairly limited in DOS compared to UNIX, although the commands that are provided can allow quite sophisticated batch files to be created. If for example you only use the computer to write, edit and execute FORTRAN programs you could write a batch file which, on switching on the microcomputer, writes a menu to the screen asking the user to choose between editing a file, compiling and linking a file, and executing a file.

The default COMMAND.COM supplied with DOS on your computer is divided into three parts. There is a part which remains resident in the microcomputers' RAM while the microcomputer is in use. An initialization section which executes the AUTOEXEC.BAT batch file and then is discarded, and the third part of COMMAND.COM is a transient part which is loaded into RAM after the microcomputer has been booted. However, the RAM used to store the transient part of COMMAND.COM can be overwritten if required when executing a program. If you own or have ever used a floppy disk based microcomputer and used it regularly, you will probably be familiar with the message requesting you to insert the operating system disk in the appropriate disk drive after running some of the larger application programs. If you have never seen this message then either you always run small programs or you have a large amount of RAM memory!

When using DOS the user is obliged to remember a number of commands before he can do anything useful. If he only wishes to execute application programs he will still need to know the following commands: how to format a disk, how to copy a disk, how to recognize and execute executable files, how to delete files, how to change directories, how to change disk drives. He may also need to know how to create data files, how to list files, and how to print files. For the programmer the learning of these commands is second nature and not a problem, but for the non-technically minded using DOS can be very daunting. A microcomputer that attempts to overcome these problems is the Apple Macintosh. The interface between the Macintosh and the user is entirely different. The Macintosh is based around a graphical interface, with a pointing and picking device called a mouse which is more important than the keyboard in the execution of commands. In this system a disk is represented as a picture with a name underneath it, called an icon. To see what is on the disk, you move the mouse until the arrow on the screen points to the disk icon and then you do a double click on the mouse button. The files on the disk are then presented to the user, like the disks as icons. To execute an application the user moves the mouse so that the arrow points at the application and does a double click—the application then starts to execute. Any commands available to the user are presented in a menu bar running along the top of the screen. Once again to execute these commands is just a question of point and click with the mouse. If for any reason the operating system or an application needs to communicate with the user then this is done through dialog boxes. These are like the bubbles that come out of mouths of cartoon characters. The user responds to these enquiries usually by pointing with the mouse and clicking. The Macintosh is very popular with non-technical users, and surveys have shown that corporate users are more productive on the Macintosh than they are on the PC.

The reason for the Macintosh success goes deeper than its operating system. The Macintosh is, and was designed to be, a graphics based system. Text and pictures are graphically based. Graphics is the natural medium, text is just pictures. On the PC there is a text mode and a graphics mode. The natural mode is the text mode—graphics has always been a little bit special. There are good reasons for this—in text mode you do not have to store every dot (pixel) which makes up a character every time you write it to the screen. You store the character set in memory and then just point to the address where a particular character resides within this character set. In text mode, only characters from the available character set can be used and the screen is limited to 80 columns by 40 rows thus the memory demands are much less stringent. However, if you have used a Macintosh you will notice the restrictions of text mode on the PC. We are used to receiving information in the form of both text and pictures. Perhaps the difference between the Macintosh approach and the PC can be likened to the difference between television and radio (although this is a bit unfair to the PC!).

So how will IBM and Microsoft respond to this radical challenge? It should be interesting to see how OS/2 and PS/2 and Windows develop on the more powerful 32-bit processors. It will also be interesting to see if UNIX will be affected by the icon revolution. As the processors get more powerful and memory gets cheaper and more plentiful there is no reason why a completely integrated text and graphics approach should not be adopted for all microcomputer systems.

3.5 THE DOS SOFTWARE INTERRUPT FUNCTIONS

The power to use the capabilities of a computer is provided by its operating system. For the IBM PC or compatible microcomputer, DOS provides services which can be invoked by an application through software interrupts. For the FORTRAN user, it is necessary to know that the software interrupt is a means of transferring control out of the FORTRAN code into code which is co-resident in the computer. Code which is co-resident with the FORTRAN program may be BIOS, DOS, or an application. An application may be a graphics system loaded from DOS before the FORTRAN program.

When DOS is loaded into RAM, the interrupt vector table is loaded into the bottom 1024 bytes of system memory. In this 1024 bytes there are stored up to 256 4-byte addresses pointing to memory locations where little programs called interrupt handlers are stored. The first 32 entries in the interrupt vector table are reserved for internal hardware interrupts. The next 32 are used by DOS. All the others can be used by either external hardware devices or application software.

Within this interrupt table are functions which allow the applications programmer to write directly to the BIOS. This is not to be recommended as it renders software extremely hardware dependent, but is frequently used by programs which require optimum speed of execution. Also DOS provides the ability for programmers to write their own interrupt handlers, either to adjust existing interrupt handlers for their own devices or to introduce new software interrupts.

Our own interest in all this is the software interrupt number 21 hex. Through software interrupt 21 hex, DOS provides a rich variety of functions which are simple to program in assembly language, and which can be built up into a library of FORTRAN utility subroutines. For a description of the facilities made available to the FORTRAN programmer through this technique, see Chapter 15, and for access to these facilities without having to program in assembler we recommend the disk set accompanying this book. A full and lucid description of the DOS operating system, the BIOS, and interrupt vector tables and handlers are given in Ray Duncan's '*Advanced MS DOS*' referenced in the bibliography at the end of Chapter 2.

Well-documented examples of assembly language subroutines callable from FORTRAN and using the software interrupt functions are presented throughout this book.

3.6 EXAMPLES USING THE DOS INTERRUPT FUNCTIONS

We shall finish this chapter by looking at three DOS interrupt functions. For most FORTRAN compilers on the PC it is difficult, if not impossible, to call the DOS interrupt functions directly. However, it is easy in assembler language. The assembler procedures (subroutines) given below are written for the Microsoft Macro Assembler MASM, and for access from the Microsoft FORTRAN compiler. If you have a different assembler or compiler you may need to make some small changes. The names of the code and data segments and the way arguments are passed from the calling routine to a subroutine and back may also be compiler dependent. You should consult your compiler manuals.

For Microsoft FORTRAN, subroutine arguments are passed by putting the 4-byte addresses of where they start in memory on the stack. The last thing put on the stack prior to the call is the 4-byte return address to the calling routine. We also need to save the base pointer (2 bytes) 'BP' on the stack at the start of the assembler routine as we will use it to point to the new top of the stack, so the subroutine arguments' memory addresses will start 6 bytes from the top of the stack. The stack is a last in first out (LIFO) structure. Thus it will be the memory address of the last argument put on the stack that will be 6 bytes from the top of the stack; the penultimate argument 10 bytes (6 + 4 for the memory address) from the top of the stack and so on (14 bytes, 18 bytes etc.). After storing the base pointer on the stack we program it to point at the top of the stack (where the stack pointer SP is). Thus the address of the last argument passed to a subroutine will be at position BP+6 on the stack, the penultimate argument's address at BP+10 and so on.

To initiate a DOS interrupt function from assembler always requires that the function number is in the 8-bit register AH before issuing the interrupt command INT 21H. Depending on the function, it may also be necessary to put appropriate values in some of the other registers. The interrupt function will typically return any information such as errors also via the registers.

In the first example below we ask DOS to identify itself by returning the version number. In this case all that is required to call the function is for the AH register to be set to 30 hex before issuing the INT 21H command. The version number is returned in the AH and AL registers. This is obviously a useful call: if for example it was contemplated that the FORTRAN program was to go on and do something that only worked under a late version of DOS, it would be essential to check that the program was not being run under an early version, where it might crash and damage something. This way, the program can at least be made to terminate elegantly! In Chapter 9, such a DOS version specific operation is undertaken. It is essential to check that DOS 3 or higher is in use: this routine makes it possible.

In the second example we expand the assembler example subroutine given at the end of Chapter 2 which zeros arrays so that it writes a message to the screen if an error is detected. This is achieved using the DOS function 9 hex which writes a string terminating in a '$' to the screen. The register DX has to be set to the offset from the start of the DATA segment where the string is stored. In the third example we poll the system clock. This is function 2C hex which returns the hours in register CH, the minutes in CL, the seconds in DH and the hundredths of seconds in DL. These functions will all be brought together into a single program.

The following assembler procedure uses the DOS function 30 hex to return the DOS version number. The DOS functions are accessed by issuing a software interrupt–interrupt 21 hex.

```
            NAME      IDDOS
;CGROUP GROUP CODE
;
CODE      SEGMENT PUBLIC 'CODE'
;         ASSUME  CS:CGROUP
PUBLIC  IDDOS
IDDOS   PROC      FAR
;
          PUSH      BP                  ;save base pointer
          MOV       BP,SP               ;load base pointer
                                        ;with stack pointer
;
          MOV       AH,30H              ;poll version of MS DOS using
          INT       21                  ;function 30 hex
;
;     the minor version number is returned in AH, and the
;     major version number in AL. First we load ES:BX with
;     the address of IMIN and put the value of AH in there
;     then we load ES:BX with the address of IMAX and put
;     the value of AL in there.
;
          LES       BX,DWORD PTR[BP+6]
          MOV       BYTE PTR ES:[BX],AH
          LES       BX,DWORD PTR[BP+10]
          MOV       BYTE PTR ES:[BX],AL
;         POP       BP                  ;restore base pointer
          RET       8                   ;4*no. of arguments
;
IDDOS   ENDP
CODE      ENDS
          END
```

For this example the interrupt 21 hex with function 30 hex returns the minor version number in AH and the major version number in AL. If you had DOS 2.11, AH would contain 11 or 0B hex, and AL would contain 2.

The FORTRAN program calls IDDOS with two arguments IMAJ and IMIN. IMIN is the last argument in the call and so its address is at BP+6. We move the values of AH and AL into the memory locations of IMIN and IMAJ, and then return to the call jumping the stack pointer over the 8 bytes used for storing the argument addresses. The following FORTRAN program illustrates how IDDOS might be called.

```
        PROGRAM TSTID
C-----------------------
C
C          Tests assembly program IDDOS
C          determines the version number of MS DOS in use.
C
C-------------------------------------------------------------
C
C       CALL IDDOS, IMAJ = major version number
C                   IMIN = minor version number
C
        CALL IDDOS (IMAJ, IMIN)
C
        WRITE (*,1000) IMAJ, IMIN
 1000   FORMAT (//'  The version of MS DOS is:   ',I2,'.',I2)
C
        STOP
        END
```

When checking the version number, remember that DOS usually increases in functionality with every new release. Some useful public domain software, written after DOS 2 was released, checks the DOS version, and instead of checking the major DOS version is 2 *or greater*, just checks whether it is 2. Otherwise useful utilities were rendered useless after DOS 3 was released. So always check the major version number with a .GE. not an .EQ.

Now take another look at the assembler routine introduced in Chapter 2, which zeros the components of a vector. The routine is going to be expanded, first of all to demonstrate how DOS can be used to send messages to the console (screen), and then to demonstrate the real time clock, being used as a timer. With the timer facility, the execution time of the assembly language code can be directly compared to that of a similar code fragment written exclusively in FORTRAN. There are a number of facets to this. First of all, when the size of vector is too large (greater than 66 000 say!) an error message is written to the screen using the DOS function 09 hex. That is the main difference between this routine and the one in Chapter 2.

```
        NAME ZERO
;
DGROUP GROUP DATA
CGROUP GROUP CODE
;
DATA    SEGMENT PUBLIC 'DATA'
        STRING  DB      'Size too large for ZERO routine!',
                DB      0DH,0CH,'$'
;
;       0D hex and 0C hex are carriage return line feed in
        ASCII code
;
DATA    ENDS
;
CODE    SEGMENT PUBLIC  'CODE'
        ASSUME  CS:CGROUP
;
PUBLIC ZERO
ZERO    PROC    FAR
;
        PUSH    BP       ;save base pointer
;
        MOV     BP,SP    ;set base pointer to point
                         ;to top of stack
;
;   initialize error flag 'IERR' to zero
;
        LES     BX,DWORD PTR [BP+6]
        XOR     AX,AX           ;make AX zero
        MOV     WORD PTR ES:[BX],AX
        MOV     WORD PTR ES:[BX+2],AX
;
;       put address of COUNT in ES:BX,
;       count is a 4 byte integer, we put the 2 low bytes
;       in AX and the 2 high bytes in DX. If DX is not equal
;       to 0 then COUNT is too large and we JUMP to ERROR
;
        LES     BX,DWORD PTR [BP+10]
        MOV     AX,WORD PTR ES:[BX]
        MOV     DX,WORD PTR ES:[BX+2]
        CMP     DX,0
        JNE     ERROR
;
;       AX contains size of vector
;       put this in CX for loop
```

```
;
        MOV    CX,AX
;
     load the address of start of vector into ES:BX
     and zero the loop counter
;
        LES    BX,DWORD PTR [BP+14]
        XOR    SI,SI
NEXT:
        PUSH   CX           ;put CX on stack temporarily
;
      we will zero a word at a time, a REAL or INTEGER is
      4-bytes or 2 words long, so we need an inner loop
      of length 2
;
        MOV    CX,2
NEXT1:
        XOR    AX,AX                      ;zero AX
        MO     WORD PTR ES:[BX]+[SI],AX ;put zero in vector
        INC    SI                         ;add 1 to SI
        INC    SI                         ;add 1 to SI
        LOO    NEXT1                      ;loop until CX is 0
;
        POP    CX                         ;get outer loop count
        LOOP   NEXT                       ;loop until CX is 0
        JMP    FIN                        ;all done
ERROR:
;     the size of vector was too large - send
;     error message to screen using DOS function 9 hex
;
        MOV       DX,offset dgroup:STRING
        MOV       AH,09H
        INT       21H
;
;     return IERR as 1
;
        LES       BX,DWORD PTR [BP+6]
        MOV       AX,1
        MOV       WORD PTR ES:[BX],AX
FIN:
;
        POP       BP     ;pop base pointer from stack
        RET       12     ;return 4*number of arguments
;
```

```
ZERO       ENDP
CODE       ENDS
:
           END
```

This time the routine expects three arguments. The first is the vector, the address of the vector being at BP+14, the second is the length of the vector at BP+10, and the third is the error flag IERR at BP+6. We first initialize IERR to zero. The length of the vector is put in the registers DX:AX (we assume that standard 4-byte integers are being used in the FORTRAN program). However, 4 bytes gives us a larger vector than can be conveniently handled, so we limit the size of vector to be that that can be described in 2 bytes (approx 65 500!), if the size passed is larger than this then we put out an error message using the DOS function 09 hex interrupt 21 hex and set IERR to be 1, before returning to the caller.

A FORTRAN program that tests this assembler procedure is set out below.

```
           PROGRAM TSZERO
C-----------------------
C
C          This test program zeros an array using an
C          assembler routine.
C
C-----------------------------------------------------
           DIMENSION XX(10)
C
           XX(1)  =  1.0
           XX(2)  =  5.345
           XX(3)  = -12345.67890
           XX(10) =  1000.9999
           WRITE(*,*) XX
           N = 10
C
           CALL ZERO (XX,N,IERR)
C
           IF (IERR .EQ. 0)        WRITE(*,*) XX
C
C                     now test the writing of the error message
C
           N = 66010
           CALL ZERO (XX,N,IERR)
C
           STOP
           END
```

Next, there is an assembler routine which reads the computer clock to an accuracy of 1/100 seconds. To measure an elapsed time, it is necessary to call this procedure, save the result, perform the operation which is to be timed, call the time procedure again, and compare the time to that at the first enquiry. It is recommended that, to minimize the length and complexity of the assembler code, the saving of the first time and the later calculation of the difference are both done in the FORTRAN section of the code. An example of this appears below.

First of all, here is the assembly language code for the time function:

```
        NAME    TIMER
;
CGROUP  GROUP CODE
;
;
CODE    SEGMENT PUBLIC 'CODE'
;
        ASSUME  CS:CGROUP
;
PUBLIC TIMER
TIMER   PROC    FAR
;
        PUSH    BP              ;save base pointer
        MOV     BP,SP           ;load base pointer
                                ;with stack pointer
;
        MOV     AH,2CH          ;interrupt returns hours in CH
        INT     21H             ;mins in CL,secs in DH,
                                ;hundredths in DL.
;
        LES     BX,DWORD PTR[BP+16]
        MOV     ES:[BX],CH
        LES     BX,DWORD PTR[BP+14]
        MOV     ES:[BX],CL
        LES     BX,DWORD PTR[BP+10]
        MOV     ES:[BX],DH
        LES     BX,DWORD PTR[BP+6]
        MOV     ES:[BX],DL
;
        POP     BP
        RET     16      ;4*no. of arguments
;
TIMER   ENDP
CODE    ENDS
;
        END
```

There are four arguments in the call. The time is read from the clock using the interrupt function 2C hex. The FORTRAN program that follows calls both TIMER and ZERO, and illustrates how the Assembler routine is quicker than using a DO loop to zero a vector 25 000 elements long (if you are using a very fast machine you may not see the difference, you would need to measure 1/1000 seconds!).

```
        PROGRAM TSTTIM
C------------------------
C
C       This test program zeros an array in two different
C       ways, one as a FORTRAN loop, the other as an
C       assembler routine.  The ratio of times taken is
C       worked out by consulting the DOS clock.
C
C-----------------------------------------------------------------
C       COMMON /TIM/ X(25000)
C
C           Use assembler routine
C
        CALL TIMER(NHRS0,NMINS0,NSECS0,NHUNS0)
        CALL ZERO(X,25000,IERR)
        CALL TIMER(NHRS1,NMINS1,NSECS1,NHUNS1)
C
        ITIMEZ = (((NHRS1-NHRS0)*60+(NMINS1-NMINS0))*60+
     1           (NSECS1-NSECS0))*100+(NHUNS1-NHUNS0)
C
C               Use FORTRAN loop
C
        CALL TIMER(NHRS0,NMINS0,NSECS0,NHUNS0)
        DO 10 I = 1, 25000
        X(I) = 0.0
 10     CONTINUE
C
        CALL TIMER(NHRS1,NMINS1,NSECS1,NHUNS1)
C
        ITIMEL = (((NHRS1-NHRS0)*60+(NMINS1-NMINS0))*60+
     1           (NSECS1-NSECS0))*100+(NHUNS1-NHUNS0)
C
C               Report findings
C
        WRITE(*,1000) ITIMEZ, ITIMEL
 1000   FORMAT(//,' Time taken by assembler routine =',I5,/,
     1           ' Time taken by loop              =',I5)
C
```

```
            STOP
            END
```

On an 8086 processor machine, we got a time of 86 hundredths of a second for the assembler routine and 168 hundredths of a second for the DO loop. The savings are only worth having in frequently executed sections of code, but all the same, they do demonstrate the inefficiency of much code derived from even quite simple FORTRAN constructs.

CHAPTER 4

PROGRAMS, FILES, AND FILENAMES

4.1 INTRODUCTION

In this chapter we look at files: FORTRAN source code files and data files. Data files take a number of forms: there are formatted and unformatted files, and there are sequential and direct access files. As part of this review, when we are looking at filenames and default file extensions, we look too at the creation and editing of files. Files which are created during the compilation process are a completely separate issue, and are dealt with in Chapter 5.

In order to see how files are stored on your PC, or more accurately how files are stored on your floppy and hard disks, you must first consider the storage media itself: the floppy and hard disks.

4.2 FLOPPY AND HARD DISKS

The processor can directly address random access memory using its registers, see Chapter 2 for the details. However, random access memory and the registers in the microprocessor chip are examples of what is termed volatile memory. When the microcomputer is turned off and the processor is starved of 'energy giving electricity', everything that was stored in the RAM and the registers is lost (unless you have a computer which has a battery back up, or uses non-volatile RAM which doesn't lose its contents).

When the microcomputer is switched on again the registers are reinitialized. Part of the RAM will be used by the operating system and the status of the remainder of the RAM is left undefined. In some machines, the value of each memory location is set to zero, or may be set to zero while loading the data area of a program. It is dangerous to rely on this, since it makes software perform erratically on machines which are not so considerate.

Programs and data can only be stored permanently if written to files which can then be stored on non-volatile memory. The most common non-volatile memory media supplied with microcomputers are hard disks, and the removable floppy disks.

The processor communicates with these disks through the operating system. The 'DOS' in MS DOS or PC DOS does after all stand for Disk Operating System.

The familiar floppy disk is a flat thin round piece of plastic with an outside layer of magnetic material. The whole is protected by an outside jacket of plastic material which is square or rectangular. Hard disks resemble a number of disks one set above the other on a spindle. The spindle of disks and the 'heads' which move over the disks either storing or retrieving data are neatly packed in a metal box. Hard and floppy disk drives can be mounted inside the microcomputer if the manufacturer has left sufficient room, or can be added to give additional non-volatile storage as external devices.

Floppy disks for DOS machines come in two popular sizes, where the diameter of the disk is 5.25 inches or 3.5 inches. The 5.25 inch disk is protected by a rather flimsy outside cover and is undoubtedly less robust (and floppier!) than the 3.5 inch disk which has a hard and durable plastic exterior, and a spring loaded metal shutter to protect the disk's surface when not in use. However, the 5.25 inch disk has been in existence far longer than the 3.5 inch disk, and is probably more widely used. As a result, the 5.25 inch disks tend to be cheaper and more widely available. With the adoption of the 3.5 inch disk as standard in IBM's PS/2 series of computers, it will no doubt come to be seen as the standard, and the 5.25 inch floppy disk will be seen as an anachronism, in exactly the same way as the earlier, and physically similar, 8 inch floppy disk has become.

At the time of writing, this expected change-over has not yet taken place. Much software is still only obtainable on 5.25 inch media, and cheap computers using 5.25 inch drives are capturing new markets. Undoubtedly the 5.25 inch disk will remain with us for some time to come.

4.3 HOW FILES ARE STORED ON DISK

When formatted, a disk is divided into allocation units (or clusters). Each allocation unit will be made up of a certain number of sectors and each sectors will be so many bytes. The number of bytes per sector and the number of sectors per allocation unit is disk dependent, but to find out these quantities for your system see the first example program at the end of this chapter. A common combination for floppy disks is 512 bytes per sector and two sectors per allocation unit—for a 360 kbyte disk this gives a total of 354 allocation units.

When a file is stored to a newly formatted floppy disk the file is written to the disk a sector at a time (the size of the sector depending on the type of disk), one sector following immediately after the previous sector on the disk. The next file written to disk will follow the first file and so on until the disk is full. A disk written to in this manner would have a very simple straightforward file storage structure. However, this nice ordered structure is destroyed when some of the files stored on the disk are deleted and replaced by other files of different lengths. When this happens the disk controller looks for the first available allocation unit on the disk. The first portion of the new file will be written to this location. The next available allocation unit is then sought for the next portion of the file. On a heavily used disk a large file will typically be stored in a fragmented fashion all over the disk. In order to keep track of the files on the disk and where each portion of a particular file is placed on the disk, a file allocation table (FAT) is constructed which contains information about the allocation units on the disk. The file allocation table is stored on the disk. When a disk is placed in the disk drive a copy of the FAT is placed into the computer memory so that the processor knows the layout of the disk.

Also stored on the disk is a disk directory. The disk directory describes files, subdirectories, and the volume label if present. The disk directory gives the address of the first sector occupied by each file and its entry point into the FAT. The FAT contains the address of the next allocation unit occupied by the next bit of the file and so on until the last sector or file marker is encountered. Thus to find the location of a file on a disk requires information from the disk directory and then repeated information from the FAT.

Notice that, however small a file, the minimum amount of disk space it will occupy is 1 allocation unit. Larger files will always occupy a whole number of allocation units.

For the purpose of clarity the description above contains a number of simplifications. For a detailed description of how files are written to disk the reader is referred to *Advanced MS DOS* by Ray Duncan, referenced in the bibliography at the end of Chapter 2.

When files are stored in a fragmented fashion over the disk file, access times are slower and it is usually worthwhile to copy a well-used disk (file by file) to a newly formatted disk so that the files will be stored consecutively over the disk.

When a file is deleted, the contents of the file are not deleted. Indeed all that happens is that the file is marked as deleted in the disk directory, making the delete operation extremely quick. This allows all the sectors pointed to in the FAT to be overwritten at some stage by a new file or files. The delete operation need not be final. It is possible to recover deleted files by merely giving the file a valid filename in the disk directory again. To do this you need to know your way around the debug program or buy one of the many admirable disk utility products that are on the market. To be fully successful in recovering a deleted file it is absolutely essential that after deleting the file no new file is written to the disk. It is highly recommended that as soon as you are aware that you have deleted a file in error you make a copy of the disk with the write protect tab firmly in place and you leave the original disk alone until the file is recovered.

It is always worthwhile having copies of useful files. Certainly any application program that you buy should be immediately copied and from then on the backup disk should be used to run the application. Even if you are only installing an application you should, where possible, do the installation from a backup disk. Those unenlightened software manufacturers who still sell their software on copy protected disks should always provide you with two sets of disks: one set for putting away in case of problems and one for using.

These days most people will be using a microcomputer with a 10 or 20 megabyte hard disk or more. Whatever the size of your hard disk it is important that you use the disk sensibly. You should separate different applications and different types of files into directories, so that you can easily keep track of all the files. You should back up your hard disk regularly—this is important. Hard disks are very reliable, but if all your work is stored on a hard disk you can't afford not to back it up. All hard disk systems should have a backup and restore facility. Indeed there is one provided with DOS. Most backup facilities allow you to perform this operation in an efficient way, so that if you do it regularly only the files that have changed will be backed up. Before you do any backing up make sure you have some idea of how many disks you will require so that you have them handy. A good backup system will check that the disk that you use is formatted and if it isn't will format it for you—however, make sure you know what your backup facility requires *before* using it.

If the idea of backing up the hard disk regularly fills you with dread—or if you know that however well intentioned you may be you will always put off the backing up of the hard disk until it is too late—then you should only keep application programs on the hard disk. You will have backups of the application programs because software is sold on floppy disks. You should keep all the data that you produce on floppy disks. In this way you will be able to recover completely from a catastrophe with the hard disk, and important data on a floppy disk can be copied easily and quickly.

4.4 FILENAMES

In the Microsoft MS DOS user guide (MS DOS v 3.2) a filename is defined as follows:

A filename can be from one to eight characters in length and can have an extension of up to three characters separated from the filename by a period (.). An example of a complete filename is "progress.rpt". Certain filenames are reserved by MS DOS and should not be used when naming your files. These filenames are: 'aux', 'clock$', 'com', 'con', 'kybd$', 'lpt', 'lst', 'nul', 'prn', and 'scrn$'.

Valid filename characters are: A–Z a–z 0–9 $ % ' - @ { } ~ ' ! # However, it is probably safer to only use letters and numbers in your filenames. Note: no distinction is made between upper and lower case for filenames.

A certain standard has evolved on filename extensions, this is largely due to particular extensions being recognized by DOS or popular applications to signify the type of file. We list most of those in regular use in Table 4.1.

The names you give to files are important. As your disk gets full, being able to instantly discriminate between files can save a lot of time, and may also prevent the deletion of precious files by mistake. It is worth taking some time and trouble when naming files. Remember that you have eight letters available to you for the filename, so try and make up names that describe the contents of the file. If you are lazy in your choice of names then when you come back to a disk full of files after a few weeks have passed you will need to print them all to discover what they do!

Table 4.1   Filename extensions

.EXE	For executable files
.COM	For command files (cf. COMMAND.COM) a special sort of executable file
.BAT	For batch files (cf. AUTOEXEC.BAT), a file containing one or more system commands, which when run will execute each system command in turn as if it were being entered through the keyboard.

To submit any of these files for execution it is only necessary to type the filename up to but not including the 'dot'.

.BAS	The extension given to files created using the BASIC interpreter
.FOR	The extension that is usually given to FORTRAN source code. (Digital Research FORTRAN is a maverick that expects .F77)
.ASM	The extension for assembler source files
.C	The extension for 'C' source files
.DAT	The extension for data files
.RES	The extension for results files
.OBJ	The extension given to object files
.LIB	The extension given to library files
.LST	The extension given to a FORTRAN source code listing
.COD	The extension given to FORTRAN object code listing
.CRF	The extension given to a cross reference listing
.MAP	The extension given to the map file
.BIN	The extension given to binary files
.TMP	The extension given to temporary files
.SYS	The extension given to files used by the operating system (cf. CONFIG.SYS)
.DOC	Common extension given to text files
.TXT	Common extension given to text files
.HLP	Common extension given to help files
.BAK	The extension commonly given by word processors/text editors to the previous version of an edited file

When you have executable programs which are in extremely regular use, it is worth giving them simple names which require the minimum of typing. More descriptive names are necessary with less regularly used software.

4.5   CREATING AND EDITING PROGRAM SOURCE AND DATA FILES

One of the utilities provided in DOS is the line editor EDLIN.COM. It is perfectly possible to create and edit your source and data files using EDLIN.COM but we cannot think of one good reason why you would want to!

The way to create and edit source and data files is to use a full screen editor, or to use your favourite word processor in 'non- document' mode. Before using a word processor make sure that it allows you to create 'non-document' files (text files). Left to its own devices a word processor will produce documents full of ESCape sequences and potentially many other weird characters (which you haven't typed). When you come to print your 'document' files, these non-printing characters will be changed to control codes for your printer, so that you get bold facing, underlining, headers and footers, and all the other wonderful features necessary for the production of nice-looking letters and swish documents.

Unfortunately your FORTRAN compiler will not ignore all these unfamiliar characters and so a program created in this way will be full of syntax errors. Reading and writing from data files produced in 'document' mode on the word processor could also lead to unexpected results.

Many word processors have a 'non-document' or text editor mode and if you are already familiar with a word processor which has this feature then we would recommend that you continue to use it (better the devil you know …). If, however, you have managed to avoid using a word processor, and you don't see any reason to learn to use one, then we would recommend you to use a purpose written program text editor. A number of such products are available commercially.

Text editors are designed for programmers, and as such they do not generally provide features such as superfix, subfix, underline, word wrap, font change, etc. which you would expect to find in a word processor. They are therefore generally cheaper than word processors and are good value for the programmer who doesn't have to provide lengthy documentation—this particular combination *should* be rather rare!

Computing departments with a mini or mainframe computer and potentially 50–100 simultaneous users are sometimes reluctant to make available screen editors or word processors for general use. This is because screen editing and word processing demands a great deal of attention from the computer's processor. The processor has to control the paging and scrolling of portions of your file on the screen. It has to control the position of the cursor relative to your file. In addition it has to handle all the features that are demanded of even the most modest screen editor. All this attention being required by one process means that other processes get less time—the response time for other users gets worse. Consequently it may only require a handful of users to be screen editing at one time to bring even a powerful mainframe system to its knees.

The beauty of personal computing is that you do not have to be bothered with issues such as these. The PC is all yours, at least while you are using it, so if you want to use all the processing power for screen editing, go ahead and use it, you will not be interfering with the response of the user on the PC beside you since they have their own processor and are not sharing yours!

When you have created your source or data file you will invariably need to edit it at some time. After editing the file and saving it, most text editors/word processors rename the original file so as to ensure that it does not get overwritten. Thus for example you may have created the FORTRAN file TEST.FOR. When you come to edit this file the edited file will become (by default) TEST.FOR and the original TEST.FOR will be preserved as TEST.BAK. Of course if you edit TEST.FOR again and again only the two most recent versions of the file will be preserved in TEST.FOR and TEST.BAK. Make sure the screen editor that you use has this backup feature. Otherwise you will need to remember to create a copy of a file before you edit. Even if your screen editor has a backup facility, it may be worth copying the original version of a file before embarking on a long complicated editing session—it is very reassuring to know that you can always return to the original version of the file!

One word of warning regarding files. Be careful when using the DOS * 'wild card' particularly when deleting files.

```
DEL *.BAK
```

will delete all .BAK files in the active directory,

```
DEL *.FOR
```

will delete all the .FOR files in the active directory. After a long session at the keyboard it is frighteningly easy to delete all the .FOR files when you meant to delete all the .BAK files to create some extra space on your disk. This is especially the case when working under pressure, or when tired. At least the operating system will not allow you to delete all the files in a directory using the command:

```
DEL *.*
```

without asking you if you are sure!

There are several procedures which help. One is to create a file called say PURGE.BAT which contains the desired command DEL *.BAK so that deletion commands are only given in a way that prevents inadvertent deletion of important material. Another is to run the editor from a batch file which saves the FORTRAN source code in another directory each time as additional security.

4.6 USING FILES FROM FORTRAN

There are essentially two types of files that you can read or write in a FORTRAN program: sequential files and direct access files. These files can be either formatted or unformatted.

If the file is formatted then you can **type** it on the screen and it will be intelligible. If the file is unformatted then it is written as a binary file and if you **type** it on the screen you will only be able to recognize an occasional word if you are lucky—frequently the binary form of the file will contain a sequence of symbols that will cause the bell on your PC to sound.

Unformatted binary files take up less storage on your disk than formatted files and so should be used for scratch files.

Like all good rules, the above has exceptions. A formatted file may have ESCape sequences in it to set up a particular printer facility, and these may interact with the screen in an undesirable way. It may assume more characters per line than the screen has, and so may not display correctly. Unformatted files will only have readable text in them if they contain **character** or **hollerith** entities. Finally, the space taken by any file is rounded to the nearest allocation unit so that for small files on large capacity hard disk systems, the savings may be illusory.

FORTRAN lacks the safeguard of being able to OPEN files for READING or WRITING. Thus, although when you write to a sequential file which has only been written to, you always write to the bottom of the file, it is possible to destroy all or part of the contents of a sequential file by reading only a part of it, then writing to it. After the record which has been written, the end of file mark is appended.

When a sequential file is OPENed for reading, a pointer is set to the first record in the file. Sequential files are read from top to bottom, in order, one record at a time. Backward movement through a file is provided by the REWIND and BACKSPACE commands. REWIND takes the pointer back to the first record in the file, and BACKSPACE moves the pointer to the previous record.

All files that are created in an editor or word processor, for example data files, are sequential formatted files.

When reading from or writing to a direct access file you can choose which line (or record) in the file you wish to address irrespective of whether the line you require is the next line in the file or not. Thus direct access files are used when lines of data need to be accessed repeatedly or when data is accessed according to some criteria which is not easily predictable.

To repeatedly access the same line of data in a sequential file would mean either that the line of data would have to be repeated as many times as required within the sequential file—thus making the file unnecessarily long—or, the sequential file would need to be rewound or backspaced frequently, meaning that even unwanted lines of data would have to be re-read, thus making the whole process exceedingly tedious.

Most databases and complex data structures which require quick access to data which may be stored anywhere within the file will make use of direct access files.

4.7 DOS CONSIDERATIONS

DOS currently supports two different file management structures. Two structures coexist because Microsoft were keen to retain some form of compatibility with the file structure used in the CP/M operating system at the same time as offering a UNIX-like operating system interface.

Thus programs, which were developed under the CP/M operating system—used on most 8-bit microcomputers—which uses a data structure called a file control block (FCB), are readily portable to the DOS environment, since DOS allows files to be defined and manipulated using FCBs similar to those used by CP/M.

At the same time DOS allows files to be referred to using file 'handles', a system developed in the UNIX operating system.

The FCB stores the files attributes such as the date and time the file was created, its name, and its length. However, FCBs cannot be used, for example, to refer to files in different directories because there is simply not enough space in the FCB data structure to define pathnames of files which may go over a number of directories. For this reason the FCB system cannot be used in a network environment.

The UNIX-like file management structure allocates to each file which is active (open) a 16-bit number called a 'file handle'. The file is then always referred to by this number. The file handle has some similarities with the use of the UNIT number to refer to files in a FORTRAN program. This is a much simpler system for the application programmer as the file is completely defined by its handle.

The disadvantage of file handles is that the number of files allowed to be active at any one time is limited.

The number of active files is limited by the 'files =' command line in the CONFIG.SYS file which is used when the operating system is started up ('booted') to configure the operating system environment, and cannot be altered without changing the CONFIG.SYS file.

Changes to the CONFIG.SYS file result in changes to the operating system environment only if the operating system is rebooted. So to change the number of active files the CONFIG.SYS file has to be edited and the operating system rebooted—clearly this operation cannot be undertaken from inside an application program.

There is an absolute maximum to the number of files that can be active at one time, and so addressable using handles. The maximum is 20 files. However, in DOS, devices such as the keyboard or the screen are referred to in the same way as files, and five of the 20 files and file handles are reserved for:

• keyboard, console, error, parallel, and serial devices

This leaves 15 files available to the application programmer. Although it is possible, but not advisable in general, to redirect the five reserved handles to files of your own choice, in some circumstances this could be used to advantage. For example, redirecting output which would by default go to the screen to go to a file. Use redirection of the default device handles with great care.

Fifteen active files at one time is ample for most applications; however, the compiler itself may reserve some of these files for its own use thus further limiting the number of active files. This limitation is only a problem if you need to have all the available active files and more open at one time. If not, the closing of a file releases that file handle for use to address another file.

Most current FORTRAN compilers use file handles for their file manipulation and thus the 'files = ' command must be used in CONFIG.SYS, and the FORTRAN programmer will be limited as to the number of files open at one time. However, the assembler programmer would be able to increase the number of active files by referring to additional files using file control blocks. These files would have to exist in the current working directory. The number of additional files referred to using FCBs would theoretically be infinite but in practice would be limited by the size of the available storage on the disk containing the current working directory.

If you use a compiler which states that it 'requires DOS 2.0 or above', then it quite probably uses file handles. If it works happily under DOS 1, then it most certainly uses FCBs.

4.8 DOS FUNCTIONS AND FILES

We finish this chapter with four assembler routines which are callable from FORTRAN programs. The routines use the DOS functions which are accessed through the software interrupt 21 hex. As before we have used the Microsoft MACRO Assembler (MASM) and the Microsoft FORTRAN compiler. The first assembly language routine uses the DOS function 36 hex to return information concerning the amount of available space left on a disk. The other three assembly language routines show how files can be created and used through file handles.

The assembly language routine IDFS is analogous to the operating system utility CHKDSK, returning information about the free and used memory on a floppy disk at a given disk drive. The disk can be either a floppy disk or a hard disk, and any drive can be addressed— even the default drive at the time of the call which may be unknown to the calling program. To be able to obtain this information from inside a FORTRAN program which performs I/O is extremely valuable. If an estimate of the size of a file to be written is calculated, then IDFS can be used to determine whether the disk at a particular drive has sufficient free storage for that file. If the free space on a disk is inadequate the file could be written to a different drive (if available) or a message could be written informing the user of the problem, and prompting the user to insert a different disk or to specify a different drive letter. At the very least the program could terminate gracefully with an appropriate error message.

The routine `IDFS` uses the DOS function 36 hex. This requires that a drive number be placed in the `DL` register prior to the interrupt. Drive number 0 refers to the default (currently logged) drive, number 1 refers to drive A, number 2 to drive B, etc. The function returns information in all the data registers, unless the drive number doesn't exist in which case an error is indicated by the `AX` register containing FFFF hex. The information returned is the number of allocation units (clusters) on the disk, the number of free allocation units, the number of sectors per allocation unit and the number of bytes per sector. The routine is shown below in full.

```
        NAME     IDFS
;
CGROUP  GROUP  CODE
;
;
CODE    SEGMENT PUBLIC 'CODE'
;
        ASSUME  CS:CGROUP
;
PUBLIC IDFS
IDFS    PROC       FAR
;
        PUSH  BP       ;save base pointer
        MOV   BP,SP    ;load base pointer with stack pointer
;
;       get drive number from stack and put it in DL
;
        LES   BX,DWORD PTR[BP+26]
        MOV   DL,BYTE PTR ES:[BX]
;
;       function 36 hex returns disk free space
;
        MOV   AH,36H
        INT   21H
;
;       is this a valid drive number? If not jump to ERROR1
;
        CMP   AX,0FFFFH
        JE    ERROR1
;
;       valid drive number
;
;       in this case function has returned:
;       number of free clusters in BX
;       number of clusters on disk in DX
```

```
;         number of sectors per cluster in AX
;         number of bytes per sector in CX
;
          LES     DI,DWORD PTR[BP+22]
          MOV     WORD PTR ES:[DI],BX
          LES     BX,DWORD PTR[BP+18]
          MOV     WORD PTR ES:[BX],DX
          LES     BX,DWORD PTR[BP+14]
          MOV     WORD PTR ES:[BX],AX
          LES     BX,DWORD PTR[BP+10]
          MOV     WORD PTR ES:[BX],CX
;
          XOR     AX,AX                   ;error = 0
          JMP     ENDDF
;
ERROR1:
          MOV     AX,1                    ;error = 1
;
ENDDF:
;
;         AX contains error value 0 or 1, put this in IERR
;
          LES     BX,DWORD PTR[BP+6]
          MOV     WORD PTR ES:[BX],AX
;
          POP     BP                      ;restore base pointer
          RET     24                      ;4*no. of arguments
;
IDFS      ENDP
CODE      ENDS
;
          END
```

The following FORTRAN program TSTDFS invites the user to enter a drive number (0 for default, 1 for A, 2 for B, etc.) and returns the allocation unit information about the disk at that drive. In addition the program calculates the total number of bytes that can be stored on the disk and the number of free bytes. This is not how the assembly language routine IDFS would normally be used—CHKDSK does this job—but it serves to illustrate how the routine can be called from a FORTRAN program.

```
          PROGRAM TSTDFS
C
C         tests assembly routine: IDFS
C         returns disk free space and additional information
C         function returns invalid drive number if IERR is set
```

```
C
100       WRITE(*,1000)
1000      FORMAT(' enter drive NUMBER,',/,
     1            ' for default drive ENTER: 0',/,
     2            ' for drive a: ENTER: 1',/,
     3            ' for drive b: ENTER: 2',/,
     4            ' etc... :',\)
C
          READ(*,1010) IDRIVE
1010      FORMAT(I1)
C
C         call IDFS, returns: NUMCL  = number of free clusters
C                             NUMCLD = number of clusters per
C                                      drive
C                             NSECTS = number of sectors per
C                                      cluster
C                             NBYTES = number of bytes per
C                                      sector
C         NOTE    clusters = allocation units
C         and     IERR = 0, successful
C                 IERR = 1, invalid drive number
          CALL IDFS(IDRIVE,NUMCL,NUMCLD,NSECTS,NBYTES,IERR)
C
          IF (IERR.EQ.1) THEN
          WRITE(*,1020) IDRIVE
1020      FORMAT(//' Invalid drive number:',I1,/,' try again!')
          GOTO 100
          ENDIF
C         WRITE(*,1030) NUMCL,NUMCLD,NSECTS,NBYTES
1030      FORMAT(//' number of free allocation units =',I8,/,
     1    'number of allocation units per disk =',I8,/,
     2    'number of sectors per allocation unit =',I8/,
     3    'number of bytes per sector        =',I8)
C
          IMUL1 = NBYTES*NSECTS
          IMUL2 = IMUL1*NUMCL
          IMUL3 = IMUL1*NUMCLD
C
          WRITE(*,1040) IMUL2,IMUL3
1040      FORMAT(//'   number of bytes free on disk =',I16,/,
     1            '   total number of bytes on disk =',I16)
C
          STOP
          END
```

The next three assembly language routines create a file, write to a file, and close a file, using file handles. The FORTRAN example that calls these three routines demonstrates that a file can be created in the default directory without recourse to the normal FORTRAN OPEN, WRITE, and CLOSE statements. Although using file handles in this way may give some speed advantage, and certainly reduces the size of executable files, these are not the main reasons why the DOS file handle routines are of interest. Using similar functions, subdirectories can be created or deleted, files can be created in subdirectories, hidden files and read only files can be written. All that is required is a change to the DOS function. The following routines provide a skeleton of what can be done. A family of such functions will be found on the disk set which can be purchased to complement this book.

The assembler routine CRHAND creates a file using a file handle. The DOS function used is 3C hex. The pathname of the file to be created has to be an ASCII zero string (a character string terminating in CHAR(0)), whose first character resides at the address given in DS:DX. To achieve this, the pathname and its length are passed through the argument list. The pathname is then copied to a local DATA area (one character at a time); after the last character in the pathname is copied, a 0 is appended to the end. A file attribute needs to be specified in CX (you could create a hidden file, CX = 2, or a read only file, CX = 1, but for normal files the attribute would be 0). If an error occurs (e.g. the pathname is not valid) the function sets the carry flag and an error code is returned in AX. Otherwise the file handle (an integer number by which the file can be referenced) is returned in AX.

```
          NAME    CRHAND
;
DGROUP    GROUP DATA
CGROUP    GROUP CODE
;
DATA      SEGMENT PUBLIC 'DATA'
;
PATHNM    DB        65 DUP(?)
;
DATA      ENDS
;
;
CODE      SEGMENT PUBLIC 'CODE'
;
          ASSUME  CS:CGROUP,DS:DGROUP
;
PUBLIC    CRHAND
CRHAND    PROC FAR
;
          PUSH    BP         ;save base pointer
          MOV     BP,SP      ;load base pointer with stack
                             ;pointer
;
```

```
;       get the number of characters in the pathname (COUNT)
;       from its address placed on the stack by the calling
;       routine, and put the value in CX
;
        LES       BX,DWORD PTR[BP+18]
        MOV       CX,ES:[BX]
;
;       now get the address of the first character of the
;       pathname, and copy characters from memory one at
;       a time into the register AL and then into the
;       local data area called PATHNM
;
        LES       BX,DWORD PTR[BP+22]
        XOR       SI,SI
LP1:
        MOV       AL,BYTE PTR ES:[BX]+[SI]
        MOV       BYTE PTR DGROUP:PATHNM[SI],AL
        INC       SI
        LOOP      LP1          ;loop until CX = 0
;
        XOR       AL,AL        ;zero AL and add to end of pathname
        MOV       BYTE PTR DGROUP:PATHNM[SI],AL
;
;       put address of local data area in DX, and get file
;       attribute from address on stack and put it in CX
;       prior to function call
;
        MOV       DX,OFFSET DGROUP:PATHNM
        LES       BX,DWORD PTR[BP+14]
        MOV       CX,ES:[BX]
        MOV       AH,3CH       ;function 3CH
        INT       21H          ;software interrupt
;
        JC        ERROR
;
        LES       BX,DWORD PTR[BP+10]      ;address of handle
        MOV       ES:[BX],AX               ;return handle
        XOR       AX,AX                    ;zero AX
        LES       BX,DWORD PTR[BP+6]       ;address of IERR
        MOV       ES:[BX],AX               ;IERR = 0
        JMP       END
;
ERROR:
        LES       BX,DWORD PTR[BP+6]       ;address of IERR
        MOV       ES:[BX],AX               ;error code in IERR
```

```
;
END:
;
        POP     BP                              ;restore base pointer
        RET     20                              ;4*no. of arguments
;
CRHAND  ENDP
CODE    ENDS
;
        END
```

This routine is called with five arguments. The first is the pathname of the file. If you put just the filename then the file will be created in the current directory. If you give a pathname then it must be a valid pathname. The second argument is the length of pathname, i.e. the number of characters in the string given as the first argument. The third argument is the file attribute, You can create read only files, hidden files, etc., but normal files have a file attribute of 0. The fourth argument is the file handle—a number like a unit number given to the file by DOS. The fifth argument is an error indicator IERR. The routine is called CRHAND and uses the DOS function 3C hex.

The Assembler routine WRTHND writes to a file referred to by a handle using the function 40 hex. Before calling this function, BX must contain the file handle, CX the number of bytes to be written, and DS:DX points to the memory of the first character in the string to be written to the file. In this example rather than using a local data area we set DS:DX to point to the memory for the character string put on the stack by the calling routine, to ensure that DS is not altered it is stored temporarily on the stack.

```
        NAME    WRTHND
;
GROUP   GROUP CODE
;
;
CODE    SEGMENT PUBLIC 'CODE'
;
        ASSUME  CS:CGROUP
;
PUBLIC  WRTHND
WRTHND  PROC FAR
;
        PUSH    BP          ;save base pointer
        MOV     BP,SP       ;load base pointer with stack pointer
;
;   put the number of bytes to be written in CX
;
        LES     BX,DWORD PTR[BP+10]
```

```
                MOV         CX,ES:[BX]
;
;       put handle in BX
;
                LES         BX,DWORD PTR[BP+18]
                MOV         AX,ES:[BX]
                MOV         BX,AX
                PUSH        DS          ;save data segment
;
;       put address of string directly in DS:DX
;
                LDS         DX,DWORD PTR[BP+14]
                XOR         AX,AX       ;zero AX
                MOV         AH,40H      ;function 40H
                INT         21H         ;software interrupt
                POP         DS          ;restore data segment
;
                JC          ERROR       ;error if carry is set
;
;       return number of bytes written (AX) to calling routine
;
                LES         BX,DWORD PTR[BP+22]
                MOV         ES:[BX],AX
                XOR         AX,AX                    ;no error
                LES         BX,DWORD PTR[BP+6]       ;IERR
                MOV         ES:[BX],AX               ;put 0 in IERR
                JMP         END
;
ERROR:
                LES         BX,DWORD PTR[BP+6]  ;IERR
                MOV         ES:[BX],AX               ;put error code in IERR
;
END:
;
                POP         BP          ;restore base pointer
                RET         20          ;4*no. of arguments
;
WRTHND  ENDP
CODE    ENDS
;
                END
```

This routine has five arguments in the call. The first is the number of characters (bytes) written to the file. This is returned by DOS and if it is not equal to the number of bytes that should have been written then an error has occurred, for example the disk might be full. The second argument is the file handle given to the file when it was opened or created. The third argument is the text to be written to the file—a character string. The fourth argument is the number of characters in the character string to be written. The final argument is 'IERR' which if non-zero indicates that an error has occurred. If IERR is 5 then the handle is not open for writing, and if IERR is 6 then the handle is not open or invalid. The DOS function used is 40 hex, and the routine is called WRTHND.

The assembly routine CLHAND closes a file opened or created with a file handle. This uses function 3E hex and the register BX must contain the file handle when the function is called.

```
NAME    CLHAND
;
CGROUP  GROUP CODE
;
;
CODE    SEGMENT PUBLIC 'CODE'
;
        ASSUME  CS:CGROUP
;
PUBLIC CLHAND
CLHAND PROC FAR
;
        PUSH    BP        ;save base pointer
        MOV     BP,SP     ;load base pointer with stack pointer
;
;       put file handle in BX
;
        LES     BX,DWORD PTR[BP+10]
        MOV     AX,ES:[BX]
        MOV     BX,AX
        XOR     AX,AX     ;zero AX
        MOV     AH,3EH    ;function 3EH
        INT     21H       ;software interrupt
;
        JC      ERROR     ;if carry is set then error
;
;       no error
;
        XOR     AX,AX
        LES     BX,DWORD PTR[BP+6]    ;IERR
        MOV     ES:[BX],AX            ;put 0 in IERR
        JMP     END
;
ERROR:
        LES     BX,DWORD PTR[BP+6]    ;IERR
```

```
        MOV       ES:[BX],AX              ;put error code in IERR
;
END:
;
        POP       BP            ;restore base pointer
        RET       8             ;4*no. of arguments
;
CLHAND  ENDP
CODE    ENDS
;
        END
```

This routine has only two arguments, the handle and the error indicator IERR. The routine is called CLHAND and uses the DOS function 3E hex.

The following FORTRAN example calls the last three assembler routines, creating a file in the current directory, writing some text to it, and closing it without apparently doing any FORTRAN I/O.

```
        PROGRAM TSTHND
C
        CHARACTER*64 TEXT1
C
C                           create a file with handle IHAND1
C
        CALL CRHAND('TSTHND.DOC',10,0,IHAND1,IERR)
        IF (IERR.NE.0) GO TO 1000
C
C       no error so write message
C       note we can write a message to the screen as if it
C       were a file with handle '1'.
C
        CALL WRTHND(IB4,1,'CRHAND OK ',10,IERR)
C
        IF (IERR.NE.0) GO TO 1000
        IF (IB4.NE.10) GO TO 1000
C
C                           write to file with handle IHAND1
C
        TEXT1 = ' You should find this message in TSTHND.DOC'
C
        CALL WRTHND(IB5,IHAND1,TEXT1,43,IERR)
C
        IF (IERR.NE.0) GO TO 1000
```

```
        IF (IB5.NE.43) GO TO 1000
C
C                       no error so write message
C
        CALL WRTHND(IB6,1,'WRTHND OK ',10,IERR)
C
        IF (IERR.NE.0) GO TO 1000
        IF (IB6.NE.10) GO TO 1000
C
C                       close file with handle IHAND1
C
        CALL CLHAND(IHAND1,IERR)
C
        IF (IERR.NE.0) GO TO 1000
C
C                       no error so write message
C
        CALL WRTHND(IB7,1,'CLHAND OK ',10,IERR)
C
        IF (IERR.NE.0) GO TO 1000
C
        STOP
1000    WRITE(*,5000) IERR
5000    FORMAT('ERROR CODE =',I5)
        END
```

We compared the executable code of the FORTRAN example using file handles and the three assembler routines CRHAND, WRTHND, and CLHAND with the executable code doing the same operations using FORTRAN OPEN, WRITE and CLOSE statements. The all-FORTRAN executable code even for this trivial example was over 1 kbyte larger.

In Chapter 9 there is an assembler routine which deletes files. Other DOS functions available on the disk set which can be purchased to complement this book are listed in Chapter 15.

CHAPTER 5

COMPILING, LINKING,
AND DEBUGGING

5.1 WHAT IS A COMPILER?

Many microcomputer programmers use interpreters, like the programs that run the majority of BASIC programs. Often, these interpreters are encoded in ROM (read-only memory) and are the main programming tool on that particular machine. Almost alone among DOS PCs, the IBM PC has a ROM BASIC. The BASIC code (which the programmer has written) is scanned line by line, and the interpreter obeys the instructions contained in it in the order in which they are encountered. A BASIC program is almost a 'data file' of commands to the interpreter.

In contrast, an assembler converts code written in easy-to-remember mnemonics into machine code. Whereas an interpreter is a fairly complex program, an assembler need not be, because there is a one-to-one relationship between the assembler mnemonics and the machine code. The next step up from a simple assembler is a macro assembler. This has the facility to replace commonly occurring code sections with predefined procedures or 'macros'. However, all that happens here is that when a call to a macro is encountered, the expanded macro code is inserted in its place.

A compiler generates machine code (eventually) just like an assembler, but is an altogether more complex operation. For a start, the source code has potentially a difficult syntax to analyse, and there may be very little equivalence between the high-level language structure and that which is eventually implemented in machine code. One line of compiler code will typically compile into a large number of lines of machine code.

Computer languages which have instructions which more closely resemble English than they do machine code are termed 'higher level languages'. As a generality, the term includes all the compiled languages and many of the interpreted languages.

FORTRAN, with its strict and relatively simple syntax, has its roots closer to machine code than most other 'high-level' computer languages, and hence the compilation process is potentially simpler and quicker than for Pascal or C (say).

5.2 WHAT A FORTRAN COMPILER DOES

This account has been written for the FORTRAN programmer who wishes to understand what his FORTRAN compiler does in relatively simple terms. For a more detailed and rigorous treatment, it is worth delving into the extensive literature on compiling techniques, or for an overview, into the chapter on compilation in Metcalf's *FORTRAN Optimization*, referenced in Chapter 1.

The way a FORTRAN compiler operates is as follows. Each line of the input file is read in, and 'parsed' into its constituent elements: reserved words, punctuation, data values, standard functions, and variables. At this stage, the compiler must decide if the syntax of the statement is permissible. Sometimes it may be difficult to decide what is what. Take for example the statement:

```
DO 10 I=1,20
```

If the comma is omitted, the statement changes to a valid FORTRAN assignment statement:

```
DO10I = 120
```

and no error will be flagged. If the first loop index is the variable J, as in:

```
DO10I = J20
```

there will still be no error, but reversing the order of indices to start from say 1 and go up to J yields:

```
DO10I = 1J
```

which should be flagged as the invalid variable name 1J.

Having decided that the syntax is inadmissible, the statement is probably rejected in its entirety. In the case of a DO loop start, it is not too serious, but if it is the terminating labelled statement, it most certainly is. A crop of later errors will be triggered. These include nesting errors in DO loops, block IFs and so on. It is particularly common to generate consequential errors when the first error is detected in a declaration statement. Some compilers are intelligent enough to only reject that part of a declaration statement *after* any error, which cuts down slightly on the number of error reports.

When a statement is admissible, the compiler adds to its tables of references to constants and variables. Further tables of forward references, to be resolved later, and backward references, which resolve earlier forward references, are also built up. Examples of forward references are when a GOTO jumps to a statement label which has not yet been encountered, or a DO loop starts, and refers to its terminating statement. Similar, but backward, references include GOTO jumps back up the program, references to already defined FORMAT statements, and so on.

The logical structure of the statement itself is represented in symbolic form and stored away.

Following the parsing of an END statement, the compiler can check that all references are satisfied, for example that no statement labels are missing. We would call all of this the first pass, or syntax check. At this point, different compilers take different actions.

Early versions of Microsoft FORTRAN were supplied with a program FOR1.EXE which could only undertake this first pass. It therefore had to generate files containing the various tables and partly processed statements. Two files were generated: PASIBF.SYM and PASIBF.BIN. The first of these two contains the symbol tables and the other the partly processed code. Assuming that the FORTRAN source file contains further subroutines, FOR1 would flush its internal data tables and then process the next module. Some symbols are carried forward, for example the number of parameters to a subroutine or function call. The compiler is then able to flag errors, provided that the call and the definition occur in the same source code file.

The second pass of the compiler was the completely separate PAS2.EXE, which finished the conversion of code to binary (i.e. generated the OBJ file), allocated space to the various symbols and so on. It was rare to have an error in PAS2 if FOR1 had completed successfully, since for obvious reasons, the files created by FOR1 had to be valid input to PAS2. Remember that many references (say to statement labels) in the generated OBJ file are relative code addresses rather than absolute ones, because the subroutines have yet to be 'linked' together. Not only that, but even if the OBJ file was a complete program, it might be loaded into different places in RAM on different machines, or if different utilities had been loaded in the same computer between invocations. Hence it contains relative, rather than absolute addresses. Also, stubs to connect to other subroutines and functions both user-written and FORTRAN-library provided, are generated at this time.

PAS2 generated the OBJ file, and deleted PASIBF.BIN and PASIBF.SYM. Other compilers, including compilers from Digital Research and Supersoft, also use this technique of generating intermediate code files, and need two separate programs, one per pass.

Microsoft FORTRAN also had a third pass PAS3.EXE for generating cross reference information.

Compare this now with Ryan MacFarland FORTRAN. Ryan MacFarland FORTRAN has a single EXE program RMFORT which contains both passes of the compiler. These are called into play alternately on each subprogram, as a result of which the OBJ file is emitted directly. Since the OBJ file is created subprogram by subprogram, an OBJ file is created regardless of errors, although it will certainly not operate correctly if errors occur. Microsoft FORTRAN's FOR1 deletes the PASIBF files if errors are detected, so that an invalid OBJ file is not created.

In principle, the Ryan MacFarland FORTRAN scheme should be quicker, and needs less manual intervention. However, the Microsoft FORTRAN scheme has smaller compiler program files, and so can operate from smaller disk media if need be. Space in the compiler is saved if the plain text compiler error lists are kept in a special file, and this has the added benefits that they can be removed if disk space is at a premium, (although this means that errors are flagged with a number rather than in words), and that the error messages can be translated to other languages or updated more easily.

Although RMFORT is not itself an overlay structured program, there is no reason why it should not be. The use of overlays would allow multipass compilers to work with small RAM, since only one part of the compiler operation need be active in the RAM at one time.

The separate passes of a compiler like the Microsoft FORTRAN compiler can be specified in the lines of a batch file, which make the overall tedium of invoking them somewhat less. One step further in this direction is to have a small EXE program which invokes the different passes of the compiler as 'chained' programs or 'child processes'. This approach has been adopted by Digital Research, Prospero, and now Microsoft in its v.4 FORTRAN.

5.3 WHAT THE LINKER DOES

Having converted one or more FORTRAN source files to OBJ files using the compiler, they have to be welded into a single program. The linker does this. It basically has three functions:

1 to incorporate start-up and close-down code which is needed by every program;
2 to incorporate library functions;
3 to interface the different modules, 'fixing up' the relative addresses where possible, so that when the program is loaded a minimum of relative addressing needs to be firmed up.

The initialization and termination code may be present in the 'library', or it may be a separate OBJ file, or it may be generated by the linker. That depends on the particular compiler/linker combination. For example, the Supersoft FORTRAN compiler *always* needs the start-up OBJ module, whereas the Prospero system only requires it if you choose not to use Prospero's own linker.

Incorporating library functions is more involved than it seems at first glance. Not only are there the standard functions like SIN, COS, and SQRT, but there are functions which may be explicitly invoked like FLOAT, or implicitly invoked when the source code calls for a type coercion. 'Coercion' is forcing a value to change its data type. For example, the code

```
A = (I+J)
```

needs FLOAT or something like it to convert ('coerce') the result of the integer addition (I+J) to real, whether it is explicitly stated or not. Note, however, that

```
A = 10
```

may be coerced at compile time, and not necessarily require such a function.

Other operations, like OPEN, CLOSE, READ, WRITE, etc., also make calls to library functions. If these are obvious, then less obvious candidates for the inclusion of library functions include addition and other apparently trivial (in FORTRAN terms) operations.

Some code is injected 'in-line', rather in the way a macro assembler expands each macro as it is encountered. Microsoft FORTRAN offers the user some control over how much code is generated this way, and how much is maintained as subroutines, with their associated calling and returning protocols. A certain amount of code is always generated in one way or the other, and there is only a limited area in the middle where the user can expect control. For example, user-defined subroutines and functions are never expanded at each call. Simple arithmetic is almost always left in-line. However, intrinsic functions, complicated maths, statement functions and so on are candidates for optional treatment either way. In-line code is always longer but faster than using subprogram calls.

Finally, the fixing up of relative addresses is simplified by the segment:offset form of addressing inherent in the 8086/8088 PC processors. The linker has the length in bytes of every code and data structure, and from the subprogram calls and how they are nested it can work out the required length of stack. These can all now be evaluated and saved in the form of offsets. Only the segment addresses need to be evaluated at load time. That is relatively easy. Imagine a program with 50 subroutines, each of which is located in its own segment. The program also has 50 independent data structures (i.e. the default data segment and 49 named COMMON blocks). It also has a stack, and a handful of segments, say 10, created for library routines. That gives 50 + 50 + 1 + 10 or 111 segments. That still only requires 111 two-byte segment addresses to be established at load time.

Overlay linkers also need to load the overlay management code. This may be held, like the start-up code, in separate OBJ modules, in a library, or it may be generated by the linker. Overlay structured programs may have all the overlays contained within a single large EXE file, or separate files (usually with OVL or OV1, OV2 etc., extensions). The special spelling 'overlayed' is used as a shorthand for 'overlay structured'. Overlaying as a technique is discussed in Chapter 10.

5.4 COMPILER OPTIONS

The precise way the compiler operates is controlled by options. You may give these as metacommands in the FORTRAN source code file. Microsoft FORTRAN has traditionally used this method. Metacommands range from the simple, like instructions to throw a new page on the printer when listing the file ($PAGE), to instructions on how to arrange data storage ($STORAGE:2 forces all INTEGERs not explicitly sized in a declaration statement to be 2 bytes in length), to what sort of code to generate. The primary disadvantage of metacommands is that they render the code less portable.

Other compilers use switches on the command line. Most of the compilers, including the latest Microsoft versions, permit this. Still others can look into the DOS environment for their switches, and others may maintain files of options, either as editable text files, or within their own code: i.e. they modify themselves, usually through a configuration program, for such things as where to search for source code, and where the various compiler elements reside in the overall disk directory structure. The Prospero compilers are perhaps the best example of this technique.

Almost certainly, the most varied set of options is given by the Microsoft v.4 compiler. It not only has metacommands, it also has command line switches and uses the environment. It is invoked by the command FL, and the program FL.EXE calls in turn a series of other programs which are analogous with the separate FOR1.EXE, PAS2.EXE, and PAS3.EXE programs of the v.3 compiler.

For example, one might

```
SET BIN=\WINDOWS\UTILITY\BIN\
```

to set the variable 'BIN' to the subdirectory path so that the v.4 FORTRAN compiler parent (FL.EXE) can find its children (F1.EXE, F2.EXE, and so on). Then, FL.EXE (the FORTRAN parent) which could reside elsewhere, could be invoked with a command line

```
FL /c /G2 /FsCON \SOURCE\TEST.FOR
```

which would (in order of switches) compile only (not link), generate 80286 instructions, and list to the CONsole, taking the file TEST.FOR in subdirectory \SOURCE\ as the FORTRAN source code. During this compilation, the compiler would also respond to metacommands, insert $INCLUDEd code fragments, and run all the separate passes of the compiler.

5.5 OPTIMIZING COMPILERS

Much of what Metcalf has to say about the subject of FORTRAN optimization in his book of the same name (see the bibliography in Chapter 1), applies increasingly to the world of PC FORTRAN.

What is really required from a FORTRAN compiler is correctness. If it generates incorrect code, then it matters not how fast it compiles and links, nor how fast it runs. We generally have to take correctness on trust, although compiler writers can, and should, submit their compilers to validation bodies for a formal verification that all is as well as it can reasonably be expected to be.

The next thing that the user is looking for depends on whether he is a developer or a user of the generated code. In the first instance, a rapid compile–link cycle is desirable, but in the second, fast run times are needed. At least once, however, a slower, more thorough, check on the source code is useful. In the following chapters some ideas are presented on how the user can influence the compile and run times of his software.

The compiler writer can influence the eventual run times by introducing optimizing features in his compiler. A typical example of this is the removal of repeated code. How the compiler performs these optimizations, and indeed what optimizations are in fact undertaken, is often a compromise between what the end-user (FORTRAN program developer) will tolerate in terms of compile time, and what vanishingly small savings are made with increasing refinement in the optimization procedure.

The reader should be able to see that following the syntactical analysis of a program, statement by statement, the whole logic of a subprogram is held in symbolic form. There are possibilities in this, and some imponderables. Possibilities for automatic optimization include strength reduction (replacement of powers by repeated multiplication), unrolling of loops, constant folding (e.g. replacing 4.*5. by 20.0), and type coercion, and so on. By way of contrast, the compiler cannot 'know' that part of the code is almost never obeyed, and so it lavishes equal attention on this as on parts of the code which are in the main logic path.

One of the most 'obvious' areas for automatic optimization, which is in the replacement of repeated subexpressions in the source code by a single variable evaluated at the outset, is in fact, quite difficult to implement. The reason for this is that the time taken to search for matches increases as the square of the length of the code, and hence the 'scope' within which a match is searched for needs to be predefined. It may be defined on the basis of a finite number of FORTRAN statements, within the length of a logical 'block' in the program, or on some other arbitrary criterion.

Some optimization is of necessity done in all compilers. The degree to which they are truly optimizing is sometimes arguable.

As well as optimizing for execution speed, we may choose to optimize to try to minimize the length of code. This is sometimes difficult to do in FORTRAN because of the effect of quite subtle features in the language specification. Take, for example, a program to send the character sequence ESCape @ to an Epson printer (which re-initializes it, or returns it to its power-on state). The FORTRAN program is simple and straightforward.

```
      OPEN   (1,FILE='PRN')
      WRITE  (1,10) CHAR(27),'@'
10    FORMAT (1X,2A1)
      STOP
      END
```

It may, however, compile and link into an EXE program of 10 kbytes length. Much of that is overhead that surely is not all necessary. It turns out that despite the fact that the FORMAT is fully defined, the FORTRAN FORMAT interpreter code is loaded in its entirety. The reason for doing so is that FORTRAN FORMATS need not be completely defined until run-time, and the mechanisms for interpreting them are included, whether needed or not.

An assembler program for doing the same thing appears longer in its source code form,

```
MOV AH,05H
MOV DL,1BH
INT 21H
MOV DL,40H
INT 21H
```

but the essential elements of it take only 12 bytes when assembled and linked. Adding the necessary preamble and closing down instructions increases the total somewhat, but not to the extent of 10 kbytes.

5.6 ORGANIZING WORK DISKS

The writers had mixed early experiences. One of us gained his early experience in PC FORTRAN with a Victor 9000/Sirius with two 600 kbyte floppy disk drives, the other with an Apricot with two 315 kbyte drives. Using almost any compiler on the former, the compiler programs, linker, and at least the appropriate libraries could reside permanently on drive A: on a bootable disk. On the other system, it was necessary to divide the files up. This organization is required on a twin 360 kbyte floppy disk drive set-up too.

With very limited disk workspace, the system was as follows:

Disk 1, which was bootable, contained the operating system and text editor (WordStar).
Disk 2, which did not have the hidden system tracks, but which did have a copy of COMMAND.COM, also contained the programs for the two passes of the FORTRAN compiler.
Disk 3 contained the linker and appropriate FORTRAN libraries. It too was not a bootable disk, but contained COMMAND.COM.

All three of these disks would be loaded one after the other into drive A:. The benefit of having COMMAND.COM on each disk is that you do not get the 'Insert disk containing COMMAND.COM into drive A:' message!

The work disks were always put into drive B:. They included one on which the source code was created using WordStar, and upon which the compiler could generate its OBJ files. For long programs, the linker could be instructed to pause for a disk change before writing the EXE file, which would go on a nearly blank (except for small test data files) fifth disk. Then, testing could be undertaken without a further disk change.

Nowadays, neither of us would seriously contemplate using such limited hardware, and we would personally consider that a hard disk was *de rigueur*. From choice, we would use machines based on fast processors and with at least 20 Mbytes of hard disk.

5.7 DEBUGGING

Apart from the inadequacies of the early FORTRAN compilers, one of the major hindrances to developing FORTRAN (or any other high-level) programs on the PC has been the lack of good debugging tools. Most mainframe and minicomputers have debuggers which can be used with high-level languages. These are very powerful, but in our experience fairly difficult to use, because they nearly all have an extremely poor human interface. They seem to have been written by the system programmer for the system programmer. However, making the effort to seek out the debugger and master some of its commands is worth the effort if you ever have the need to write long or complex programs.

What, then, is a debugger, and how will it help? A debugger instruction is actually provided with the microcomputer processor. This instruction causes the processor to process one line of machine code and then stop. After each line of machine code the contents of the registers, and the state of the flags can be examined, and also the contents of any memory location in the RAM can be looked at. So potentially you have the means to execute your code in this debugging mode and at any stage discover the value of any variable stored in memory.

Of course there has always been a debugger on the PC, the humble 'DEBUG', and this works as described above at the assembler level. That is to say, when an executable code is loaded into DEBUG the user gets to see the machine code and the assembler mnemonics; however, what the FORTRAN programmer wants to see is his FORTRAN source code. It is possible with some compilers on the PC to obtain an assembler listing of your FORTRAN code, and this is quite instructive if you want to get some idea of what assembler code looks like, and how assembler code differs from FORTRAN. However, the assembler code that you see is incomplete, so even with the assembler listing in front of you when you load your executable code into DEBUG it is still unrecognizable. It is quicker and more cost effective to fill your source code with write statements than to try and use DEBUG for debugging FORTRAN programs.

The DEBUG program may be a COM or EXE program on your system. There are many versions of it. You might be lucky and have it included with your version of DOS, or you might be expected to purchase it separately. Public domain groups usually offer something pretty much like it at a reasonable price. If you write programs in assembler code, DEBUG is surprisingly powerful. It is also useful for detailed explorations in the operating system, undeleting files, patching software, and the like, but that is another story (the most famous story-teller being Peter Norton, with his associated software 'the Norton Utilities', and his books on the IBM PC and DOS; these are mentioned in the bibliography of Chapter 2).

A debugger is a software tool which allows the programmer to execute his program one instruction at a time, and provides facilities which allow him to examine the state of his program variables after any instruction. This is the essence of the debugger: for efficient debugging we will expect a few more facilities than these, especially when debugging our FORTRAN programs, where one FORTRAN instruction will generate a number of machine code instructions.

5.8 WHAT IS REQUIRED FROM A HIGH-LEVEL CODE DEBUGGER

Some debuggers allow you to work as though you were operating on the source code. These are high-level code debuggers. DEBUG is not a high-level code debugger: several of the FORTRAN compiler packages contain high-level code debuggers. Examples of software firms whose FORTRAN compiler product includes a high-level code debugger are Microsoft (CodeView), Ryan MacFarland, and Prospero.

There are basically two types of error that the FORTRAN programmer soon becomes familiar with. The first type of error is the syntax error which the compiler should spot for you. Except of course, the syntax error in the FORMAT statement, which might not become apparent until run time with some compilers. FORTRAN 77 allows FORMAT statements to be defined at run time, and it is sometimes the case that all checking of FORMAT statement syntax is done at that time, and none at compile time.

The second type of error is the run-time error which the FORTRAN programmer has to find for himself. Run-time errors can be obvious, but more typically are extremely tedious to find. When faced with the latter sort, all one can do is to find out as much information as possible. In the past, without a debugger, we put WRITE statements at appropriate points in the program. This allowed us to gradually narrow down the area of search, by alerting us to variables which obviously had the wrong values. Although very effective, the problem with this approach is that unwanted WRITE statements are added to the source code. They will have to be deleted when the error has been found. Also it is unlikely that the first batch of WRITE statements will be sufficient to unearth a determined run-time bug. With luck it will narrow the field of attack. It is not unusual to have to go through the edit–compile–run cycle a number of times before obtaining a program that will execute correctly.

So what is really required from a high-level code debugger? Not very much really. The ability to STEP through our code one FORTRAN instruction at a time. The ability to GO quickly to any particular point of our FORTRAN code—with even a moderately short program we would soon get bored with stepping through the program one instruction at a time to get to the section of code where we think the bug might be lurking. The ability to look at and scroll through FORTRAN source code in the debugger, before executing the next section of code. The ability to get the value of any variable within a program unit at the point in the code at current location. This is all that we require. It doesn't seem an impossible wish list, does it? Most debuggers offer quite a lot more, but the facilities described above are the ones that we use most, and will be provided by all debuggers. What should be the strategy in using a debugger? First run the program through to the first section of code where the error may be hidden. Then find the values of all relevant variables at that point. That should indicate any problems that may have happened prior to this section of code, and will then allow the code of each subsequent FORTRAN instruction to be inspected and 'tried out', by stepping through the code one FORTRAN instruction at a time, checking each variable as it changes, and seeing if the changes are as expected (more often, whether they are as it is hoped!). After having inspected one section of code in this way, continue execution normally to the next section of code designated for checking, and so on until the error or errors are found.

Of course, it is possible to inadvertently skip over the section of code where the error is, and so an initial strategy would be to isolate the section or sections of code where errors lay, before doing an in-depth search for the error. With a debugger the source code does not need to be altered each time to do this.

Now consider this debugging strategy in a little more detail. First call up the debugger with the executable program it is wished to examine. To run a program with the debugger usually requires the debug option to be set at compilation time. The high-level debugger needs access to source code, line numbers, and usually non-optimized executable code. To carry this overhead when a program is error free would be extremely inefficient, and so there is a difference in compilation. In contrast, a low-level debugger operates on any executable code, but it is more difficult to decipher its display.

Once the debugger is active, look at the FORTRAN source code of various program units in the executable file, so that 'BREAK POINTS' may be set prior to the areas of code where it is thought the error might be hiding. When the debugger executes the code it will continue execution until a break point is encountered, at which juncture it will stop the program, and wait for a command at the terminal. Break points are usually set by specifying a line number in the program unit where it is wished to stop. The line number is not always obvious, so the debugger must be able to show the code for the program unit in question with line numbers. Some debuggers allow cursor selection of lines in FORTRAN rather than line numbers, for example, Microsoft CodeView.

Having set one or more break points, instruct the debugger to start the execution of the program. This is usually done by issuing the command 'GO'. The program will then execute up to the first break point, where it will halt.

It is now necessary to examine the values of various (all) variables in the program unit up to this point. If the break point has been set sensibly, all values at this point will be 'right', so check that values are believable. Very often when something is wrong it is obviously wrong, but check carefully nevertheless.

Having checked the variables, step through the code, one FORTRAN instruction at a time. The command for stepping through the code is usually 'STEP'. However, there are nuances that you should be aware of. Suppose that while stepping through the code a call to a subroutine is encountered. Does the debugger execute all the instructions in the subroutine and only hand back control to the user on the line of code after the subroutine call in the program unit being stepped through? Or does the debugger stop on the first instruction of the called subroutine? Sometimes the debugger will offer two different commands for these two situations: otherwise the default will be stepping to the line below the subroutine call in the current program unit, and debugging will only switch to the called subroutine if a break point is set within that subroutine.

In some debuggers the 'STEP' command will take a following parameter which allows the user to specify how many steps should be executed before the program is halted again. This is useful for stepping over WRITE statements or trivial lines of code. Be careful though, otherwise you may step over the instruction that you were interested in, and have to start again.

STEPping through DO loops of no interest can be very tedious and it is usually quicker to set a break point at the end of the DO loop and GO to the break point.

Normally on each step through the code we will want to examine the values of the variables that are being manipulated to ensure that they are changing in the way in which we expected when we programmed this bit of code. If we get through a section of code which we thought might contain an error without finding anything then by issuing the command 'GO' again we will cause our program to continue executing normally up to the next break point.

In this way sections of our code can be rigorously examined, and usually run-time errors can be picked up very quickly. The debugging process is particularly effective if it is possible to choose input data for our program which gives us a known answer, or which is simple enough for us to work through by hand.

While the debugger is working it needs to present the following information to the user: a portion of source code including the line that is about to be executed; a command line area where the user can issue commands; a display area where the values of variables are shown; and possibly another display area where program output to the standard output device (the screen) is written. This is too much information for one screen, particularly if your program writes a lot of information to the standard output device, and the better debuggers put program output on a separate screen, and allow the user to switch easily and quickly from one screen to the other.

5.9 OTHER COMMON UTILITIES PROVIDED IN DEBUGGERS

The 'WATCH' command is provided by most debuggers and can be very useful. You set a watch on a particular variable. Then whenever that variable changes value, the old and new values are displayed and execution of your program is halted. The debugger will display the source line which gave rise to the change. Although useful this command should be used sparingly. Speed of execution is badly affected by the WATCH command—the debugger has to check the variable after each line of code is executed to see whether it has changed. Also in a section of code where a variable changes a lot it can become very tedious with all the stopping and starting. The best approach is to use the WATCH command only after you have isolated a variable which is going wrong and a section of code where you know the error occurs. You can then set the WATCH on the variable over that section of code only.

Most debuggers have a 'SEARCH' command. This searches the FORTRAN source code for the next occurrence of a particular expression, in the same way in which a word processor would work. This is useful for quickly locating a point in the source code where a break point is to be set.

Most debuggers will allow the values of variables to be changed. Thus if you have reached a break point where you suspect that a variable has the wrong value, and you think you know what the right value should be, you can change the value of the variable, and then continue execution of the program. If you get the right answer then you should be able to work your way back to the error.

All debuggers allow the addresses of variables in memory to be displayed, and dumps of the memory, registers. and flags to be examined. How useful this is when debugging an ordinary FORTRAN program is debatable. However, if you call assembler routines from your FORTRAN code then this facility is extremely useful for ensuring that variables pass correctly across subroutine calls, and for debugging the assembler code.

5.10 THE MICROSOFT 'CODEVIEW' DEBUGGER

Microsoft market a debugger called 'CodeView'. It is supplied free with all their languages, and provides a common debugging interface for all of the Microsoft languages. Unfortunately it will not work with other compilers. The reason for highlighting this debugger here is simply because it is the best debugger that we have come across on mainframe, mini or microcomputers. It is the best in our opinion because of the human interface which makes it a pleasure to use. CodeView does not necessarily have the broadest range of commands, but nevertheless it does have a rich collection of features which include everything that any FORTRAN programmer will require, and the presentation is such that he/she will be encouraged to use them. To get the best from CodeView you must have an IBM PC or closely compatible computer. This allows you to run CodeView through a windows interface, which has a menu bar with drop-down windows containing all the commands, and also extensive use is made of the function keys. A mouse can also be used to good effect if you have one, but do not be put off if you haven't. Also intelligent use is made of colour for those of you with colour monitors.

Apart from the drop-down menus, the main screen has up to four windows: the display window which shows the source code of the program being debugged; the dialog window where you enter commands and where the debugger writes the responses to appropriate commands; the watch window, an optional window which displays the status of specified variables or expressions; and the register window which shows the current status of the registers and flags.

A separate screen is used for output from the program, and help which is available at the touch of a function key, or from one of the drop-down menus displayed on a series of help screens. The help information is comprehensive.

The next line of program to be executed, if visible in the display window (it will normally be visible, but you have the ability to scroll backwards and forwards through your program), is displayed in reverse video. Lines containing previously set break points are shown as bold on monochrome screens, and in a different colour on colour screens.

All the commands described in the sections above, plus many additional features, are available to the programmer debugging his program, and because it is so easy you will find yourself using most of them.

Apart from giving praise where praise is due (and goodness knows those of us who have used Microsoft FORTRAN from version 2.* days, have had occasion to criticize Microsoft many times in the past, and so it is nice to be able to redress the balance a bit), the other reason for mentioning CodeView is that Microsoft distribute freely (or for a small media cost) a demonstration version of this product. Not only is this a good advertisement for CodeView it is also a very good way for people unfamiliar with debuggers to learn the capabilities provided by these products. You do not need Microsoft FORTRAN to use the demonstration, but if you have a friend with Microsoft FORTRAN he can (with Microsoft's blessing) give you a copy of this demonstration diskette.

5.11 SUMMARY

In the early days of microcomputing, FORTRAN compilers had a very bad reputation, and many FORTRAN programmers either gave up PC programming or started programming in assembler or 'C'. Nowadays there are at least half a dozen good quality FORTRAN compilers available on PCs and compatibles, and even multifunctional cheap compilers (like those pioneered by Borland for languages such as Pascal and 'C') are starting to emerge. If you feel that you will need support, then do not expect much from your computer dealer—most have never heard of FORTRAN, and it is our experience that the large multinationals are very skilful at keeping customers at arms length ('that problem is fixed in the next release' is a common response), so your best bet is probably a product like Prospero FORTRAN 77. If you want access to most of the third party libraries or utility software you would do best to stick to a high profile product such as Microsoft FORTRAN 77.

If your programs are likely to be long and complicated, then you will sooner or later wish you had access to a good debugger, these are becoming more common and once again we would mention both Prospero FORTRAN 77 (who have always had good debugging facilities obtained via their PROBE program) and Microsoft FORTRAN 77 in its latest incarnation.

If we have not mentioned your favourite compiler, we apologize. We know that both the Lahey F77L compiler and Ryan MacFarland compiler RMFORT have many friends, and that new compilers or new versions of existing compilers, are emerging every month. Incidentally you may wonder why we haven't mentioned the IBM FORTRAN compiler. The current IBM FORTRAN compiler is in fact the Ryan MacFarland FORTRAN compiler, although IBM do make some modifications to interface to their graphics primitive library in order to make it appear different. Often you will find that the current release of the IBM compiler is an older version than the current Ryan MacFarland FORTRAN compiler.

CHAPTER 6

PRECISION, ACCURACY, AND THE RIGHT ANSWER

A commonly held misconception is that DOS computers are small, cheap, and therefore inaccurate. This has even been authoritively stated by people who should know better. Once, indeed, one of the authors was told by a fairly eminent Professor from a large and rich university that only the privileged few with access to supercomputers should be doing engineering analysis at all. In fact, the evidence is that DOS microcomputers have the capability to actually generate more precise results in many situations than do supercomputers like the Cray, or CDC Star, and combined with the convenience of using a machine which is so versatile, the PC must be the choice of the majority.

6.1 WHY DATA IS STORED IN DIFFERENT FORMATS

Basically, memory on any computer is a series of 'on–off' switches. In a DOS PC these are organized into groups of eight, called bytes. To store any information, take as many bytes as you need, and set the little switches to represent that information. This of course presupposes that there is a coding and decoding system which is capable of interpreting that pattern of switches, or bits, into numeric data. There are many possible coding systems, depending on what sort of data is to be stored.

One of the greatest steps towards the modern computer was the realization that the information stored inside the memory of the computer could equally well be program steps as data items. Hence, systems of encoding and decoding a variety of things would be required. The FORTRAN programmer could easily envisage a multiplicity of data types: CHARACTER, REAL, DOUBLE PRECISION, COMPLEX, LOGICAL, INTEGER, and so on. We need to add program code to this list.

The eight 'binary' switches in a byte (if on = 1, and off = 0, the switch pattern can be viewed as a binary number) can be set in 2 to the power 8 different combinations, or 256 different ways. If, then, a byte is used to store CHARACTER Information, up to 256 different CHARACTERS could be stored. Since this exceeds the number of characters in (most) alphabets, a byte is a good character holder. Indeed, with only upper and lower case and punctuation, not

---

all the switches, or bits, in each byte need to be used. In the same way, if a byte was used to store a program instruction, there is a potential instruction set of 256 different processor operations. We will not complicate matters by suggesting that the instruction in a particular byte could be somewhat conditional on the values in preceding bytes, but that would then open up a whole new range of possibilities. In Chapters 12 and 14, we will discover the **escape sequence**. This is a slightly limited way of extending the range of apparent values for a byte beyond its 256 different meanings.

LOGICAL data in FORTRAN may only have two values, true or false, represented in FORTRAN style as .TRUE. or .FALSE., and so only needs one byte: and of that only one bit is strictly required. LOGICAL*4 is therefore a waste of 31/32 of the data space it consumes, and LOGICAL*2 scarcely much better. Even LOGICAL*1, which many compilers do not accept, wastes effectively 87.5 percent of the available space. One is tempted to wonder whether a human dimension to programming as well as a better utilization of memory overall could be achieved by having 'relatively true or false on a scale of 1–256'. Bytes are therefore more than adequate for characters and logical data.

It is when numbers have to be stored that bytes are not good enough. Since a byte can only cope with 256 different bit patterns, a byte can only be used for 256 different numbers—and they all have to have the same sign (positive) or else one of the precious bits is used up to represent + or -. For floating point numbers the position of the decimal point needs to be known, and this requires more bits. Suppose we assume initially that only integer numbers are to be stored. These do not have a decimal fraction. Even then, more than 256 different numbers will certainly be needed. The answer is to use more bits, and that means more bytes. Examine the number of unique bit patterns in multiples of a byte, taking one off for 'sign' to see what might be obtained, there are some examples in Table 6.1.

Table 6.1 Range of values that can be stored in integers of different lengths

Bytes	Range	Comments
1	−128 0 +127	
2	−32 768 0 +32 767	(16 bit word)
3	about 8 million	not common today (24 bit word ICL mainframes used this at one time)
4	about 4000 million	
5, 6, 8, etc.	enormous	

For unsigned numbers the bit pattern in an INTEGER number represents the binary value of that number. For signed numbers, which is all that is available to the FORTRAN user, the 'two's complement form' is used. Positive numbers are the same as their unsigned equivalent except that their leftmost (most significant) bit cannot be 1, this is reserved for negative numbers which makes them easy to recognize. But beware the rest of the bits are not the same as in the equivalent positive number. The rule for changing from a positive to a negative number (or vice versa) is to reverse all the bits (1 to 0, and 0 to 1) and then add 1. This representation of INTEGERS is normally transparent to the user, unless he wishes to use the radix 2 method of specifying a constant, so as to represent a bit pattern in the code—an example of this is covered in Chapter 13, where a bit pattern for describing a cursor is handled in this way.

Now whereas there are only a limited number of sensible strategies for holding such an integer number, in contrast, there is much more flexibility in storing FLOATING POINT numbers. These floating point numbers are the REALs of FORTRAN, or half of a COMPLEX pair. We will assume for now that these numbers are stored by using some of the bits to store the **characteristic**, and some of them to store the **mantissa** (sometimes termed the 'exponent'). For those to whom this is Greek, the number is represented in the form:

$0.345\,678 \times 10 \times 10 \times 10 \ldots n$ times

The mantissa is the .345 678 part, and the characteristic is n. As an example, if n was 4, the number would be $0.345\,678 \times 10 \times 10 \times 10 \times 10$, or 3456.78. In actual fact, both the mantissa and characteristic will be in binary, but take them in decimal for the time being, as this makes things easier to comprehend. Sign bits are needed for both the characteristic and the mantissa: a negative characteristic implies **dividing** by 10 n times.

Given a certain number of bytes, bits in the characteristic can be traded for those in the mantissa: effectively changing the **precision** with which a number is held in inverse ratio to its **range**. One further refinement is whether or not the '0.' part of the mantissa is stored: normally it isn't. Also, numbers in the mantissa need only be stored in the range 0.100 000 ... to 0.999 999 9 ..., because 0.099 999 9 can be shifted with the appropriate modification to the characteristic. This is called 'normalization'. Remember too that all this is done in the binary system, and is just a coding system for the binary switches in the bytes allocated to store the number. The computer itself makes no assumption about how data is coded into the bytes, that is entirely software dependent.

There is, however, a standard for this coding: the IEEE standard. Whether or not a particular piece of software adheres to this standard (or any other) is of course, not guaranteed. Most modern PC FORTRAN compilers do, especially those that support numeric coprocessors, because although the main CPU chip merely manipulates bytes, the coprocessor actually works in terms of those standard data types.

Typically, at least 4 bytes is used to store a single floating point number; 6, 8, 10, or even more bytes can be used in particular circumstances. Suppose the sort of precision and range that each of these options gives is examined in the same way as was done for integers earlier. Some examples are given in Table 6.2.

Most FORTRANs for PCs have the option of using the 4- or 8-byte forms: one compiler (Digital Research FORTRAN 77) allows the 10-byte form too, but only in special circumstances. There is a good reason for this. Assume that your PC has a numeric coprocessor. This has a number of internal 10-byte (80-bit) registers. Loading any real number from memory into these registers (providing it is in Intel form: Microsoft started its FORTRANs using the Microsoft representation of real numbers, which wasn't compatible with the Intel format, and had to revise this with later versions of the Microsoft FORTRAN compiler) is done with a conversion to the internal 80-bit form, which has a mantissa of 64 bits. The result is computed by the coprocessor to this precision, regardless of the precision of the source numbers. On transfer of the results back to RAM, truncation/rounding occurs: however, the end result must be better, even for REAL*8 arithmetic, than computing totally in 64 bit mode.

Table 6.2 Range of values that can be stored in a REAL variable of different lengths

No of bytes per data value	Significant figures (decimal)	Range of numbers i.e. 10 to the power of ...
4	typically 7	−38 – +38
(6)	10 – 11	−76 – +76
8	6 – 17	−308 – +308
10	about 20	−2466 – +2466

Remember that it is possible to gain increased precision at a cost in range, and vice versa.

Now, the Digital Research FORTRAN 77 compiler recognizes that this is going on, and allows for 80-bit real numbers to exist, to be loaded into the coprocessor's registers and back, without any conversion. This must result in an increased precision for a numeric computation. However, since the layout of the bits in this 80-bit variable is that which suits the mode of operation of the numeric coprocessor, input and output conversion is difficult unless the number is first truncated to one of the standard forms, either REAL*8 or REAL*4 (the 8- or 4-byte REAL).

Most FORTRAN compilers offer an option to emulate the 8087 numeric coprocessor in software for those without coprocessors. The Microsoft FORTRAN compiler is one of them. It means more than just doing numeric operations and computing transcendentals using the main processor; it also implies operating at the intrinsically higher 80-bit precision. That this is slow is widely recognized, and Microsoft provide an alternative maths package for the no-coprocessor case. This computes to a precision appropriate to the declared variables (4-byte or 8-byte REALS), and so is less accurate than coprocessor emulation. It is, however, significantly faster.

6.2 ERRORS IN HANDLING NUMBERS

So where is all this leading? Well, having discovered that the computer only holds real numbers approximately, it is easier to see why some errors creep in. Take for example a simple test: make a loop to add 0.000 000 1 to 1.0 ten million times. the answer ought to be 2.0, but it isn't: the answer you get will often surprise. (Do it with 4-byte integers for the loop count, and 4-byte reals.) Here is the test program:

```
C
C       Test program to try out repeated addition of a small
C       number using low precision arithmetic. The answer is
C       unexpected.
C

        INTEGER*4 I
        REAL*4     A
        A     = 0.0
        DO 10 I=1,10000000
        A     = A  +  0.0000001
10      CONTINUE
        WRITE(*,*) ' FINALLY, A=',A
        STOP
        END
```

Repeat the test first by taking 8-byte REALs, and then by doing a multiply instead of the repeated add. These are the test programs.

```
C
C       Test program to perform the addition using higher
C       precision arithmetic.
C

        INTEGER*4 I
        REAL*8     A
        A     = 0.0D0
        DO 10 I=1,10000000
        A     = A  +  0.0000001D0
10      CONTINUE
        WRITE(*,*) ' FINALLY, A=',A
        STOP
        END
```

and

```
C
C       Test program which does the whole operation as a
C       single multiply.  It is significantly quicker too.
C

        INTEGER*4 I
        REAL*8     A
        A     =  0.0000001D0*10000000.0D0
        WRITE(*,*) ' FINALLY, A=',A
        STOP
        END
```

In the first case, adding the 0.000 000 1 was effectively adding zero each time: it didn't matter that you did it so many times, the answer was still 1. Even with the better precision, the answer still isn't perfect, and it is nowhere near as good as the multiply—especially if you do that with 8-byte precision too.

It is possible to do the operations using the stack of registers on a numeric coprocessor chip without saving the results to ordinary RAM until the very end of the calculation process. This not only speeds things up considerably, it also improves overall accuracy—unless you save the 80-bit intermediate results too. The reader interested in such exotica should consult Startz' book *8087 Applications and Programming* (see the bibliography in Chapter 2) for details.

The end result of the foregoing is a set of observations.

1 The answer is better if you use higher precision.
2 The errors are dependent on the algorithm (calculation sequence) used.
3 Addition of very different sized numbers is particularly bad.

6.3 SOME EXAMPLES

Frankly, 4-byte precision is just on the margins of acceptability for many purposes: sometimes it works and sometimes it doesn't. It is fine, for instance, if you want to locate the coordinates of a pixel on the screen, or a pen on a piece of paper—even 2-byte integers can be good enough for that. What is fine for playing computer games often just isn't good enough, however, for many scientific and engineering calculations.

Here are just a couple of examples. Suppose an engineer made a survey of the English Channel for the new tunnel, and did the 'setting out' calculations in 4-byte precision. Two sets of tunnellers starting from England and France would almost certainly miss each other somewhere in the middle of the Channel! This would occur mainly as a result of round-off in his calculations, since in a distance of about 40 000 metres, the basic precision of a REAL*4 variable is plus or minus a number of millimetres. That would then be a problem of **accuracy**.

A second example concerns coordinates more directly. The United Kingdom has a National Grid map coordinate system with an origin South West of the Scilly Islands, so that the whole country, especially the mainland, has positive coordinates. Any point in the country may be located according to this system: the more figures, the greater the precision of reference. However, consider locating the position of an aeroplane with respect to the National Grid in 4-byte precision and it will be fine in the Scillies, Southern England and the Midlands, or Wales. However, as we move into Scotland, and the coordinates increase in magnitude, positional accuracy decreases. A flying accident would surely result. A better **precision** is certainly required. (Citizens of larger countries would appreciate the need for better precision sooner than those in the UK—the loss in aeroplanes would quickly become catastrophic!)

Consider now 8-byte precision. As an example of what this can do, it can represent the distance from the Earth to the Moon to better than 0.000 05 mm in the 400 000 km distance—or to better than a thousandth of the diameter of a speck of dust. Do we need that? Particularly since every variable in the program takes up twice the space, the program will be longer, and will run slower. Admittedly, it makes little difference to the numeric coprocessor what accuracy is requested, it always works to the 80 bits, but data is still fetched from RAM 16 bits at a time (8 bits at a time on the 8088 as used in the IBM PC), so the memory access is longer. If the value 10 to the power 308 is examined, it gives such an enormous number that it is probably debatable whether there are that many atoms in the observable Universe.

The ideal compromise is 6-byte precision. All British mainframe computers traditionally used this 48-bit REAL from the original Atlas, and in some cases offered 96-bit DOUBLE PRECISION. Results are much more likely to be 'right' when using 6 bytes without too much worry at the coding stage, and both the code and data sections of programs are as compact as they can reasonably be expected to be.

Just holding a number in encoded form to a fixed precision causes a loss of accuracy. Now do some calculations with it, and the errors grow. This is because we do not compute to enough digits, and get an additional error or 'round-off'. All computations are subject to this to a certain extent, but some computational procedures are more prone to error than others. (A few exercises with the trigonometry of a right-angled triangle with one sharp or small-angled apex using Pythagoras or the sine and cosine formulae is instructive.)

Now comes a big difference—do you have a numeric coprocessor on your PC or not? If you do, this is what happens. Your application takes your 32- or 64-bit number and expands it to a special 80-bit form for the numeric operation in the coprocessor. The rounding down to the appropriate precision is done after the completion of the computation. Effectively, this 80-bit internal form has a 64-bit mantissa. Now this is much better than many Supercomputers (e.g. Crays) so the eminent Professor (alluded to at the start of this chapter) was talking through his pipelined processor!

If you do not use a coprocessor, then the main processor has to be instructed just how to do the arithmetic operation. This takes a number of steps, and you have a choice how you do it. When using 32-bit numbers (24-bit mantissa) you can stop at 24 bits, or carry on and round later. Or with 64-bit REALs, you can stop when the 53-bit mantissas have been dealt with, or go on and completely emulate the coprocessor's function. This is a software choice, and even if the high-level language programmer doesn't have control over this (he does with some compilers), the compiler writer has. Stopping the arithmetic short accelerates the growth of round-off errors and needs to be watched, although it does speed up the computations. 'Short' arithmetic is faster than 'long' if you do not have a coprocessor, but the difference when one is fitted is very small, and has more to do with fetching and carrying the data from memory.

The last thing that causes problems with precision is the Trojan Horse left by the compiler writer. In most microcomputer languages, 32-bit precision is the default. Thus, to operate in 64-bit precision, not only do variables need to be explicitly TYPEd in the program, but all constants do too. In the FORTRAN context, this means writing *every* constant with a D exponent, so that (for instance) 0.5 becomes 0.5D0; 1.0E-8 becomes 1.0D-08, etc. Otherwise, the compiler is likely to interpret this as an invitation to insert single precision code there in the program. Putting expressions in subroutine calls is another pitfall: some languages compute the result to single precision before passing it over *even if the result is obtained by operating on double precision variables and is picked up as double precision in the subroutine.* Using generic forms of trigonometric functions (always advisable where possible) may also be a pitfall: FORTRAN 77 is supposed to be context sensitive to put in the correct precision function when a generic name is used: some PC FORTRAN implementations are not.

The essence of getting the right answer can be summarized with the following.

- Precision
- Control of round-off
- Selection of an appropriate algorithm
- Careful coding

To sum up, the PC (particularly when equipped with a coprocessor chip) is capable of such precision in its calculations as to exceed virtually everyone's needs. But this can be degraded quite easily by carelessness so that the end result is just not good enough for any purpose. The solution is programmer vigilance.

6.4 MATHS LIBRARIES FOR USE WITH FORTRAN COMPILERS

Microsoft FORTRAN probably gives its users more choice over the way it performs mathematical operations than do other compilers. In view of this, the details of the Microsoft FORTRAN system will be described.

Very early versions of Microsoft FORTRAN offered virtually no choice of library. A coprocessor, if present, was simply not used. Real numbers were held in Microsoft's own format, rather than the IEEE format, and would have needed time-intensive conversion each time the coprocessor was accessed. Version 3 of the compiler (3.10 and 3.13) offered IEEE formats, and two libraries. These respectively supported a coprocessor, or emulated it in software. Programs linked to the emulation library would use a coprocessor if one was present in the target system, by first checking for its presence, and if found, the code is modified 'on the fly'. A choice of whether to perform math operations via subroutine calls (slower, but more compact) or by the insertion of in-line code (faster, but longer) was made by means of a compiler metacommand.

In these versions, subroutines were provided to reduce the computation precision in the emulator: the default was the full 80-bit precision of the numeric coprocessor. Using the reduced precision had the effect of speeding up the emulator, at the risk of increased round-off error, and of obtaining different results if the same program was run twice, once on a coprocessor equipped computer, and once without.

Unfortunately, the method of detecting coprocessor error and exception conditions relied on interrupts, and the handling of these is hardware dependent. A number of DOS machines fell into this trap, and would 'hang-up' when such a condition occurred. Because there was no way of switching off the use of the coprocessor in the emulation library, it would happen no matter which library was selected. Later (post 3.30) releases have information on patching the libraries, or replacing machine specific code, to overcome this problem.

Version 3.20 brought a larger memory model, but was a stopgap. Versions 3.30 and 3.31 (minor improvements only) brought the most changes. Primarily, this was because the maths code library was separated from the logical code, the former occupying MATH.LIB, and the latter FORTRAN.LIB. One of three supplied libraries had to be renamed MATH.LIB, these respectively offered coprocessor essential, coprocessor optional—if not found then software emulation of its functions, and an alternate maths package offering single precision maths only, done in software, and not an emulation of the coprocessor at all. Once again, in-line code, or subroutine calls, could be specified via a metacommand.

Versions 3.30, and later, of the compiler support mixed language programming, with interfaces to C and Pascal, along with a subset of C functions supplied in CEXEC.LIB.

With version 4 of the compiler, Microsoft have released an installation program that builds the requisite libraries from a series of 'building blocks'. The target libraries include maths support, and so include emulator and coprocessor flavours, but creation options include choosing memory model (medium or large), C compatibility, and compatibility with 3.3 versions of the compiler. ALTMATH and DECMATH have been effectively dropped.

When compiling with version 4, the selection between in-line code or subroutine calls for maths operations may be made with a parameter on the command line, or with metacommands in the source code as before.

Other FORTRANs offer a less confusing choice. Digital Research's compiler has four libraries with large and small memory model, with or without coprocessor support. Ryan MacFarland and Supersoft have two each: with and without coprocessor support. Prospero have six: three memory models, all with or without the coprocessor.

6.5 SUMMARY

There is a great deal of confusion between precision and accuracy. We could say that the two authors live 7.3498 miles apart, which would be more than precise enough for most purposes. Adding a few decimal places not only wouldn't improve matters for practical purposes—it wouldn't improve accuracy either, since the 'correct' answer is more like 15! Accuracy encompasses precision, but not vice versa.

The computer can only yield the 'right' answer from a calculation if:

- it has correct input data
- it uses an appropriate mathematical model
- it computes to an appropriate precision

Your PC (especially with a numeric coprocessor), no matter whether it is the cheapest and slowest 8088 floppy disk machine or the latest 80386 hard disk equipped and correspondingly more costly 'business' computer, has the necessary hardware to do this, and any PC FORTRAN gives it the required 'system' software. The rest is up to you.

CHAPTER 7

READABLE AND MAINTAINABLE CODE

'Why do I need to bother with comments cluttering up my code? Why should I split my code up into subroutines? I only write programs once in a while. The programs do specific jobs, once I've got them to work I'll never need to look at them again. Structured Programming? What's that?'

This sort of complaint is often voiced by the tyro programmer, the engineer or scientist anxious to get results quickly, and (sadly all too often) the academic or loner who programs for himself. We hope by the end of this chapter to have convinced you (and him!) that it is desirable to always write readable and maintainable code, and to demonstrate that, with a consistent approach, code can be written so that it can actually save time and wasted effort.

7.1 WHAT IS READABLE AND MAINTAINABLE CODE?

Readable code is code which can be picked up and almost completely understood by someone with no knowledge of the FORTRAN language. This inevitably means that the code is liberally commented in English—not FORTRAN!—but it also means that variable names should be chosen with some thought, and that the FORTRAN is written and set out in such a way that it is clear and easy on the eye.

Maintainable code is first and foremost readable code. Code which is easily understood by a layman should be simplicity itself for the programmer!

Maintainable code is code in which errors can be quickly found. Code which, on the wakening of a 'sleeping bug', can be 'debugged' efficiently, even though it may have been written at some remote time in the past. Inevitably, the intimate familiarity that one has with a piece of code that has been newly developed soon fades, and the purpose of what seemed quite straightforward at the time, becomes completely obscure.

Maintainable code is a piece of code, no bigger than a subroutine, doing a specific and well-defined task. This exploits one of the most powerful features of the FORTRAN language—modularity. Subroutines which do small well-defined tasks can be written independently of the other fragments of code which go to make up a program. Each subroutine

---

can be compiled and checked syntactically. Each subroutine can be tested thoroughly to ensure that it carries out its task correctly, and, once checked, the subroutine can be placed in a user-defined library ready to be called from any program, not just the one under development. The source code for individual subprograms can be kept in small files which are easy to edit or list and rapid to recompile.Code written in this way can be (and typically is) used over and over again in many different programs, and used with increasing confidence that it performs its task correctly under a variety of input data.

People who write code for one purpose only, like the hypothetical doubter at the beginning of this chapter, often have to program the same basic operations time after time. Hopefully, with such an evolutionary process, the code can become better each time. More often than not, the same inefficiencies are recreated repeatedly. Not only that, but each time the code has to be debugged, and that is wasted time.

The programmer can easily utilize the tools that are needed to create readable and maintainable code. We have already mentioned some of them. These are the ones which come from an organized and efficient attitude of mind, and which are automatically reflected in the code, rather than rules which, blindly followed, lead to the desired end. There are such rules too. Perhaps the simplest of these is in the use of layout and comments. Using white space and nicely laid out, informative, comments will make our code more interesting to look at. If you can bear to look at it, and read its content, then you are much more likely to be able to get at the meaning.

Brackets should also be used to enforce meaning, and intrinsic functions such as 'INT' and 'REAL' to make the results of mathematical expressions unambiguous.

In order that code can be kept together in manageable and distinguishable blocks we should use where possible the 'IF THEN ELSE ENDIF' in place of 'GOTO' using indentation to mark which 'IF' goes with which 'ELSE' and 'ENDIF'.

COMMON blocks should be studiously avoided, by using argument lists and dynamic dimensioning and by choosing variable names which exploit default types (i.e. INTEGER variables start with letters I–N), and which have meaning, many of the errors associated with using subroutines and functions disappear.

These guidelines may well be unpopular with programmers who started their FORTRAN programming with FORTRAN IV (FORTRAN 66) since they attack some of the more commonly used constructs in FORTRAN IV. Some of the alternatives listed above were not available under FORTRAN IV. However, we do urge FORTRAN IV, programmers to adopt the structures available in FORTRAN 77, it is our (painful) experience that the old structures can lead to silly errors which can be hideously difficult to find, whereas the new structures and commands, used properly, enhance the readability and maintainability of FORTRAN code.

Now look at the ideas set out above in more detail. Some of the code used to exemplify the benefits and pitfalls may look a bit contrived but it is difficult to convey the import of the above strategy in small fragments of code without recourse to extreme examples.

7.2 COMMENTS

Start with comments because they are simple and they so obviously make FORTRAN code (or any other code that we can think of!) more readable and easier to maintain. Comments can appear anywhere within a FORTRAN program and they should appear in most places. Comments should be used to explain the code not just mimic it.

Consider the following snippet of code:

```
C       set up W1
        W1 = 2.0
C       set up W2
        W2 = 3.0
C       set up W3
        W3 = -2.0
C       put W4 as W2*W2 - 4.0*W3*W1
        W4 = W2*W2 - 4.0*W3*W1
C       take the square root of W4
        W5 = SQRT(W4)
C       take W6 as (W5+W2)/(2.0*W1)
        W6 = (W5+W2)/(2.0*W1)
C       take W7 as (W5-W2)/(2.0*W1)
        W7 = (W5-W2)/(2.0*W1)
```

Not a very inspired piece of FORTRAN! Almost anyone with an elementary mathematics knowledge could eventually work out what the programmer was trying to do, but seeing whether or not there any errors, especially if this fragment was part of a long subprogram, might not be easy. The comments are no help at all and the variable names do not give any clues.

A more helpful way to code the same thing could be:

```
C       ------------------------------------------------
C       This bit of code calculates the roots of the
C       quadratic equation:
C               A * (X*X) + B * X + C = 0
C       where in this case A = 2, B = 3, and C = -2
C
C       start by setting up the coefficients A,B and C
C       ------------------------------------------------
```

```
      A = 2.0
      B = 3.0
      C = -2.0
C
C     The 2 roots are given by:
C           X1 = (-B + SQRT(B*B - 4*A*C))/(2*A)
C     and   X2 = (-B - SQRT(B*B - 4*A*C))/(2*A)
C     first calculate D as SQRT(B*B - 4*A*C)
C
      D = SQRT(B*B - 4.0*A*C)
C
C     and now the roots X1 and X2
C
      X1 = (-B + D)/(2.0*A)
      X2 = (-B - D)/(2.0*A)
C
C     ---------------------------------------------------
```

We hope the improvement is obvious! The code takes a few more lines and a bit more thought was given to the variable names and the comments. It is very unlikely that any 'bug' would be left alive in this code for very long. So although it might have taken a bit longer to write, it will take a lot less time to debug. Well-commented code is easy to fix, and that can save a lot of time. (The fragment does not check that the $B*B-4.0*A*C$ is neither zero nor negative. It is not strictly necessary here, since the coefficients of this quadratic do not give rise to the problem. In the general case, all values given to a function should be checked for admissibility first.)

Also one not so obvious advantage of writing well-chosen comments frequently is that as you type the code and comments you will pick up lots of mistakes along the way. You might not make any fewer syntax errors caused by 'typos', but we guarantee that you will have a lot less run-time errors to find!

We will see many more examples of how comments can and should be used to make code more understandable in the examples that follow in this chapter.

It is a good idea to use lower case for comments: this separates the comments from the code. Standard FORTRAN demands that code is in upper case although most PC compilers permit lower case to be used anywhere. There is no problem with comments in lower case though, since everything after the 'C' in column 1 (which should be in upper case) is ignored. This also means that comments can start anywhere after the 'C'. This may mean that comment lines can be 'outdented', like this fragment:

```
C This is the program initialization stage
C Here all the variables are set to zero
      DATA A,B,C/0.0,0.0,0.0/
```

or alternatively, extra indentation (often by using tabs) can be just as effective:

```
C                           calculate the distance from the
C                           satellite to the shuttle
C
      DIST = SQRT (DELX**2  + DELY**2 + DELZ**2)
```

Notice too that the comment and code are separated much more visibly by that extra blank comment line. Other emphases can be obtained with the (sparing) use of underlining. The extensive underlining with asterisks that one saw in code written in the 1960s, was directly the result of the limited character sets on the line printers of the time, and should be avoided nowadays. On the other hand, it is possible to generate exquisite boxes and rulings within FORTRAN source code comments with the aid of the block graphics characters residing at ASCII codes 127 on most DOS computers. Resist the temptation! The least that can happen is that your printer will have a different character set, or will strip off the high bit, rendering the 'box' an untidy sequence of letters and numerals. The worst is that you move to a compiler where the source code is unreadable.

A slight problem with the use of **tabs** to layout a program neatly is the interpretation placed on tabs by the compiler. Some compilers do not accept tabs in source code (not PC FORTRANs thankfully). Microsoft FORTRAN accepts the first tab in a line as tabbing to column 8—a little further than the standard FORTRAN layout which commences in column 7 normally. Thereafter, tabs are treated pretty much as space characters. As a result, a compilation listing will lose its nice layout. One solution is to use a text editor which inserts the requisite number of space characters rather than an explicit tab each time. The other is to use a print formatter to generate listings rather than use the compilation listing.

7.3 BRACKETS, LAYOUT, AND THE USE OF WHITE SPACE

Use brackets to enforce meaning, making your code a lot easier to read and a lot more understandable. Use them in complex arithmetic expressions, and in IF statements, and wherever they make the code more legible. For example:

```
C     convert: theta from deg. - radians
C              omega from revs/sec - radians/sec
C
      ANGLE = THETA/360.0*TWOPI
      W = OMEGA * TWOPI
C
C     con-rod centre of gravity point acceleration (m/s**2)
C     in the x direction
C
      ACCGX = W**2*B/1000./4.*RN**2*COS(2.0*ANGLE)
C
```

```
C      in the y direction
C
       ACCGY = -W**2*B/1000./RN*SIN(2.0*ANGLE)
C
C      piston acceleration
C
       ACCP = -W**2*R2/1000.*COS(ANGLE)+1.0/RN*COS(2.0*ANGLE)
```

These equations need not have physical meaning for the programmer, but if the correct expressions were available, and the FORTRAN was coded properly and well-commented it would be possible to pick out any mistakes.

The above example of programming is horrible. From the way the equations are coded above we have no idea how they will evaluate since we do not care to remember all the rules governing the priority given to add, subtract, multiply, divide, exponentiate, etc.

The code may well be full of mistakes but without help from the programmer we certainly wouldn't be able to say what was right and what was wrong. One further step in the right direction might improve the code to the following version:

```
C      convert: theta from deg. - radians
C               omega from revs/sec - radians/sec
C
       ANGLE = (THETA/360.0) * TWOPI
       W = OMEGA * TWOPI
C
C      con-rod centre of gravity point acceleration (m/s**2)
C      in the x direction
C
       ACCGX = (W**2) * ((B/1000.0)/(4.0 * (RN**2))) *
      1        COS(2.0*ANGLE)
C
C      in the y direction
C
       ACCGY = - (W**2) * ((B/1000.0)/RN) * SIN(2.0*ANGLE)
C
C      piston acceleration (m/s**2)
C
       ACCP = - (W**2) * (R2/1000.0) *
      1        (COS(ANGLE) + ((1.0/RN) * COS(2.0*ANGLE)))
```

This second fragment of code is much clearer and the expressions have a fair chance of being correct. At least we can see what the FORTRAN will evaluate and compare it with the formulae written down on paper. It is extremely difficult to debug bits of code when you have to think about what the FORTRAN is doing at the same time as thinking about what you are trying to achieve. If it is obvious what the FORTRAN is doing then errors are easier to find.

Finally, the code is easier to find amongst the comments if you do not comment each individual statement. In the above example the two accelerations, and the resultant piston acceleration are part of a logical block in the program. Not only is there no need to separate the code lines, it may be better if you do not:

```
C
C       con-rod centre of gravity point acceleration (m/s**2)
C
C                - in the x direction
C                - in the y direction
C                - leading to: piston acceleration (m/s**2)
C
C
        ACCGX =    (W**2) * ((B/1000.0)/(4.0 * (RN**2))) *
     1             COS(2.0*ANGLE)
        ACCGY = -  (W**2) * ((B/1000.0)/RN) * SIN(2.0*ANGLE)
        ACCP  = -  (W**2) * (R2/1000.0) *
     1             (COS(ANGLE) + ((1.0/RN) * COS(2.0*ANGLE)))
C
```

If you use brackets to enforce meaning in mathematical expressions you will be less likely to make silly mistakes, your code will be much easier to read and you need not memorize the rules concerning the priorities FORTRAN uses in evaluating expressions. One of life's rules for doing any activity well is to make it simple! (As an aside, spaces in the source code can have a hidden benefit. Many text editors have a 'jump to next word' facility. WordStar is one such. This facility is implemented by searching for spaces or punctuation in the text. Extra white space not only makes it more readable, it also makes it easier to jump to the precise point of interest!)

Now another example which illustrates the use of brackets to make FORTRAN code more understandable:

```
C
C       calculate DSTAR = [D] or [Dep] depending if gauss
C       point is plastic. [Dep] must also be used if we
C       are using the implicit creep algorithm on the
C       first iteration ISFLAG is 1 when restarting with
C       initial stiffness algorithm DEINT contains elastic
C       stiffness matrix at temperature defined at the
C       beginning of the loadcase
C
        IF (ISFLAG .EQ. 1) THEN
            DO 60 J = 1, 6
```

```
            DO 60 I = 1, 6
            DSTAR(I,J) = DEINT(I,J)
60          CONTINUE
C
C     [Dep] matrix required if there is plasticity or
C     implicit creep on the first iteration and not initial
C     stiffness algorithm (NALGO = 1)
C     [Dep] also required if initial stiffness algorithm and
C     we are restarting.
C
      ELSE IF IPLAST.EQ.1.AND.NGPYLD.EQ.1.OR.ICRPLC.EQ.1.AND.
     1          NGPCRP.EQ.1.AND.IMPLIS.EQ.1.AND.ITER.EQ.1.AND.
     2          NALGO.NE.1.OR.NALGO.EQ.1.AND.ISRSON.EQ.1) THEN
            DO 70 J = 1, 6
            DO 70 I = 1, 6
            DSTAR(I,J) = DPMAT(I,J)
70          CONTINUE
      ELSE
      ...
```

This is a section of code from a finite element program. It is not easy to understand what is going on even if you are very familiar with the variables and the subroutine that it comes from. As coded above it is almost impossible to predict when the ELSE IF statement will be executed, except possibly by trial and error.

This is better:

```
C
C     calculate DSTAR = [D] or [Dep] depending if gauss
C     point is plastic. [Dep] must also be used if we
C     are using the implicit creep algorithm on the
C     first iteration ISFLAG is 1 when restarting with
C     initial stiffness algorithm DEINT contains elastic
C     stiffness matrix at temperature defined at the
C     beginning of the loadcase
C
      IF (ISFLAG .EQ. 1) THEN
            DO 60 J = 1, 6
            DO 60 I = 1, 6
            DSTAR(I,J) = DEINT(I,J)
60          CONTINUE
C
C     [Dep] matrix required if there is plasticity or
C     implicit creep on the first iteration and not initial
C     stiffness algorithm (NALGO = 1)
```

```
C      [Dep] also required if initial stiffness algorithm and
C      we are restarting.
C
       ELSE IF ( (IPLAST .EQ. 1 .AND. NGPYLD .EQ. 1)
     1           .OR.
     2           ( (ICRPLC .EQ. 1 .AND. NGPCRP .EQ. 1) .AND.
     3           (IMPLIS .EQ. 1 .AND. ITER   .EQ. 1) .AND.
     4                                 (NALGO  .NE. 1) )
     5           .OR.
     6           (NALGO .EQ. 1 .AND. ISRSON .EQ. 1)  ) THEN
C
         DO 70 J = 1, 6
         DO 70 I = 1, 6
         DSTAR(I,J) = DPMAT(I,J)
  70     CONTINUE
       ELSE
       . . .
```

It is still fairly complicated, but by using brackets and white space at least you can see which expression goes with which. Even though the ELSE IF expression is still one long statement we have broken it down into more manageable parts. Much improvement is gained by aligning similar parts of consecutive expressions: even just aligning the position of the '=' signs can bring about some improvement.

Always put spaces on each side of logical operators, more for the operators .AND. and .OR. than for the comparison operators. This helps identify what they are more clearly.

7.4 INTRINSIC FUNCTIONS

We have seen above how the use of brackets can make an equation in FORTRAN more readily understandable and less prone to error. The intrinsic functions, INT, REAL, etc., have a part to play in arithmetic expressions as well as the more obvious ones which we automatically use when required, such as SIN, COS, TAN, etc. Consider the following example:

```
C      set up some real and integer variables
C
       X = 33.9
       Y = 3.0
       N = 7
       M = 2
C
C      now some arithmetic
C
       IXY = X/Y
```

```
      FNM = N/M
      INX = N * X
      IXN = X/N
C
C     do you know what the computer would evaluate for
C     all of these - and would you be sure to remember
C     if they were to appear in a more complicated
C     expression?
C
      Z = X/Y
      IXY = INT(Z)
      FNM = REAL(N)/REAL(M)
      INX = N * INT(X)
      IXN = INT(X/REAL(N))
C
C     there is less scope for error in these expressions!
C     if you can't remember what the intrinsic functions do,
C     at least they are easy to look up in your manual or
C     a FORTRAN text book
```

7.5 IF...THEN ELSE ENDIF

The IF...THEN ELSE ENDIF structure has the virtue of giving a logical sequence to your code, whereas overuse of the humble GOTO statement can force a tortuous journey through the program.

Of course the conditional GOTO and the unconditional GOTO statements cannot be dispensed with altogether, but they should be used sparingly. Computed GOTOs and assigned GOTOs can and should be replaced without exception by the IF...THEN ELSE ENDIF structure, as they can be a source of much misunderstanding and error.

The one disadvantage of the IF...THEN ELSE ENDIF expression is that when a number of these expressions are nested it is not clear which ENDIF goes with which IF. This disadvantage is completely overcome if 'indenting' is used. Let us look at an example:

```
C
C     In this example we are in the middle of an interactive
C     session. We have just prompted the user for 1 integer
C     and 2 real variables which have to be entered all on
C     one line. The program must not 'fall over' under any
C     circumstance so we read the response as an 80-byte
C     string. We then split this string into 3 substrings
C     and finally if all is well encode these strings.
C     The variables EMPTY and FAIL are logical.
```

```
C
C       first using GOTOs only
C
        CALL GETSTR (EMPTY,80 STRING,FAIL)
C
C       was there a failure in reading string if so report
C       error and give user another chance to enter
C       string correctly
C
        IF (FAIL) GO TO 40
C
C       check if the string entered was empty - this is an
C       error there is no default response so report error
C       and ask question again
C
        IF (EMPTY) GO TO 50
C
C       split string into substrings
C
        CALL SUBSTR (3,NUMSTR,STR,STRING,FAIL)
C
C       were we unable to split the string successfully
C       if so report error and ask question again
C
        IF (FAIL) GO TO 60
C
C       were 3 strings entered
C
        IF (NUMSTR .NE. 3) GO TO 70
C
C       is the first string an integer
C
        CALL CTOI (STR(1),INT1,FAIL)
C
C       were we able to encode an integer
C
        IF (FAIL) GO TO 80
C
C       is the second string a real
C
            . . .
C       and so on
            . . .
  40    CALL ERRREP (10.UNAME)
C
```

```
C       report error number 10, and name of routine
C       we would now need to check how many times the user
C       had made errors - if more than 3 then quit
C       otherwise ask question again
C

         . . .
        GO TO 20
 50     CALL ERRREP (20,UNAME)
C
C        and so on  and so on
C
C        note how far apart the GOTO and its target label can
C        become making it difficult to follow the logic of
C        the program. Also we will produce lots and lots of
C        labels which will make the  code messy and also the
C        choice of label numbers more and more bizarre
```

And now how the same code might look if written with IF...THEN ELSE ENDIF and
GOTO:

```
C
C        read response into 80-byte string
C
        CALL GETSTR (EMPTY,80,STRING,FAIL)
C
C       check for failure to read string
C
        IF (FAIL) THEN
C
C       failed to read string correctly report error
C
           CALL ERRREP (10,UNAME)
C
C       check number of times error made, if less than 3 say
C       return to ask question again
C
         . . .
           GO TO 20
        ELSE IF (EMPTY) THEN
C
C       string is empty, this is an error since there was no
C       default report error
C
           CALL ERRREP (20,UNAME)
C
```

```
C      check number of times error has been made etc.
C
         . . .
         GO TO 20
      ELSE
C
C     string read correctly split into 3 strings
C
         CALL SUBSTR (3,NUMSTR,STR,STRING,FAIL)

         IF (FAIL) THEN
C
C     report error
C
            CALL ERRREP (30,UNAME)
C     etc.
         . . .
            GO TO 20
         ELSE IF (NUMSTR .NE. 3) THEN
C
C     the response didn't contain 3 strings - report error
C
            CALL ERRREP (40,UNAME)
C
C     etc.
C
         . . .
            GO TO 20
C
C     and so on
C
         ELSE
C
C     string decoded successfully confirm
C     entry
         .
         .
         .
C     etc.
C
         ENDIF
      ENDIF
C
C     continue with next bit of program
```

It is much easier to locate errors when the code is set out like this with bits of code which are logically related all in one place. Note how almost every condition gave rise to a series of operations which finished with a GOTO. Not only that, but the GOTOs were all going to the same place. They might even be superfluous, if statement 20 happened to be the next statement after the ENDIF! In any case, it is better to 'fall through' to the terminating ENDIF and to have just one GOTO if at all possible.

You should also try to avoid a 'hanging' ELSE...ENDIF at the bottom of a long IF THEN construct. If you think that such a condition should never arise, program defensively, and put in an error message of the sort 'THIS MESSAGE IMPLIES AN ERROR IN THE PROGRAM'.

7.6 VARIABLE NAMES

Great care should be taken when choosing variable names. By choosing variable names which relate to the entities that they represent, equations written in FORTRAN are readable and can be instantly understandable. Apart from the normal FORTRAN restrictions on variable names you should without exception choose names that reflect the default variable type.

Integer variables should always begin with letters from the range I to N, and real variables with the letters A to H or O to Z. If you use double precision everywhere instead of real then use A to H and O to Z for double precision variables. If you need to mix real, double precision, and complex then choose a convention for each of these types and stick to it. For example you could use variables names beginning with D for double precision variables and variable names beginning with Z for complex variables.

There is nothing more certain to lead to errors than an integer variable starting with the letters A to H or O to Z, or a real variable having an integer variable name. For example in the more mechanical branches of engineering, a parameter known as Poisson's ratio is very often referred to as NU (the Greek letter). Call it GNU or PNU or PR or POISSN or whatever in your program, otherwise disaster lies ahead.

It is sometimes convenient to use LOGICAL variables in your program. LOGICAL variables can very often make a program more readable, but choose the names of your LOGICAL variables wisely. LOGICAL variables can only be TRUE or FALSE so choose names which are obviously TRUE or FALSE. We have already used two LOGICAL variables in the code examples above, these were EMPTY and FAIL. There is only one alternative to empty and that is not empty, FAIL similarly is obviously either true or false. SUM for example would be a hopeless name for a LOGICAL variable, SUM implies an equality to an as-yet-unknown value which could be anything.

7.7 SUBROUTINES

As we shall see, subroutines offer many advantages, in fact the only reason we can think of why people may not use subroutines is that they are too lazy. The answer to this is to have a template subroutine that you can read into your text editor and adapt for any use. The template that we use is shown below:

```
      SUBROUTINE
C     ----------------------------
C     purpose of routine:
C
C     arguments
C      input :
C
C     output :
C
C     called by:
C     subroutines called:
C     functions called:
C     COMMON blocks used:
C     Revision History:
C     -----------------------------------------------------
C

      RETURN
C
C     -----------------------------------------------------
C
C     ERR condition detected
C
      END
```

This template, and others like it, are at the heart of code widely used in the construction and aerospace industries. We would have liked to show all our examples with such full comments, but that would have made the book unacceptably long.

Notice that we have an information section below the SUBROUTINE statement. Having this information section and keeping it up to date has a cost—it takes time and effort particularly in the development of a new subroutine. However, we have found that it is well worth the effort involved when it comes to the maintenance of our subroutines. If you are involved in documenting your code—particularly if you need to write manuals for people who have to develop and maintain your code—you will find that the information sections below the subroutines are invaluable.

Although this template contains little FORTRAN it has a large psychological effect when it comes to writing a new subroutine. There is no need to start from scratch—there is a structure there to help you, to get you out of the starting blocks. Most text editors can read another file into the current file, and do so several times. It is an easy way to generate code. Now consider the four main reasons why subroutines are worth using.

Look at an example:

```
        PROGRAM MAIN
C
C       start with the declarations etc.
C
        PARAMETER .......
        DIMENSION ......
        CHARACTER ......
        LOGICAL ........
        DATA .......
C
        CALL INDAT(........)
        CALL CHKDAT(..........)
        CALL WRTDAT(..........)
        CALL SOLVER(.........)
        CALL STRAIN(..........)
        CALL STRESS(..........)
        CALL OUTPUT(.........)
C
        STOP
        END
```

If you plan your program and adopt a modular approach it is quite feasible that your main program could be like that shown above, with a few details and comments added. By choosing appropriate names for your subroutines the main program will read like the contents page of a book.

Even without comments it is fairly clear what is happening in the program outline shown above. The problem data is read in in subroutine INDAT. Subroutine CHKDAT checks the data, and subroutine WRTDAT writes out the data to the output file. Subroutine SOLVER solves some equations, subroutine STRAIN works out the strains, and subroutine STRESS works out the stresses. Subroutine OUTPUT writes the results to the output file.

2 IT MAKES THE PROGRAMMING TASK LESS DAUNTING

Each subroutine called by the main program will most probably call other subroutines, and these subroutines may call other subroutines, and so on depending on the complexity of the programming problem. By using subroutines in this way a major complex problem can be split into a number of small problems, each subroutine undertaking its own little task. By consigning a small problem to a subroutine, one is isolating that problem.

When assigning a task to a subroutine, it will become clear what variables are required to solve that task. There will in general be input variables and output variables—these are put in the argument list. The subroutine need not know anything about the routine calling it; provided it is called with the correct variables in the argument list it will perform its task.

3 IT MAKES CODE TESTING EASIER

Each subroutine can be tested independently by calling it with the appropriate variables in the argument list from a small test program. The subroutine can be called with a range of values for the input variables and so checked for reliability.

4 IT MAKES THE WRITING OF PROGRAMS AN EASIER, QUICKER, AND MORE INTERESTING TASK

(a) By adopting a modular approach to writing programs it is possible to quickly build up a library of well-tested subroutines which carry out small primary tasks, which can be used over and over again. Even in the development of one program you will find that you use some subroutines many times. For every subroutine which is called more than once you have saved yourself from repeating a number of lines of code, saved yourself from introducing unnecessary errors into the program, and given yourself extra time to spend on the more interesting tasks before you.

(b) Since each of your primary subroutines in your subroutine library is used frequently, and has been well tested it is—inasmuch as any piece of code can be—bug free. Since these subroutines form the foundations of any new program or program module that you write, you will spend less time debugging your programs, and more time testing your working program on interesting problems!

7.8 ARGUMENT LISTS—NOT COMMON BLOCKS

The problem with COMMON blocks is that subroutines that share COMMON blocks do not in general have to be related in any way. It is not clear which subroutines contain a particular COMMON block.

If argument lists are used for transporting variables about the code, then the argument list is shared only by the subroutine and the routines that call it.

COMMON blocks typically appear in a number of routines throughout a program. While developing a program there are frequently changes of mind. The code is more complicated than was first thought. It becomes apparent that there is a simpler way of coding something. A problem arises which was not anticipated. These and other reasons lead to new variables being introduced into the code, and existing variables being moved around.

If you use COMMON blocks for your variables then these may need to be amended to reflect the new requirements. If a COMMON block does alter, then it will need to change in every subroutine in which that COMMON block appears, even those subroutines which are finished, tested, and 'put to bed'. If one subroutine is forgotten then it will lead to an error—but where will that error occur and how will it manifest itself?

If you use argument lists for your variables, then a change to the argument list in one subroutine will only, at worst, lead to a change to the argument list in those routines which call it. There is a direct relationship between the subroutines which have to be altered. And how do you go about finding the error when one of your COMMON block variables has the wrong value? In which subroutine was that variable set up, in which subroutine was it changed?

When there is an error in a variable in an argument list, then you can check its value in the calling routine, just before the CALL statement. If it is wrong in the calling routine then you can look in the routine that called that, and so on. There is a methodical way in which you can track down the error. *And* you can do this with a symbolic debugger if your FORTRAN system supports one, rather than introducing extra printout lines whilst debugging manually.

Of course there are some problems associated with variables in argument lists. The error that occurs most frequently is where the argument list in the CALL statement does not match the argument list in the subroutine. This is the first thing to check when a variable passed through the argument list has a strange value.

We always like to have our arguments in alphabetical order in serious programming work. This has a number of advantages particularly where there are many variables in the argument list. It is easier to spot if an argument is missing, you can see immediately if a particular variable is in the argument list because you know precisely where to look. Ordering your variables in alphabetical order can be a nuisance sometimes, but you will find yourself making less errors, and finding those that you do make more quickly.

The other error that is frequently made with argument lists (and COMMON blocks) is that a variable or variables are declared wrongly. The dimension statement is wrong. All variables in one subroutine are REAL and in aother subroutine DOUBLE PRECISION. This is the second thing to look for when variables have unexpected values.

Having, we hope, convinced you that COMMON blocks should not be used for the mass transfer of information from one routine to another, we should say that COMMON blocks can be useful when used to carry system constants around the program. For example you might have a program that has a number of output files: a 'log' file, to give information on how the analysis is progressing and to record any error messages; a file to hold the complete program results; a file which contains data for a restart, and a file which has selected results for input to a graphics program, say. We would need to OPEN all these files with associated unit numbers. These numbers would then be used in write statements throughout the program: let us say unit 8 for the log file, 9 for the results file, 10 for the restart file, and 11 for the graphics data file. Half-way through a subroutine, well away from the OPEN statements, you might well be heard mumbling under your breath 'what on earth was the unit number for the results file'. How much easier to have ILOG = 8, IRES = 9, IRST = 10, IGRP = 11; put ILOG, IGRP, IRES,

IRST (in alphabetical order of course) in a COMMON block and carry these variable names around the program. 'Of course the unit number for the results file is IRES'! This would also have advantages for portability.

It is quite common in FORTRAN to have unit number 5 as the standard input device and unit number 6 as the standard output device (note this is *not* in the FORTRAN 77 standard). On some computers you may be able to assign unit 5 and 6 to any file, on other computers units 5 and 6 may be reserved for standard I/O.

If at the start of your program you had IDAT = 5, with the intention of using unit 5 for your input data file, then when transporting to a machine where unit 5 was reserved, only one number in your main setup routine would need to be changed—IDAT = 21 say. If, on the other hand, you had explicitly referred to unit 5 each time you read from the input data file you would be faced with a lengthy editing session changing 5 to 21. On each edit that you perform there is a mistake waiting to be made!

A further example of the good sense in making all READ and WRITE statements refer to variables for the unit number arose from an unexpected source while transferring code from Microsoft Fortran version 3.31 to version 4.0. In the earlier version, several files could be OPENed and connected to (say) NUL. For example, unit numbers 7 and 8 could both be connected to the same file or device by consecutive OPEN statements. In v. 4, it became impermissible to connect more than one unit to a given file.

The program at issue generates extensive results files from a long and complicated input file. It might take several test runs before the input file is free from errors. Debugging may not exclusively apply to programs: large data files may need debugging too! To safely dispose of extensive and unwanted results files generated by a program during this debugging stage, they would be connected to NUL, and no data would be saved. The program used explicit unit numbers, and needed extensive editing to introduce variables, which could be allocated the same unit number, when connected to NUL, or different numbers, connected to the appropriate files, when the results were really wanted.

As it happens, the extra work would not have been needed had the two units been referred to by symbolic names.

7.9 STATEMENT NUMBERING AND ORDERING

Code is much easier to follow if a consistent ordering is maintained. Always declare data in short statements, and do not mix them up. For instance, declare CHARACTER data of different lengths in different statements, and declare *all* of it before declaring other data types:

```
CHARACTER*1   ANSWER
CHARACTER*40  LABEL
CHARACTER*80  TITLE
```

```
LOGICAL       YES,    ACCEPT,    FATAL
DOUBLE PRECISION X(5000)
```

Declare the data types *before* using DATA statements to set values, and always dimension your variables when they first appear, rather than waiting to put them in an explicit DIMEN-SION statement. Get all of this out of the way before writing executable code, even if you have access to a compiler that does not protest at declarations mixed up in the executable statements.

Number the statement labels in an ascending sequence throughout the subroutine. You have to be pretty confident to do this consecutively at first writing: we suggest increments of 10 to leave space for afterthoughts. Use low numbers for executable statements, high ones for FORMATs. Only put statement labels on CONTINUEs and FORMATs if you can so arrange it—a statement label on the last executable statement in a loop, for example,

```
      DO 30 I=1,NV
      SUM = 0.0
           DO 30 J=1,NV
30         SUM = SUM + X(I,J)*Y(J,I)
```

makes it so much more difficult to jump to the loop end as in:

```
      DO 30 I=1,NV
      SUM = 0.0
           DO 20 J=1,NV
           IF (I .EQ. J) GO TO 30
           SUM = SUM + X(I,J)*Y(J,I)
20         CONTINUE
30 CONTINUE
```

and such a change might be required as part of the debugging process.

In short subroutines, statement numbers may not need to exceed 99. That leaves the hundreds for FORMATs. Why not use numbers starting with 5 for input and 6 for output, reflecting the commonplace old 'standard' for unit numbers? Then you will always know that 500, 501, and so on are input FORMATs, 600, 601, etc. are for output. We find it convenient to group all our FORMATs at the end of a subroutine. They are often easier to lay out if grouped together, apart from always knowing where to find them.

7.10 SUMMARY

You will find it very beneficial to adopt some if not all of the advice given above in your coding, if you do not already. However, there are times when the constraints of developing FORTRAN programs on the microcomputer conspire against us. For example if you use the

Microsoft FORTRAN compiler you will find that named COMMON blocks are allocated a segment to themselves. If you have a number of large arrays then you may well find that it is less of a problem to allocate each its own named COMMON block, than to declare them locally in some calling routine and pass them through the argument list. Also the default memory size allocated to the addresses of variables passed through the argument list is only 2 kbytes. If you use argument lists extensively you may exceed this limit and need to reallocate this memory size. If you use COMMON blocks you would avoid any such problems. In later chapters of the book where we discuss the problems of coping with a slow microcomputer or small memory you may well get advice which conflicts with some of that given in this chapter. The best approach is to adopt a coding strategy based on the principles in this chapter. Where you are forced to deviate from this strategy, use COMMENTs liberally and wisely so that readability is sustained in your comments. You will find that the effort involved in writing readable and maintainable code is amply rewarded by the time saved in debugging your programs.

CHAPTER 8

CODE TRANSFER AND PORTABLE CODE

8.1 INTRODUCTION

There are several aspects to the transfer of FORTRAN from machine to machine. For a start, there is the physical transfer of the code. It is worse than useless transferring executable code unless between extremely similar machines: it simply will not run. The exception should be made for all DOS machines, because they run on a family of compatible processors, but even here there may be incompatibilities. (Some machines can emulate the processors in DOS computers to a greater or lesser extent.)

We concentrate then on the transfer of FORTRAN source code. There is first of all the mechanics of the transfer, then having ported our source code to the new machine we are faced with recompiling the code with a new compiler. Of course FORTRAN 77 (and FORTRAN 66 before it) are defined standards, but even if we stick rigidly to the standard we will still find that the code does not compile cleanly first time round. The problems arise mainly because of bad programming habits, but also, to a lesser but probably more annoying degree, from the restrictions, extensions, and downright perversion of the FORTRAN standard perpetrated by the compiler writer. We need to get into the habit of writing *portable* code, so that although we will not eliminate compilation errors altogether after moving our source code, the problems that do arise will not be our fault! What's more, they should normally be confined to known areas of incompatibility such as FORTRAN input/output (I/O).

Writing portable code also allows us to move between two different compilers on the same machine. Although it is difficult to contemplate wanting to do this on a mainframe computer, there are often benefits to be obtained by doing so on the DOS microcomputer. Not only are new or improved products with extra facilities still regularly coming onto the market, but software prices are comparatively modest, and the quest for speed in execution or compilation leads to regular changes. More to the point, changing compilers can often reveal an obscure bug, because a different system sometimes has a clearer error message than the one normally in use.

On mainframe computers there still exists a lot of code written in FORTRAN to the 1966 standard, referred to variously as FORTRAN IV or just FORTRAN 66. This poses its own problems when porting to DOS microcomputers, since the best compilers (and they are improving all the time) are all FORTRAN 77 compilers. For future portability it would be just as well to convert old codes to FORTRAN 77, and we look at some important aspects of this conversion procedure. We also list the differences between the two FORTRAN standards.

Finally we look at the new FORTRAN 8x standard, and what we would like to see included in this standard.

8.2 LINES OF COMMUNICATION

In the early days of FORTRAN, computers communicated to the outside world through the media of punched cards, or punched paper tape (the latter being very common in Britain in the early days of computing, although the use of punched cards became more widespread later). Both input and output were via the punched paper media, and separate machines existed to print out from a 'deck' of cards, or from a punched tape. Even then, there were transfer problems. Machine X used cards, and machine Y, tape. Even among two machines which used the same medium, there could be differences.

Take first the tape. Tapes very soon standardized on 8 holes across the tape: each representing a bit in a byte. A 7-bit code was usually used, corresponding to at most 127 characters in the character set. For example, a hole was punched in a position to denote '1', or the tape was left whole in that place to denote '0'. Since the punches were mechanical, and often unreliable, a hole could be left out. There was almost no way of checking this, since whatever hole pattern was selected probably still had a valid, if different, meaning.

This is where the eighth hole comes in. Using a 7-bit code for characters allows the eighth bit to be used for parity checking. This is a simple, quick, but by no means complete method of checking each character. For example the computer may be instructed that a character from the paper tape will not be accepted as valid unless an even number of holes is received for the 8-bit code. A character which had a 7-bit code, resulting in an odd number of holes being punched, would have a hole punched for the eighth bit to make the total number of holes even. For a character with a 7-bit code giving an even number of holes the eighth hole would not be punched. After checking that the number of holes was even, the computer would then strip off (ignore) the eighth bit before encoding the character.

This form of parity checking is called 'even parity', also used was 'odd parity' where each 8 bits always had an odd number of holes, and for optimum speed and no checking, or where additional non-standard characters using 8-bits were required, 'no parity'. These terms are still used in today's electronic communications.

Unfortunately, as with so many other aspects of computing today, the manufacturers of computers which were able to accept their input from paper tape, did not agree on a standard method of coding. So it wasn't necessarily possible to transfer code from one such computer to another simply by feeding the paper tape containing the code on one computer into the other computer.

The situation was pretty much the same with punched cards, where there were at least two 'standards' in common use. One corresponded to ASCII, the other termed EBCDIC, commonly used on IBM computers, had different codes for some of the symbols. These were punctuation mainly: numerals and upper case letters were the same. There were different card sizes, but by and large the card format settled down to the 80-column standard.

On mainframe and minicomputers code transfer is usually achieved using magnetic tape. Here too ASCII and EBCDIC codes are used as well as a number of others; however, most mainframes are able to cope with the more common codes used, so that provided that it is known how the magnetic tape has been encoded it is usually possible to successfully transfer the code, and most mainframe to mainframe (or mini) communication is done in this way.

None of this is really useful to the PC owner whose code is on a mainframe, or who wants to transfer his code to a mainframe, or to another type of microcomputer—a tape drive may cost many times as much as a PC, and the floppy disks (some mainframes have floppy disks as well) will almost certainly not be compatible.

Most microcomputers use floppy disks as portable storage media, although external hard (Winchester) disks and cassette tape streamers are also used on some DOS microcomputers.

Code transfer between microcomputers is probably most easily, and for large files most quickly, achieved using an external hard disk. However, not only are they expensive, but they don't travel too well and should probably only be used if the two PCs sit side by side. Indeed hard disks can be shared by microcomputers (even two or more of different types) and, of course, large capacity hard disks are used as the central storage media in microcomputer networks.

Cassette tape streamers are used primarily as large capacity back-up devices for hard disks. They are also expensive, and encoding of data to cassette tapes is machine dependent.

Floppy disks are cheap and plentiful, but so are the number of different types. Even if two microcomputers will accept the same type of disk there is no guarantee that one will be able to read data from a disk created on the other. The old Apricot XI microcomputer, the Macintosh microcomputer and some IBM AT microcomputers all use 3.5 inch disks, but none will be able to read data encoded on a disk by the other. This is because the method of storing data (the **format**) of the disk is different in each case.

IBM alone have manufactured machines which have used single-sided, double-sided, double-density and high-density disks, and both 5.25 inch and 3.5 inch varieties. These microcomputers all use the same operating system—PC DOS—but still pose a number of problems for file transfer. A 5.25 inch drive will not be able to read a 3.5 inch disk, a single-sided drive can not read both sides of a double-sided disk, and a drive that reads double-density disks will not be able to read data stored on high-density disks.

So what do we do if we want to transfer our FORTRAN source code from our microcomputer to another microcomputer with an incompatible storage media, or to a mainframe computer? Or if we want to transfer code from a mainframe computer to our microcomputer?

There are a number of different aspects to these problems and we start by looking at two specific cases before discussing general purpose communications.

However, for short programs, you should consider retyping! The effort in making communications links and using unfamiliar software may exceed the effort in a little rekeying. Add to that the opportunity to understand the code as you type it, and to add extra comments, and there may be additional benefit in doing so.

8.3 TRANSFER FROM 5.25 INCH DISKS TO 3.5 INCH DISKS OR VICE VERSA

If you are moving from a machine with 5.25 inch disk drives to one with 3.5 inch disks (or vice versa) then you may need help getting your program on the other type of diskette. If you only need to do the operation once then ask your local dealer to do the copying for you. If you need to transfer a lot of programs then we suggest you consider obtaining an external disk drive for one of your machines which will allow you to use both types of disks on the same machine. For example you could buy an external 5.25 inch disk drive for your 3.5 inch machine. The software provided with the external drive will allow you to 'format' disks and 'diskcopy'.

One of the strengths of DOS version 2 and above is in the simplicity of installing different hardware: just plug the controller card into any vacant expansion slot (sometimes the physical size and shape of the card may restrict where it goes, and some of the 80286/80386 machines have different types of slot, so your card can only fit into an expansion slot of the correct type). Then copy the supplied driver on to your boot disk, and add the appropriate DEVICE= line to the CONFIG.SYS file. When DOS boots, the device driver will be loaded.

The theory of loadable device drivers is beyond the scope of this book, but if you are interested in pursuing it further, we suggest you refer to Ray Duncan's *Advanced MS DOS* (Microsoft Press—see the bibliography in Chapter 2).

8.4 TERMINAL EMULATION

We believe that microcomputers can be used successfully for running most FORTRAN programs, and indeed the latest microcomputers based on the 80386 Intel processor are as powerful as most minicomputers. Moreover the time between submitting a program and getting the results is very often *shorter* on a microcomputer than a multi-user mainframe, where certain jobs are scheduled to run at off-peak times, and where there may be a delay in getting the results (particularly graphics results) due to the mainframe (and the graphics terminals) being at a different geographical location. However, there are still some programs which are better suited to mainframe computers, particularly those which have large storage requirements. Even with these programs microcomputers still have a role to play.

Multi-user mainframe computers are usually very heavily used, particularly during the daytime—there has to be a demand to justify the large capital outlay. But in addition to doing the jobs that they are good at, such as 'number crunching', the mainframe also spends a lot of time doing jobs for which it is less well suited such as editing. The ideal solution is for the editing (and the initial program development) to be done by the microcomputer, and only the final compiling, linking, and execution to be done by the mainframe.

Microcomputers can be considered as computer terminals with added intelligence. They have most of the components of dumb terminals, and indeed many of the components of some of the cleverer graphics terminals, but in addition they can of course be used as general purpose computing devices and they have local storage facilities.

For reasons of cost, many mainframe systems communicate with their terminals using only two wires. One for signals to the terminal, and one for the opposite direction, with circuits being completed via earthing. Of necessity, such communications links are serial, in other words the data bits in each byte are sent one after the other, and control of sending information is by software: the receiver sends a message to stop sending shortly before it is overwhelmed.

This type of terminal communication is very simple to emulate, and appropriate software is often bundled with PCs. Unfortunately, it demands that the terminals (and hence the PC) are physically close to the mainframe. When the computer is remote, or data transfer is at higher speeds, better error checking and signal enhancement are required. This normally demands the use of devices called modems at each end of the communications link.

Some terminal emulations need hardware in the PC. Examples of this are common in the IBM mainframe world. They take the form of boards which fit into the PCs expansion slots. The cost of this hardware can be considerable. However, using the PC as a dumb terminal is a waste of resource, we only need to add file transfer and the PC can be used in the ideal way we postulated above.

The mainframe may expect only 'dumb' terminals to be connected, but with the right software the PC can still transfer files with its host. Hence, for example, a program on the PC could send a source code file to the mainframe as if it were a programmer typing it in line by line! Similarly, the mainframe might be commanded to send a listing of the source code, and instead of (or as well as) sending it to the screen, the PC might store it away on a disk.

This is usually so easy that microcomputer to microcomputer communications are often better done by sending things via a mainframe first! PCs do not normally expect a terminal to be connected.

When contemplating general communications with and without modems, the purchase of appropriate communications software is advisable. In the next section we describe what is probably the best choice for the PC user. This does not rule out the use of other commercial products: many of them have their own special features which have a particular application. We will concentrate on the transfer of FORTRAN source code because that is our objective here.

8.5 GENERAL PURPOSE COMMUNICATIONS

If you want to transfer a program from your IBM PC or other DOS computer to a number of completely different machines, such as an Apple Macintosh or a Digital VAX, you will need a more general tool. As before you will need a cable and some software, but this time you will need software on each of the machines involved in the transfer. If the computers are in different physical locations you will also need a telephone line and a couple of modems (more about this later). The cable will give you the physical link between the machines. The software will allow the machines to talk to each other.

The cable will connect the RS232 serial port on your PC to the appropriate serial port on the particular computer to which you are currently transferring files. 'Standard' RS232 serial ports have 25 different channels or pins on the connector, but don't be dismayed if you have less than this—you don't normally require more than three or four channels to successfully transfer data from one machine to another and the IBM AT computers have nine pin serial ports which are physically smaller. The number of channels required and the precise cable connections will be dependent on the two machines that you are using—it may also depend on the software. If you are communicating for the first time between two machines then be prepared for one or two setbacks. You should have a cable made by a professional who knows the 'pin outs' required on the two machines. You should have a lot of patience—and ideally you should have a 'break out' box and a soldering iron. A break out box allows you to see visually when one of the wires in your cable is being used for communication, and it will allow you to set up any combination of connections between the wires in your cable from one end to the other.

There are a large number of communication software products available. Some are expensive and sophisticated, some are cheap and get the job done. The best one to use is called 'KERMIT', named after the frog in the children's TV programme. This program was developed for terminal emulation and file transfer at Columbia University in the United States. Regardless of its other merits, it has one of overriding importance. It is free! You only have to pay for the disks or tape—you will find the PC version on the disk set accompanying this book. It is available on almost all popular computers and works adequately as a file transfer program. How well KERMIT works on a particular machine will depend entirely on who implemented it on that machine and how good a job they have done. Good implementations of KERMIT are available on most popular machines.

Once you have an appropriate cable (if this is the first time you will not know whether the cable is appropriate or not yet, only that it plugs into both machines—so keep your fingers crossed) and KERMIT running on both machines, you will need to look at the 'status' of all the variables that KERMIT gives you control over (these may be presented differently on the two machines). You will be able to set such quantities as:

- the speed at which the communication between the two machines will take place, known as the 'baud' rate, measured in bits per second;
- whether there is any parity checking: even parity, odd parity, no parity—they are analogous to the hole patterns in punched paper tape referred to earlier;
- local or remote echo: are the characters you send (assuming that you are sending readable text) going to appear on your screen because your computer puts them there when they are sent, or because the remote computer sends them back as a check?
- block checking: will your software check that data has been correctly transferred, and how?
- handshaking—carriage return, line feed, ESC, bell, XON, XOFF, none—these are protocols to stimulate the sender into sending or stop sending information;
- character at start of packet (start bit);
- character at end of packet (stop bit);
- packet length;

etc.

You should ensure that everything is set the same on both machines. The 'baud' rate settings usually vary between 300 and 9600. Some machines, particularly those that run with 8088 chips and slow clock rates (like the original IBM PC for instance) may have difficulty coping with the fastest rate. File transfer over a serial port is quite slow at the best of times, so you want the baud rate to be as fast as possible. However, the faster you go the more likely that errors will occur. If your two machines are in the same room then you should be able to communicate at the fastest speeds. If you are communicating via a modem (a telephone link) then, particularly when the lines are busy (e.g. in the morning), you may find that errors occur even at 1200 baud.

Having ensured that all the parameters are set the same on both machines, you simply issue the command 'send' followed by the file name of the file you wish to transfer, and the command 'receive' on the destination computer. Either you get file transfer or you don't. If you don't get file transfer, recheck the baud rates on both machines. If this is all right then the cable is probably wrong. If you get file transfer then you are in business, even if the data transferred is rubbish! Your two computers are communicating—they just aren't speaking the same language. Recheck that the status variables are set the same on both machines.

What other errors can occur? The most likely errors are loss of data or spurious data. Quite a common effect when transferring files is repeated end of file markers at the end of the file. Most errors can be simply put right in the editor on the target machine, but if you get a lot of errors try transferring the file again at a slower baud rate.

KERMIT also usually includes one or more terminal emulators. Thus having transferred your file from IBM PC to Digital VAX 11/780 you can then edit the file transferred using your PC as a VT100 terminal.

We have used the term 'modem' a couple of times in the foregoing without defining what it is. 'Modem' stands for *mo*dulator/*dem*odulator which is its function. When Alexander Graham Bell invented the telephone he didn't foresee that at some time in the future computers would want to converse using it, so he didn't build in the necessary tolerances for accurate digital communication. Enter stage left, the modem. The modem sends a constant tone over the telephone line called the carrier. To send data, the modem varies the tone (modulation)—of course there needs to be a modem at the other end to interpret (demodulate) the variations in tone as data, and also to send back data from the remote machine. There are many different modems, the main variables being speed and method of communication (asynchronous—in which each byte is sent separately with its own start bits and stop bits; and sychronous—where the transmitter and receiver are exactly sychronized so that data can be sent in continuous streams with no start or stop bits allowing much faster data transfer). The finer details are beyond the scope of this book, but for the uninitiated this is a very confusing subject. If you need to buy a modem, make sure you know as much as possible about the modems you will be communicating with. If you are buying a modem for your PC then it should come with all the communication software that you need for the PC end but make sure it is compatible with the software at the other end—most good communications packages include the 'KERMIT' package mentioned above.

KERMIT will transfer binary files as well as ASCII text files. If you transfer binary (EXE, COM, etc.) files between DOS machines, they probably will work. If you transfer them to anything else, they will not.

8.6 SOME UNEXPECTED PROBLEMS

Having transferred your program to the target machine you are then typically faced with compiling your program with a different compiler. Even if the compilers on the two machines were produced by the same company, there is no guarantee that they will be the same on both machines. If both are DOS machines and the compiler is manufactured by the same company, then it is more likely that the compiler will be the same–however, there still might be local nuances.

For example, the Microsoft FORTRAN compiler has code to handle error conditions in the numeric coprocessor. This makes assumptions about how the coprocessor and the rest of the hardware fit together. Some DOS computers used other hardware configurations, and the Microsoft FORTRAN would hang up on those machines if an error condition, such as attempting to divide by zero, occurred. A software patch was developed, and applied to the standard software libraries issued with Microsoft FORTRAN. Machines known to be affected, and which need the patch, include the Victor 9000/Sirius 1, Apricot, TI Professional, and NEC APC3 and PC9801 machines. Patched code will not run correctly on an IBM PC or strict compatible. Other FORTRAN compilers, which handled the error conditions in another way, were not affected by the hardware differences.

8.7 PORTABLE CODE

Having transferred your FORTRAN source code to another machine you now need to compile your program on the new machine. Suppose that this transfer was from a mainframe to your PC. What problems will you face? 'None. FORTRAN 77 is meant to be a standard, and if I stick to the standard there should be no problems!' We wish that were true. Coding your FORTRAN within the 77 standard will certainly help when you come to use a new compiler but unfortunately the standard is not very tightly defined in certain areas. The problems will be similar to those if you had stayed on the original computer, but decided to use a different compiler.

It is very easy at the beginning of a project to convince yourself that you will never change computers and compilers, that you might as well take advantage of those extensions to the standard that your compiler offers—but our advice is to always stick to the standard. If the program that you write is useful to you then it will probably be useful to someone else—and that someone else may well use a different compiler. At the very least put all subroutines containing non-standard software in their own library so that you can easily identify those routines that will need attention when you change compilers.

The main stumbling block of portability with FORTRAN code is file manipulation: the standard is simply not strict enough. Most of the problems are related to the fact that different operating systems have different rules governing the naming and storing of files on the computer. This general area is one to which order should have been brought by the FORTRAN 77 standard. Sadly it wasn't. This gives rise to a number of problems.

Take the OPEN statement first. When moving from computer system to computer system, you will find that file naming conventions vary. Friendly 'CON' under DOS becomes 'SYS$INPUT' and 'SYS$OUTPUT' under VAX/VMS. Similarly, file names with a name of up to eight characters and a three character extension are common: but VAX/VMS allows a generation number as in DATAFILE.RES;32. It also allows more than eight characters for the file name if required.

Other operating system file names (and directory extensions) are completely differently to DOS. An example from the microcomputer world is UNIX, where it is normal (but not compulsory) to have just a one-letter extension after the name, thus a data file may be called 'OUTPUT.D', whereas in comparison under DOS it is normal (but not compulsory) to use three letter extensions, such that a data file might be called 'OUTPUT.DAT'. Also the characters that you are allowed to use in file names might vary from operating system to operating system.

When using direct access files, you will almost certainly have to change the size of record length. This is because the units used for defining the record length are not defined in the standard. Thus on some computers the record length is measured in bytes, and on others in words. On the VAX the units for record length actually change depending on what sort of file you are opening.

Other factors that change are the elements permitted in the parameter list of an OPEN statement, and the permitted values that can be assigned. This changes not only across machines and compilers, but sometimes across two versions of the same compiler. As an example, all version 3.xx Microsoft FORTRANs have permitted a file to have STATUS='OLD' and STATUS='NEW'. This meant respectively that it either had to exist for the program to run successfully, or that it was created if it didn't. The latter STATUS is normally described as 'UNKNOWN'. Version 4 introduced 'UNKNOWN' status, but redefined 'NEW' as meaning 'the program will crash if the file exists'.

At least as extensive a range of problems is associated with CLOSE and INQUIRE statements, and for the sake of brevity we shall not dwell on them further. Other things to look out for when changing machines and compilers are reserved unit numbers and IOSTAT error numbers. Remember that on some machines certain UNIT numbers may be reserved for specific tasks such as I/O (input/output) to a particular device, also the range of numbers that can be used as UNIT numbers may differ from compiler to compiler. Often DOS based compilers reserve 5 and 6 for console I/O, but unit 0 is sometimes reserved for this, along with the standard preconnected unit *.

If you use the IOSTAT=IERR statement in your I/O statements then you should be aware that the error numbers will mean different things for different compilers and different machines.

Now all of these things are so fundamental to writing FORTRAN code, which controls files from within a program, that you might be forgiven for believing that the standard is of no use whatsoever, and for porting all but the simplest codes you would be right. There seems to be no good reason why the standard in this area should not be tightened. Could it be that (as always) the vested interest of the major computer manufacturers is being put before the interests of the humble programmer?

A good programming tip you might like to adopt is to put all your OPEN statements (and INQUIRE statements) in one subroutine. Then if you do need to change compilers most of your work will involve the changing of just one routine. To take this one step further you will find it useful to put all non-standard subroutines in one or two marked files or libraries, so at least the problem of re-identifying non-standard code is removed.

Another tip contained in the following fragment of code may prevent you from overwriting a valuable file:

```
CHARACTER*10 FILNAM, STAT
CHARACTER*1  ANS
```

```
      ...
      STAT = 'NEW'
30    OPEN (INUNIT, FILE=FILNAM, STATUS=STAT, ERR=100)
      ...
100   WRITE(*,*) 'File:',FILNAM,
     1            '    already exists - overwrite (Y/N) ?'
      READ (*,'(A1)') ANS
      IF (ANS .EQ. 'Y' .OR. ANS .EQ. 'y') THEN
                      STAT = 'UNKNOWN'
                      GO TO 30
                      ENDIF
      STOP
      ...
```

Other areas of non-portability are usually quickly identified: the use of tempting extra facilities beyond the standard provided by the generous compiler writer, used so automatically that it is a shock to find that the new compiler doesn't support them; or code written in assembler which will not work with the new compiler because the new compiler uses different calling conventions, or which needs to be rewritten in the assembler code native to the new computer.

8.8 THE ACCURACY OF PORTED CODE

Code which works to a particular accuracy on one machine or under one compiler will not necessarily work to the same accuracy under a different compiler or on a different computer.

The accuracy of your calculations will be dependent on the number of decimal places to which your real (and double precision) numbers are stored. A real number is stored as a mantissa and a characteristic (exponent). A real number on most machines is stored using 32 bits with so many bits for the mantissa and so many bits for the characteristic. The number of bits used for the mantissa and characteristic can vary from machine to machine. The number of bits used for the mantissa and the number of bits that remain for the characteristic determine to what precision each real number is stored and the largest positive and negative number that can be addressed as a real number. The proposed IEEE (the Institute of Electrical and Electronics Engineers Inc.) standard for floating point numbers defines a 32-bit real number as follows: 1 bit for the sign, 15 bits for the exponent and 23 bits for the mantissa. (There are actually 24 bits for the mantissa, the first bit is always assumed to be 1 and is never stored.) This gives a precision of 7 decimal digits. The largest real number is approximately 3.40E38 and the smallest positive real number is approximately 1.175E-38. The largest negative number is -3.4E38.

The IEEE standard is used in the Microsoft FORTRAN compiler on the IBM PC for REAL and DOUBLE PRECISION numbers. If you were moving to the CRAY-2 computer you would find that the real numbers occupy 64 bits. A real number on the CRAY-2 has pretty much the range and precision of a double precision number on the IBM PC although one or two precision bits are traded for an extended range. (One way to slow down the superfast CRAY-2 computer is to demand double precision for your real variables!). On the VAX, double precision numbers have the same range as single precision numbers but the precision to which each number is stored is 16 decimal places. On the other hand if you had an 80*87 mathematics coprocessor fitted to your microcomputer you would find that real numbers stored on the coprocessor occupy 80 bits - giving you both a large range and an amazing degree of precision. For a more lengthy discussion please consult Chapter 6.

You may find that if your program contains floating point arithmetic, you get different answers when you change from machine to machine, and you need to go from real to double precision numbers on some machines in order to obtain a reasonable accuracy for your calculations. If you put your program on a CRAY-2 you will almost certainly want to reduce double precision variables to real variables to obtain optimum speed without loss of accuracy. If you need to alter the precision of your real variables you will have to change any intrinsic functions you have used which are not generic. A good tip is to always use generic intrinsic functions if possible.

8.9 CHANGING FORTRAN STANDARDS

FORTRAN has evolved through several stages to become the language it is today. There must be very few programs written in the early days of FORTRAN that are still in use, but there are thousands written for compilers which attempted to meet the FORTRAN 66 standard. Of the features in that standard which caused most troubles, one could probably name two: firstly the inconsistent handling of Hollerith data, and secondly, the poor or non-existent control over files from within an application. Both of these were addressed in FORTRAN 77, but sadly, without complete success.

In FORTRAN 66, the only way to handle textual data was to read in the stream of characters and pack them into numeric variables and arrays. The problem with this was that the packing factor varied between the data types, and also between machines which might use different arrangements of memory to contain those variables. Some compilers only permitted this packing in INTEGER variables, others allowed it anywhere. Where that was the case, the packing factor might be different between data types. For instance, a string of 20 characters might be read into four variables on one machine, with a packing factor of 5, and into five variables on another with a packing factor of 4. Hence one saw FORMATs in the form of 5A4 for basically one string of data. The safest way was always to pack Hollerith data with a packing factor of 1.

The replacement of Holleriths by CHARACTER data was greeted by cheers of delight in the FORTRAN camp, until it was seen quite what the compilerwriter had done with it! In many implementations of FORTRAN 77, they had outlawed Holleriths entirely. This meant often quite extensive recoding of long-established code. Happily, in later editions of most PC compilers, Holleriths and their packing into numeric variables have put in a new appearance. Hence old code will work. You are warned, however, to take it out at the first opportunity.

The widely implemented ENCODE and DECODE statements from FORTRAN 66 compilers have been replaced by 'internal files', or as one of the compiler manuals puts it: 'core to core I/O'. Digital Research FORTRAN 77 has ENCODE and DECODE for backward compatibility, and even permits an optional syntax much more like FORTRAN 77. Avoid these constructs in new code if you do not want problems in the future. As an exercise, try writing subroutines called ENCODE and DECODE with a similar syntax to the ENCODE/DECODE statements, so that you can make the transition more smoothly if you have to.

The need to put CHARACTER data in its own COMMON blocks is also something else which can cause difficulty, especially where old code is being massaged into shape. This requirement is often relaxed as an extension to the strict standard.

Another feature which causes more difficulty in contemplation than it does in reality is FORTRAN 77's introduction of the 'zero trip DO loop'. In FORTRAN 66, a loop was executed at least once: this could be envisaged as a result of making the 'test' at the end of the loop. The later standard acts as though the test were made at the start. Hence, in

```
      L = 10
      J = 20
      DO 10 I=J,L
      ...
10    CONTINUE
```

the loop would not be executed at all in FORTRAN 77 whereas in FORTRAN 66 it would have been executed once. Genuinely portable code will always make a test and jump over the loop explicitly if it is not required.

Sometimes the loop index retains its final value on exit from the loop. This is by no means always the case. Indeed, many compilers generate code that makes the loop index finish up after exiting the loop in the normal way containing the value -1. There is nothing in FORTRAN to say what it does: the standards state that it is 'undefined'. Portable code always assumes that the loop index does not contain sensible values *unless* the program flow includes a jump from inside the loop. In that case one can rely on the loop index variable retaining its proper value.

Much of the benefit of CHARACTER data was missing from the Microsoft FORTRAN package until version 4, which implemented the LEN and INDEX functions, concatenation (whoever set up concatenation using // when Basic's syntax of using the + operator is more rational and simpler?) and CHARACTER* (*). Without these, one can only use CHARACTER variables as glorified Holleriths (which is what they were!), and the introduction of substrings (present from v. 3.30) gave little improvement.

There are a number of other differences between the two standards which are listed in Appendix 2. Each of these can cause problems, although the most important difficulties do appear to lie with CHARACTER data and the file handling. The table which forms Appendix

2 is reprinted with only a few amendments from Appendix E of the Digital Research FORTRAN 77 compiler manual, and is as elegant and succinct an appraisal as one could wish to find.

As a matter of record, the table lists differences between the two standards. Compilers which offer extensions, or suffer restrictions, may differ in even more particulars.

8.10 FORTRAN 8x

The sad tale of the latest attempts to bring FORTRAN in line with modern computer science is recounted by Metcalf and Reid in their book *FORTRAN 8x Explained* (see the bibliography at the end of Chapter 1). The good news is that the whole of the FORTRAN 77 standard is incorporated in the FORTRAN 8x standard (88 would have fallen nicely in the series after 66 and 77). The decision to include it all guarantees (!) that existing FORTRAN 77 programs will compile under the new standard.

Changes from FORTRAN 77 to the proposed new standard fall into a number of areas. Firstly, there are new features. Foremost among the new features are an enhanced set of standard procedures, some functions, but many subroutines. Most FORTRAN programmers will welcome such additions, except where the names clash with subprogram names in their FORTRAN code. Other new features include additional data types and control constructs.

More contentious is the suggestion that certain FORTRAN language constructs be labelled 'deprecated', or headed for removal in the next language revision cycle, and 'obsolete', probably becoming 'deprecated' the next time around, and removed the time after. Some of those constructs or features declared 'deprecated' for FORTRAN 8x have only just been introduced into the language for FORTRAN 77, and it is odd that they should so rapidly be declared redundant. One or two of the 'new' features, such as NAMELIST, were widely implemented in FORTRAN 66 type compilers, and had been dropped for FORTRAN 77.

We sense, in the disagreement amongst the ANSI X3J3 committee members, struggles between certain vested interests.

Our position on the new standard is that we welcome efforts to increase functionality, but not if they impair portability. We suggest reading Metcalf and Reid's book. Some of it you will not recognize as FORTRAN. It is as though one day you opened a newspaper and found that the English was no longer comprehensible. It might lead to progress in the long term, but is guaranteed to cause chaos at first.

CHAPTER 9

INVOKING FORTRAN PROGRAMS AND OTHER DOS INTERFACES

FORTRAN programs are usually invoked from DOS by giving their names on the command line, or summoning them from some 'user interface' like GEM or Windows by highlighting their name and giving a mouse button click, or pressing the return key. Sometimes the input to a program is contained in a data file, and it is galling to have to wait for the program to load, and then prompt on the screen for the data filename. Wouldn't it always be better to be able to give this data filename on the command line, and let the program pick it up? In this chapter, we consider how this might be done.

In Chapter 10, among other things, we consider how a 'user friendly interface' program can invoke other programs, but in the more general context of chaining to other programs, and so we can leave that subject for the time being.

9.1 USING DOS AND BATCH FILES

Metcalf, in his *FORTRAN Optimization* (see the bibliography of Chapter 1), makes the suggestion that the OPEN statement should be eschewed in favour of using 'Job Control Language' to connect files to logical units for later use in a FORTRAN program. The reasons he gives for this include the variations in the implementation of parameters in OPEN statements. In the context of DOS, one might follow the spirit of this suggestion in one of several ways.

The first of these ways is to explicitly name the files in the FORTRAN OPEN statements in your program, and make sure that wherever you have created and stored your data files, copies of them, with the appropriate name, exist where the FORTRAN program expects to find them.

For example, you create your data files in a subdirectory named \DATAEDIT, and have your executable FORTRAN program 'STATS.EXE' in a subdirectory \RUNTIME. The data file in \DATAEDIT is named according to some formal naming system 'DERBYWIN.088'. In your FORTRAN program, this data file of statistics might be named something else completely, via an OPEN statement of the kind:

```
OPEN (10, FILE='GENINPUT.DAT', STATUS='OLD')
```

The following batch file will ensure that the appropriate files are on line and ready, and then tidied up on completion, as follows:

```
COPY \DATAEDIT\%1 \RUNTIME\GENINPUT.DAT
CD \RUNTIME
STATS
DEL \RUNTIME\GENINPUT.DAT
CD \DATAEDIT
```

Suppose the batch file was called RUNSTATS.BAT. Then to invoke the file we would issue the following command at the DOS prompt:

```
RUNSTATS DERBYWIN.088
```

The batch file would first copy DERBYWIN.088 to the file GENINPUT.DAT in the \RUNTIME directory. Then the \RUNTIME directory would be made the current working directory and the program STATS.EXE would be executed. After execution of STATS had been completed the input file GENINPUT.DAT would be deleted and the file \DATAEDIT would be made the current working directory. Of course, RENaming is a possibility, instead of copying. The problem with that is that you might be faced with renaming back manually if the program crashes, and in any case, for valuable data, you would be advised to always work on a copy anyway.

The possibilities are endless. The big advantage of all this is that the data file name is given on the command line, the computing overhead is low, and thereafter little or no user intervention is required.

9.2 USING I/O REDIRECTION

A similar effect can be achieved by the use of what is termed 'I/O redirection'. In short, at least three 'files' are 'preconnected'. These are known in the literature as 'standard input', 'standard output', and 'standard error'. Basically, they all relate to the CONSOLE device. In other words, input is expected from the keyboard, output of normal program results to the screen, and, similarly, error messages also go to the screen. It is possible to reassign the standard input and standard output devices, and this is a useful facility. For example, if a program STATS.EXE sends voluminous output to the screen, one can redirect this off to oblivion (to the NUL device) by using the '>' redirection operator:

```
STATS > NUL
```

and off goes all the output. This is useful too in batch files where some commands would echo their 'results' to the screen. Redirection is useful too, in the case of programs which normally send their results to the screen, and which can be directed to send them to a file by this simple command. During development, for instance, output can be directed towards the screen by default. For production runs, output can be directed to the printer or to a file. Note that redirection to a printer is sometimes superfluous, since pressing CTRL-P causes what comes up on the screen to be directed to the printer until CTRL-N is pressed.

Redirecting output also means redirecting any ESCape sequences there may be in the output. Beware. They can make files uneditable and unprintable.

In the same way as one can redirect output, it is also possible to change the input stream from the keyboard. For example, a program which expected keyboard input (say by expecting input as responses to a 'READ (*, . . .' statement), could be made to accept input from a file, by use of

```
STATS  < TEST.DAT
```

Such a terminal interactive program would still print its prompts to the screen if written with 'WRITE (*, . . .' instructions. They can be removed too by a simultaneous output redirection:

```
STATS  < TEST.DAT > NUL
```

This is particularly useful at the development stage of a program, where the general interactive facility is still required, but in the edit–compile–test cycle, the need to retype that same data each time begins to pall. It is sometimes useful to have the output on the screen to remind you of where the program has got to (or had got to before it crashed). The file 'TEST.DAT' must contain the exact keypresses that you would have used if replying explicitly to the prompts.

Some observations on the limitations of this procedure need to be made. First of all, take the case where input is redirected, but output isn't. Even supposing WRITE statements have been used to generate the prompts, you may have used the non-standard feature in FORMATs where they terminate in a special character (sometimes $, but more often \) which inhibits line advance, so that when the computer echoes input characters on to the screen, they follow on the same line as the prompt. The actual instruction to go to the next line is contained in the user response, i.e. when the user hits the RETURN key. Hence, all the screen layout disappears if the data comes from a file, and the prompts follow on from each other in a mess.

In that quest for speed of response, you may have chosen to write direct to the screen by using one of several techniques. Firstly, you might have used a DOS service, rather than a FORTRAN formatted WRITE. That is certain to be redirectable, and is in accordance with the advice given in Chapter 12 on screen handling. Alternatively, you might use a BIOS service. That might or might not be redirectable, but do not rely on it. We do not recommend using direct calls to the BIOS. For a start, your programs will not be universally portable, even if they work on most DOS machines (the strictly IBM compatible ones, if you have used the IBM BIOS). Using a BIOS software interrupt, if you must know, is very similar to using a DOS software interrupt. Use the data section in Ray Duncan's *Advanced MS DOS*, or one of Peter Norton's books on the subject (Chapter 2 has a bibliography) for details. Finally, you might have written direct to the screen RAM. That is certain not to be redirectable, *not* to be portable, even between some types of video adaptor, and *not* to co-exist with memory resident utilities like SideKick. Some of these techniques are dealt with in Chapter 12, and the rest are referred to here for completeness.

The 'standard error' device is not normally redirectable under DOS 2 and 3. However, when running something like 'CodeView', Microsoft's new standard debugging environment, it would be unfortunate to have error messages breaking though a carefully designed screen layout. Accordingly, Microsoft have included a standard error redirection utility with their FORTRAN v. 4.0 or later.

9.3 OTHER USES OF REDIRECTION

File operations, including directory searches, can be made from within a FORTRAN program, but they all assume the use of fairly extensive, assembly language coded routines. We show how to do this later in this chapter. The simplest way for the FORTRAN programmer to do a directory search is to redirect the output of DOS 'DIR' to a file. Then that file, which contains plain text, can be OPENed, and searched in the ordinary way using standard FORTRAN facilities. For example, if a batch file is used to invoke a particular program, the line

```
DIR > DIRECTRY.LST
```

may be included. In the FORTRAN code, this may be accessed by

```
OPEN (8, FILE='DIRECTRY.LST', STATUS='OLD')
```

and so on. Careful examination of the format of the directory entries in this file will show exactly where filenames, dates, sizes, and times lie, so that the directory can be sorted or otherwise handled in what appears to be a sophisticated way, but is nothing of the sort.

Indeed, since it is possible to invoke COMMAND.COM from within a FORTRAN program (again, using the facility to create a child process, which will be described further in Chapter 10), a directory can be obtained in this convenient form at any time.

It is sometimes possible to do this without assembly coded routines at all. Both Microsoft and RM FORTRANs now invoke the command processor COMMAND.COM after a FORTRAN PAUSE statement. The PAUSE operates in the time honoured fashion if one just presses the RETURN key. Then program execution restarts. On the other hand, if a valid DOS command is given, COMMAND.COM is brought into action. Implementations vary: COMMAND.COM may be invoked for a single command, or it may be loaded as a separate 'child' process, so that it takes over until the 'EXIT' command is given. This obviously demands that a second copy of COMMAND.COM is loaded, and in turn, that requires some free memory.

The program author can then instruct his program to write on the screen

```
WRITE (*,*) 'Type the following: DIR > DIRLIST.DOC'
PAUSE
```

which prompts the user what to do. The technique is available for changing directory, or whatever.

Beware: using redirection sometimes doesn't work, particularly when using Microsoft FORTRAN. The reason for this is the way in which child programs inherit their parent's environment. If redirection has not been used in the parent program, it is not available for a child. The information given in the supplementary README file in the Microsoft FORTRAN manuals applies to child FORTRAN programs, and not necessarily to others, so it is always worth a try before abandoning the idea.

Sometimes it is possible to put the desired command string into the keyboard buffer. This is obviously possible using DOS software interrupts, although on some machines there is an all-FORTRAN (if not entirely portable) way. This involves the use of ESCape codes. For instance, on the Apricot microcomputer, the ESCape sequence is ESC \ n, where "n" is the character to put into the keyboard buffer. Hence, sending ESC \ D ESC \ I ESC \ R ESC \ CHAR(13) to the SCREEN has the bizarre effect of putting 'DIR RETURN' in the keyboard buffer. This could be a part of a formatted or unformatted WRITE to the console, or, alternatively, use a DOS interrupt as recommended in Chapter 12.

One caveat in using the above technique is that for maximum control the keyboard buffer needs to be emptied first, or you never know quite what mayhem can break loose, including formatting the hard disk.

9.4 USING THE 'ENVIRONMENT'

DOS 2 and 3 have inherited something termed the 'environment' from their Unix parent. It is possible to put plain text into the environment, where it can be interrogated later. For example, the command line goes into the environment space for a particular program. Similarly, filename 'aliases' can be set here. In principle, one should be able to use the SET command to create these aliases, so that one could initially have

```
SET INPUT=DERBYWIN.DAT
SET OUTPUT=BESTBETS.LST
```

and use the aliases INPUT and OUTPUT in the OPEN statements in your program. Unfortunately, this demands that the compiler understand what the environment is all about, and so too must the implementation of DOS.

9.5 GETTING FILENAMES FROM THE COMMAND LINE

You might expect Microsoft to know DOS best, although sometimes one has doubts. They do know some of the inner workings, and make use of them in their FORTRAN compiler. One of these inner workings is to do with command line arguments.

If a filename specified in an OPEN statement is blank, for example: FILE = ' ', then Microsoft FORTRAN programs will attempt to read a valid filename from the command line. So, suppose your program STATS.EXE was invoked with

```
STATS
```

then a filename won't be found, and as a result, will produce the message

```
File name missing or blank
Please enter name
UNIT **?,F255
```

in which ** represents the unit number from the OPEN statement. Of course, if you had invoked the program as

```
STATS DERBYWIN.DAT
```

the file DERBYWIN.DAT will be opened as the appropriate file. Successive OPEN statements with blank filenames will look for successive command line arguments.

Furthermore, if no OPEN statement is encountered before the first READ or WRITE operation on a unit, then it is treated as above, as if the program contained an OPEN statement but the filename was left blank, and the command line is first searched for a filename before issuing the prompt.

If the environment and file handles in DOS 2 and up reflect the Unix side of DOS' parentage, the above facility reflects the CP/M ancestry. Under CP/M, the first two entries in the command line were always parsed into filenames ready for use as input and output files.

PROSPERO FORTRAN

Prospero FORTRAN has an elegant subroutine GETCOM which finds the command tail and returns it as a CHARACTER string. The syntax of this is:

```
CHARACTER*80 LINE
. . .
CALL GETCOM (LINE)
```

The CHARACTER variable LINE is filled with the whole of the command tail from the first non-blank character after the program name. Naturally, if this is less than the 80 characters

---

we have assigned above, `LINE` is space-padded at its end. If the command tail is longer, then the remaining characters are left out: `LINE` contains the first 80 only. Successive calls to `GETCOM` may return longer or shorter substrings.

Provided that one only requires a single filename, the syntax of the Microsoft and Prospero compilers is little different.

Microsoft:

```
OPEN (10, FILE=' ', .....
```

Prospero:

```
CHARACTER*30 LINE
...
CALL GETCOM (LINE)
OPEN (10, FILE=LINE, ...
```

The benefit of the Prospero system over the Microsoft FORTRAN strategy is that it is possible to parse the command line for option switches as well as filenames, and also, if the parsing is sufficiently intelligent, to permit switches and filenames to occur in any order. What is more, the Microsoft error message breaks into whatever designed screen layout you have, and it would be better to trap the failure to put a filename on the command tail as part of an overall program strategy, not just as an accident. It would be useful, therefore, to have a facility equivalent to Prospero's `GETCOM`.

9.6 ASSEMBLY LANGUAGE PROGRAM TO CATCH THE COMMAND TAIL

Now wouldn't it be nice to have a `GETCOM` subroutine in Microsoft FORTRAN? This is how it ought to be done.

When an `EXE` program is loaded, the `ES` register points to the start of the program environment. Microsoft FORTRAN saves this, in a globally accessible variable named `CESXQQ`. In general, however, this address is not available, and one of the first things you must do, after entry to the program, is to find and save this segment address.

Under DOS 3, there is a special DOS function call (062hex) to find the start of the environment at any stage in program execution. To use this, first check if DOS 3 or higher is in use before making the call, otherwise grab the `ES` register as above, and hope you haven't changed its contents first. Next of all, go to offset 80h, and look for the command tail.

The command tail is in fact held in a particularly useful format. It is preceded by a 'length' byte. This is one of the three simplest means of implementing a character string (one is just a set of bytes, one is preceded by a length byte or bytes, and the other is terminated by a special character, say ASCII 00h, or sometimes '$'). By examining this byte, it is possible to return the number of character bytes in the command tail as well as its contents.

Here is the assembler routine; it expects two arguments from the calling routine: N which will contain the number of bytes in the command tail, and TAIL a character string which will contain the command tail.

```
        NAME    GETPSP
;
CGROUP  GROUP   CODE
;
CODE    SEGMENT PUBLIC 'CODE'
        ASSUME  CS:CGROUP
;
PUBLIC  GETPSP
GETPSP  PROC    FAR
;
        CMDTAIL EQU 080H  ;define position of command tail
        PUSH    BP        ;save BP on stack
        MOV     BP,SP     ;put SP in BP
        PUSH    DS        ;save DS and ES which we will use
        PUSH    ES
        MOV     AH,62H    ;function 62 hex gets PSP
        INT     21H       ;interrupt 21 hex
;
        MOV     DS,BX     ;put returned address (BX) in ds
        MOV     SI,OFFSET CMDTAIL        ;offset of command
                                         ;tail
;
; now read address of command tail length variable N off
; stack
;
        LES     DI,DWORD PTR [BP+10]    ;load ES:DI with N
        MOVSB                           ;move a byte from DS:SI into N
;
; now read character string (TAIL) address off stack
;
        LES     DI,DWORD PTR [BP+6]      ;load ES:DI with TAIL
        MOV     CL,07FH   ;use CX for count
        XOR     CH,CH     ;put CH to 0
        CLD               ;clear direction flag
        REP     MOVSB     ;move a byte from DS:SI to TAIL
                          ;until CX zero
        POP     ES        ;pop the registers off stack
```

```
        POP     DS
        POP     BP
        RET     8               ;return to FORTRAN 2 arguments in
                                ;call
;
GETPSP  ENDP
CODE    ENDS
;
        END
```

The following FORTRAN program can be used to call GETPSP:

```
        PROGRAM CMTAIL
C
C program to test GETPSP.ASM
C which returns command tail
C
        CHARACTER*127 TAIL
C
C N is length of command tail
C
        CALL GETPSP(N,TAIL)
C
C write length and command tail to screen,
C
        PRINT *, N,TAIL(1:N)
C
        STOP
        END
```

Try running this program with the command:

```
CMTAIL I can now pass data into my program using the command tail
```

The string following the program name can be up to 127 characters long: don't worry about word wrap after 80 characters on the line—just keep typing.

9.7 DOS FILE OPERATIONS FROM FORTRAN

The DOS in MS DOS and PC DOS means 'disk operating system'. Many of the facilities of this system are apparently not available to the FORTRAN user, at least, not immediately. We saw in the above how it is possible to use some of the facilities in DOS to create directory listings and so on, for use within a FORTRAN program, using the facilities of COM-MAND.COM, but this is not what is done, for example, when you use file operations in a word processing or spreadsheet program. Take humble WordStar for instance. That can copy, delete, and rename files. How does it do it? The answer for the FORTRAN programmer must be to use an assembly language coded subroutine which does the appropriate operation.

The DOS file operation functions are extremely powerful. In the disk set which can be purchased to complement this book, we have prepared a library of file handling functions. For brevity, only one is presented in full here. It is a subroutine to delete a file entry from a named (sub)directory. Study it carefully, and you will see that all that is done is to set up the appropriate parameters, and then transfer control to DOS via software interrupt 21H. This is sometimes known as the DOS interrupt.

The names of the other file handling routines are given in Chapter 15, and, for precise details, either consult the comments in the assembler source code in the disk set that can be purchased to complement this book, or read Ray Duncan's *Advanced MS DOS*, referenced in the bibliography at the end of Chapter 2.

```
            NAME      DLDIRE
;
DGROUP    GROUP DATA
CGROUP    GROUP CODE
;
DATA      SEGMENT PUBLIC 'DATA'    ;space is reserved for the
                                   ;path
PATHNM    DB        65 DUP(?)      ;which will be sent from the
DATA      ENDS                     ;calling FORTRAN routine
;
;
CODE      SEGMENT PUBLIC 'CODE'
;
          ASSUME    CS:CGROUP,DS:DGROUP
;
PUBLIC    DLDIRE
DLDIRE    PROC FAR
;
          PUSH      BP             ;save the base pointer on the
                                   ;stack,


          MOV       BP,SP          ;because we will use BP to get
                                   ;params
          LES       BX,DWORD PTR[BP+10]  ;address of path length
                                   ;-> ES:BX
          MOV       CX,ES:[BX]     ;and its value into CX
          LES       BX,DWORD PTR[BP+14]  ;address of pathname ->
                                   ;ES:BX
```

```
        XOR     SI,SI                      ;offset from start of
                                           ;pathname=0
LP1:
        MOV     AL,BYTE PTR ES:[BX]+[SI]   ;move pathname byte
                                           ;by byte into local
        MOV     BYTE PTR DGROUP:PATHNM[SI],AL ;data
        INC     SI                         ;segment, increasing the
        LOOP    LP1                        ;count, until CX = 0
        XOR     AL,AL                      ;getting a zero to put
        MOV     BYTE PTR DGROUP:PATHNM[SI],AL    ;at end of
                                           ;pathname
;
        MOV     DX,OFFSET DGROUP:PATHNM ;address of pathname
                                           ;->DS:DX
        MOV     AH,41H                     ;function 41H
        INT     21H                        ;software interrupt
        JC      ERROR
;                                          no errors...
        XOR     AX,AX                      ;zero -> AX
        LES     BX,DWORD PTR[BP+6]         ;address of IERR
        MOV     ES:[BX],AX                 ;IERR = 0
        JMP     END
;
ERROR:                                     ;errors...
        LES     BX,DWORD PTR[BP+6]         ;address of IERR
        MOV     ES:[BX],AX                 ;error code -> IERR
;
END:
        POP     BP                         ;restore BP
        RET     12                         ;clear stack of
                                           ;4*no of args
;
DLDIRE  ENDP
CODE    ENDS
;
        END
```

This routine deletes a directory entry. That is it deletes a file in any subdirectory, from the current directory. The pathname of the file from the current directory needs to be specified in the call.

Before we give a brief description of the assembler routine, we will look at how the routine is called from a FORTRAN program.

DLDIRE is called as if it were a FORTRAN subroutine with three arguments. The first argument is a character string with the pathname of the file, the second argument is the length of the character string, and the third and last argument is the error code returned by the assembler routine.

Thus, for example, if the file FRED.DOC existed in a directory called \UTIL\TEST, it could be deleted with the following call to DLDIRE:

```
CALL DLDIRE('\UTIL\TEST\FRED.DOC',19,IERR)
```

The function used is available under DOS version 2.11 or later.

9.8 A BRIEF DESCRIPTION OF THE SUBROUTINE DLDIRE.ASM

The GROUP directives for the data and code segments are required so that the FORTRAN can communicate with the assembler routine. The assembler routine has been written so that it can be called from a Microsoft FORTRAN program. To work with a different compiler these GROUP directives may need to be changed.

In the data segment the variable 'PATHNM' has been declared to be 65 bytes long, and will hold the pathname of the file to be deleted.

'PROC FAR' indicates that DLDIRE is a subroutine (or procedure) and that the calling routine will probably not reside in the same segment as DLDIRE and so will need a FAR call.

With Microsoft FORTRAN the arguments in a subroutine call are passed by placing the segment and offset of the memory where they are stored on the stack. For a subroutine call, the memory address for the last argument in the call will start 6 bytes beyond the stack base pointer (BP+6). Since the segment and offset take 2 bytes each, the memory address for the next argument will start at BP+10, the next at BP+14 and so on. The second argument is the number of bytes in the pathname character string. This is placed in CX which is the count register. The first argument, the pathname, is then read into 'PATHNM' in the data register, byte by byte, a loop CX times.

To delete the file with the given pathname the interrupt 21 is performed with 41H (41 hex, 65 decimal) in the AH register.

If there is an error, then the error code is returned in the register AX and the carry flag is set. The mnemonic JC jumps to the given label (in this case ERROR) if the carry flag is set. At the label ERROR the error code in AX is put in the memory at the location of the last argument in the call (IERR) and control is returned to the calling routine. If there is no error, IERR is returned as 0. The names of the data and code segments, and how arguments are passed to subroutines are compiler dependent.

This routine could easily form the template for a number of allied routines for renaming files, copying them, and so on. Such a suite of subroutines would be potentially very useful. So much so, in fact, that they will be found in their entirety on the disk set which accompanies the book.

The reason that this particular routine is especially useful is that in Microsoft FORTRAN v. 4.0, the artifice of OPENing a number of unwanted files and connecting them to NUL simply doesn't work, at least, not in the same way as it did in earlier versions of MS FORTRAN. We can OPEN another file to say NUL1, and when we are finished with it, explicitly CLOSE it, using DISPOSE='DELETE'. Experience shows that this leaves a zero length file called NUL1 in the directory. We can then delete this by invoking the file deletion subroutine above. The bug was fixed in v. 4.01.

CHAPTER 10

USING MEMORY EFFECTIVELY

10.1 INTRODUCTION

The FORTRAN programmer faces two major problems when developing his programs on DOS computers. Both problems are related to the amount of random access memory (RAM), which is limited to 640 kbytes on IBM-compatible DOS computers, very much smaller than the core memory found on most mini and mainframe computers.

The first problem is 'is there going to be enough memory on the target system?'. Of course, you will always know how much there is if you are developing software for your own computer, but if you want your code to run on other computers, you will sooner or later hit this problem. There are two considerations here. The first concerns the amount of code–'Will the executable code fit into the available RAM?' The second concerns the amount of storage required–'Will all my arrays fit into RAM, and how will the amount of RAM affect the size of problem I can analyse?' The size of executable code depends to a great extent on the facilities and attributes of the compiler (and linker), and the size of code included from FORTRAN libraries.

If you do not have enough space for all your arrays then either you resign yourself to solving smaller problems, or you design your code, if possible, to write intermediate results off to a file which will be stored on disk and use the released space to calculate new results (an 'out of core' solution). If you use an 'out of core' solution, be patient—the time taken to access data stored in a file on disk will be appreciably longer than the time taken to access data already in RAM.

The second major problem is 'how can I write a program which works on a 256 kbyte machine (say) but also can take advantage of the extra memory on a 640 kbyte machine?'. This is very much a FORTRAN problem, the old chestnut of having to define the size of arrays explicitly in the source code. For the software developer it would be much more convenient for the program to discover how much memory there is available and then to allocate it accordingly. The only alternatives for the software developer are to either insist that his customers have a certain amount of RAM, thereby losing potential customers who do not have sufficient and who are not prepared to upgrade; or to maintain several different versions of the program, which is confusing, expensive, and to be avoided if possible. It is not surprising that the

FORTRAN language has been abandoned by some software developers in favour of the 'C' language which gives the programmer more control over memory.

On mini and mainframe computers, programs which are designed to solve very large problems (as well as small problems) usually use dynamic dimensioning. All the variable length arrays are stored in one (or two) vector(s), and a driver subroutine is supplied in source code in which the size of the vector(s) is declared. The user can edit the size of vector(s), recompile, and relink, and run the code for any problem that will fit within his memory constraints. This approach will not be successful in general on DOS computers because even if your user has a FORTRAN compiler, he will probably not have the same one as you used to compile the rest of the program. Different compilers are not compatible; supplying the compiler with your program would be prohibitively expensive. The use of dynamic dimensioning, however, is well worth persevering with.

A neat solution to this problem is presented later in the chapter where an assembly routine is used to find the amount of available memory, and to set the dimension of a vector dynamically to that required by the problem, if there is enough space. This works on any DOS computer.

We start the chapter by looking at some general points concerning compilers, and follow with a discussion of the way in which compilers allocate memory to code and data. We then show how memory can be dynamically allocated to a FORTRAN program at run time. The problem of 'shoehorning' a potentially large executable code into limited memory using the techniques of 'overlaying' and 'spawning' is discussed. Finally we consider the impact of the latest Intel processors on the problems faced by DOS programmers.

10.2 THE COMPILER

When discussing the problems of small memory one should remember that early PCs had very small quantities of RAM (as little as 64 kbytes), and even quite recently, the standard was as little as 128 kbytes (typical of PCs sold with DOS version 1), rising slowly through 256 kbytes (most DOS 2 machines) to the now ubiquitous 512 or 640 kbytes.

Early FORTRAN compilers for PCs used the very minimum of memory, and generated frugal code. This was partly because the compiler author knew that RAM was in short supply and expensive, and partly because the first compilers offered fewer facilities. As compilers developed a bigger range of facilities in line with the full FORTRAN standard, and as they moved from restrictive memory models towards a situation where the FORTRAN programmer could code more or less what he liked within reason, RAM prices moved downwards, and suddenly compiler writers came to expect plenty of free RAM. Since all computing expands to fill the memory, and twice the time, allotted to it, not long elapsed before the problem of too little RAM appeared again: this time not due to cost, but to physical limitations—the placement of the video RAM at the 640 kbytes position in PC DOS which is also a limitation on IBM compatible machines running MS DOS. (You may be one of the fortunate few whose computer does not hit this barrier—at least, not for a few hundred kbytes more!)

During compilation and linking, most FORTRAN compilers can use as much memory as they are given. Once over a certain minimum threshold, below which they will not work at all, they can use the extra RAM to hold tables of intermediate results. If there is no free memory, they have to resort to disk storage of the intermediate results, or just crash, elegantly (with a message) or not (without a message!). The first and best answer to all of this is for the program developer to equip his machine with the maximum possible amount of RAM. This is cheap today, and will be even cheaper tomorrow, but it is still a good buy.

Compiling is speeded, and its memory demands reduced, by compiling small source modules. It is further reduced if in these modules, the individual FORTRAN statements are short, easy to parse, and do not need forward references to resolve. An example of this comes about in explicit type definitions. Suppose an INTEGER array is to be defined with a name which is implicitly REAL, take 'A' for instance – not good practice, and certain to confuse an experienced programmer at some stage, but a good example. The processes of compiling will be delayed, and unnecessary table space will be occupied, if instead of:

```
        SUBROUTINE DEMO
C--------------------------
C
C       The routine exists to set the context for some
C       type and dimension declarations.
C
C--------------------------------------------------------
        INTEGER   A
        DIMENSION A (50, 60)
        .
        .
        .
```

we were to write:

```
        DIMENSION A (50, 60)
        INTEGER   A
```

or even worse:

```
        COMMON / NEXT / A
        DIMENSION A (50, 60)
        INTEGER   A
```

Similarly, long and complicated arithmetic and logical expressions are difficult to decipher, and should be replaced with shorter forms wherever possible.

Optimizing compilers are supposed to make short work of code such as

```
X = (A-B)*(C+D)
Y = (A-B)*(C+D)*2.0
Z = (A-B)*(C+D)/2.0
```

because they can identify that the (A-B) and (C+D) elements need only be evaluated once. However, the above is more lengthy to type than

```
X = (A-B)*(C+D)
Y = 2.0*X
Z = 0.5*X
```

and certainly takes longer to parse. Indeed, if you should replace (C+D) by (D+C) or worse, (A-B) by -(B-A), then it is doubtful whether the optimizer will make any improvement and may well leave less efficient code than the manual optimization of reducing the number of operations. On some mainframes, the optimizer may well assign registers for the storage of these common subexpressions, rather than storing the result in RAM, and repeatedly fetching it. Even though there is a small register stack on a numeric coprocessor, it is quite likely that even the better PC compilers will fail to make use of it effectively. In a situation such as this, hand optimization of coding is still useful, and should be used.

10.3 THE SEGMENTED MEMORY MODEL AT THE HEART OF THE INTEL CHIPS IN DOS COMPUTERS

To understand some of the problems experienced in programming FORTRAN and using the memory effectively, it is essential to understand how the Intel processors manipulate the available memory. This should come as a reminder if you have already read Chapter 2.

Part of the initial success of the 8086/8088 series of processors was due to the ease with which 8-bit software, designed to run under CP/M on its 8-bit microprocessor predecessors the Intel 8080 and the work-alike, but generally improved Zilog Z80, could be ported on to the new processors. These micros grabbed two bytes for each address, and interpreted the 65 536 different bit patterns as an address space of 64 kbytes (remember, 1 kbyte is 1024 bytes). That gave 64 kbytes for operating system, program code, *and* data. Program and data compression techniques were obviously *de rigeur* on those machines.

The designers of the 16-bit microprocessors were faced with a quandary. Should they start with a clean sheet of paper, or try to provide a compromise, one which offered an easy upgrade path from the earlier systems? They chose the upgrade path, and this was at the same time a strength and a weakness. A strength, because it enabled a flood of software to appear early on, and a weakness, because it put an obstacle in the way of using the capacities of the then new microprocessors to the full.

In the same way as the 8-bit micros had grabbed 2 bytes to form an address, the 16-bit microprocessors grabbed two *words*, each of 2 bytes. If these 4 bytes had been combined into a 32-bit integer, it would have given an address space of 4000 million bytes: that is what some families of 16-bit and all families of 32-bit microprocessors do. The Intel designers chose a technique of 'bank switching'. One pair of bytes was used to give a 16-bit address relative to the start of a bank of memory, or 'segment'—these are known as the 'offset'. The other pair, the 'segment' address, were used to flag the start of that segment in the overall memory space. This restricts the size of each segment to the 64 kbytes of the 8-bit micro. At the time, memory was expensive, and no doubt the Intel designers of the time felt justified in their choice: segments could start at any multiple of 16 bytes in RAM.

With this mode a total address space of a megabyte, or 1024 kbytes, was possible. Effectively, it means that a 20-bit addressing mode has been chosen. In naming the basic storage units, a **word** was 2 bytes, and the 16-byte multiple was a **paragraph**. All segments are therefore 'paragraph aligned' in that they start on a paragraph boundary.

In the design of the chip, four registers were provided within which segment addresses could be stored. Effectively, this means that the chip can address four separate segments of memory using the data stored in its registers without swapping any segment address, and since many code and data structures would almost certainly be shorter than 64 kbytes long, whole sequences of operations could be undertaken without changing the contents of those segment registers. In view of this, the diseconomies of the method of building the addresses could be ignored. Indeed, early DOS micros were lucky if they had enough data for four complete segments, and the possibility of superimposing the four separate 'frames' almost anywhere on to the available address space was of considerable appeal.

The constraints that this memory model has on the FORTRAN programmer are considerable. For the newcomer, they are more apparent than real, but as one tries to extract the maximum from a given system, the restrictions imposed may be important.

In addition, the designers of the IBM PC chose to place the video screen RAM at what must have seemed to be an impossibly high position at 640 kbytes. This effectively sterilized 384 kbytes of the available address space, and has given rise to a whole new industry in overcoming it. A few maverick computer designers ignored the IBM PC standard, and located their memory maps elsewhere. These machines, notably the Victor/Sirius 9000 and the Apricot family of machines, enjoyed a measure of success in the early years, prior to the widespread adoption of 'IBM compatibility', particularly in the UK, where IBM were slow in introducing their PC. Both of the present authors regularly use such machines, and lament their passing as a serious contender for the *ipso facto* standard.

10.4 MEMORY MODELS IN PC PROGRAMMING

At the simplest level, a program could start, run, and terminate, having left the segment registers unaltered. Such a program would be small, and involve less than 64 kbytes each of code, data, and stack (a segment reserved for the storage of intermediate results passed from one subprogram to another). Indeed, because there are four segment registers on the chip, it is easily possible to arrange two segments of data. At the minimum level, all of the registers could refer to the same physical segment.

Such a memory model is known as 'small'. It is obviously efficient, in that addresses are always only 2 bytes long (i.e. only the 'offset' relative to the start of the segment needs to be obtained), whether one is fetching instructions or data. Execution might also be expected to be fairly quick.

A more complex model might be to have a number of modules of code, and a number of blocks of data, each organized so that no module or block exceeded a full segment in length. Jumping from one module of code to another (e.g. by a subroutine call) could require a change to the value held in the code segment (CS) register, and accessing data in a different data block, a change to the data segment (DS) register, but such changes would be relatively infrequent. This is the 'medium' model.

Finally, there is the 'large' model. In this, code and data structures can transcend the boundaries of segments. Segment register contents can be expected to change frequently, and 4-byte addresses are needed for all code and data. Four-byte addresses are needed in the medium model too, but by carefully structuring the compiler, it is possible to keep the register changes to a minimum. Large model code must be expected to be longer and more turgid than for the other two models because of the superfluity of addressing information.

Hybrid schemes, in which the code is small, and the data large, can be conceived and implemented with a greater or lesser degree of success. The nomenclature is confused, and one can never be sure precisely how a particular FORTRAN compiler places code and data in memory without a careful reading of the documentation and detailed study of the map produced by the linker.

A single stack segment is usually allocated to a FORTRAN program. This may impose some constraints on the programmer, principally by restricting the number of subroutine calls and their parameters—the stack is the mechanism of passing the addresses of the parameters, the return address, and for saving intermediate results where necessary. These intermediate results include a subset of the contents of the processor's registers so that on returning from a subroutine or function the original program context may be restored. When returning from a subroutine the contents of the processor registers stored on the stack and the return address are read from the stack as well as the memory location of the variables passed through the argument list. Storage on the stack taken by that subroutine is then released and can be used on a subsequent call to a subroutine or for any future intermediate results. A limit on parameter passing is contrary to modern ideas of structured programming, which prefer parameter passing to the use of COMMON; it does, however, tend to make execution somewhat faster if the latter is used.

A stack segment of 64 kbytes will be able to store 16 384 four-byte memory addresses (remember arguments in subroutine calls are passed by memory address in FORTRAN not by value), so whether the limitation of a single stack segment is restricting in reality is debatable. The programmer who meets this restriction may find it more rewarding to contemplate redesigning his program rather than looking at ways of increasing stack storage. Indeed in the Microsoft FORTRAN compiler the stack segment is controlled internally by the compiler and a space for storing variables passed through the argument lists is allocated in the default data segment. A length of only 2 kbytes is reserved for this 'stack' by default by the Microsoft compiler.

10.5 IMPLEMENTATION OF MEMORY MODELS IN PC FORTRANS

The memory model of version 3.xx Microsoft FORTRAN is typical of the broad spectrum of FORTRAN compilers for DOS. The variants of this compiler are roughly variants of the large model, and are implemented as follows:

Code Each subprogram can be up to 64 kbytes long. It therefore seems evident that the CS register is set on entry to a particular subroutine, and (except for further subprogram calls) the CS register remains set for the duration of execution of that subprogram. Subprograms must therefore, by definition, be paragraph aligned if they are FORTRAN subroutines or assembler routines called from FORTRAN. (assembly language subroutines, called only from another assembler routine, do not have this restriction.)

Data All variables and arrays which have local scope, that is, are declared and used within a single subprogram, are allocated space in the default data segment. Data variables and arrays may also be declared in COMMON blocks, each of which may occupy up to a complete segment in length. One might view this simplistically as supposing that the segment information resided in the common block name, and the offset information in the variable list of the COMMON block! Blank COMMON was allocated within the default data segment in Microsoft FORTRAN version 3.x, although in later versions it can be placed in its own segment or segments. Furthermore, since the subroutine parameter passing convention involved 4-byte addresses, data arrays could be passed as parameters even if the data resided in named COMMON blocks. Hence, a shortfall in space in the default data segment could easily be accommodated by putting data into named COMMON blocks even if it was to be manipulated as subprogram parameters later.

Stack This by default was part of the default data segment, but could under user control be allocated up to a complete segment of memory.

Later versions of Microsoft FORTRAN permit not only the use of LARGE model arrays, but also a degree of control over the allocation of data items and even entire COMMON blocks, but at the cost of the introduction of non-standard FORTRAN code. This involves tagging individual arrays with [HUGE], thus denoting that trans-segmental addressing is needed, or COMMON blocks with [NEAR], denoting that they are to be packed into the default data segment. The compiler does, however, yield the correct [HUGE] or trans-segmental addressing mode if the size of the array is self-evident at compile time. Global declarations of [HUGE] ness may be made via metacommands embedded in the source code, or even specific arrays may be thus named if the placing of the [HUGE] attribute in the source code offends.

To be specific, the $LARGE metacommand is used. This takes the form

```
$LARGE
```

if it is merely required to make *all* arrays in that source code module addressable across segment boundaries, or

```
$LARGE: BIGONE
```

if, for example, the array 'BIGONE' was to be the sole recipient of [HUGE] ness. (Some arrays are just [HUGE], others have [HUGE] ness thrust upon them ...)

It has always been the case that the allocation of memory to FORTRAN programs has been static, that is, it should be obvious to the compiler what are the sizes of all data structures. One area in which confusion arises is in the use of 'assumed size' and 'adjustable' arrays. Suppose within a subroutine an array is passed as a parameter. FORTRAN passes the address of the start of the array, and array bounds checking is usually an extra overhead option, so is not normally enabled. So the length of the array should be of little consequence. FORTRAN permits the length to be passed as a parameter, or even to be ignored, as in the following:

```
SUBROUTINE ASU (ARR)            SUBROUTINE ADJ (ARR, N)
DIMENSION ARR (*)               DIMENSION ARR (N)
```

Both subroutines may be called giving *different* arrays as parameters. In neither case is it obvious what is the maximum size for the array. We must either assume that all such arrays must be less than a segment in length, or give them all the flexibility to be longer. This latter choice is at the expense of longer, slower, code. Those FORTRANs which do permit the use of trans-segmental addressing usually have an option to specify the treatment of adjustable and assumed size arrays.

How this evolves into more usable facilities as later versions of a compiler are released can be seen in the development of Microsoft's FORTRAN. Prior to v. 3.20, arrays could not be bigger than a segment, and v. 3.20 introduced the facility for the first time. In v. 3.30 the [HUGE] attribute could be put in the source code as well as the $LARGE metacommand: in v. 4.00, as in Ryan MacFarland FORTRAN, a compiler command line argument may be used.

Version 4.00 of Microsoft FORTRAN, newly released at the time of writing (but superseded twice before we reached the end of the book...), extends the facilities both to smaller and larger models. The successful use of such a range of choice is dependent on not only a depth of understanding and a range of experience, but also on a degree of luck. This also permits the compiler to deal with all assumed size arrays as [HUGE], or not, depending on a compiler option.

10.6 USING SPACE EFFECTIVELY

Data structures in FORTRAN are fixed length, and therefore inflexible. In times past, programmers guessed the maximum size for arrays, with a little fine tuning to accommodate memory limitations in whatever computer they were using. Inevitably, users wanted bigger and bigger arrays. During the 1970s a technique known as 'virtual memory' was developed, and widely implemented. What this does is to treat the overall data area as a series of 'pages'. Data not available in RAM can be loaded from disk, swapping a page in memory for one on disk. A problem known as 'thrashing' occurs when, for every data item, a disk swap is needed. This can be caused by a trivial fault in programming style, such as accessing elements of an array in a non-optimal order!

There is a temptation on a virtual memory system to dimension everything to 100 000 or more, with a consequent degradation of system response not only for the program in question, but also for every other user as the system thrashes pages on and off backing store. This is not an available option for the PC programmer. For a start, virtual memory management isn't a function of DOS, nor is there unlimited RAM which is easy to access. At the very best, a program that just squeezes into the PC DOS limit of 640 kbytes can be written, and the programmer has to pray that the next release of DOS is smaller. If past record is a guide to the future, it won't be. Often, a large data structure is declared, just so that a program can handle the infrequent large problem. Most of the time it deals with smaller commonplace problems and the overall utilization of the data structure is poor. If only the data structures were dynamic, only one version of the program would be needed; and only when a particularly large problem demanded it would it be necessary to obtain time on a fully RAM equipped machine.

So a problem exists. We may wish the same program to run on many different machines, each of which might have a different total memory size, or have a different mix of operating system and memory resident utilities installed. Thus the amount of free memory is variable, even between apparently similar machines of equivalent specification.

The elements of a memory management system which can be accessed from FORTRAN are presented in the following sections. Remember that DOS knows how much memory is free, even when a FORTRAN program is loaded and running. It does this by keeping a set of constants relating to the overall system down at the low end of RAM.

The Intel processors expect that in the first 1K of RAM there will be a table of 256 addresses, each of the 4-byte segment:offset form. The processors recognize 256 different interrupts, and when one of these is detected, the table is examined for the four byte address of a service routine. Some of the 256 different interrupts are reserved for use by DOS, and yet others are completely unused: the FORTRAN programmer who does not dabble in assembler will not be able to use them for his own purposes, but they are nevertheless available. Immediately above this 1K block is an area in which DOS keeps system constants All DOS variants make use of this facility to a greater or lesser extent.

It is quite easy to look into this area to find the size of installed RAM, if you know where to look, but it really isn't worth the effort, since different machines use a different address for the same data, or even hold the amount of memory in a different way: number of bytes on one, paragraphs on another, or even number of 64K segments on a third. This machine specific operation prevents software portability.

DOS version 3 has a function which may be used to enquire the amount of system RAM. In due course, the majority of applications will use this function, but while DOS 2 is so commonplace, another technique must be used.

The method that we are going to outline works with all versions of DOS greater than 2, with UNIX/Xenix, with VAX VMS—indeed, with many operating systems: the details, and the coding, vary of course. On PCs, it works with any FORTRAN: it works best with those that permit greater-than-a-segment data structures, but for the old fashioned, or impecunious, it will work with early versions of a number of FORTRAN compilers. Some coding nuances do have to be applied to cope with this range of compilers, and we leave the implementation details of this to the reader.

The method is to ask DOS direct how much space is free. Not how much there is in total, but how much is free. Remember that this will be *after* the FORTRAN program has loaded, so that free space is entirely (with a few caveats) at the disposal of the programmer. The operations cannot be done direct from the FORTRAN, as the necessary facilities are not an explicit part of the language, and so we will need assembler. (Some variants of FORTRAN can be interfaced to C or Pascal, which have facilities for doing the following. However, this is a real minefield, and needs to be approached with caution.) As in many other examples in the book, Microsoft FORTRAN is the vehicle for exploring the ideas.

DOS has a function to do what is required. The function has a UNIX name: 'malloc'. You ask DOS for so many paragraphs (units of 16 bytes), and it allocates them, or returns an error message *and* a note of how many paragraphs are free. If you know how many are wanted, it is possible to make a simple request. Doing it the following way also yields important information on the total memory resource. If you have skipped the sections on assembly language programming in the foregoing chapters, a discussion will be found in Chapters 2 and 3. For other brands of FORTRAN, you may find that the particular protocols are slightly different.

Before looking at the strategy in detail, consider the particulars of calling subroutines and passing parameters.

10.7 PARAMETER PASSING AND SUBROUTINE CALLING IN MICROSOFT FORTRAN

When a subroutine or function is called by Microsoft FORTRAN, 4-byte segmented addresses of all the parameters are pushed on the stack, followed by a 4-byte, segmented, return address.

There is no traceback data (as there is in Ryan MacFarland FORTRAN), and indeed no check by the recipient that the correct number, let alone type, of parameters are passed. FORTRAN always sends the addresses of parameters via the stack, but on return those addresses are popped off the stack into oblivion. This makes it difficult to pass addresses *back* from a subprogram, but they can be passed *forward* once they are known.

That makes it difficult to carve data structures out of memory as and when you need them, unlike in those languages like C and PASCAL with 'pointer' data types, and a generally richer syntax for data allocation. What would be useful is to merrily go along until an array of, say, 10 000 four-byte elements was needed. Then, the operating system could be asked to reserve this RAM, handing back a pointer to its start, so that it could be accessed. DOS has the technology to do it, FORTRAN has not; extensive assembler, or interfaced PASCAL or C, sections would be required.

To use the facilities within DOS for carving out data areas, it is possible to pass their addresses onwards to subroutines which are called later, even if they cannot be passed back. Hence, a program structure such as is shown in Figure 10.1 will fail, whereas one structured like Figure 10.2 will work.

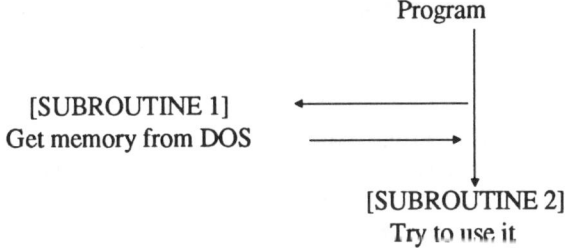

Figure 10.1. Unacceptable structure for dynamically allocating RAM to a FORTRAN program

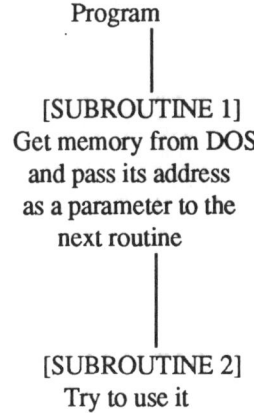

Figure 10.2. Ideal structure for dynamically allocating RAM to a FORTRAN program

It is worth noting that an assembler coded subroutine can quite easily call FORTRAN—as easily as the reverse. Some types of function return their values in registers, but we are not concerned with passing values *back*, so will ignore this for the time being.

10.8 THE CODE FRAGMENTS

We have written some code fragments. The first is in FORTRAN, and then some in assembler, and then some more in FORTRAN. Examine the first FORTRAN code. This comprises the root program called 'CALLER'.

```
        PROGRAM CALLER
C-------------------------
C
C
        This program allocates and uses memory dynamically.
C
C
C  --------------------------------------------------------------
        INTEGER*4 NBUF
        CALL MEMMAN (NBUF)
        WRITE(*,*) 'CALLED FROM "CALLER", NBUF=',NBUF
        STOP
        END
```

A 4-byte integer is declared, and passed to an assembly language subroutine 'MEMMAN'—the memory manager. MEMMAN need not have parameters sent to it: if it does, then it has a way of passing information back to CALLER. MEMMAN is an interface between CALLER and the main part of the FORTRAN program. It is necessary to have CALLER so that FORTRAN creates the necessary program entry protocols—if you are capable of writing those, then you probably don't need to read the following!

Now examine MEMMAN. This is in Microsoft macro assembler. Another procedure MEMOD is also shown in the assembler code: we will come on to that presently.

```
        NAME MEMMAN - MEMORY MANAGER
;
        EXTRN   MASTER:FAR
CSMEM   SEGMENT PUBLIC PARA 'CODE'
        ASSUME  CS:CSMEM
;
PUBLIC  MEMMAN
PUBLIC  MEMMOD
;
MEMMAN  PROC    FAR
        PUSH    BP              ; saving BP so it can be reused
        MOV     BP,SP           ; to address the parameters
```

```
        MOV     AH,48H               ; Function code for DOS
                                     ; interrupt
        MOV     BX,0FFFFH            ; Gimme a megabyte!
        INT     21H                  ; Get hand slapped ...
;                                    ; BX now has all DOS's got
        MOV     AH,48H               ; OK, I'll have that ...
        INT     21H                  ;
        MOV     CX,BX                ; Save the reply
        LES     BX,DWORD PTR [BP+6]
;                                      Move it into NBUF
        MOV     ES:[BX],CX
;                                      Restore the stack
        MOV     SP,BP
        POP     BP
        PUSH    ES
        PUSH    BX                   ; NBUF on stack for call
;                                    ; to master
        PUSH    AX
        XOR     CX,CX                ; Best way of zeroing IBUF to
        PUSH    CX                   ; put on stack for call to...
;
        CALL    MASTER
        RET     04
MEMMAN  ENDP
;
MEMMOD  PROC    FAR
        PUSH    BP
        MOV     BP,SP
;
        LES     BX,DWORD PTR [BP+6]  ; Put NBUF into
        MOV     CX,ES:[BX]           ; CX for safety
        LES     BX,DWORD PTR [BP+10] ; Cheap way of
                                     ; loading
                                     ; ES with segment of
                                     ; IBUF
        MOV     BX,CX                ; Now required
                                     ; length in BX
        MOV     AH,4AH               ; DOS call
        INT     21H                  ;
        MOV     SP,BP                ; Restore the stack
        POP     BP
        RET     08
MEMMOD  ENDP
CSMEM   ENDS
        END
```

We define a code segment, named CSMEM, which will be aligned on a paragraph boundary when loaded into memory. It consists of two procedures, MEMMAN and MEMMOD, each of which is called with a far call, i.e. the procedure needs a 4-byte, segmented address.

The strategy is as follows. In MEMMAN, DOS is asked to allocate 0FFFFH paragraphs (a megabyte) of extra data space. Of course the request must fail, because there is DOS, the FORTRAN program, and all the video stuff taking up memory. DOS will return a fail code in the AX register, and the size of free memory in the BX register, again in paragraphs.

This time it is known what to ask for, and providing no other process has claimed it in the few microseconds taken, the request must be successful. DOS also returns the segment address of the memory area it has allocated, on a successful request in the AX register. Put this size into the lowermost 2 bytes of the size variable passed to MEMMAN, and start to build the stack to call a FORTRAN subprogram 'MASTER' with the good news! Now give MASTER a start address (add a zero offset to the segment, which makes it, too, paragraph aligned) and a length, also in paragraphs. MASTER will read this data from the stack into its argument list (see subroutine MASTER). Macro assembler and the linker look after the 4-byte return address.

However, before looking at MASTER, another factor needs to be addressed. It has claimed all of free memory. This means that no other memory allocation will work—including other processes, opening file control blocks, or anything else. (Some FORTRANs other than Microsoft FORTRAN dynamically allocate buffers for I/O.) It is essential to release unused memory as quickly as possible so that such operations do not fail. This is undertaken by the procedure MEMMOD. This assembler coded routine will be called as quickly as possible to free resources. In our example it is called from MASTER with the arguments NBUF and IBUF, where NBUF is the amount of memory required and IBUF is the array which starts at the beginning of the sector allocated. Thus the memory location of the start of the sector of memory allocated to IBUF will be passed in the argument list. Of course, if one knew in CALLER the memory required, one could perform this function immediately.

Now is the time to examine MASTER. This has the length parameter NBUF, and the 'array' starting in the reserved memory area, IBUF. IBUF has been declared to be [HUGE]—this is an undesirable step, since it uses non-standard FORTRAN—and with other compilers might be done with a compiler metacommand. An equivalent procedure in say Ryan MacFarland FORTRAN or Microsoft FORTRAN version 4 would be to use a compiler directive to the effect that assumed size arrays were bigger-than-a-segment. Now suppose that it was desired to use this additional memory for four arrays, K, M, R, and D, of different data types, and problem specific length.

This is all done in the FORTRAN code, which should be examined in conjunction with the following explanation. First of all, convert the lengths to paragraphs (units of 16 bytes). This is done in FORTRAN for maximum readability. If data variables are all short, part of a paragraph is wasted in each, but at least it is known that no data item can be allocated space so that it spans a segment boundary, as the arrays are all paragraph aligned.

When the desired lengths are obtained, they are summed, and compared to the amount available. If insufficient, the program terminates, and DOS takes care of releasing all the memory allocation. If there *is* sufficient memory, then it can be partitioned for the program's use, but it is timely to release whatever is not required. At that point, MEMMOD is called. MEMMOD performs the UNIX function named 'realloc'.

It was not necessary to claim all free memory in the second 'malloc' function in subroutine MEMMAN, if it was known at the outset precisely how much memory was required. It would be a straightforward test to see if available memory was large enough for the program. Then it would not be necessary to relinquish the unused portion.

Coding it as we have done has some benefits to offset what seems at first sight to be a slightly convoluted approach. Firstly, the assembler code is kept short and simple. Secondly, there is negligible delay in between the two 'malloc' calls, so we have confidence that the second request will be successful, even in a busy system. Finally, control is rapidly returned to FORTRAN code where deciding on a solution strategy can be rationally based on what resources there are. For instance, in solving systems of equations, one might opt for a disk based solution, or one which is entirely in RAM. Even if there is insufficient RAM for the latter, it might be possible to perform the disk based solution more efficiently if there is an appropriate size of RAM workspace.

Without a dynamic memory management scheme like this one, conservative assumptions about available memory have to be made, leading to inferior performance at all times.

```
        SUBROUTINE MASTER (NBUF, IBUF)
C --------------------------------
C
C       To be called from an assembler routine 'MEMMAN'.
C
C -------------------------------------------------------
        INTEGER*4  NBUF, IBUF(*)[HUGE]
        WRITE(*,*) 'Maximum NBUF=',NBUF
C
C       let's suppose we want array K as: Integer*4 length
C                                                   LK items
C                                M as: Integer*2 length LM
C                                R as: Real*4     length LR
C                                D as: Real*8     length LD
C
C       assumed LK, LM, LR, LD come from an input routine...
C
        CALL INPUT (LK, LM, LR, LD)
C
C       sort out lengths of arrays in para.
C
```

```
        LENK = (LK-1) / 4 + 1
        LENM = (LM-1) / 8 + 1
        LENR = (LR-1) / 4 + 1
        LEND = (LD-1) / 2 + 1
        JBUF = LENK + LENM + LENR + LEND
        IF (JBUF .GT. NBUF) THEN
                WRITE(*,*) ' Insufficient memory '
                STOP
        ELSE
                NBUF = JBUF
                CALL MEMMOD (NBUF, IBUF)
                WRITE(*,*) ' Shortened to NBUF=', NBUF
        ENDIF
C
C       sort out start positions in IBUF
C
        M1 = 1
        M2 = M1 + LENK*4
        M3 = M2 + LENM*4
        M4 = M3 + LENR*4
C
        CALL FOLLOW (IBUF(M1), IBUF(M2),
     1               IBUF(M3), IBUF(M4),
     2               LK,   LM,   LR,   LD)
C
        RETURN
        END

        SUBROUTINE INPUT (LK, LM, LR, LD)
C---------------------------
C
C       not for real ...
C
C -------------------------------------------------------------
        LK = 500
        LM = 1500
        LR = 1000
        LD = 12800
        RETURN
        END
```

Towards the end of MASTER, compute the offsets from the start of IBUF which will correspond to the four arrays. IBUF is a 4-byte integer array, so the start positions are obtained by incrementally adding four times the length in paragraphs of each array to get the offsets M1 ... M4. IBUF is known to be bigger than a segment, so the correct addressing will be generated, and the addresses of the four start points passed to the subroutine via the stack, from whence they are picked up as the addresses of four quite separate arrays... Length information is also passed, which is used in the array size declarations, although you may use 'assumed sizes' at this point.

This data is picked up in the next program down the chain:

```
      SUBROUTINE FOLLOW ( K, M, R, D, LK, LM, LR, LD )
C------------------------------
C
C
C      To be called from FORTRAN routine 'MASTER'
C
C ------------------------------------------------------------------
C
      INTEGER*4   K(LK)
      INTEGER*2   M(LM)
      REAL*4      R(LR)
      REAL*8      D(LD) [HUGE]
C
C      perhaps we know that only 'D' can possibly be
C      bigger than a segment ...
C
              .
              .
              .
      RETURN
      END
```

A subtlety in 'FOLLOW' arises because it may be the case that most of the 'arrays' used in the dynamically allocated memory might always be less than a segment. If this is the case, then use of code which allows addressing across segment boundaries is an added overhead which we can well do without. In the example, K, M, and R are less than a segment. If it is known at the outset that this must be the case, a shorter addressing mode can be forced. On the other hand, arrays that are always, or sometimes, bigger than a segment need to have the correct address mode. Again this has been done with a [HUGE] reference, an undesirable, non-standard feature. (The fact that rules demanding that such features be avoided make good sense can be seen when you move up from versions 3.3x to 4.x of Microsoft FORTRAN. Some of the [HUGE] declarations have to be moved from after the dimension information to before it.) However, substantial economies can be gained, both in storage as well as processing time, with such non-standard usage—if you use these declarations make sure they are well flagged by comments in the source code.

Previously, it was stated that the technique would work even if your compiler was limited to data structures of less than a segment in length. It only needs a simple variation of the code in MEMMAN as presented to allocate memory for each array as it is required, in up-to-a-segment blocks. However, it is recommended that memory allocations be made as soon as possible into the program, to prevent the case arising that much time is spent on an analysis which will eventually fail due to shortage of space.

It is also possible to call any routine from MEMMAN, not just simply the one called 'MASTER'. Microsoft FORTRAN contains a standard INTEGER*4 function named LOCFAR. Give this a subroutine name as a parameter, and the segmented 4-byte address of the entry point of the subroutine is returned. With this address on the stack, and therefore available to MEMMAN, it is possible to make the call refer to any routine.

Microsoft FORTRAN interfaces well with Microsoft C, and the 'malloc' function exists in the C library. Hence, the procedure above could be implemented equally well in C, and interfaced with Microsoft FORTRAN using the implementation details outlined in the documentation. Other FORTRANs, notably Prospero FORTRAN, even have the requisite functions in their run-time libraries.

10.9 OVERLAYS

In the foregoing, it has been assumed that program code fitted easily into the available RAM, and that there was generally enough data space too. What do we do if the data structures are fixed in size, but the code is very long and complicated? It may well be that not all of this code is executed every time the program is run: it exists as a series of 'options'. A method for dealing with this was developed early on in the history of computer programming. It is known as overlaying. In an overlayed program, sections of program code are usually kept on disk as subsidiary files, only to be brought down into RAM when required. An overlay management scheme is needed, to ensure that a section of code is not overwritten when it is needed.

If you use a program such as WordStar, or dBase, or many of the programs which were adapted from an 8-bit computer environment to run under DOS, you will see that the program itself consists of a series of files, often with an OVL or OVn extension (n is usually an integer digit, running from 1, and effectively numbering the files). These are overlays. Overlays are very necessary when only up to 64 kbytes of RAM exist!

There is nothing in *any* version of FORTRAN for DOS computers that prevents overlaying. Building the overlaying structure is a function of the linker which is used, not the compiler, although some compilers have overlay management functions built into their libraries. Those that do, assist the overlaying process. Let us examine a simple overlay structure by means of an example.

In this example, the MAIN routine can call three subroutines: LEFT, MIDDLE, and RIGHT. In turn, LEFT calls A, B, and C, MIDDLE calls P, Q, and R, and RIGHT calls X, Y, and Z. This might be represented as in Figure 10.3.

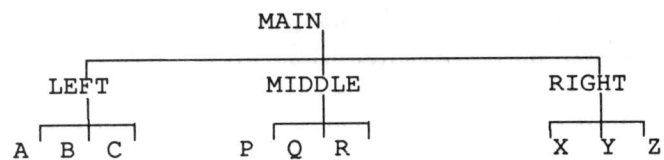

Figure 10.3 Tree structure of a program which is suitable for overlaying

This is a simple tree structure, and many programs are much less well organized than this. Nevertheless, to keep things simple in the first instance, consider this one. When MAIN is loaded into memory, it performs some processing, and then calls LEFT. It is evident that for LEFT to have somewhere to return to, MAIN must remain in memory. Similarly, when LEFT calls A, LEFT too must remain in memory. However, no room needs to be allocated for MIDDLE, P,Q,R, RIGHT, X,Y, or Z—or, for that matter, for B or C. When A finishes processing, the code space it occupies may be released, and reused for B. Similarly, B could relinquish its space for C.

On completion of C's operations, program control returns to LEFT, and ultimately back to MAIN. At this point, the code space used for LEFT is no longer needed, and can quite easily be used for MIDDLE, in due course, using the second area for P, Q, and R in turn, and then repeating the process with RIGHT, X, Y, and Z. Obviously, two 'overlay areas' are required, one for LEFT, MIDDLE, and RIGHT, and one for A,B,C,P,Q,R, X,Y, and Z. The size of the first area would be controlled by whichever was the largest out of LEFT, MIDDLE, and RIGHT; a similar argument would apply to the second area, which in turn would be controlled by the largest of the routines to fit in it.

This structure would be ideally suited to a program where LEFT, MIDDLE, and RIGHT all had approximately the same length, and each of the next level of subroutines also had similar sizes.

This is unlikely to be realized in practice. We may find, for example, that P was as big as A, B, and C together, and so instead of filling each of the overlay areas with just one subroutine, we might fill the second area with A, B and C on the first occasion A is required, then replace them with perhaps P (a particularly large subprogram) when the middle branch was being followed. That would cause only one reference to be made to the overlay file on disk instead of three separate ones for A, B, and C individually, and there would be a slight gain in overall efficiency.

We now have the concept of 'overlay units', each comprising one or more subprograms, which may be loaded into a given area. There are obvious merits to this, in that the total number of new disk operations is minimized.

Suppose that RIGHT was particularly small, and so were X, Y, and Z. They might all fit into the first overlay area. In this case, there is nothing to stop them being in the same unit. The only restrictions on what goes where are the following:

1   The return path must be held in memory.
2   A subprogram may call another further down the path, or in its own area *and* unit.

For obvious reasons, a subprogram cannot call another that needs to be loaded in such a way as to overwrite any part of the return path. In the event that two subprograms need to call the same general procedure or function, there are two choices: firstly, the procedure can be included twice, under different names, and secondly, it might be loaded along with MAIN in what is known as the 'root' area. We will therefore extend the two rules above to include:

3   Any subprogram may call one in the root area.

This is, of course, subject to the proviso that the routine in the root area does not itself violate the first two conditions.

The simplest overlay memory management scheme would partition the required amount of code RAM into fixed size overlay areas. A really smart scheme would make the partition between the areas dynamic, or even blur the distinctions between what constitutes an 'area' and a 'unit'.

Such a scheme is implemented in the Prospero FORTRAN overlay manager. The executable code is divided into modules, and those modules are handled as a 'last-in, first-out' or LIFO stack. This is best visualized by taking each subprogram to be a module. When control passes from one subroutine to another via a CALL, the calling routine stays in memory, but when control passes via a RETURN, the code space used by the called routine may be safely relinquished. Modules made up of a number of subroutines pose little extra implementation difficulty.

These patterns only apply to the code space. We also need to consider what should be done with the data. This includes data local to each subroutine, and that which is 'common'. The latter includes arrays and data passed between routines, as well as data in COMMON blocks.

Overlay structures can allow the local data areas to be overlayed too. (We use the term 'overlayed' in preference to 'overlaid' to denote this specific memory management strategy.) It should at least be an option. Of course, the most secure, if least economical, scheme is to make the storage of local data completely static, and not overlayed. This does mean that data values are preserved across invocations of a subroutine, a feature that should *not* be relied upon in really portable software.

FORTRAN 77 has a new feature in the SAVE statement that may be of relevance in the overall context of overlaying. It is not necessarily the case that COMMON block data allocation is static (i.e. data storage is allocated at the time the program is first loaded, and not altered until execution terminates). Indeed, the standard only demands that a memory allocation is made for a COMMON block across invocations of subprograms that reference it, unless it exists in the main program or is explicitly SAVEd. As far as the present generation of FORTRAN compilers is concerned, all this is academic, as COMMON block allocation is entirely static in all the PC compilers tested at the time of writing. However, that is no guarantee for the future...

10.10 DESIGN OF PROGRAMS TO MAKE THE BEST USE OF OVERLAYING

A program that is modular in design and construction is the best for overlaying. Space is used most economically if the main program module, and the associated routines that need to reside in the root area, are as small as possible. A good memory map is the second essential. This must specify the length of code (and of local data if it is possible to overlay that too) and a full list of called routines. It is possible to purchase program analysers which make maps of the structure of complex FORTRAN source code files just to ease this process. The use of these in just one or two cases can repay an initial modest outlay on their cost.

A program that has a large monolithic main section, or an involved interlinkage between the different subprograms, especially with prolific use of ENTRY statements, will cause trouble with overlaying.

Overlayed programs can also provide an easy means of issuing demonstration versions of software to prospective purchasers. One merely deletes essential overlays from the demo disk, and the program runs fine until that particular element is invoked. This will not work if you are using a linker which binds all of the overlays into a single EXE file.

For reasons which will appear evident in the next section, the source code needs to be divided into separately compiled modules which should not span the boundaries of a particular overlay unit. It is permissible for these separate source code files to contain less than the contents of a complete overlay unit, but not more.

10.11 OVERLAY LINKERS

Sometimes one has to wonder whether compiler writers and distributors begrudge having to provide linkers at all. (Some didn't, especially in the early days when Microsoft LINK was an integral part of DOS.) It may well be worth obtaining a specialist linker to complement a particular compiler. Take for instance the Microsoft LINK linker. In recent versions, this has supported overlaying; but only to the extent of permitting a single overlay area in addition to the root. While useful, it can scarcely be termed an effective overlay capacity.

A similar facility is provided by Ryan MacFarland in their latest release. This is a cut-down version of Phoenix's PLINK86. Again, it only supports one extra level of overlaying. This should not be mistaken for the full PLINK86 plus, a highly professional product, which among its other abilities can nest overlays deeply.

Only two of the commonly available PC FORTRANs provide an effective overlay capability with the linkers included as part of a FORTRAN system. These are Digital Research FORTRAN 77, and Prospero FORTRAN. A good overlay linker, such as the full version of PLINK86, is a worthwhile investment if the program requires an extended overlay structure, and the linker supplied with the compiler in use does not support overlaying well.

Most overlay linkers generate a series of files for the 'executable program'. These are likely to be the root module, with file name extension EXE, and a series of OVL files. The root module will normally be large in size, because it contains all the library routines required by the root and overlays, and the routines which are resident in the root anyway, as well as the linkages for loading overlays from disk when required. The names for these overlays are chosen at link time, either explicitly, or as a function of the name of the first module in the overlay unit. They are not normally renameable in the same way as are executable files.

The overlay versions of Microsoft LINK operate somewhat differently: all the overlays are held within a single EXE file. This makes such files very large and unwieldy, possibly too large to copy on to a single 360K floppy disk. On the other side of the coin, however, individual overlays will never become lost in copying, or inadvertently renamed. To distribute on 5.25 inch floppy disks executable programs which are more than 360 kbytes in length, you need to cut them up into sections.

You can do this dismembering by treating the program as a binary data file, reading it in in blocks, and writing them out to however many files are necessary. Microsoft FORTRAN supports the binary file type. Then they can be reconstituted on the target computer's hard disk by use of the DOS COPY command, not forgetting to let DOS know it has to join the files as binary files with the /B option:

```
COPY FILE1.exe+FILE2.exe /B FILE3.exe
```

Some archiving software can compress even programs that have been EXEPACKed, and it may be possible to distribute an archived version of the program. Archiving and file compression programs are available in the public domain, and as 'shareware'.

Both the Digital Research linker LINK86 and Microsoft's LINK use a similar syntax to denote the subdivision into overlay units. When linking the structure shown in Figure 10.3, the subdivision into units for Digital Research LINK86 would be:

```
MAIN + (LEFT + (A+B+C)) + (MIDDLE + (P+Q+R)) + (RIGHT + (X+Y+Z))
```

(Note that this is only a part of the command line. To discover details of the full syntax of linker invocation consult the documentation issued with the compiler or linker.)

The above assumes that *each* of the subroutines is in a separately compiled object module. If subroutines A, B, and C were in one object file, then the name of that would be given in place of (A+B+C). Indeed, since the linker is combining object files, and the instructions are given to it in terms of files, it is obviously not possible to put subroutines from one object file into different overlay units. Hence the source code must be allocated to the different FORTRAN files in a way that reflects the final overlayed structure. This is obviously desirable from a point of view of maintenance, but may not be the obvious subdivision after, say, porting a FORTRAN source as one large file from a mainframe.

In Microsoft Link, although up to about 64 overlay units may be specified, there can only be one overlay area in addition to the root. Thus, the parenthesized overlay units may not have a nested structure as in the Digital Research linker. PLINK86 can be given a 'script' in which the overlay structure is defined in detail.

10.12 A SORT OF OVERLAYING: SPAWNING A SUB-PROCESS

When COMMAND.COM is instructed to load and execute a FORTRAN program, with control returning to COMMAND.COM on completion, a DOS function known as 'EXEC' is involved, and the procedure is known as 'spawning'. The name EXEC, like so many other things in DOS, owes its origins to UNIX, although the concept is an essential part of all operating systems. COMMAND.COM is no different to any other program running under DOS. Any program can in fact 'spawn' another.

The EXEC function is not only used from COMMAND.COM to load and run the FORTRAN application—it may be used in reverse, to load a second copy of COMMAND.COM from the application program. Both Ryan MacFarland FORTRAN, and from v. 4.00, Microsoft FORTRAN, invoke the EXEC function after a PAUSE statement (Ryan MacFarland were the originators of this brilliant idea). Basically, on terminal access systems, a FORTRAN PAUSE can be used to stop results scrolling off the screen, and in a PC context, a PAUSE may be used to enable one to change paper or pens in a plotter or suchlike. It is possible to denote which of a series of PAUSEs has been invoked by giving an integer code, or optionally, a character string, after the PAUSE keyword. This is then displayed before the 'Press any key to continue' or whatever.

However, in the implementation of PAUSE, the compiler writers at Microsoft and Ryan MacFarland have made it operate by spawning a second copy of COMMAND.COM so making available all the directory functions, changing the default drive, all internal and external DOS commands, especially deletion and renaming of files, and the facility to run other programs. COMMAND.COM is enabled for one command only: a series of commands can be entered by using the one opportunity you have to give a DOS command, to invoke a further copy of COMMAND.COM, making it stay resident and available to process a series of DOS commands. Termination of that copy of COMMAND.COM is by use of the EXIT command. We have seen in Section 9.3 how useful this facility can be.

Explicit calls to the EXEC function may also be made, with the deliberate intention of transferring control to another program. This might be useful if you wanted to write a program as a 'front end' to invoke other programs you had written, perhaps based on selections from a menu. The following explains how.

Microsoft FORTRAN is one of a family of related languages. Each module, in whatever language, can call, or be called by, a module in any of the other languages. However, the FORTRAN source code must contain so-called INTERFACE units, which set up the relationships between the FORTRAN call and the data structures expected by the Microsoft C or Microsoft Pascal module. A further complication is that these languages expect values for data to be passed, while FORTRAN expects addresses of variables to be passed. There is therefore considerable work in coding such an interface. Since version 3.30 of Microsoft FORTRAN, the facility to interface with Microsoft C has been provided, and a subset of the C library to support the general 'spawning' process and the calling of DOS internal commands is included.

The interfacing with C has a couple of undesirable side-effects. Firstly, detailed treatment of this using the Microsoft FORTRAN protocols would be useless to users of other FORTRANs, and second, one is forced into the use of a bizarre variant of FORTRAN to do, what is after all, only a function that all operating systems must have. We shall, therefore, write our own interface, in assembler, to the EXEC function. Although this is in a form compatible with Microsoft FORTRAN, it could easily be converted to match some other compiler.

The assembler routine EXEC is called from FORTRAN as follows:

```
CALL EXEC ( PROG, TAIL, IRET )
```

where PROG is a CHARACTER variable containing the path and name of the program to be executed, terminated with an ASCII zero.

TAIL is another CHARACTER variable, but one which has an odd format. It has to start with a count byte (i.e. a byte containing the number of characters in TAIL). The next characters are the program command tail, comprising the options on what would normally go on the command line after the executable program name. The characters in the main body of TAIL start at the first non-blank character that you would give. The string is terminated with a CR (ASCII 13).

When working out what value to give to the count byte, do not include the count byte itself, or the terminating CR. Hence, in the typical DOS command

```
CHKDSK /V
```

PROG is a CHARACTER*6 variable with the contents 'CHKDSK', and TAIL is a CHARAC-TER*4 variable with the contents CHAR(2)//'/V'//CHAR(13). Thus TAIL is actually 2 bytes longer than is given in the count byte. Finally, IRET is an INTEGER*2 variable which will contain the return code from the execution of PROG. Many FORTRAN programs will not return such a code, and so IRET may not be needed, in the case that we are EXECing a FORTRAN program.

Alternatively, since the return code is left in register AX, EXEC could be converted into a FUNCTION. However, such a practice would be contrary to the rules of good FORTRAN programming which demand that all routines which do (or potentially do) I/O operations be made into subroutines.

We make some fairly sweeping assumptions to keep the code simple. Firstly, we will assume that the spawned program is content to use a copy of the environment block used by the calling program. Secondly, all file-to-unit connections will be done explicitly by OPEN statements in the called program. It is possible to specify on the command line (i.e. in TAIL above) two files, these would be specified as file control blocks, and could only be used by the spawned program if they existed or were created in that program's working directory.

The operations are to save BP and DS on the stack, put the address of the command into ES:BX and of the command tail into a parameter block structure. When this is done, the stack information is saved to a couple of local variables, and the DOS EXEC function is called (EXEC corrupts SS:SP). The first thing to do after calling EXEC is to restore the stack, so that the return information can be handled.

In the demonstration, the DOS external command (program) CHKDSK is used. All versions of DOS supply this program, which might be a COM or EXE program. It is used in the example because it always exists. Nothing is done with it, or with the information it returns, it is just used to demonstrate the EXEC function in a simple way. You could just as easily invoke FORMAT, and this could be useful if a program expected a floppy disk change, and you had none available which were preformatted. It would be useful to be able to pause the program to format one.

The example of using EXEC to FORMAT a disk is too dangerous to experiment with before seriously considering what side-effects there might be.

```
TITLE   EXEC - Spawn another program
;
CSEXEC  SEGMENT PUBLIC PARA 'CODE'
        ASSUME  CS:CSEXEC
;
PUBLIC  EXEC
;
STK SEG DW      0
STK PTR DW      0
;
EXEC    PROC    FAR
        PUSH    BP                              ;
```

```
        MOV      BP,SP                          ;
        PUSH     DS                             ;
        LES      BX,DWORD PTR [BP+14]           ; put command into
                                                ;     place
        LDS      DX,DWORD PTR [BP+10]           ; get command tail
                                                ; info
        MOV      TAI OFF, DX                    ; post it into the
        MOV      TAI SEG, DS                    ; locations in
        MOV      DX,      OFFSET PAR BLK        ; param block, then
        MOV      DS,      SEG     PAR BLK       ; get seg:off of
                                                ; this
        MOV      STK SEG, SS                    ; put SS, SP
        MOV      STK PTR, SP                    ; somewhere safe
;
        MOV      AH, 4BH                        ;
        MOV      AL, 00H                        ; DOS EXEC function
        INT      21H                            ;
;                                               Restore the stack
        MOV      SP, STK PTR
        MOV      SS, STK SEG
        MOV      BP, SP
        LES      BX,DWORD PTR [BP+6]            ; get address for
                                                ;   ret
        JC       NO ERR
        MOV      [ES:BX], AX                    ; code and put in
        JMP      NEX FLG
NO ERR: MOV      [ES:BX], 0
NEX FLG:POP      DS
        POP      BP
;
        RET      12
;
        PAR BLK EQU $
                DW   0      ; this would be seg of environment
        TAI OFF DW   ?
        TAI SEG DW   ?
                DD  -1      ; this would be seg:off of fcb1
                DD  -1   ;          ditto           fcb2
EXEC    ENDP
;
CSEXEC  ENDS
```

An example of the FORTRAN code to call up CHKDSK is as follows:

```fortran
      SUBROUTINE DSKCHK
C----------------------
C
C     note the cautious use of CHARACTER: no concatenation in
C     MS FORTRAN 3.3x, even worse in earlier versions!
C
C     ------------------------------------------------------------
      CHARACTER*7 PROG
      CHARACTER*4 TAIL
      INTEGER     IRET
C
      PROG(1:6) = 'CHKDSK'
      PROG(7:7) = CHAR(0)
C
C                CHKDSK assumed to be in default subdirectory
C
      TAIL(1:1) = CHAR(2)
      TAIL(2:3) = '/V'
      TAIL(4:4) = CHAR(13)
C
      CALL EXEC (PROG, TAIL, IRET)
C
      IF (IRET .EQ. 1) THEN
          WRITE(*,*) ' FUNCTION INVALID'
      ELSE IF (IRET .EQ. 2) THEN
          WRITE(*,*) ' FILE NOT FOUND OR INVALID PATH'
      ELSE IF (IRET .EQ. 5) THEN
          WRITE(*,*) ' ACCESS DENIED'
      ELSE IF (IRET .EQ. 8) THEN
          WRITE(*,*) ' INSUFFICIENT MEMORY'
      ELSE IF (IRET .EQ. 10) THEN
          WRITE(*,*) ' INVALID ENVIRONMENT'
      ELSE IF (IRET .EQ. 11) THEN
          WRITE(*,*) ' INVALID FORMAT'
      ENDIF
C
      RETURN
      END
```

This FORTRAN subroutine DSKCHK, and its use of the DOS facility CHKDSK, has been used as a demonstration, and since every DOS system has the program CHKDSK, you can run this example. It is not a good example, in that if CHKDSK finds errors, it will break through any carefully designed screen layout you have made, to ask for the 'F' response. You can use the EXEC function to run other FORTRAN programs, not just DOS programs.

10.13 ADVANTAGES AND DISADVANTAGES OF SPAWNING AGAINST OVERLAYING

A spawned child must carry all the overheads of fresh copies of all the system subroutines that come from the FORTRAN library. These include the I/O formatting routines, mathematical functions, error messages, and so on. This information needs only to be loaded once for an overlayed program, so overlaying must be preferred when RAM is in short supply.

Spawned programs can be developed, modified, and released completely independently of other parts of the system, in contrast to overlayed programs, where the correct protocols are established at link time, and it is inadvisable to issue overlays created at different times.

Overlaying is a natural response too, when the data structures for the different phases of the program are entirely common, and memory resident. Spawning the different phases of the analysis as different programs is preferable when the different modules use different data structures, and communicate via disk files.

By perverting DOS' intentions, a spawned program could re-use its own parents' code and data space. In this case, arrangements for return on termination are likely to be difficult to organize!

10.14 THE 80*86 PROCESSORS AND EXTENDED AND EXPANDED MEMORY

Machines which are fitted with 80286 or 80386 processors can either access the megabyte memory of the preceding 8086/808 or 80186/80188 processors in 16-bit segmented addressing, or they can address a much larger address space in 'protected mode'. New operating systems will enable programmers to make use of this enlarged or 'extended' memory space in due course, although this will be of little use to the very many owners and users of earlier machines.

If you have an 80286/80386 machine with plenty of extended memory, then you can run other operating systems than DOS to use all of it, or you can treat the surplus above a megabyte as 'RAM disk'. Again, this is of little use to the owner of one of the more primitive machines.

One solution to this allegedly lies in the use of 'expanded memory'. Expanded memory is memory addressed outside the 8086 1 megabyte limit and copied into or out of a single segment in the megabyte normal address space as and when required. This copying is done in small blocks. In order to do this transfer, 'intelligent' add-on boards with their own specific loadable device driver are required. You will often see this referred to as LIM EMS which stands for Lotus/Intel/Microsoft Expanded Memory Specification. Access to expanded memory is achieved through the driver by means of a software interrupt, and will need an assembler routine or routines. We have not attempted to include this software in the book for a number of reasons. First and foremost, expanded memory is a technological blind alley. Secondly, expanded memory is expensive for what it is. Thirdly, it is slow in comparison to main memory, and finally, the specification keeps changing.

We have high hopes of OS/2, Microsoft's successor to DOS, in overcoming restrictive barriers on available memory. Under OS/2, DOS applications can run happily in a 'compatibility box', but that is a complete emulation of DOS, with all its limitations as well as its benefits.

CHAPTER 11

COPING WITH A SLOW COMPUTER

11.1 INTRODUCTION

What do we mean by a slow computer? We don't mean that it is intrinsically slow—although that may be your problem—we mean that you are *finding* the computer slow. This may be when you run a particular application, or, you may find the code development cycle tediously slow, either way we hope that this chapter will give you real practical help in speeding things up.

Some of the advice in this chapter you may have seen elsewhere in books on code optimization, but most of the information comes from many years experience of FORTRAN code development on microcomputers by the authors.

We start with the hardware. If you are buying a microcomputer to run a large heavily mathematical program, such as a 3-dimensional finite element stress analysis program, then, if you or your dealer knows what they're doing (don't depend on it!), and you can afford it, you will probably buy a microcomputer with an 80386 processor running at 25 megahertz with a 100 megabyte hard-disk and an 80387 coprocessor. This would be the most powerful IBM compatible DOS microcomputer that you could buy at the time of writing. If this microcomputer is too slow then either you'll need to optimize your code or you should consider buying time on a fast mainframe computer.

If, like the rest of us, you find yourself with a twin floppy Amstrad PC, which you bought for word processing and subsequently discovered could be used to develop FORTRAN programs, then you might find that, for a modest hardware investment, both the code development cycle and the running of programs can be greatly enhanced. Of course you should also consider some code optimization strategies which we will suggest below.

On the microcomputers with the slower, less powerful, processors (the PC compatibles, as opposed to the AT compatibles), you will find, particularly for large programs, that the code development cycle edit–compile, edit–compile, ... edit–compile–run, edit–compile–run, etc. can become exceedingly tedious. The best solution to this of course is to write bug-free programs, and your attention is drawn to the chapter on readable and maintainable code. For those of us that are human, however, there are ways in which code development can be speeded up. The compiler environment is important in this respect. Certainly one of the major criticisms of FORTRAN compilers on microcomputers in the past is that they haven't had the debugging tools that one takes for granted, perhaps, on mainframe computers—at least, on modern ones!

This is changing rapidly. Microsoft, for one, have come up with their CodeView debugging system for Microsoft FORTRAN 4.0 and later, and so too have one or two of the other compiler writers. CodeView, which makes use of colour graphics if you have it, is invaluable when you need to track down an evasive run-time bug, and makes techniques such as filling your code with WRITE statements totally redundant.

Finally, in this chapter we look at efficient coding techniques. Some of these techniques can give spectacular improvements in the execution speed of your program, but often at the cost of making the code less readable and more difficult to maintain. Other techniques may only give modest improvements to the running speed of a program, but can always be adopted without impairing the readability of the code. You should try and incorporate these latter techniques in your programming style so that you naturally write efficient code. The other techniques should perhaps only be adopted when speed becomes a major criteria in the running of a program.

If running speed is still a problem after writing efficient but readable code, the best strategy is to time various sections of the program (there are a number of products commercially available which give a breakdown of the time spent in different routines of a program—or you could simply use the timing routine on the accompanying disk), discover the section of code which takes the most time (usually a big DO loop) and then fine tune this section of coding.

Of course you may find that none of the techniques suggested below give you an acceptable running time for your program. In this case you will need to check the algorithms that you are using to make sure that they are the best available. Finally, before throwing your microcomputer into the dustbin you should consider writing the computationally intensive parts of your program in assembly language. This is not as difficult as you may think, and may be very cost effective.

11.2 HARDWARE

In writing this chapter we have had in mind, as a minimum hardware configuration, a twin floppy disk drive IBM PC or compatible, with only perhaps 256 kbytes random access memory (RAM), and without a numeric coprocessor. Such a machine is usable for FORTRAN development, but only just. The reason for this is lack of disk capacity: twin 360 kbyte disk drives are simply not large enough to keep the requisite files and workspace on-line. (Single-sided 3.5 inch microfloppy disk drives suffer the same problem.) It is, however, a problem that can be solved in part by a move to a more appropriate (i.e. smaller) compiler, although that may generate slower code. The later 1.2 megabyte, 720 kbyte or 1.44 megabyte disk drives are much more suitable for use with the larger, 'professional' grade compiler software.

A quantum leap in productivity can be obtained by fitting a Winchester disk (hard disk), especially for use during program development, or when running any program which requires access to large files. Hard disks are relatively cheap—the performance differential between the twin floppy and 20 megabyte hard disk versions of a PC is well worth the extra investment. Whether you have a hard disk or not it is desirable to have as much RAM memory in the system as possible. Some of the compilation and linking processes can make use of extra RAM, and only if they run out of space resort to slow disk operations. Extra memory also makes the programmer's job easier, as he does not need to be so very careful about each memory location. Note, however, that the RAM in add-on boards might be slower than that which is fitted to the motherboard of the computer, leading to a surprising degradation in overall system performance.

If you have a large amount of RAM, particularly if you have extended memory installed starting at the 1 megabyte boundary or if you have an extended memory board that meets the Lotus/Intel/Microsoft Expanded Memory Specification, or if you have a non-IBM compatible computer which allows you to use the RAM between 640 kbytes and 1 megabyte, you should consider using a RAM disk and you may also want to consider disk cacheing.

DOS v.3.1 or later comes with an installable device driver called RAMDRIVE.SYS, on PC DOS it is called VDISK.SYS (a RAM disk is sometimes called a virtual disk), by including a simple command in your CONFIG.SYS file you can define one or more RAM disks. A RAM disk can be used just like any other disk drive with two differences. The first difference is that information on the RAM disk is accessed much faster than information on a floppy or hard disk. This is because the information is already in memory. The second difference is that when you switch your computer off all information stored on the RAM disk is lost. So remember to copy any important files back to your floppy or hard disk before switching off. There is actually a third difference over floppy and hard disks and that is that you can control the format of your RAM disk—how many bytes to a sector, etc.

RAM disks will speed up any I/O bound operation. For example, you can greatly speed up the development cycle by copying source file(s) to RAM disk, compiling them and putting the object file(s) on the RAM disk too, then linking the file(s) and putting the executable file on the RAM disk. Finally, you can run the executable file from the RAM disk. You will have to ensure that your RAM disk is big enough to store all these files, *and*, that, after defining the RAM disk, there is still enough memory left for the compiler and linker to load. You will probably need to experiment with different combinations of RAM disk and residual memory before you get the optimum benefit.

Disk cacheing is similar to using a RAM disk in that RAM memory is used to buffer input and output (I/O) to disk. In this case, however, a clever piece of memory resident software is used to create the RAM buffer and control the contents of the buffer so that the most frequently used files are always there. Disk cacheing software is readily available in the microcomputer market-place. Incidentally some of the fastest IBM compatible computers automatically use disk cacheing, which explains their remarkable speed.

Then there is the numeric data coprocessor chip. This has the largest effect on run times for programs which do a lot of numerical work. It is particularly effective where trigonometric and exponential ('transcendental') functions are involved, as these are hard coded into the structure of the chip. Very few software development applications make use of it, however, and a coprocessor chip will not make much, if any, difference to the program development cycle.

Finally, there is the move to a faster architecture overall. This might involve installation of a different processor chip, or an add-on 'turbo' board, or even the move to a faster machine— upgrading to an 'AT' or 80286 machine, or to one of the newer 80386 machines, for instance. Numeric coprocessors can be obtained for these machines, and indeed may be driven faster than the clock rate of the main chip to gain the final few microseconds in any numerical operation.

11.3 DEVELOPMENT

The work of the program developer is assisted by subdividing the program into small modules, and compiling these separately. We have already seen, in Chapter 10, that this enables large programs to be compiled where there might otherwise not be enough memory. Individually compiled program units, each of which consists of one, or possibly more than one, subroutine are then bound together with the system libraries by the linker. Linking is normally quite a rapid operation: each object module is generated in exactly the right form for the linker to read it, there is no ambiguity, and no alternate forms to be considered. In contrast, compilation stages take much longer because of the very nature of parsing and syntactical checking.

During program development, a change to one module requires only the recompilation of that module, not of the whole program. This greatly reduces the time for the edit–compile–link–run cycle.

When using an 8086/8088 based PC, the optimum size of a source code file is between 100 and 200 FORTRAN statements, not counting comments, which are processed very rapidly. The value of 200 is very much an upper limit if compilation times are to remain reasonable. The limit for an AT (80286 or better) style machine is between 500 and 700 FORTRAN statements, although the lower limits applicable to the slower machine lead to files that are easier to review and to edit. If these limits are adhered to, the compilation takes only a few seconds.

Compilation time depends on the amount of RAM in your machine. With 640 kbyte RAM you may find that you can exceed the limits given above and still compile in a reasonable time. However, we would nevertheless urge you to keep to small modules since the effort in editing a large source file may be considerable.

The naming convention for files which form a part of a larger whole is important. The name may reflect the program to which the module belongs, e.g. GRAPH12.FOR, or it may reflect the name of the subroutine(s) contained within the module. In either case, a block of comments somewhere in the file should give a 'directory' so that you can easily trace back to where the module was called from, or find subroutines named in that module. Ideally, these 'directories' need to be accessible elsewhere, either on-line, in the form of a file, or in your own documentation, or preferably both. A text editor which allows two files or more to be open simultaneously can open a window on to this general directory.

You may wish to consider, however, naming the object modules arising from the compilation of these source files with an abbreviated name. A short name, for example A.OBJ, given to each object module means that more modules can be cited on the command line for the Microsoft LINK. In order to avoid confusion, keep all related object modules in the same subdirectory, or on their own floppy. When using a twin floppy machine, use Microsoft LINK's /P option, so that the linker will pause before writing the EXE file. This gives the programmer the chance to change floppies so that the EXE file can be written to a completely empty one.

The worst that can occur is the following scenario. The linker and libraries are on drive A:, and the object modules are on drive B:. The default drive is specified as B:, so that the object modules can be cited without a drive letter, otherwise the command line overflows. Finally, memory is limited so that Microsoft LINK then wishes to create a temporary file on the default drive. That prevents the disk in drive B: from being switched, even though the /P parameter has been given. If you find yourself in this situation then beg, borrow, or steel yourself to buy, a hard disk machine!

Modules whose development is complete, and which have been properly tested and verified, can be held in libraries. This is better than keeping them as named object files because it cuts down the total number of names that you need to recognize.

Software to create and maintain libraries is either supplied with the compiler, or is available separately at little extra cost. A library is simply added to the list of libraries to be searched at link time, rather than quoting the names of the object modules explicitly. Note, however, that some linkers do not search libraries recursively. This means that if you have libraries A and B, and the FORTRAN system uses library F, it may be necessary to specify libraries in a special order. If A contains subroutines that call those in B, and both use the system functions in F (as will usually be the case), the libraries must be invoked in the order A + B + F, not in a random order. If B contains a subroutine which calls one in A, this may crash, and the list of libraries may need multiple invocations, e.g. A + B + A + F. This is not required with the more sophisticated linkers.

Some linkers permit the use of 'response files'. These contain, for instance, a list of the object modules to link in a given case. This saves retyping, and may allow a longer list than either the linker, or DOS, permit on the linker command line. Microsoft LINK for instance, allows a response file name to be given as in

```
A>LINK@OBJECTS,PROGRAM,CON,@LIBRARYS
```

where `OBJECTS.RSP` contains a list of the object files to link, and `LIBRARYS.RSP` contains a list of libraries to search. The file extension, if not `RSP`, needs to be given.

Alternatively, batch files may be used.

11.4 MAKE

There is a program developer's tool called 'MAKE' on UNIX systems that has been extensively copied in the DOS environment. Essentially, it checks the constituent source and object file creation dates and times. Those object files which do not exist, or pre-date the corresponding source code, are recreated by running the compiler before an automatic linking. Thus one never needs to specifically invoke particular operations on specific files to rebuild a program after editing.

Facilities of this sort are included with Microsoft FORTRAN (v. 4.0 or later), or are available from suppliers of utilities. They are at their best on hard disk machines, but in particular circumstances can fail disastrously. The most common cause of failure is for the DOS clock/calendar to be set incorrectly, so that the date and time stamp given to a source file is wrong.

11.5 CODING FOR COMPILATION SPEED

Just as in the previous chapter you are advised to use simple statements which are easy to parse, and which use up only a limited amount of the compiler's internal tables, also keep coding simple if you want rapid compilation. Short statements, using a minimum of variables and no implicit type conversions, will always compile more rapidly than complicated expressions. `DATA` statements in particular can be extremely complicated, and it will usually be the case that a number of `DATA` statements compile quicker than one long one with many continuation lines.

11.6 PROGRAM EXECUTION

Much has been written on the subject of FORTRAN optimization. In the latest, and most comprehensive, book on the subject, Metcalf (1985, see the bibliography in Chapter 1) delivers a homily on the social irresponsibility of a minority of programmers who steal the majority of computing resources in a large establishment. Those with university experience know only too well what this means. However, the humble PC programmer or user is in a different position. She or he has no responsibility to other users (unless they are queuing for the machine, or are one of the unlucky few who have networked PCs), but will be faced with the wait while a program loads, and the even longer wait while it executes unless certain steps are taken. This waiting is a sterile and boring occupation, and needs to be minimized.

The smaller the executable code is, the faster it loads. There are two elements to this: the physical size of the EXE file, and the amount of code space claimed in RAM. It is therefore desirable to use the 'packed file' utility (EXEPACK with Microsoft, COMPEXE with Ryan MacFarland FORTRAN) to shorten the size of executable files. These operate by replacing repeated bytes with a counter, but do it in such a way that the file can be unpacked when it is loaded. The principle is simple and obvious (we all say 'three apples' and not 'an apple, an apple, an apple'), and the utilities are small and quick. Both Microsoft and Digital Research offer the facility to output a packed file from the linkers they supply with their FORTRAN packages. We have found that early versions of EXEPACK usually beat COMPEXE by a few bytes, but EXEPACK was more likely to yield a corrupt file: this occurred both when using the utility in stand-alone mode, and when invoked in the linker. Whatever bug caused this was removed by the time version 4 of Microsoft FORTRAN was released.

It is often better to use the packing option in the linker direct because the link process (actually it is the generation of the EXE file) is much shortened. A FORTRAN programmer using a floppy disk machine may find the use of a packing option vital if an executable file for a large program is to be created. Personal experience suggests that the savings are in the data structures, and we have known EXE files shortened from about 620 kbytes to about 130 kbytes.

Similarly, the use of the smallest memory model will shorten the executable code, and provide further savings in time. An additional benefit is that disk storage is saved. This saving will be useful, but is nowhere near as great as can be achieved by packing. We have saved 3 megabytes of a 20 megabyte hard disk by packing a relatively small number of programs. Remember, however, that the disk space taken by a file is an exact number of sectors so that packing small files may not yield a real saving if less than a sector is freed.

11.7 SOFTWARE CONSIDERATIONS

Research has shown that the maximum wait that a terminal user will tolerate is about 5 seconds, before becoming impatient. It is therefore important that activities which take longer than this are accompanied by some sort of display on the screen. For example, a program which normally operates 'instantly', may for a particular data set spend a long period processing. A program that uses transcendental functions, on a machine without a numeric coprocessor, can take a surprisingly long time to execute. The following subprogram uses the screen handling routines of Chapter 12 to show how the user may be kept informed of the progression of such a lengthy series of operations, we envisage in this example that a 500 * 500 matrix is being manipulated.

```fortran
      SUBROUTINE COMPUTE
C--------------------------
C
C                  blank the screen (it might be 'dirty')...
C                  go into reversed video...
C
      CALL CLS
      CALL REVID
C
C                  explain what is going on...
C
      CALL PUTTXT(10,10,' Monitoring progress: ',22)
      CALL PUTTXT(12,10,' Row  ',6)
      CALL PUTTXT(14,10,' Col. ',6)
C
C                  now get into the computational loops...
C
      DO 100 I=1,500
      CALL PUTINT(12,20,I,3)
C
      DO 50 J=1,500
      CALL PUTINT(14,20,J,3)
C
C                  manipulate the 500*500 matrix here
C
 50   CONTINUE
100   CONTINUE
C
C                  reset a normal display, and
C                  'clean the blackboard'...
C
      CALL NORMAL
      CALL CLS
C
      RETURN
      END
```

It is assumed that the subroutines called in the above code have the following functions:

CLS   clear the screen
REVID   turn on inverse video
NORMAL   switch off inverse video
PUTTXT   jump to row and column defined by parameters 1 and 2, print the text in the
         third parameter to the number of characters given in the fourth
PUTINT   similar to PUTTXT, only relating to the integer in the third parameter

The issues involved in access to the screen functions of DOS, bypassing FORTRAN formatted output and thereby avoiding explicit carriage control, are covered in Chapter 12. There we have separated the individual functions of placing the cursor at specific screen coordinates, and displaying text. In the above code fragments, we have combined the two.

Note that the choice has been made consciously to clear the screen on entry, and again on exit. This involves a minuscule additional overhead, and means that the code is tolerant, in a program with multiple authors, of a failure elsewhere. It is thus entirely self-contained and fault-tolerant, both desirable attributes.

The moving figures output by the code do attract the eye, and a monitoring display such as this can be quite effective in a box on the screen, or on the 'status line' (line 25). The details for this are left to the reader.

Such procedures actually make programs run more slowly, but in keeping the user informed of progress, rather than bored and looking at an immobile or blank screen, give a psychological appearance of activity.

11.8 CHOICE OF COMPILER

Switching compilers to gain speed is a search for the Holy Grail. It is often better to stick to just one for production work, and fine tune the source code to suit it. We are not in favour of using extensions to the language standard, however, and the use of test compilations with a range of compilers is very beneficial in catching abstruse errors, or non-portable coding.

The differences between the run times of short programs compiled using different compilers can appear large if expressed as a ratio–for example if compiler A gives a run time of 8 seconds and compiler B gives 5 seconds, A is '60 per cent slower'. (Note if output is direct to a printer, the run times of the two will be identical: the printer will slow them down to a common level.) For large compute-bound or disk-bound programs, with much more of a mix of operations, a more realistic comparison of compilers can be made and the differences in run times may be smaller. This is because a compiler which is slower than its rivals for some operations may produce more efficient code for other operations.

The following example illustrates that for extra speed a change of hardware is usually more cost effective than a change of compiler.

A numerically intensive program (actually a finite element analysis for geomechanics) was transferred from a mainframe to be run on a floppy disk, no coprocessor, 5 MHz 8086 machine. The code was so complicated, that only one compiler would run it. It ran for three hours! Transferring it to an 8087 coprocessor equipped machine, the run time came down to 45 minutes. The coprocessor cost half as much as the cheapest discounted price which could be found for the compiler which would successfully compile and link the program. Here, spending the money on hardware was the right choice, although in order to get the program to run, several compilers had to be investigated.

Moving on to a hard disk AT style machine, with an 8 MHz 80286 processor, the run time came down to about 15 minutes, and when an 80287 coprocessor was fitted, a further reduction in run time to about 7 minutes was achieved. The cost of that 80286/7 hard disk machine was about the same as the sum total of the discounted prices of five leading compilers. Again, the advisability of spending the money on hardware is well shown.

On the AT style machine, the compile–test–modify cycle came down to a reasonable time, so that it became practical to undertake the necessary modifications to enable one of the other compilers to work. Ultimately, the run time was reduced to below 5 minutes, but at a cost of many man-days of effort, largely in getting to the bottom of undocumented, or poorly explained, non- standard features in the compiler. If you have a compiler that will compile your routines, then the cost–benefit equation is clearly weighted on the side of hardware purchases.

The difference in run times on the AT style machine with fully developed versions for different compilers turned out to be about plus or minus half a minute: a variation found with the same code depending on whether the hard disk is relatively full or empty. So the little gain that was achieved with the fastest compiler was barely significant statistically speaking. Spend the money on hardware.

Compilers do take different amounts of time to compile, and for the developer, this might be important. However, for really serious work, one runs a source program through several compilers. If it is of any length, one or other compiler will protest at something. It might be a bug in your program, or merely something that will affect future portability. A favourite example was an exam results processing program. Every novice writes one of these as a first task—for the academic, they can be real headaches. A program evolves over many years with patches added by colleagues of greater or lesser competence and imagination. A colleague had added three DO loops which terminated on IF statements. This got by the VAX, Microsoft FORTRAN, and Ryan MacFarland FORTRAN compilers but was finally caught by the Digital Research compiler.

11.9 SOURCE CODE FEATURES

Actually making the program run faster demands sensible coding, and an appreciation of what takes the time in a computer program. Even the slowest of the processors which support DOS is amazingly fast at some operations. What slows it down are the layers and layers of program which it has to support. For instance, a FORTRAN application program calls a DOS function. This does a little processing, then transfers control to the BIOS which actually does the work. Finally, control is returned back up the chain. Sometimes activities summed up in a single FORTRAN statement can give rise to dozens of these transfers of control: input/output being a case in point. Apart from the delays induced by the mechanical elements of a printer or disk drive, the operating system and all the other 'middlemen' take their slice of the action too.

This might be seen as an argument for making calls via assembly language direct to the BIOS of a computer. Despite the attractions of this, it is highly undesirable from the point of view of program portability: indeed, there may be subtle differences between BIOS details on quite closely related machines, let alone between the myriad of similar specification 'clones' that one sees marketed. Operating system calls make the software an order of magnitude more portable, if several times slower.

Most of the time taken by a program is used in a tiny part of the code. This is likely, on a no-coprocessor machine, to be where there is a heavy numerical load, particularly where transcendental functions are evaluated. Another significant time consumer is I/O. On coprocessor equipped machines where mathematics is much faster, I/O is likely to be the major bottleneck. In the following sections, we consider the areas where the FORTRAN programmer can make real improvements to the speed at which his program runs.

11.10 CHOICE OF LIBRARY

Many of the operations in a FORTRAN program use the same code expansions over and over again. Each compiler keeps these as a 'library' of functions and subroutines which are bound to the generated code at link time. Often, compilers have alternate libraries which can be selected for use by the programmer, and the decision needs to be based on factors such as speed of execution, precision, and size of EXE file.

As a FORTRAN user, you will normally have only a few choices to make. You can choose a bigger or smaller memory model, and you can choose whether or not to have 8087 code (which will *only* run when a coprocessor is present) or 8086 code (which will not make use of a coprocessor even if one is available). Most compilers have moved away from the latter option to a system where a 'no-coprocessor' program first tests to see if one is present. If there is a coprocessor fitted, then the program updates some tables and values internally so that the coprocessor can be used. The overhead of the test is small, and is saved many-fold if a coprocessor is found.

The no-coprocessor code is designed to emulate the coprocessor's operations, to yield very high precision in its results. This leads to slow processing where the full coprocessor precision is not required, and it may be possible to develop a still satisfactory, but reduced precision, support library. Microsoft have done this, and include it with their compiler. It is known as the ALTMATH library, and is a complete replacement for the coprocessor emulation library.

In speed terms, we have the following:

Fastest

     Coprocessor library
     Emulation library, coprocessor found at run time
     Alternate maths library
     Emulation library, no coprocessor

Slowest

Microsoft also at one time supported a binary coded decimal library but this has now been discontinued.

When compiling, one has the choice to generate 'in-line' code, or subroutine calls to access intrinsic mathematical functions. The first is fastest, but generates lengthy code containing repetitive sequences of the same instruction, the second choice is more compact, but slower. It has the further advantage that the choice of library (coprocessor, emulation, or alternate maths mode) may be selected at link time. If memory is not a consideration, it is suggested that the 'in line' emulator code is chosen, since this gives the maximum flexibility and speed on which machines will run a particular executable code (EXE) file.

All of the other FORTRAN compilers that we know of give less control over the generation of the precise form of the code, and whether or not this is beneficial depends on whether one views simplicity as a greater virtue than control. Ryan MacFarland, for instance, offer a coprocessor library, and a no-coprocessor library of the 'use it if it's there' type. So also does the Supersoft FORTRAN 66 compiler. Digital Research's FORTRAN offers the choice of small and large models, in both coprocessor and no-coprocessor forms, a total of four libraries. A similar format is followed by the Prospero FORTRAN 66 and 77 compilers.

As well as an improvement in executable file size and memory requirement, using the small model also gives code that loads and runs faster. If processing time is critical, a change of model might give the desired improvement.

Some compilers generate code for particular Intel processors. Microsoft FORTRAN v. 4.00, for instance, has a switch to generate 8086, 80186, or 80286 code. Some improvement in performance, and in code size, but with a loss of portability, is the direct result of processor specific code; 8086 code is universally portable.

11.11 DATA STRUCTURES

Any FORTRAN program in which the data is all in a single segment must run faster than one where it is stored in separate segments. This implies use of the small model if that is possible, or where not, say in the Microsoft FORTRAN compiler, the use of the [NEAR] attribute to COMMON block names to force them into the default data segment. The reasons for this are clear. The DS (data segment) register is loaded with the segment address of the default data segment at program initialization, and there is never any need to change it, or to fetch another address for it.

Failing this, operations should concentrate on the manipulation of data from within the same segment. In the 'medium' model, where common blocks are less than a segment, it implies the minimum of operations which draw data from different common blocks. These operations all cause repeated swapping of the contents of the DS register.

If it is imperative to use the 'large' model, with trans- segmental addressing, operations should try as much as possible to organize their use of the data in such a way as to minimize the need to move from segment to segment in accessing the [HUGE] arrays. An example may illustrate this. Suppose there is a large REAL*4 array named BIG, and dimensioned BIG (300,300). Accessing this using the leftmost index first, as in, for example,

```
        DO 10 J = 1, 300
        DO 5  I = 1, 300
        BIG (I,J) = ...
    5   CONTINUE
   10   CONTINUE
```

as against:

```
        DO 10 I = 1, 300
        DO 5  J = 1, 300
        BIG (I,J) = ...
    5   CONTINUE
   10   CONTINUE
```

shows a speed advantage. Why? Because the segment address for BIG changes only six times, whereas in the second case, it changes once every (65 536/(4*300)) or 54 operations, a total of 1800 times in 90 000 operations.

11.12 OPTIMIZING LOOP STRUCTURES

The first important step in optimizing loops is to remove invariant code. It may well be that the compiler will optimize this itself, but in reorganizing the code, the sequence of computations may be altered. The traditional example goes something like this:

```
        DO 10 I=1,1000
        IF (ABS(X) .LT. 0.000001) GO TO 10
        Y(I) = Z / X
   10   CONTINUE
```

Since neither Z nor X is dependent on the loop, the result of Z/X is a constant, and needs only to be computed once, outside the loop. The optimizing part of the compiler is not normally clever enough to read the programmer's obvious check, and when X is 0.0, the program crashes. Such a thing can be hard to debug, because the code clearly shows a check. However, if one manually rearranges the loop, one takes the check too (or rapidly appreciates why the inevitable crash happens).

Of course, repetitive execution of IF statements inside DO loops is itself an inefficient programming practice. It is often possible to rewrite the code to remove the need for this sort of construct.

So-called optimizing compilers also replace repeats of a constant sub-expression within the scope of a single DO loop. However, the parser cannot tell (as we can) that (A + B) is identical to (B + A), and even subtle syntax changes can fox it. Code also becomes clearer if this sort of replacement is made manually. Besides, the code may need to run through the compiler a number of times, and each time the optimizer is called, extra time is needed. One could go further, and point out again that FORTRAN compilers work most rapidly on short, unambiguous, statements. Any manual refinement of the code must be worthwhile.

As an addition to this point, the compiler, or the run-time code, has to make many 'coercions' of type when processing constants if the programmer is casual in his coding. For example, the statement

```
IF ( X .LT. 1 ) GO TO 30
```

demands the coercion of the INTEGER constant 1 to REAL type (assuming X is REAL) before the comparison can be made. This coercion might be done at the compilation stage, or at run time. In any event, it is an unnecessary operation. The places where most programmers are thoughtless in this respect include both IF statements and arithmetic assignment statements. The type change is usually from INTEGER to REAL, or on occasion INTEGER to DOUBLE PRECISION. Another problem area is in the assignment of REAL constants to DOUBLE PRECISION data types in DATA statements. One may be lucky and have the extra bits set correctly, but it is better not to trust to luck.

The next enhancement one can make is to examine the order of DO loops. For example,

```
        DO 20 I=1,500
        DO 15 J=1,10
        .
        .
        .
15      CONTINUE
20      CONTINUE
```

involves the overhead in setting up the inner loop being invoked 500 times. Merely reversing the order of the loops

```
         DO 20 J=1,10
         DO 15 I=1,500
            .
            .
            .
15       CONTINUE
20       CONTINUE
```

creates a much more favourable loop environment.

Short loops can easily be unrolled, for instance replacing:

```
         DO 10 I=1,2
         X(I) = Y(I)
10       CONTINUE
```

with

```
         X(1) = Y(1)
         X(2) = Y(2)
```

Partial unrolling, computing two or more operations from the sequence in each loop cycle, may also be undertaken. This goes against the rules of elegant coding, but can gain speed in crucial areas.

It is obviously inefficient to have consecutive loops where they might be amalgamated. For instance compare:

```
         DO 10 I=1,20          and          DO 10 I=1,20
         X(I) = …                           X(I) = …
            .
            .                               Y(I) = …
            .                                  .
10       CONTINUE                              .
         DO 15 I=1,20                          .
         Y(I) = …                     10       CONTINUE
            .
            .
            .
15       CONTINUE
```

The example on the left even takes more coding, as well as longer to execute, than the one on the right, which lacks the second loop overhead. Of course, if the second loop needed to access array elements of X with a higher subscript than I, then the first structure is the only one possible. The technique of amalgamating loops is sometimes termed 'jamming'.

11.13 IF STATEMENTS

Early FORTRAN compilers translated arithmetic IFs more efficiently than logical IFs. One would naturally expect compilers implemented on PCs to mimic the earlier compilers in this respect, as in so much else. However, compiler techniques have advanced significantly, and this statement may be true or false for a particular compiler or version. One way of testing it is to command the compiler to issue assembler code for the two alternatives and to compare them. This is easily done for Microsoft FORTRAN v. 4.0 and Ryan MacFarland FORTRAN v. 2.11.

However, the issue of program readability is much more important than slight inefficiencies, and this is as much a matter of taste as anything else. The facility to jump three ways in code is a useful attribute of the arithmetic IF, but is, surprisingly, rarely used. It is much improved in readability if the statement numbers in the referenced section of code ascend, with a moderately large interval (say at least 10).

For example,

```
  2 A = 100.98
  9 B = 2.345
102 X(2*N-1) = A + B
    IF (A-B)   3,7,4
  7 CONTINUE
    .
    .
    .
  4 ...
```

gives no hint of where to look for statement labels in a jumble of numbers. Whereas:

```
 10 A = 100.98
 20 B = 2.345
 30 X(2*N-1) = A + B
    IF (A-B)   70, 40, 60
 40 CONTINUE
    .
    .
    .
 60 ...
```

should be easy to follow.

One cautionary note in this. The arithmetic IF is one of the statements earmarked for termination in the next (or maybe the one after the next...) FORTRAN standard.

The block IF feature of FORTRAN 77 can be used to good effect in complicated logical constructs, but we find that too many ELSE IFs, especially when separated by a large number of statements, are quite difficult to follow. In addition, the modern tendency to have indentation for just one or two statements is equally as distracting, and un-FORTRAN like.

Sometimes, IFs are redundant. An example of this is

```
      IF ( A .GT. B ) THEN
            L = .TRUE.
      ELSE IF ( A .LE. B ) THEN
            L = .FALSE.
      ENDIF
```

can quite easily be replaced by the logical assignment

```
   L = A .GT. B
```

but possibly at the expense of readability.

11.14 USE OF DATA STATEMENTS

Excessive use of initialization code, for example:

```
         DO 25 I=1,10000
            A(I) = 0.0
   25    CONTINUE
```

leads to a slowing down at run time. The alternative is to initialize in a DATA statement:

```
   DATA A / 10000*0.0/
```

Be warned, however, that long numeric lists in DATA statements cause slow compilation, and large EXE files. The small penalty at run time might be more acceptable. Points to watch out for include unnecessary initializations, for example in the above where the elements of A are immediately assigned some other value without using the zeros so laboriously placed there. There is little merit in replacing single variable assignments by DATA statements, as in:

```
   X = 5.923498
```

to

```
   DATA / X / 5.923498
```

once the code is written and working, although there is merit in so doing at the program development stage, if it can be remembered. It saves keeping a copy of the constant just to assign it to X, rather than a measurable amount of processor time. Remember too, that excessive precision in a constant assigned to a single precision variable leads to the need for a coercion at compile or run time.

The PARAMETER statement is a new feature of FORTRAN 77 which can be used to give a permanent value to a name and also initialize such things as array sizes. PARAMETER statements have just been introduced to Microsoft FORTRAN with the release of v. 4.0, although they have been implemented in the other full FORTRAN 77 compilers for some time.

Where a DATA initialization is inappropriate, for example when the compilation delays are excessive (on occasion, it has been thought that an 8 MHz 80286 machine has hung up during compilation of a big DATA statement), or where an array has to be repeatedly re-initialized, there is a compromise. This applies to multidimensioned arrays. It is illustrated in the following fragment:

```
          DIMENSION A(100, 100, 5)
          DIMENSION B(50000)
          EQUIVALENCE (A(1,1,1), B(1))
              .

              .

              .
          DO 10 I=1,50000
          B(I) = _
10        CONTINUE
```

The overhead of computing the array element position from its indices is avoided, and of course, partial loop unrolling may give further speed gains.

11.15 USING FUNCTIONS

Many FORTRAN programmers seem never to use the intrinsic functions properly. The following is commonly seen:

```
          A = -10000.0
          IF (B .GT. A) A = B
```

Whereas the IF statement in its entirety could be replaced with the assignment

```
      A = MAX (A, B)
```

This will execute much faster. Note that in this example the generic function name, MAX, has been used. Later compiler versions are better at handling the generic names: early versions often needed explicit invocation of a function which matched the types of its parameters and intended result. This even happened where the documentation listed the generic functions.

Efficient use of functions may be made where they are reducible, or return the same value when called with the same parameters. For instance, we would expect

```
X = SIN(Y) + SIN(Y)
```

to return the same result as

```
X = 2.0 * SIN(Y)
```

On a coprocessor equipped machine, the latter will be slightly faster than the former, but on a machine without a coprocessor, the difference will be enormous. That is, unless the compiler has chosen to replace the former expression with the latter as part of an optimization procedure. That would be fine in this context, but what about

```
Z = RANDOM(X) + RANDOM(X)
```

where RANDOM returns a number in a random sequence. This would most certainly not work if 'optimized' into the form of the previous example. This function RANDOM is irreducible.

Take too a further example. The function INKEY returns a value sampled from the keyboard buffer. Consider

```
        CHARACTER*1 A, B, INKEY
        A = INKEY()
        B = INKEY()
```

What happens if the optimizer saves the result of the first call in a temporary variable? Total failure! Fortunately, PC optimizers haven't reached that level of 'sophistication' yet—evidence from the mainframe world suggests that they just might!

Some functions can be combined. For example,

```
R = LOG (X) + LOG (Y)
```

can quite easily be coded as

```
R = LOG (X*Y)
```

without loss of readability, and with major time savings in the computation stage.

The normal rule which is to give constants in the correct type to prevent the need for type coercions at either compile or run time needs to be extended to indicial powers. Thus where it is better to write

    2.0 * X

than

    2 * X

it is better to write

    X ** 2

than

    X ** 2.0

In the latter case, logarithmic functions will almost certainly be invoked, although in the former, more efficient methods, perhaps involving multiplication, may be used.

Indeed, the manual replacement of powers with repeated multiplication may be worthwhile. This is extended to the general concept of strength reduction. In a particular example

    ((A * X + B) *X + C) *X + D

replaces

    $A X^3 + B X^2 + C X + D$

giving a minimum of costly multiplications. Where a series of polynomials is required, however, it might be preferable to compute the multiples of 'X' explicitly at the outset.

11.16 CHOICE OF ALGORITHM

Many FORTRAN programmers give this scant attention, except in some particular. An example that springs to mind comes from a colleague who spent much time refining his matrix inversion procedures to solve large problems, but who left simple bubble sorts for his data. The bubble sort algorithm, although easy to code, and quite good for short lists, can be very poor on long ones, and should be replaced by more complicated, but faster algorithms like Quicksort and Heapsort.

The movement of the thrust of academic work in computer science departments away from FORTRAN and into Pascal or C has deprived the FORTRAN community of many interesting and useful ideas. A knowledge of which parts of a program take the longest to execute and a willingness to experiment are useful in this context.

11.17 IMPROVING I/O PERFORMANCE

In this section, we consider formatted output to screen, printer or data file, basically as a form of 'results' presentation, and the use of disks as mass storage devices. First of all, consider the formatted write statement.

In a formatted write statement we have a unit number, format statement number and a list of variable names. The format statement itself consists of 'edit groups' which describe how the value stored in each variable is to be organized into characters on output. Complicated format lists take a relatively long time to execute. For FORTRAN 77, where the interpretation of format information is done at run time, this can be a major factor in running speeds, particularly when compounded over many repeats of a write-and-format combination.

On inspection, one may find that lists are printed out with (say)

```
    FORMAT ( 2X, F8.3, 3X, F7.2, 2X, F8.2 )
```

which might easily be converted into the simpler-to-interpret

```
    FORMAT ( 3F10.3 )
```

or similar at the expense of gaining or losing one decimal place on output. Any savings from this form of rationalization will be small, and only need to be sought when the writing operation is in an inner loop, and so is repeated many times. It is certainly not worth making the change for those WRITE statements which are executed once or twice per run.

Much bigger gains can be obtained by rationalizing the output list itself. Suppose that the above FORMAT was accompanied by a WRITE statement of the form:

```
    WRITE (5, 100) A, B, C
```

This will generate separate calls to system functions for each of the variables A, B and C. We often find that a single array reference, to D, where D is a three element array, only makes one call to the system functions. We can even save ourselves the overhead of the three assignments by EQUIVALENCEing the variables to the elements of D, as follows:

```
        DIMENSION D(3)
        EQUIVALENCE (D(1),A), (D(2),B), (D(3),C)
        .
        .
        .
```

```
            WRITE (5, 100) D
                  .
                  .
                  .
```

Note, however, that there is little to be gained by indexing D in the WRITE statement, as in

```
    WRITE (5, 100) (D(I), I=1,3)
```

because that reintroduces the separate system function calls. As before, maximum benefit is obtained in oft-repeated WRITE statements.

The purpose of EQUIVALENCE statements is not always obvious on reading through a program listing, and they can be overlooked when a new programmer attempts to read and understand the listing. Where the above technique is used, it is advised that a comment should be placed nearby to explain what has been done, for example

```
C               following WRITE is optimized version of
C               WRITE (  )  A, B, C  (see EQUIVALENCEs)
C
            WRITE (5, 100) D
```

and so on.

11.18 USING DISKS AS BULK STORAGE

The speed of data transfer is enhanced if the data is stored in the computer's internal binary form, i.e. is unformatted, rather than formatted where it first has to be converted to readable ASCII characters. In some cases, where the user wants to read the file using the DOS commands TYPE or PRINT, or where the file is to be used by other programs not written in FORTRAN, possibly even an application such as Multiplan or dBase, it is necessary to use formatted files.

When using unformatted files, one has two choices: to make them sequential or direct access. A sequential file is best visualized as a 'tape'. In fact, sequential files originated when magnetic tapes were the primary mass storage medium. Conventional wisdom is that one should write as long blocks or records on a tape as one can, because it minimizes the 'inter-block' gap thus shortening the re-read time. The FORTRAN statements BACKSPACE and REWIND have a genuine physical meaning when applied to a tape!

Most PCs do not have tapes, and even if they do, tend to use them for backing up purposes only. However, FORTRAN has retained the sequential file. How is this implemented on disk?

Most compilers fail to say. The following account is based on Microsoft FORTRAN. This writes sequential files as a set of logical records preceded by a single byte which has the value 75. This is of no significance (sic!). Each logical record (created by a single unformatted WRITE) is made up of 130-byte long physical records, with possibly a shorter final record if the logical record length is not an even multiple of 128 bytes. Each of the 130-byte records starts and ends with a single byte containing the value 129 (in unsigned, INTEGER*1 mode, which FORTRAN doesn't have...it has to be read as a CHARACTER*1 and deciphered using ICHAR); the possibly shorter last record has these 'parenthetical' bytes containing a value 1 more than the number of bytes in the last record. There is no 'end of logical record' mark, unless the logical record happens not to be a multiple of 128 bytes, in which case the short physical record suffices. If this description were correct then Microsoft FORTRAN would seem to be incapable of correctly executing

```
            DIMENSION A(128), B(128)
            OPEN (9,FILE='TEST',FORM='UNFORMATTED',
    1            ACCESS='SEQUENTIAL')
            .
            .
            .

            WRITE (9) (A(I), I=1,128)
            WRITE (9) (B(I), I=1,128)
            .
            .
            .

            REWIND 9
            READ (9) X
            READ (9) Y
            .
            .
            .
```

This should result in X containing A(1), and Y containing B(1). If the documentation is correct, it won't because it would not be able to distinguish where A ends and where B begins. As it happens, it *does* execute correctly. This is because the last physical record in a logical record shows the exact length in the 'length bytes'. It is not so much that the last physical record contains an 'end of record' mark, rather that the others contain 'not end of record' information! So beware documentation on files even when it is given.

Microsoft FORTRAN also has another sequential, unformatted file mode termed 'binary'. This contains no record separators whatsoever, and should device 9 be connected to a binary file the code above would place A(2) in Y.

In order to read B(1) in the above example we would need to store the length of A on the record, viz:

```
WRITE (9) NBLK, (A(I),I=1,NBLK)
```

and to READ it back in the same way. This makes the transfer slower than

```
WRITE (9) A
```

but of course, in this case, the length of A is known anyway since the whole of A is stored and A must be declared in the routine. The binary type file is particularly used when reading files which were created by programs written in other languages since these files will not have a particular internal structure which corresponds to one of the standard FORTRAN structures.

The record is assembled in memory in a dynamically allocated part of memory in the 'heap' above the top of the program area. It is thus essential that there is some free space left when the program is loaded. Under Microsoft FORTRAN v. 3.3x, the buffer is allocated a size of 1024 bytes for sequential access files, which is effectively the maximum length of an unformatted sequential record. In v. 4.0, this buffer can be increased in size, using the non-standard BLOCKSIZE directive in your OPEN statement. By increasing the BLOCKSIZE I/O, can be speeded up but at the expense of increasing the amount of memory that has to be reserved on the heap for I/O operations.

A similar mechanism is found in RM FORTRAN, where the unformatted record length is assumed to be 512 bytes. To extend this, up to a maximum of 65 536 bytes, the switch /Rsize is given when invoking the program. For instance, to make a program run using 20 000-byte record lengths, the following invocation is made:

```
A>program /R20000
```

Only use BLOCKSIZE or /Rsize if your program is very I/O bound and only then after you have tried using a RAM disk or disk cacheing explained earlier in this chapter. The use of either a RAM disk or disk cacheing is liable to be more effective in speeding up I/O bound programs with the additional benefit that your code remains standard.

11.19 USING DIRECT ACCESS FILES

The sequential file can only be read in a certain order, that is, the order in which it was written. Admittedly, one can BACKSPACE, which returns to the start of the record last read, or REWIND, to go to the start of the file, but these are crude controls compared to the ability to READ and WRITE records in any order, as permitted in a direct access file.

However, to gain this random access, all the records must be of the same physical length, which is specified on OPENing the file. The facility to write variable length records is, of course, lost. If you write less information to a record than the defined record length the record will be padded with undefined characters.

To make efficient use of the hardware which positions the read/write head(s) on the disk, the record size should be a multiple or sub-multiple of the number of bytes allocated as a cluster. The common (and some less common) arrangements are given in Table 11.1.

Table 11.1 Cluster sizes on some DOS disks

Disk format	Cluster size (bytes)
360 kbyte d/s 5.25 inch (IBM PC)	1024
720 kbyte d/s 3.5 inch	1024
1.2 Mbyte d/s 5.25 inch (PC AT)	1024
10 Mbyte Winchester	4096
20 Mbyte Winchester	8192
315 kbyte s/s 3.5 inch (Early Apricot)	512
1.44 Mbyte 3.5 inch	2048
600 kbyte s/s 5.25 inch (Victor Sirius 9000)	512
1.2 Mbyte d/s 5.25 inch	1024
120 kbyte s/s	512
180 kbyte s/s	512
320 kbyte d/s	1024
5 Mbyte Winchester	2048

For a first guess, take one sector of 512 bytes for the cluster size on single-sided floppy disks, and two sectors giving a total of 1024 bytes for double-sided floppy disks.

11.20 ORGANIZATION OF DISKS

DOS attempts to use disk space effectively, by reusing the space released as files are deleted. On the first writing, the disk is filled sequentially. After a period of deletion and rewriting, files become fragmented, that is, scattered over the surface of the disk. This becomes particularly noticeable with hard disks, and the larger capacity floppy disks. The time taken to read a file can significantly increase as this fragmentation takes place. The answer is a complete backup, deletion of all files and directories, possibly by reformatting, and the recreation of the directory structure from the backup disks. Backing up is not just a security measure, but can genuinely enhance the systems performance.

The user with a low capacity floppy disk based system may gain some benefit from a well-organized disk, but nothing like the benefit that a hard disk user will gain. Published disk performance benchmarks normally fail to take into account the degradation in performance that fragmentation brings, and as they are usually carried out on new, evaluation machines reveal the best that can be hoped for, rather than what will be achieved in practice.

It is possible to purchase software which will compress the data on a disk, by closing up the spaces. This can be time consuming initially, but may be worthwhile eventually.

11.21 SUMMARY

In the beginning, we said that you should use the fastest and best-equipped microcomputer you can get your hands on. This will certainly make a big difference. However, adopting some of the techniques outlined above can make a real difference to your productivity, and that of your software.

CHAPTER 12

SCREEN HANDLING: TEXT MODES

12.1 INTRODUCTION

In the dim and distant origins of FORTRAN, both programs and data were prepared on punch cards, and these were normally handed to the computer operator as a 'batch'. He then instructed the computer to read in the decks of cards, and to undertake compilation, linking and execution steps. The turn round time for this process might be as little as a couple of hours! In the early days, output too was on punch cards, and these might have to be run through a printer as a separate operation to produce a listing. Later, fast computers were able to provide 'instant turn round' or 'fast batch' services, where the individual submitted his card deck with control cards which instructed the computer what to do, and separated program from data, and fast line printers produced output on demand. Essentially, however, the same processes were involved.

Input was laid out fairly formally in specific columns on punched cards, as expected by FORTRAN, and interpreted on input by means of a rigid FORMAT specification. Data records were separated by being placed on consecutive cards. Output was equally rigid, and was spaced across the page by the edit fields in an output FORMAT, and down the page by the simple carriage control built into the first character of each output statement.

The first major change came when computers became capable of handling the requirements of more than one user. This owed little to the scientific or engineering FORTRAN user, but was a response to the needs of a part of the business community who needed simultaneous access to the same data. The problems met and solved by the early pioneers of multi-access computers are now being handled again by microcomputer systems programmers. Whereas until recently the micro was a standalone, single-user machine, more and more emphasis is currently being placed on multi-user machines, and networks of single-user machines, as methods of sharing expensive hard disk space, and giving real- time access to the same data files.

The newcomer to PC computers is often amazed at the variety of 'user interfaces' with which he is presented. At one end of the scale this involves purely graphics based methods, like those of GEM and Windows, which owe their origins to research into user interfaces done at the Xerox Palo Alto Research Center (PARC) and popularized by Apple with their LISA and

Macintosh computers, right through to the opposite end of the scale where the user prepares a data file using a text editor, and then runs this with a program in 'batch mode'. The latter method gives the ultimate in program portability, but with no concessions whatever to the user. However, it is relatively easy to go part-way between the two in order to develop a degree of user friendliness without making a program entirely machine dependent.

We start by looking at the standard display available to us in FORTRAN. We see that by making use of the VT52 or ANSI (supplied with DOS) device drivers we can control movement of the cursor and produce an interesting screen display with effects like reverse video, bold, faint, and italic type, etc. We then look at more sophisticated input and output to our FORTRAN program by using DOS system calls. The DOS system calls are coded in assembly language routines which are accessible to any FORTRAN program simply by subroutine calls. A number of examples of these assembly routines are given in the text, and a complete library of these subroutines are available on the accompanying disk set. The main advantage of these routines in the context of this chapter is that strings can be written to the screen quickly without needing to worry about carriage control characters, and characters can be read from the keyboard buffer (one character at a time if required) without requiring the user to press the RETURN key after each data item. This opens the way for data entry screens to be handled from a FORTRAN program, allowing the user to enter data in different character fields in different parts of the screen, and to edit individual data items without needing to re-enter a complete line of data. The issues involved in editing a data entry screen are discussed and the skeleton of a FORTRAN code to handle the editing of a data field is presented. Finally we consider the design of a general input screen and the use and design of menus is discussed.

12.2 SCREEN DISPLAYS

It is possible to send FORTRAN formatted data to the screen. This is done in a variety of ways. A number of compilers have preconnected units, five to keyboard for input and six to screen for output at program initialization. Some others also have device 0 preconnected to keyboard and screen for both input and output. Naturally, in a FORTRAN 77 context, the * device is assumed to be the screen for output and the keyboard for input, and a PRINT statement too is expected to relate to the screen. The connection of units 0 and * are relatively fixed, but using the I/O redirection facility of DOS (v. 2 and above), assignment of the 'standard input' and 'standard output' devices can be made. Suppose a program normally expects input and output to and from the keyboard and screen (termed the 'console' and given the DOS device name 'CON' in most documentation). This can be made to accept data from a file INFILE.DAT and to send its output to OUTFILE.RES by a command such as

```
A>program <INFILE.DAT >OUTFILE.DAT
```

The < and > symbols are termed 'redirection' symbols and denote a reassignment of the standard input and output channels to these files. Indeed, using 'piping', a whole series of programs can be made to pass output from one to input of another, as in

```
A>prog1 <INFILE.DAT |prog2 |prog3 >OUTFILE.DAT
```

where program `prog1` now accepts input from `INFILE.DAT`, passes its output to `prog2` as input, expects `prog2` to pass its output to `prog3` (again forming a new input) with the results of the third program in this chain being sent to `OUTFILE.RES`. The 'piping' symbol is `|`.

Only the standard preconnected input and output units can be redirected in this manner. Explicit connection of units to files and devices is made after program loading and initialization, and is not therefore subject to redirection. It is normally only possible to redirect `STDIN` and `STDOUT` (names given to the standard input and output devices) and not `STDERR` (a preconnected device through which errors are normally reported). Confusingly, `STDERR` is usually the screen, and its output cannot be redirected. (Microsoft FORTRAN v. 4 includes a simple program to change the file/device assignment for `STDERR`.)

Unlike FORTRAN, which permits different logical unit numbers for screen (output) and keyboard (input), DOS lumps them together as the 'console', and gives them the device name `CON`. The alternative name or alias of `USER` is sometimes available to allow you to name the two separately.

12.3 FANCY EFFECTS ON SCREEN OUTPUT

The most immediate effect on a monochrome monitor is 'reversed video'. Typically, on a green screen monitor, the letters appear as green on a black background. Going into reversed video makes black letters appear on a green background. This is relatively easy for the screen driver software to do—all that is needed is to turn off the pixels that are normally lit, and turn on those that aren't. As a means of highlighting important data, reversed video is hard to beat. Virtually all PC monitors will support this effect. On colour monitors, it is usually possible to set both the foreground and background colours. In this context, background means the colour of the 'box' in which the character is displayed, and foreground, the pixels which make up the character itself. This is generally even more effective, unless too many colours are selected, in which case the screen simply looks muddled.

Depending on what screen option is installed on a PC, it may be possible to have faint or emphasized characters, to have them underlined, displayed in different fonts (e.g. *italic*), or other options. Moving the screen display into these fancy modes is done by means of escape codes, or by going behind DOS to the BIOS or underlying software.

First of all, we shall consider escape codes. These are so named because one of the ASCII codes (actually number 27) is named `ESCape`. This is usually taken to indicate that the following byte or bytes are **commands**, and not **data** which has to be displayed. Some of the other ASCII codes are commands in their own right, of course, and one of the escape sequences tells the screen to **display** them, rather than to **obey** them! In the following, we refer to the `ESCape` code itself as `ESC`, and to the sequences which include `ESC` as `ESCape` sequences.

There are two main conventions for ESCape sequences. The first of these is supported on a minority of computers, the latter on a majority, but they are sometimes difficult to use. The first set is 'VT52' compatible.

Early microcomputers had either proprietary operating systems, or 'CP/M'. CP/M was an operating system which performed very much like a subset of the operating system for PDP minicomputers produced by Digital Equipment Company (DEC)—it should come as little surprise that CP/M came from a very similarly named company, Digital Research! Since many PDP computers used DEC's own terminals, especially the VT52, CP/M was usually configured to drive this sort of terminal, or one like it. Then, with 16-bit microcomputers, a new version of CP/M was launched. This was popular initially, especially in the UK, where it was available on the Sirius/Victor 9000 computer before IBM began serious exports of their PC. The Sirius/Victor 9000 supported the VT52 control (or ESCape) codes. However, the IBM PC, and its many imitators, used a set of control codes produced by an ANSI committee, and these eventually became the effective standard, although Apricots were marketed able to obey both types of control code, as indeed are Amstrad PCs. The Apricot did it to complement the Sirius, and the Amstrad, because it is marketed with an operating system, DOS PLUS, emanating from Digital Research which emulates MS DOS.

Some DOS machines are configured capable of interpreting ESCape codes by means of code inserted in the BIOS, others need to have the line

```
DEVICE=ANSI.SYS
```

added to the CONFIG.SYS file, so that the ESCape code handler is loaded as a device driver at system boot time. The facilities of ANSI.SYS may vary from machine to machine, and in any case are fairly rudimentary compared to those machines which had a full set of enhanced VT52 escape codes in their BIOS. It is possible to purchase substantially improved device drivers for PCs, both commercially and as 'public domain' or 'user supported' software from user groups. We have included a VT52 device driver in the accompanying disk set.

As an alternative to using a loadable device driver like ANSI.SYS, it is possible to use 'terminate-and-stay-resident' programs which intercept the stream of characters being sent to the screen driver, and which filter out the ESCape codes before sending BIOS interrupts to drive the particular required effect. ANSI.SYS can only be removed by editing CONFIG.SYS and rebooting.

The principle behind the VT52 ESCape codes is that when the screen driver receives the ESCape code, which is 27 (decimal) or 1B (hexadecimal) in the ASCII sequence, the next character, or number of characters, are interpreted as commands to switch some special mode on or off. The majority of these ESCape sequences involve just one extra character, although a minority involve extra data. Take for example the sequences to turn inverse video effects on and off. This is done with the sequences

ESCape   p

and

ESCape   q

An example of a WRITE statement using this facility is:

```
        WRITE (*,100) CHAR(27),'p',' MESSAGE ',CHAR(27),'q'
100  FORMAT(10X,2A1,A9,2A1)
```

Note in this that the ESCape code is generated by means of the CHAR function, because the ESCape character on its own may not be inserted into a FORTRAN source. It is, of course, valid to assign it to a CHARACTER*1 variable, or an element of a longer CHARACTER entity.

The organization of the different functions within the VT52 set is not necessarily rational, and indeed computers which support a VT52-like set of ESCape sequences may in fact have reused some of them for special purposes. A list of these ESCape sequences is given in Appendix 3.

By and large, there are two types of ESCape code. There is first of all the sort described immediately above in which the following character goes up to make the command. Then there is the sort which needs some following data. Examples of this include functions to 'go to screen x,y coordinates of: ' and 'set colour to: '.

The ANSI ESCape sequences have a more consistent philosophy, but are usually longer, and often more difficult for the FORTRAN programmer, than the VT52 type. They use the concept of a 'lead- in', followed by numeric parameters, and terminated by a particular letter code. Take, for an example, the screen clearing functions to clear from the screen origin to the cursor position, to clear from the cursor position to the end of the screen, or to blank the entire screen. All the ANSI sequences commence with the lead in sequence:

ESC [(27 decimal, 1B hexadecimal)

and the screen clearance sequences end with the capital J. The three functions listed have parameters 0, 1, or 2, for example:

ESC [0 J–clear from screen top left to cursor
ESC [1 J–clear from cursor to screen bottom right
ESC [2 J–clear screen completely

Since the ANSI sequence has cursor positioning operations, and the first two of these leave the cursor position unchanged, it would be consistent to leave the cursor unmoved after ESC [2J. However, the majority of implementations 'home' the cursor to the screen 'origin' in the top left hand corner following this operation. Table 12.1 gives the ANSI ESCape sequences for setting screen text and graphics attributes: all of these terminate with lower case 'm'.

Table 12.1 ANSI ESCape sequences for setting screen text and graphics attributes.

ANSI ESCape sequence (assumed preceded by ESC [	Function
a; b; ... ;c m	Where a, b, c, etc. take the values:
	0 all attributes off
	1 bold on
	2 faint on
	3 italic on
m terminates the	5 blink on
ESCape sequence	6 rapid blink on
	7 reverse video on
	8 concealed on
	30...47 set foreground and background colours
	48 subscript
	49 superscript

Note that, although it is possible to switch the special attributes on one at a time, they have to all be switched off together, and selections reinstated. VT52 compatible screens have 'on' and 'off' ESCape sequences for each function.

The analogue of the VT52 ESCape sequence example given above to write a simple message in reverse video can be achieved using ANSI ESCape sequences thus:

```
WRITE (*,100) CHAR(27),'[7m',' MESSAGE ',CHAR(27),'[0m'
100  FORMAT(10X,A1,A3,A9,A1,A3)
```

As well as creating these special effects, ESCape sequences have one other major use; that is to position the cursor on the screen at particular coordinates, or to move it relative to its present position. Table 12.2 gives the ANSI ESCape sequences for cursor movement.

Since the ESCape character is not a valid carriage control character to appear first in a FORMAT, the initial character is interpreted according to the FORTRAN rules regardless of whether or not the list includes cursor positioning information. Virtually all PC FORTRANs interpret carriage control characters for the CON, USER, LPT, and PRN devices.

It is possible to WRITE with a FORMAT that thereafter inhibits carriage control on the next statement, by use of either the backslash (\), or, less commonly, the dollar ($) symbol sent to the FORTRAN screen driver. Experience has shown that this is relatively useless in the majority of cases, because we need to inhibit the carriage control at the start of the FORMAT, not at the end of the preceding FORMAT.

Table 12.2 ANSI ESCape sequences for cursor movement and direct addressing

ANSI ESCape sequence ESC [	Function
n A	Move cursor *up n* rows, unless at the top of the screen already. If *n* is omitted, it is assumed to be 1
n B	Move cursor *down n* rows, unless at the bottom of the screen.
n C	Move cursor *right n* columns
n D	Move cursor *left n* columns
m; n F	Position cursor at row *m*, column *n* the F is replaceable by H in some implementations

We therefore need to write some assembly language routines for sending characters and strings to the screen driver without using FORTRAN formatted or list-directed I/O. We show how the screen can be fully controlled later on in this chapter.

Examine first what happens when a character is sent to the screen driver by a FORTRAN program. This calls a DOS service to display the character. DOS checks to see if redirection is in effect, and, if not, calls a further routine in the BIOS. 'Screen accelerators' work by bypassing the check for redirection. For obvious reasons, the actual display must be slowed by these many levels of handling. The FORTRAN application can make significant gains in the speed at which text is displayed by bypassing the FORTRAN formatter, and using the DOS or BIOS services direct. If the DOS services are used, I/O redirection and piping still work; an additional benefit is that the program will work correctly on any DOS computer, not only one which has a compatible BIOS. Furthermore, FORTRAN carriage control is now irrelevant.

We recommend using the DOS service rather than that offered by the BIOS for the reasons above. Only if the application is to be used on 8088 machines (e.g. the original IBM PC and XT), *or* if the effect of animation is required, is it worth going direct to the BIOS for speed. Later machines are sufficiently fast to cope with DOS' overhead.

Basically there are two output services: output a single character and output a string. Naturally, for the output of a number of characters, the latter is going to be faster than the former, even considering the overhead in the FORTRAN code of building the string. Using assembler code to perform these functions is particularly effective, and some examples are given below in the next section.

(There is a similar set of DOS and BIOS services for the output of characters to a printer. In contrast to the screen which can easily accommodate any updates that DOS or the BIOS can throw at it, and whose response is governed by software considerations, printers are unlikely to be able to outrun DOS. There are printers which can, but they invariably cost many times as much as a PC, and are unlikely to be found connected to one. Furthermore, the carriage control conventions are nothing like so inconvenient on hard copy devices: spacing over an already printed line does not cause deletion, and data scrolled off the top of the page can be recovered with little more than a few backward line feeds. The use of normal FORTRAN formatted output is therefore recommended for printers. There is little or no merit in writing equivalent code to circumvent normal FORTRAN outputting procedures for printout. However, it could be done, using facilities little different from those presented here.)

12.4 CHOOSING ESCAPE SEQUENCES OR BIOS OPERATIONS FOR SCREEN EFFECTS

For every operation that can be called up via an ESCape sequence, the computer has its appropriate code in the BIOS. Why, then, not cut out DOS completely and call the function in the BIOS? After all, that is what Peter Norton, the doyen of PC programmers, recommends. (He also recommends not using FORTRAN, but that is a separate issue.) The reason for sticking with ESCape sequences is program portability. (And that is the reason why most of us continue to use FORTRAN.)

Most mainframe computers these days use terminals which are connected to the processor via simple communications links. We often find VT52 or VT100 compatible terminals, and, less commonly, ANSI terminals are in use. A FORTRAN program running on such a machine must use ESCape codes to get fancy effects on those terminals: there is no equivalent of a BIOS service. (The equivalent is in the terminal itself, and is accessible to your program only through the ESCape sequence.) In the future, many DOS PCs are going to run terminals via simple, serial communications links. It will be tragic if your FORTRAN program only works on the central computer in a network, and not on one of its terminals.

You can run your PC through a separate terminal. It could be one which offers VT52 ESCape sequences—many of them do. Connect it to the serial port on the PC, set the communications parameters to match the terminal's setting by use of the MODE command, and transfer control to the terminal with the command CTTY AUX:. That will give you access to a screen which might have much better resolution, and thus be more restful on your eyes, than a PC screen. Many programs circumvent DOS in their screen operations, however, and they will almost certainly not run with the terminal. Your FORTRAN programs will if you use ESCape sequences.

A further advantage of ESCape sequences, particularly those which require numeric parameters, is that you need not worry about whether the parameter is INTEGER*2 or *4 (or *1): this may be a problem if you are sending values to an assembly language BIOS function.

The drawback of using ESCape sequences is that your program will simply not work correctly on a computer that does not have ANSI.SYS or another ESCape sequence handler installed as a DOS loadable device driver.

Sometimes enhanced screen driver programs are supplied as terminate-and-stay-resident programs. Unlike a DOS loadable device driver, they can be removed from memory for critical applications. They are easier to set up, as they can be installed during the operation of a batch file which invokes your FORTRAN program, and cleared away on completion.

To summarize, there are four choices. The simplest and slowest is to use the FORTRAN formatter. That gives least control over position on the screen (or what control there is is gained with the most difficulty). Secondly, some gains in control and screen effects may be achieved through the use of ESCape sequences embedded in the formatted output. The next easiest alternative is to use a DOS output function, called by means of an assembler subprogram, and making use of ESCape sequences in the screen driver. The final choice is to circumvent even DOS, and use the fundamental characteristics of the computer BIOS.

Our recommendation, implemented in the code and examples that follow, is to use the third of these methods.

12.5 INPUTTING DATA TO A FORTRAN PROGRAM

FORTRAN expects that input to a program comes via a sequence of character strings. Ideally, these are expected to form a series of 'card images', reflecting FORTRAN's origins as a card based computer language. With first terminal access to mainframes and minicomputers, and latterly microcomputers, which are 'terminal' based as well, the strictness in formatting these 'card images' has been relaxed—instead of expecting a string of precisely 80 characters, what is now expected is a string of greater or lesser length, terminated by a CR LF sequence (i.e. the ASCII codes 13 and 10), or just CR on its own (ASCII 13).

As input from a data file, this is scarcely a problem, and almost any word-processing or text editing program, from humble EDLIN upwards, can be used as easily to create data files as to write program source code or batch files. An early enhancement on terminal based FORTRANs was to allow data to be formatted with commas separating the data items. This is similar to, but not always the same as, FORTRAN 77's 'list directed I/O'. Comparing most, if not all, PC keyboards to those on mainframe terminals, we find one important omission: there is no comma close to the numeric keypad on the PC. Hence, comma-separated data items are not so convenient to produce on the PC, as they are in terminal input to a mainframe. The nearest key on the average numeric keypad that can be used as a data separator is the RETURN key.

It is when direct input from the keyboard is required that most problems arise. In order to send the input string to FORTRAN, it must be 'terminated', and this termination normally comprises pressing the RETURN key. Not only is this an extra chore each time data is input, it also means that if there is some fault with the input string, and if this is intercepted by the FORTRAN program without a crash, the user must repeat the complete line (keying the correct keystrokes, as well as replacing the incorrect ones). What is required is the ability to intercept individual keypresses, validate them, and build them into a string which can (if the data item is numeric) be interpreted into the correct value. Another advantage of reading input from the keyboard, a character at a time, is that a help facility could be provided with a help screen being presented to the user at the touch of a function key (say), this facility could be set up so that help was available at any time during data entry even in the middle of inputting a data item.

12.6 READING KEYPRESSES

DOS itself intercepts keypresses, and puts them into a buffer. The length of this 'type ahead' buffer varies from computer to computer, and on some it is configurable. Memory-resident programs filter out certain characters from this buffer for their own purposes: these are usually particular combinations not normally in use. Both DOS and the BIOS have routines for getting the keypresses and other keyboard characteristics. As mentioned above in respect of the screen driver, the use of BIOS services renders software non-portable and should be avoided. Using BIOS services may well interfere with the use of memory resident utilities like SideKick as well.

In contrast to the screen driver, where the use of the BIOS service is attractive where speed is required, there is little to gain in reading keypresses directly through the BIOS—unless, of course, the application needs to cope with the entry of text at trained typist speeds.

The act of intercepting keypresses from FORTRAN involves an assembly language subroutine, which will be described in Section 12.10.

The input buffer is both useful, and dangerous. This is because the user tends to learn the responses, and types ahead. Where a wrong keypress is made, data and input get out of step. The best that can happen is that the program catches up and emits an angry beep: the worst is that the user finds that he has confirmed a deletion operation.

Where critical operations such as file deletion are concerned, the input buffer should be cleared **before** reading in the confirmation, as a general safeguard.

In the following assembler routines, we consider the different elements of reading from a keyboard and writing to the screen.

12.7 WRITING TO THE SCREEN

We will start with the preamble and winding up statements in assembler. These make the declarations, and force all the screen and keyboard utilities to occupy a single code segment. As usual, the code is written for the Microsoft Macro Assembler and expects to interface to Microsoft FORTRAN.

```
                NAME  SCREEN  AND  KEYBOARD  UTILITIES
;
CSSANDK    SEGMENT    PUBLIC      PARA 'CODE'
           ASSUME CS:CSSANDK
;


           the individual procedures go in here


;
CSSANDK    ENDS
;
           END
```

Within this frame, the individual utilities form separate procedures. Their names must be declared PUBLIC, so that they can be referred to from the FORTRAN code. The DOS system calls are available through software interrupts. To make use of a particular function we need to initialize one or more of the registers and then issue software interrupt 21 hex. The AX register determines which function is to be called, usually we need only configure the high byte AH of the register. The procedure should be apparent in the assembler code that follows.

Consider first a routine which outputs a simple string which we know in advance, and do not wish to change. An example of this is the 'clear screen' function, which requires the sending of 'ESCape [2J' to the screen driver ANSI.SYS.

```
PUBLIC     CLS
CLS        PROC    FAR
PUSH       DS                  ; save DS on the stack
           MOV     AH, 9       ; function code 09
           MOV     DX, SEG CLRSTRG     ;
           MOV     DS, DX             ; address of CLSTRG goes
           MOV     DX, OFFSET CLRSTRG ; into DS:DX
           INT     21H         ; DOS software interrupt
           POP     DS          ; restore DS
           RET
CLRSTRG    DB      1BH.'[2J$'  ; define ANSI sequence
CLS        ENDP
```

Here we have used the DOS system call function 9.

CLS is the name of this subroutine, which will be actioned with a

```
   CALL CLS
```

from FORTRAN. Hence the name CLS is defined to be PUBLIC. Furthermore, CLS is a PROCedure addressed from outside its own segment (FAR). Within the procedure, the DS register must be used, so its contents are pushed on to the stack for retrieval later (the POP instruction near the end). Any register which we wish to preserve and restore can be handled in this way. The registers DX and AX (actually just the high byte AH of the 16-bit register AX) are going to be used by the call to DOS. AH is given the function code (9), DS:DX is given the segment and offset of the string of bytes making up the message, and which we have defined in the define bytes (DB) instruction. Note that the last byte is the dollar symbol. The DOS function will go on sending bytes until it finds this.

Although it has been decided that this is a SUBROUTINE, and is called without parameters, CLS itself can be called as a FUNCTION. The assembler code cannot decide what is the correct mode, and the Microsoft compiler will do no more than to check across invocations in the same FORTRAN source code file, taking the first one it encounters to be correct. When using assembly language coded subroutines beware of this. Ideally, use no functions, or use them with care.

A whole family of screen control primitives may be defined in this way: it is perfectly adequate to have a subroutine for each. In the disk set accompanying this book, such a family of subroutines will be found. Perhaps the only caution that the tyro assembler programmer should heed is that each string defined by 'DB' needs a unique name—its name is not local to the procedure as it would be if coded in FORTRAN.

12.8 GENERAL PURPOSE STRING OUTPUT ROUTINES

We can display a string held as an array of CHARACTER*1 data by means of a program like the following:

```
        SUBROUTINE PUTSTR (STRING, NCH)
        CHARACTER*1 STRING (NCH)
          .
          .
        DO 100 N=1, NCH
        CALL PUTCHR ( ICHAR (STRING(N)) )
  100   CONTINUE
          .
          .
```

in which PUTCHR is a single-character output routine, coded in assembler and detailed below.

This is far from the most efficient way to do the job, but is appealing for a variety of reasons. Firstly, the assembler coding is minimized, and uses the most elementary code which must be duplicatable on all computer operating systems: it will be very portable. Secondly, regardless of the way the CHARACTER string is held, it still works. Different ways in which CHARACTER data may be held include the following:

- A simple string of bytes
- A 'count' byte or bytes, followed by the character bytes
- A string of character bytes, terminated by a particular character—usually ASCII zero (00h) but in some specific contexts (see Chapter 14) it might be ASCII 03 or something else. DOS itself has a string output function that expects the byte stream to be terminated with a '$' (ASCII 24h) which we used in CLS
- A pointer and length (the actual characters may be stored in a string space not actually at the address of the 'start')

It is therefore better (in the sense that it will prove less implementation sensitive) to pass an INTEGER giving the character number in the ASCII set. Indeed, this is shown in the FORTRAN code fragment above. It removes any problem with leading count bytes, or with pointers. However, pretty much the same result will be obtained with Microsoft FORTRAN if the CHARACTER*1 byte itself is sent! All that is needed is the assembler code for PUTCHR:

```
        PUBLIC  PUTCHR
PUTCHR  PROC    FAR
        PUSH    BP
        MOV     AH, 02H      ; interrupt 21h function 02
        MOV     BP, SP       ;
        LES     BX, [BP+6]   ; address of parameter - ES:BX
        MOV     DL, ES:BX    ; parameter itself - DL
        INT     21H
        POP     BP
        RET     04H
PUTCHR  ENDP
```

How this differs from the CLS procedure is that now there is a parameter. The address of the character is pushed on the stack, followed by the 4-byte return address. Hence the stack pointer SP points at the return address, and the address of the character is at SP+4. The BP register is used to address this, so it has to be PUSHed onto the stack to save its contents for later restoration. BP is 2 bytes long, so the addresses must each be 2 bigger after it is pushed. The square brackets mean to fetch the *contents* addressed, and these wind up in DL eventually, noting some of the vagaries of what registers may be used for what purposes. AH has been preloaded with the function code 2, and the DOS interrupt completes the picture. It is the job of the assembly language routine to clean up the stack on exit, by removing the 4-byte address of the parameter. (Note that Digital Research FORTRAN demands that this is done by the calling procedure. Beware!)

This routine may easily be modified to send characters to the serial port or printer using software interrupt 21H function codes 4 and 5 respectively. Function code 6 can be used for input or output, except that there is no CTRL-C detection. Loading DL with the value 0FFH is a signal that input, rather than output, is requested.

The immediately obvious alternative to single-character output, is to use the string output function. The string needs to be 'doped up' with a terminating '$' (24H) and leading length byte(s) have to be stripped off. Microsoft FORTRAN just sends a byte string, without any prefix count or terminating character, and so is easy to deal with. For simplicity, the assembler coded string output routine assumes this mode, and the user is left to make the necessary adjustments to suit his compiler and implementation.

The following incomplete FORTRAN sequence

```
        SUBROUTINE SHWTXT ( PAR, LENGTH )
        CHARACTER LIST(81), PAR(80)
        .
        .
        .
        DO 10 I=1,LENGTH
        LIST (I) = PAR (I)
10      CONTINUE
        LIST (LENGTH+1) = '$'
        CALL SHWBYT ( LIST )
        .
        .
        .
```

which interfaces with the assembler routine SHWBYT

```
        PUBLIC  SHWBYT
SHWBYT  PROC    FAR
        PUSH    BP
        MOV     AH, 09H      ; function 09
        MOV     BP, SP
        LDS     DX, [BP+6]   ; address of start - DS:DX
        INT     21H
        POP     BP
        RET     04H
SHWBYT  ENDP
```

demonstrates the general principles.

Further alternatives, which include sending the byte count to the assembler routine, and repeating the DOS function 02 in a loop, will not be proceeded with.

Any problems in using assembly code lie in the FORTRAN interface. The CHARACTER*1 definitions enable the routine to be used with early versions of Microsoft FORTRAN. Later versions support the substring operation, so that one could have

```
        SUBROUTINE SHWSTR ( PAR, LENGTH )
        CHARACTER LIST*81, PAR*80
        .
        .

        .
        LIST (1:LENGTH) = PAR (1:LENGTH)
        LIST (LENGTH+1:LENGTH+1) = '$'
        CALL SHWBYT ( LIST )
        .

        .
```

and with full FORTRAN 77 including the concatenation operator:

```
        .
        .
        .

        LIST (1:LENGTH+1) = PAR (1:LENGTH)//'$'
        CALL SHWBYT ( LIST )
        .

        .
```

Screen control functions which require the output of a fixed string can be built up from calls to PUTCHR, or to PUTSTR, or to the more complicated string operation subroutines SHWBYT and SHWTXT. The latter will optimize performance, and, once written and incorporated in a library, keep source code simple.

When one is operating with ESCape sequences, explicit assembly language subroutines like CLS (above) are not required. They can easily all be coded in FORTRAN with a call to SHWBYT, e.g.

```
        SUBROUTINE CLS
        CHARACTER*5 LIST
        LIST(1:1)=CHAR(27)
        LIST(2:5)='[2J$'
        CALL SHWBYT (LIST)
        RETURN
        END
```

You may note from this a reluctance to use concatenation for compatibility with Microsoft FORTRAN v. 3, and a desire to see as much code as possible in FORTRAN.

12.9 Cursor movement

Using VT52 conventions for direct cursor placement is easier in FORTRAN than using ANSI escape sequences. The reason for this is that the VT52 sequences involve a lead-in 'ESCape Y' followed by two bytes giving the row and column number. These bytes are positioned in the ASCII set in such a way as row and column number 1 are represented by the first 'printable' (i.e. not a control character) character in the sequence, row/column 2 by the second, and so on. Hence one merely has to add 31 to each of the row and column numbers to get the relevant bytes (32 if you like to number rows and columns from 0).

The ANSI sequence involves the standard 'ESCape [' lead-in, followed by row and column numbers given as ASCII digits. These obviously need one or two bytes each, depending on whether the cursor is to be placed in the first 9 rows or columns. There are a variety of ways of generating these: we shall use the ASSIGN statement in conjunction with internal files.

Here then, is the first attempt at a cursor positioning subroutine, GOTOXY.

```
        SUBROUTINE GOTOXY ( ICOL, IROW )
C-----------------------------------
C
C       Subroutine gives direct cursor addressing via ANSI
C       escapes.  The formats could terminate with 'F$'.
C       Method 1 of 4.
C
C-------------------------------------------------------------
        LOGICAL ICLT10, IRLT10
        CHARACTER*9 STRING
C
C                   checks on the validity of ICOL, IROW
C                   could be carried out
C
        ICLT10 = ICOL .LT. 10
        IRLT10 = IROW .LT. 10
C
C                   depending on whether col < 10, and/or
C                   row < 10, select the format and length
C
        IF (ICLT10 .AND. IRLT10) THEN
            ASSIGN 100 TO NFORM
            NL = 7
        ELSE IF (ICLT10) THEN
            ASSIGN 110 TO NFORM
            NL = 8
```

```
            ELSE IF (IRLT10) THEN
                ASSIGN 120 TO NFORM
                NL = 8
            ELSE
                ASSIGN 130 TO NFORM
                NL = 9
            ENDIF
C
C                       using selected format, store in STRING
C
            WRITE (STRING,NFORM) CHAR(27), IROW, ICOL
C
C                       use string output routine to display
C
            CALL SHWTXT (STRING, NL)
            RETURN
C
  100       FORMAT(A1,'[',I1,';',I1,'H$')
  110       FORMAT(A1,'[',I2,';',I1,'H$')
  120       FORMAT(A1,'[',I1,';',I2,'H$')
  130       FORMAT(A1,'[',I2,';',I2,'H$')
            END
```

It is quite practical to program cursor addressing in assembler, as the following alternative subroutine shows. Here, the BIOS services of an IBM PC or compatible are used.

```
            SUBROUTINE GOTOXY ( ICOL, IROW )
C-------------------------------------------------------------
C
C       subroutine to give lead-in to IBM PC BIOS cursor
C       positioning  :  Method 2 of 4.
C
C-------------------------------------------------------------
            CALL CURPOS (CHAR(ICOL-1), CHAR(IROW-1))
            RETURN
            END
```

Well, perhaps it is not all assembly language. This FORTRAN code subroutine converts the row and column numbers from whatever type of INTEGER they are to simple byte values. This is easier to do with the simple CHAR function already provided in FORTRAN than in the assembler code. Of course, the coordinate system for the ESCape codes begins at (1, 1) in the top left-hand corner of the screen. For the BIOS code, this is (0, 0). Next we need the assembler routine CURPOS:

```
            PUBLIC   CURPOS
CURPOS      PROC     FAR
            PUSH     BP

            MOV      AH, 02H
            MOV      BP, SP
            MOV      DL, BP+6  ;  this loads DL - we don't
                              ;  want DH
            MOV      BL, BP+10 ;
            MOV      DH, BL    ;  put required byte in DH
            MOV      BH, 0     ;  display page 0
            INT      10H       ;  IBM ROM BIOS screen driver
            POP      BP
            RET      08H
CURPOS      ENDP
```

Perhaps the reason we prefer the VT52 ESCape sequence is its sheer simplicity. The next routine should demonstrate it.

```
            SUBROUTINE GOTOXY ( ICOL, IROW )
C------------------------------
C
C           Subroutine to use VT52 ESCapes to position cursor
C           on machines with a VT52 screen driver. Method 3
C           of  4. Sadly, this routine will fail for row or
C           column 5!
C
C----------------------------------------------------------------
            CHARACTER*4 STRING
C
C           STRING =
C            CHAR(27)//'Y'//CHAR(31+IROW)//CHAR(31+ICOL)
C
C                      Wouldn't it be nice if concatenation
C                      worked in ALL PC FORTRANs ?
C
            STRING(1:1) = CHAR(27)
            STRING(2:2) = 'Y'
            STRING(3:3) = CHAR(31+IROW)
            STRING(4:4) = CHAR(31+ICOL)
            CALL SHWTXT (STRING, 4)
C
            RETURN
            END
```

That would have been wonderful if the occurrence of row or column 5 did not give rise to ASCII 36 in the output string. The value of that ASCII code is '$', and that interferes with the DOS output string function. Accordingly, single-character output using the PUTCHR subroutine is required.

```
            SUBROUTINE GOTOXY ( ICOL, IROW )
C-----------------------------
C
C      Subroutine to use VT52 ESCapes to position cursor on
C      machines with a VT52 screen driver.  Method 4 of 4.
C
C--------------------------------------------------------------
C
          CALL PUTCHR(27)
          CALL PUTCHR(ICHAR('Y'))
          CALL PUTCHR(31+IROW)
          CALL PUTCHR(31+ICOL)
C
          RETURN
          END
```

12.10 READING FROM THE KEYBOARD

Basic procedures outlined above can be applied to the input of single keypresses. There is much more temptation to put these in a FUNCTION, so that, for example, code could be written as

```
CHARA = INKEY()
```

The temptation is even more difficult to resist when one realizes that the DOS call which returns the keypress value leaves its data in the AX register, which is where Microsoft FORTRAN expects to find the results of some types of FUNCTION. Remember, however, that this demands the definition of INKEY to be of CHARACTER TYPE in every subroutine in which it is invoked. The initial appeal wears off after a dozen or so compilation failures where you have forgotten to put it in! As always, a SUBROUTINE is to be preferred.

This is the subroutine:

```
          PUBLIC  GETCHR
GETCHR    PROC    FAR
          PUSH    BP
          MOV     AH, 08H
          INT     21H
          MOV     BP, SP
```

```
              LES      BX, BP+6
              XOR      AH, AH        ;this zeroes AH better than MOV
              MOV      ES:BX, AX
              POP      BP
              RET      04H
GETCHR        ENDP
```

Software interrupt 21H function 1 is an alternative, but it echoes the character read to the display. Ideally, look after the display separately. Function 6 offers generalized input or output: place an 0FFH byte in the DL register, and expect results to be returned in AL. The zero flag is cleared if input occurs (i.e. a character was waiting), or it is set if there was none. It is obviously better for polling whether input occurs or not. GETCHR waits for a keypress.

Some keypresses generate extended data. We will explore this as follows by reference to the IBM PC's keyboard. If the IBM PC BIOS software interrupt 16H is used (no, we do not recommend doing so, for reasons we will see later), then two bytes are returned in the AX register. The first of these, in the case of an 'ASCII' key, or a key on the normal QWERTY section of the keyboard, has the key number in AL, and a set of flags in AH. They show the state of CTRL, ALT, SHIFT, and so on. The BIOS function can be invoked in several ways, corresponding to the function we have used, which waits for a keypress, or polling the state of the keyboard to see if a key is pressed.

Should one of the 'non-ASCII' keys be pressed, such as a function key, or a key on the numeric keypad, then the function returns a NUL in AL, and the key number in AH. The status of SHIFT, ALT, and CTRL, etc. is also available for the really determined keyboard interrogator.

The key numbers relate fairly logically to the position of the keys on the keyboard of the original IBM PC, but may seem randomly distributed on later keyboards, such as the enhanced, AT style, keyboard now in popular use.

Calling the DOS function causes the transfer of the characters to ASCII codes as follows. If CTRL is pressed with an ASCII key such as 'A', then CTRL-A, ASCII 01, is returned. If SHIFT is pressed, then upper case letters or the upper symbol on the key top is returned. Non-ASCII keys send a 2-byte sequence via DOS. This packet is made up of the byte NUL, followed by the key number as an ASCII code.

It is simpler to accept a stream of bytes than to decipher which bits are set in a flag byte. Certainly, to detect CTRL and SHIFT combined with another key, the deciphering is done for us (although the method we use cannot detect CTRL–ALT–etc. combinations). If a cursor or function key occurs as we read in the characters, it is signalled by the occurrence of a NUL byte. We throw that one away, and look at the next byte which is extracted from the keyboard buffer with GETCHR. That tells us which key actually was pressed.

The method we use has further merits. DOS computers incompatible with the IBM PC (notably the Victor/Sirius 9000 and the Apricot family) do not respond to IBM PC BIOS software interrupt 16H, although they respond perfectly to the DOS equivalent. Normally, single bytes are returned from function keys, and these correspond to ASCII codes greater than 127. Cursor keys on those machines normally return an extended sequence to DOS, starting with the ESC (ASCII 27). The method we use works fine for those. In other words, for maximum portability, even at a slight cost in speed, use the DOS function. It is quite easy on Sirius and Apricot machines to configure any key to generate a series of bytes. Again, using GETCHR, they can be read one-by-one.

One disappointing feature of the original IBM PC keyboard is that the DEL key generates an extended sequence and not ASCII 7 (CTRL-G) or 127 which are used on other computers for deletion under the cursor. Some ostensibly IBM PC-compatible DOS computers, such as the Amstrad PC 1512/1640, permit this key to be reassigned to CTRL-G, and the assignment to be remembered in battery-backed RAM. You may therefore need to examine all three combinations to decide if a deletion operation has been requested.

Given the difficulties in deciding what a keypress will do, use this program to show what ASCII values are returned.

```
        PROGRAM KEYCODE
C---------------------------
        INTEGER*2 N
        CALL CLS
        WRITE(*,*) 'Press your desired key.. (CTRL-C)'
     1             'finishes)...'
10      CONTINUE
        CALL GETCHR (N)
        WRITE(*,*) 'Key code is ',N,''
        GO TO 10
        END
```

Inspection of the FORTRAN code in the MENU subroutine will reveal a subset of the extended codes. The subject of extended codes is Summarized in more detail in Table 12.3.

Note that the Apricot's sequences are identical to the ESCape sequences which, sent to the screen, would move the cursor as required—the IBM's need to be interpreted. Apricot and Sirius keyboards are so readily configurable that further information is likely to be incorrect. Use the KEYCODE program to determine what the assignments are.

Extended codes are also generated on the IBM PC keyboard for the following:

- ALT + an ASCII key
- Function keys, in their base case, or with SHIFT, CTRL, or ALT
- Certain CTRL + a non-ASCII key combinations
- PgUp, PgDn, Home, End, PrtSc, Ins

Use the KEYCODE program to determine these for yourself.

Table 12.3 Some extended key codes

Key	IBM PC	Apricot Sirius	
Up	00 72	27	65
Down	00 80	27	66
Left	00 75	27	68
Right	00 77	27	67
Delete	00 83		127

Decimal codes are used. In hexadecimal, 27 is 1BH, 65 is 41H, and 80 is 50H.

DOS also has an input string function (number 10). We recommend handling the keypresses one by one, and not using this function.

The idea was earlier introduced of clearing the input buffer before reading a keypress. This could prevent a type-ahead from confirming a potentially disastrous operation. DOS function number 12 (0CH) does both the clearing and character reading. A subroutine to do this would be

```
            PUBLIC   CLRCHR
CLRCHR      PROC     FAR
            PUSH     BP
            MOV      AH, 0CH
            MOV      AL, 08H   ;this means we want to input with
                              ;function 08 when the time comes
            INT      21H
            MOV      BP, SP
            LES      BX, BP+6
            XOR      AH, AH
            MOV      ES:BX, AX
            POP      BP
            RET      04H
CLRCHR      ENDP
```

In addition to the 'low numbered' DOS system functions used here, it is possible to use the input and output functions 63 and 64 (3FH and 40H) for I/O to devices which have been opened with handles.

12.11 GENERAL INPUT SCREEN DESIGN

The features that are required from an interactive, text based, system are of two types. Firstly, the program may offer choices, and the appropriate selections will control the flow of the program logic. Secondly, the program will require numeric or textual data.

It is often found desirable to separate the two operations, although many older FORTRAN programs make program choices based on numeric input data values.

Mainframe systems used in banking, airline booking, and so on have displays laid out as forms. Input is placed in particular areas in these forms. The systems are designed to be easy to use, and to aid in getting correct and complete data at the point of collection. This sort of display is known as an input screen.

PCs have introduced the techniques to a wider audience. Input screens are the rule, rather than the exception. They can be programmed in FORTRAN.

Input screens which enable the user to make choices are often implemented as menus. In Section 12.12, details of the programming of a menu screen are given. The other type of input screen, which is designed to simplify the input of numbers and text, consists of a whole series of elements. The programming of these elements is complicated, and an example is explained in the remaining sections of the chapter.

Some of the features found in input screens are as follows:

- A title
- An area for status information; this includes the setting of the INSERT/OVERTYPE toggle
- An area for help information; this might include the assignments for the function keys
- The input fields, with plenty of room for labelling information
- Borders around the whole screen, and/or to subdivide the area logically according to function

The programmer may find it helpful to reserve certain lines on the screen for the different categories of information to be displayed. Help information may not be required in certain situations.

You should examine commercial (probably not FORTRAN) programs. See how the user interface is structured. Whatever effect has been used, you can do it too.

When you use large areas of inverse video, the cursor can get lost, particularly if it is the first or last character in a data field. If you have hardware which supports a blinking cursor (and more importantly, have hardware which permits you to turn off the blinking), then it is a useful effect to create an invitation to input data. Alternatively, highlight the current data entry area block in a screen mode that draws attention. Colour is good for this.

12.12 MENUS

Many programs have multiple choices at one or more stages in their execution. In a batch mode of operation, the data file will contain a series of flags to select the operations required. These are often simple numerics (e.g. 1 for 'yes' or 'on', 0 for 'no' or 'off'), but may be more complicated, including pseudo binary switches (e.g. 10 for option 1, 01 for option 2, and 11 for both). Character data is much less common—perhaps because apostrophes are needed if list-directed I/O is involved, and perhaps because more complex tests are required. For example, the same might be implied by:

```
<space> X, <space> x,  X <space>, or x <space>
```

It is desirable to offer choice menus in many PC applications. In the following section, a number of methods of dealing with menus will be given. However, it is worth noting that the more sophisticated the facility, the more machine specific it is likely to be.

A simple way of showing the menu options is to display the available choices in such a way that it is 'obvious' what key selects what option. For example, the following lines could be displayed:

```
Program XXYYZZ      E)xecute, P)rogram, Q)uit, Z)ap, N)ew file
-------------------------------------------------------------------
Input option>
```

Once it is understood that only the initial letter needs to be typed to select a menu item, the rest of the word acts as an *aide-memoire*. In case the little one- or two-word explanations are not enough, more information can be summoned by typing, for example, the ? key. The principle advantage of this mode of presenting a menu is that it is almost completely machine independent, using no ESCape sequences at all (except maybe 'clear screen', although that is not absolutely necessary, as screen contents can be scrolled off the screen by a series of line-feeds). It is also extremely compact, and is ideally suited to menus which control minor choices in program flow. Menus which cause major changes in program flow are better given more prominence.

It is desirable to intercept single keystrokes with the assembly language GETCHR function rather than with a FORTRAN formatted read from the keyboard which uses A1 format. The reason for this is that the formatted read needs a RETURN keypress as well as the choice letter. Much PC software written other than in FORTRAN does not need the last keypress, and the shorter form is desirable for consistency (and for an appearance of somewhat greater polish!)

Another approach is shown by the following subroutine, and accompanying calling program fragments, which details a step-through menu. In this, a series of mnemonics may be shown at arbitrary screen coordinates. The first is highlighted in 'emboldened' or 'reverse video' display mode. By pressing cursor keys, the user can step through the menu item by item. The highlighting is transferred from item to item during this process. Finally, pressing the RETURN key selects the currently highlighted operation.

In implementing the menu subroutine, it is desirable that the menus are 'circular', i.e. dropping out of the bottom of a list transfers control to the top, and vice versa. It is also desirable, or so experience shows, to keep the mnemonics short, if necessary supplementing them with a line of text in normal display mode, explaining each choice.

In principle, the system is simple. The menu subroutine is passed a series of start coordinates, mnemonics, and the mnemonic length. The individual mnemonics are displayed at the given coordinates, and the first is rewritten in reverse video. Keystrokes are intercepted, and filtered for cursor up or down keys. As each is found, the following or preceding option is selected and highlighted, and the just-abandoned option is rewritten in normal mode.

It is desirable to hide the cursor, or else it makes the currently highlighted menu item appear that extra character longer. On some hardware, the cursor may be hidden or revealed with ESCape sequences. An alternative ruse is to send it to a part of the screen currently blocked out in inverse video each time it is not required. This may mean a little extra effort in coding. Some hardware permits the hiding of a cursor by sending it to coordinates which lie off the screen.

Some additional refinements, not all of which are implemented in the illustrated code, are to permit movement with a '+', '−', or spacebar key, or to allow selection of menu items by pressing the key corresponding to the first letter of their mnemonic.

Here is a little program to call the menu routine:

```
      PROGRAM TSTMEN
C-----------------------
C
C        Program exists to demonstrate the MENU selection
C        routine.
C
C-------------------------------------------------------------
      CHARACTER*7 MNEMON(4)
      DIMENSION IX(4), IY(4)
      DATA MNEMON /' Eddie ',' Tim ',' Wiley ', 'FORTRAN' /
      DATA IX, IY / 32, 32, 32, 32, 5, 10, 15, 20 /
C
C                     Invoke the menu
C
      LENGTH = 28
      CALL MENU (4, MNEMON, 7, IX, IY, IOPT)
C
C                     Return the choice
C
      CALL CLS
      WRITE(*,*) 'Selected option number:', IOPT
```

```
        WRITE (*,*) 'Option:   ',MNEMON(IOPT)
        STOP
        END

        SUBROUTINE MENU (NVALS, MNEMON, LENGTH, IX, IY, IOPT)
C---------------------
C
C       To display a menu, select an option.
C
C-------------------------------------------------------------
        INTEGER IX (NVALS),  IY (NVALS)
        CHARACTER*(*) MNEMON (NVALS)
C
C         display the mnemonics: switch cursor off later...
C
        DO 10 I=1,NVALS
        CALL GOTOXY (IX(I), IY(I))
        CALL SHWTXT (MNEMON(I), LENGTH)
  10    CONTINUE
C
C         highlight the first menu option 'retrospectively'
C
        IPOS = 1
  20    CONTINUE
        CALL GOTOXY (IX(IPOS), IY(IPOS))
        CALL REVID
        CALL SHWTXT (MNEMON(IPOS), LENGTH)
        CALL CURSOF
C
C                 test for RETURN key
C
  30    CONTINUE
        CALL GETCHR (N)
C
C                 terminating event; switch cursor back on...
C
        IF (N .EQ. 13) THEN
            IOPT = IPOS
            CALL NORMAL
            CALL CLS
            CALL CURSON
            RETURN
C
C                 up the menu...
C
```

```
           ELSE IF (CHAR(N) .EQ. '-') THEN
                CALL NORMAL
                CALL CURSON
                CALL GOTOXY (IX(IPOS), IY(IPOS))
                CALL SHWTXT (MNEMON(IPOS), LENGTH)
                CALL CURSOF
                    IPOS = IPOS - 1
                    IF (IPOS .EQ. 0) IPOS = NVALS
                GO TO 20
C
C                       down the menu...
C
           ELSE IF (CHAR(N) .EQ. '+' .OR. CHAR(N) .EQ. ' ') THEN
                CALL NORMAL
                CALL CURSON
                CALL GOTOXY (IX(IPOS), IY(IPOS))
                CALL SHWTXT (MNEMON(IPOS), LENGTH)
                CALL CURSOF
                    IPOS = IPOS + 1
                    IF (IPOS .GT. NVALS) IPOS = 1
           GO TO 20
C
C          IBM cursor key... throw away leading zero...
C
           ELSE IF (N .EQ. 0) THEN
                CALL GETCHR (N)
                CALL NORMAL
                CALL CURSON
                CALL GOTOXY (IX(IPOS), IY(IPOS))
                CALL SHWTXT (MNEMON(IPOS), LENGTH)
                CALL CURSOF
C
C                       decide if up or down...
C
           IF (N .EQ. 72 .OR. N .EQ. 75) THEN
                IPOS = IPOS - 1
                IF (IPOS .EQ. 0) IPOS = NVALS
           ELSE IF (N .EQ. 77 .OR. N .EQ. 80) THEN
                IPOS = IPOS + 1
                IF (IPOS .GT. NVALS) IPOS = 1
           ENDIF
           GO TO 20
C
C          Apricot/Sirius cursor key... throw away leading ESC...
C
```

```
      ELSE IF (N .EQ. 27) THEN
          CALL GETCHR (N)
          CALL NORMAL
          CALL CURSON
          CALL GOTOXY (IX(IPOS), IY(IPOS))
          CALL SHWTXT (MNEMON(IPOS), LENGTH)
          CALL CURSOF
C
C                   decide if up or down...
C
      IF (N .EQ. 65 .OR. N .EQ. 68) THEN
          IPOS = IPOS - 1
          IF (IPOS .EQ. 0) IPOS = NVALS
          ELSE IF (N .EQ. 66 .OR. N .EQ. 67) THEN
          IPOS = IPOS + 1
          IF (IPOS .GT. NVALS) IPOS = 1
      ENDIF
      GO TO 20
C
      ELSE
C     defensive programming would put an error handler here
      ENDIF
      GO TO 30
      END
```

We have pretended that routines CURSON and CURSOF exist for switching the cursor on and off. The reader is given the task of preparing these. The routines REVID and NORMAL for setting reverse video and returning to normal are ESCape sequence generators.

12.13 LOGICAL SEQUENCE OF DATA ENTRY SCREENS

Once the building blocks have been obtained, it is possible to create data entry screens and menus of any level of complexity. There are some guidelines in the design of these systems. Firstly, consider a menu driven system, with a tree structure of further menus. Ideally, each individual menu should be structured so that the most often traversed path through this tree should only require pressing the RETURN key as each menu is displayed (i.e. the most likely choice should come first, cf. Lotus 1-2-3). Destructive options, for instance file deletion commands, need to be relatively inaccessible. This is done by positioning them at the centre of the menu, or just below. (The extreme bottom of a 'circular' list is easily accessible by pressing the 'cursor up' key, but the mental gymnastics required for this make the bottom of the menu less accessible in practice than the top of the menu, despite only requiring the same number of keystrokes.)

It is better not to remove an option from a menu when it is no longer selectable, but rather to indicate its status by colour or screen intensity.

Next, remember that sometimes it is necessary to move backwards through the menus. This situation arises when the user remembers an operation which should have been undertaken earlier.

Finally, consider the experienced user who may find all this scrolling through menus wearisome in the extreme. It is worth providing him with some 'hot-key' combinations, at least for the commonest operations, so that he can progress at maximum speed.

12.14 'DROP DOWN' OR 'POP UP' MENUS

Sometimes it is desirable to make certain program options display 'help'. If you erase the current screen contents completely, novice users in particular may be distressed to see their work vanish, however momentarily, when a help screen is summoned. It is often better to make the help information drop down or pop up over part of the screen. Menus of choices can similarly be made to appear on only part of the screen.

Programming the effect may necessitate storing the contents of the affected part of the screen, and rewriting after the menu or whatever has been deleted. In most cases, however, it will be found simplest to rewrite the whole screen, since each different screen type will be generated by a separate subroutine call. Systems like Windows and GEM save a bitmap of the affected area of the screen, and on closing a menu or dialog box, only that area is restored. If that degree of sophistication is required, and some portability, it is better to latch into one of the proprietary graphics interface systems such as the two mentioned.

Text systems can operate at two levels. Firstly, by using ESCape sequences or BIOS calls, it is possible to set the display area to be a window on the whole screen. Subsequent operations affect only that window until full screen modes are restored. Even with direct cursor addressing, this is the best thing to do, since it both freezes the rest of the display, and prevents it from being overwritten.

Certain keypresses would be used to cause the program to display such information. Software using this facility normally assigns the function to a combination of keys which are unlikely to be pressed together by accident.

12.15 SELECTION OF KEYPRESSES TO INITIATE PRO-GRAM OPTIONS

Any designed input screen will consist of a set of elements. In the remainder of the chapter the principles behind one element of such a designed input screen are presented. That element is a box into which a single integer data item can be input, with a data editing facility. In the code, use is again made of the assembly language character input and string output routines already developed.

It may be desired that data can be input into the various data entry areas in an arbitrary fashion. Hence, interspersed with data, there may be controlling keypresses to switch from one data entry area to another. Additionally, certain functions may be selected at any time during program operation. Switching between insertion and overtyping modes is an example of this.

We believe that the programmer should be aware of the conventions used by other software when selecting his/her own control function keys. There are some quite involved issues here, and they are dealt with in the following sections.

The subroutine presented below as an example of a data input element is the minimum required to do the job, which is to demonstrate the principles. Enhancements to the code are almost certain to be required for production programs. We recommend that such routines are set up to permit several types of keypress to be made. For example, moving around a data entry box or screen. Use cursor keys by all means. They are logical. But also allow CTRL-and-a-key options, as in WordStar, or some other favoured program.

There are at least two desirable spin-offs from this. Firstly, your users (and the most important one being you) will find that similar keypresses perform similar functions in all the software use. That decreases mistakes and shortens the learning process. Secondly, the software will be more robust, and probably more portable. Having alternatives makes it much more likely that your program can still run on a machine with a slightly defective key (board), or after a program that reassigned a key, and didn't give it back on completion. It also makes it likely that your program will run on a machine with a physically different keyboard—one which has a different number of function keys, for instance.

12.16 GENERALIZED INPUT DATA AND EDITING

In any element of a data entry screen (implemented as one or more SUBROUTINEs) it is sensible to combine the 'input of a new data item' routine with one to 'edit an existing data item', if only to economize on coding. However, matters are simplified if a suite of routines are written, one to input each data type, merely to prevent an overcomplication arising in the routines. We will use the INTEGER data type as an example here, but in the disk set that accompanies the book will be found a family of routines for the input of a variety of data types.

Imagine a section of the screen blocked out in reverse video, and containing a data item which we might wish to alter. This data item might be a character string, an integer value, or a real value. (A FORTRAN LOGICAL would appear similar to any other character string, and a COMPLEX, merely two REALs.)

We present a subroutine GETINT in skeletal form, which may be used to read an INTEGER from a data field on the screen. The subroutine reads the INTEGER, one character at a time, checking for errors. It also allows the user to edit characters in the field being input.

The subroutine statement includes five parameters. The first two of these are the screen location coordinates at which the input field commences, the third is the integer numeric variable through which the initial value is passed to the subroutine, and through which the result is passed back to the caller. The fourth parameter gives the field width within which editing is permitted, and the final LOGICAL variable affects the interpretation of all blanks. This is not the same as BN and BZ in a FORMAT, but is a way of setting the initial contents of the field to blanks, rather than zero (remember, we are going to use the same function to create *and* edit data), and to permit the user to return all blanks, which the program will interpret in turn as zero.

In the executable part of the program, no attempt to initialize the screen (e.g. by clearing it) needs to be made, as it is to be expected that this subroutine forms part of an overall data entry screen. The first action of the routine is to jump to the data entry field start coordinates, and set reversed video characteristics. We will keep the data entry field in reversed video, and expect the rest of the screen to be in normal mode, although a normal block within an entirely reversed video screen is equally as clear cut. Where video monitors permit, a combination of colours, or emboldened display, may be effective. The choice depends on design decisions taken for the program as a whole, and which have an impact on the appearance and style of the program's user interface. The next step is to initialize a character string as a workspace.

The length of the character string exceeds that of the data field within which 'digits' are to be entered. The reason for this is that during editing, one might insert a certain number of characters, leading to the remaining characters being pushed 'out of the box'. Then, if other characters are deleted, it would be preferable if those excess characters 'reappeared' in the box. This would not occur if the workspace was too short. Another character string is used for the storage of a temporary format, so that, on completion of the first few statements, the integer number has been displayed in the appropriate field on the screen, and the cursor appears at the first character position. Left justifying is a feature that users always appreciate.

At this point the subroutine needs to repeatedly read in keypresses and interpret them, exiting an infinite loop only when a terminating key is pressed. The computer actually stores the keypresses in a buffer, and the assembler subroutine fetches them (using a service provided by DOS) one at a time. It would be rather better to leave the screen updating until the buffer had been emptied, merely to speed the response, but for simplicity, the screen will be updated after each keypress. Some 'keypresses' place more than one character into the input buffer. Such 'string keys' normally generate a flag code (ASCII 0 or 27), followed by an operation code. Typical examples of this are the cursor keys, which generate the codes listed in Table 12.3.

Tests need to be made for the following operations:

- Toggle the 'insert' and 'overtype' modes (toggling means changing from whatever is set to the other option)
- Perform a deletion operation
- Perform a cursor movement operation
- Exit the process of editing or insertion (i.e. perform a 'terminating event')
- Input a character which is invalid in the context of the data item

It is only when these operations have been discounted that one can assume that all that remains is:

- Input a character which is part of the data

Dealing with some of these operations is simple, and with some of them difficult. Take the first, to 'toggle' the insert/overtype mode of input. What key(s) will we use to indicate this? Will it be a function key, or a combination of a special key (ALT, CONTROL, SHIFT) and a letter? Function key assignments are appealing, after all, this is what the function keys are provided for. There are, however, two pressing arguments in favour of a combination of special key and normal letter. The first of these is that the implementation of function key codes can vary slightly between machines. The second is that certain keypress combinations have come to represent particular operations as a result of being used in 'industry standard' software.

As an example of the latter, the combination of CONTROL and V (or v) has been used in WordStar and many other pieces of software for just such a purpose. This probably reflects early keyboards which were not amply supplied with function keys. Even if a function key is associated with a particular action, it is worth making the CONTROL-and-a-letter combinations from WordStar or other leading packages an easy alternative. In the following subroutine, the insert/overtype toggle will be associated with CONTROL-V.

One final matter is to decide whether or not to display the current status of the insert or overtype toggle somewhere on the screen. It is worth examining some word-processing packages to see how they tackle this: most have a nearly inconspicuous flag somewhere—after a while the user only sees this when he looks specially.

The subject of deletion is a somewhat more complex operation. Again, we will take the WordStar model. This permits deletion in front of, or behind, the cursor (actually, 'in front of' means 'under'), or delete a string of characters from the cursor to the next following blank, or to the end of the line. These would all be useful operations in the context of editing our data field, although, except in the context of editing a string of character data, the last two of the deletion operations are effectively the same. WordStar has CONTROL-and-a-key combinations for these, although a number of machine specific implementations have forward and backward delete keys, and can be made to do the longer deletions by the use of SHIFTed DELete keys.

To understand the program code for deletions, it is probably important to consider cursor movement as well. The subroutine must keep a record of the current cursor position in the data field. On entry to the editing operation, it is best to position the cursor at the start of the field, and expect some movement. Should this be via WordStar-like key combinations, or is this an opportunity to use the cursor keys? When we intercept a cursor keypress, the first byte signals extended data and must be 'thrown away', and the second key examined to determine the cursor movement direction. That keycode cannot be carried forward, since it may be a 'valid' ASCII code for something else. We would be advised to change it to the WordStar CTRL combination, which means that the demonstration code services WordStar-compatible cursor movements by default.

A second difficulty is that the cursor keys offer a selection of 'terminating events', each of which conveys some directional information. One cannot view a data entry screen as consisting of a single box or data input field. Keeping the cursor arrows free for use as terminating events means that the user can select not only the end of editing for the particular data item in hand, but can indicate his desires as to which data item elsewhere on the screen he would like to modify. In the example code, we will not reach such heights of sophistication: many FORTRAN programs have a fairly sequential type of input, and the code fragments exist to demonstrate techniques. Dealing with the multi- character, or string, keys is one of these. The RETURN key is a good, general purpose, 'terminating event' key.

By the time it has been decided that a keypress is not a control function, then it must be a data character, or invalid. If an invalid character is received, it must be discarded as quickly as possible. This is a good reason for having separate subroutines to treat each data type, as they each have a different range of valid characters. An integer input field, for instance, can only accept the digits from 0 to 9, and the signs + and -. Real numbers might also include the decimal point, the letters E or e (and possibly D and d), and a second sign. Character data, on the other hand, may validly be any character, printable or otherwise.

Not only does numeric data have a restricted range of valid symbols, but their sequence is restricted too. For instance, a sign must be the first non-blank character in an integer field, and cannot appear elsewhere. In a real number, there may be two signs: the first appearing as in the integer, the second following an E or D, may not be followed by a second decimal point. And so on. In the subroutine GETINT, a sign key may be pressed at any time. If it is '+', it cancels any negative sign, and if '−', puts a negative sign into the first character string in the data entry box. A negative sign can be removed by typing '+', or by deleting or overtyping the character '−'.

It is trivial to test whether or not the keypress is a valid symbol overall, but more difficult to immediately see whether or not it fits in context. This may need a number of flags to be held in memory, and continually updated, or for the data to be repeatedly tested.

Let us first examine what happens if a valid character (both in type and context) is presented to the program. If the 'overtype' mode is in force, the character replaces the one at the current cursor position, the string is redisplayed, and the cursor position updated both in memory and on the screen. With 'overtype' off , and 'insert' mode selected, a substring from the cursor position to one character short of the end of the buffer is shifted one character forward, and the new character inserted into the 'vacated' place, before the various updates are attempted.

Suppose now that the keypress is obviously invalid, for example a letter key is pressed in an integer data entry field. The best option is to merely ignore the keypress. The user with poor keyboard skills will become rapidly annoyed if each transgression of this sort causes a bell or buzzer to sound: audible warnings should be restricted to serious errors only, and ideally be subject to user control. The problem is what to do about a valid symbol improperly placed in the field. Complete context checking could be time consuming, and will prevent the user from producing an invalid intermediate step while editing. It is probably simplest, and most convenient all round, to build the data field following the whole sequence of keystrokes, exercising discretion only when the 'terminating event' keypress is made. At this point, a data error is quite easy to detect and trap in the conversion of the character string from the input buffer to a numeric data item using the internal files facility of FORTRAN with the ERR= parameter. A data error at this point is worth giving an audible warning, because the user may be typing ahead and be out of synchronization with the editing process. Strictly speaking, the keyboard buffer should be cleared at this point for safety.

A FORTRAN subroutine containing code relating to all of the above points is shown below. A program to call the routine is as follows:

```
        PROGRAM TSTINT
C---------------------------
C
C       Calling procedure to examine how GETINT works.
C
C-------------------------------------------------------------
        LOGICAL NULL
        CALL CLS
C
C                       set a screen location for the start
C
        IX = 20
        IY = 15
C
C                       initialize a value for editing
C
        IVALUE = 10
        LENGTH = 5
        NULL    = .FALSE.
C
C                       call the subroutine to permit IVALUE to
C                       be modified
C
```

```
        CALL GETINT (IX, IY, IVALUE, LENGTH, NULL)
        CALL CLS
C
C                        return the edited value
C
        WRITE(*,*) ' The number was ',IVALUE
        STOP
        END
```

```
        SUBROUTINE GETINT (IX, IY, IVALUE, LENGTH, NULL)
C---------------------------------------------------------------
C
C       Input an integer number into a field of length LENGTH
C       and return the numeric value in IVALUE, or edit a
C       value passed via IVALUE. The input field starts at
C       column IX and row IY.
C
C---------------------------------------------------------------
        CHARACTER*20 WORKSP, TFORM, TEMP, BLANK
        LOGICAL      INSERT, NULL, SIGNED
        DATA         BLANK/'                    '/
C
C                        Set all the initial flags
C
        IF (IVALUE .LT. 0) THEN
            SIGNED =.TRUE.
            ELSE
            SIGNED = .FALSE.
            ENDIF
        INSERT = .TRUE.
        IPOS   = 1
C
C                        This step emplaces the INTEGER value
C                        as a string for editing
C
        IF (.NOT. NULL) THEN
            WRITE (TFORM,100) LENGTH, 20-LENGTH
100         FORMAT('(I',I2,',',I2,'X)')
            WRITE (WORKSP,TFORM) IVALUE
C
C                        now left justify in the available
C                        field
C
            DO 10 I = 1,20
            IF (WORKSP(I:I) .NE. ' ') GO TO 20
```

```fortran
10              CONTINUE
                I = 21
20              IF (I. LT. 21) THEN
                        J = 21-I
                        TEMP(1:J)    = WORKSP(I:20)
                        WORKSP       = BLANK
                        WORKSP(1:J) = TEMP(1:J)
                        ENDIF
        ELSE
                WORKSP = BLANK
        ENDIF
C
C                       display the workspace
C

        CALL GOTOXY (IX, IY)
        CALL REVID
        CALL SHWTXT (WORKSP, LENGTH)
        CALL GOTOXY (IX, IY)
C
C       now we will poll the keyboard for keypresses...
C       VALID choice keys are:
C               INSERT      CTRL-V    toggles INSERT/OVERTYPE
C               DEL         <127>     deletes at cursor CTRL-G
C                                     too
C               BS          <8>       deletes behind cursor
C               CR          <13>      terminates
C               Any INTEGER           added to data field
C               CTRL-T                blank data field R of
C                                     cursor
C               CTRL-Y                blank whole data field
C               Cursor key or CTRL-S/CTRL-D
C
30      CALL GETCHR (N)
                IF (WORKSP(1:1) .NE. '-') SIGNED=.FALSE.
C
C                make all the special key reassignments
C
        IF (N .EQ. 0) THEN
                CALL GETCHR(N)
                IF (N .EQ. 83) N = 7
                IF (N .EQ. 72  .OR.  N .EQ. 75) N = 19
                IF (N .EQ. 77  .OR.  N .EQ. 80) N = 4
                ENDIF
C
```

```
C                    these function key assignments are
C                    for Apricot/Sirius
C
      IF (N .EQ. 27) THEN
          CALL GETCHR(N)
          IF (N .EQ. 65  .OR.  N .EQ. 68) N = 19
          IF (N .EQ. 66  .OR.  N .EQ. 67) N = 4
          ENDIF
C
C                    CTRL-V returns key code 22
C                    toggle INSERT/OVERTYPE
C
      IF (N .EQ. 22) THEN
          INSERT = .NOT. INSERT
C
C                       operations to cover sign of field
C
      ELSE IF (CHAR(N) .EQ. '+') THEN
          IF (SIGNED .AND. WORKSP(1:1) .EQ. '-') THEN
              SIGNED = .FALSE.
              TEMP(1:19)   = WORKSP(2:20)
              TEMP(20:20)  = ' '
              WORKSP       = TEMP
              IPOS = IPOS - 1
              ENDIF
C
      ELSE IF (CHAR(N) .EQ. '-') THEN
          IF (.NOT. SIGNED) THEN
              SIGNED = .TRUE.
              TEMP(2:20)   = WORKSP(1:19)
              TEMP(1:1)    = '-'
              WORKSP       = TEMP
              IPOS = IPOS + 1
              ENDIF
C
C                    DELETE key returns keycode 127, or CTRL-G
C                    perform deletion at the cursor...
C
      ELSE IF (N .EQ. 127  .OR.  N .EQ. 7) THEN
              TEMP     = WORKSP
              TEMP(IPOS:19)   = WORKSP(IPOS+1:20)
              TEMP(20:20)     = ' '
              WORKSP   = TEMP
C
C                    BS key returns keycode 8, del BEHIND
```

```
C                      cursor
C
          ELSE IF (N .EQ. 8) THEN
                    IF (IPOS .GT. 1) THEN
                    TEMP     = WORKSP
                    IPOS     = IPOS - 1
                    TEMP(IPOS:19)    = WORKSP(IPOS+1:20)
                    TEMP(20:20)      = ' '
                    WORKSP = TEMP
                    ENDIF
C
C                    delete all to the right of cursor with
C                    CTRL-T
C
          ELSE IF (N .EQ. 20) THEN
                    TEMP     = BLANK
                    TEMP(1:IPOS)     = WORKSP(1:IPOS)
                    WORKSP = TEMP
C
C                    Delete all the data field with CTRL-Y
C
          ELSE IF (N .EQ. 25) THEN
                    WORKSP = BLANK
C
C                    terminating event
C                    now test to see if we have a valid
C                    INTEGER in WORKSP
C                    - it is desirable not to cancel the
C                    'invisible' part of WORKSP if we don't
C                    have to, hence the use of TEMP
C
          ELSE IF (N .EQ. 13) THEN
                    TEMP = BLANK
                    TEMP(1:LENGTH) = WORKSP(1:LENGTH)
                    IF (TEMP .EQ. BLANK) THEN
                         IVALUE = 0
                         ELSE
                         READ (TEMP, 200, ERR=40) IVALUE
                         ENDIF
 200      FORMAT(BN,I20)
                    CALL NORMAL
                    RETURN
  40      CALL BEEP
          GO TO 30
```

```
C
C                       here we service WordStar style
C                       CTRL-key cursor movements, substituted
C                       for cursor keys above
C
      ELSE IF (N .EQ. 19) THEN
                IPOS = MAX0 (1, IPOS-1)
      ELSE IF (N .EQ. 4) THEN
                IPOS = MIN0 (LENGTH, IPOS+1)
C
C                       invalid key:  many users hate to be
C                       beeped at!
C
      ELSE IF (N .LT. 48  .OR. N .GT. 57) THEN
                CALL BEEP

      ELSE
C
C                       it must be a valid numeral!
C
      IF (INSERT) THEN
                TEMP      = WORKSP
                TEMP(IPOS+1:20)   = WORKSP(IPOS:19)
                WORKSP  = TEMP
      ENDIF
                WORKSP(IPOS:IPOS) = CHAR(N)
                IPOS    = MIN0 (LENGTH, IPOS + 1)

      ENDIF
C
C                       at the end of the loop, always redisplay
C                       if screen update is too slow, maintain
C                        a CHANGED? flag, and only rewrite if
C                       CHANGED? is .TRUE.
C
                CALL GOTOXY (IX, IY)
                CALL SHWTXT (WORKSP, LENGTH)
                IPOS = MIN0 (LENGTH, IPOS)
                IPOS = MAX0 (1, IPOS)
                CALL GOTOXY (IX+IPOS-1, IY)
      GO TO 30
C
C
      END
```

```
      SUBROUTINE BEEP
C----------------------------
C
C        sounds the bell or buzzer by sending ASCII 07
C
C--------------------------------------------------------------
      CHARACTER*2 BELL
      BELL(1:1) = CHAR(7)
      BELL(2:2) = '$'
      CALL SHWBYT (BELL)
      RETURN
      END
```

The valid range for an integer is dependent on its size in bytes. This can be catered for by having different GETINT routines, or by conversion afterwards. For simplicity, we suggest the latter.

Analogous GETTXT and GETFLO routines could be created. Examples appear in the accompanying utility disk set. We developed these from GETINT. The text editing subroutine GETTXT requires only a subset of the operations in GETINT, although to edit REAL numbers with GETFLO requires rather more.

Some observations regarding the extra operations might be a help if you want the exercise of coding it yourself. In GETINT, we can check if the leading minus sign has been set merely by looking at the first character in the display field immediately after each keyboard interrogation with GETCHR. The same sign control is needed, and implemented, in GETFLO, but an additional problem appears with the decimal point. That can occur anywhere, and so can be deleted by any deletion operation anywhere in the editing field. We have found it helpful to check any character overtyped or deleted to see if it is the decimal marker.

Next, we ducked out of accepting D and E formats. Typically, we expect that very large and very small numbers will be input with a GETFLO for the characteristic *and* a GETINT for the mantissa or exponent. That saves a lot of FORTRAN code!

CHAPTER 13

SCREEN HANDLING: GRAPHICS MODES

13.1 INTRODUCTION

One of the most exciting areas for the microcomputer programmer and user alike is the field of graphics. On the principle of 'a picture is worth a thousand words', graphics can be used to summarize many pages of numerical results in just a single illustration. Such a picture can be produced on a large variety of different devices, from printers (which produce the picture as a set of more-or-less closely spaced dots, or a 'raster image'), to plotters, which draw the picture as a series of vectors.

All hard-copy drawing devices have two main drawbacks: slowness, and there is a finite media cost per copy. The time taken to produce a hard copy might be a function of the native speed of the device, which in turn is usually (but by no means always) a function of cost. This is usually low compared to that of the program which is producing the graphic image, and is a combination of the speed with which the printer head or pen moves, and the data transmission link between computer and device. Media costs may turn out to be surprisingly high if several attempts are necessary to produce a finished illustration.

The amount of processor time expended to produce the patterns sent to the hard-copy device is an overhead which is lessened if that device possesses 'intelligence'. In this respect, most plotters are superior, since they can be instructed simply to perform a range of graphic operations, whereas for dot-matrix printers whole lines of the dot or bit image must be assembled. New generations of laser printers, capable of graphics, and provided with large amounts of processor capability *and* RAM, overcome this problem to a certain extent.

The screen of a DOS microcomputer is capable of displaying graphical images at many times the speed of the fastest hard-copy device compatible (in price, as well as behaviour) with a PC, and has an almost negligible media cost. It is thus ideally suited to the procedure of pre-viewing illustrations destined for copying onto a permanent medium, especially where the development of such illustrations is incremental. However, the screen resolution is usually poor in comparison to that of a hard copy device, and so the final 'fine tuning' may still require a number of copies.

The speed at which the screen can display graphical images enables the user to interact with the computer in a way impossible on all but the most powerful terminal access mainframe computer systems. Nowhere is this more evident than in the fields of computer-aided design and draughting, where microcomputer based systems are the standard, and in the so-called 'desktop' user interfaces which are the foundation of 'desktop publishing' systems. In principle, all that these systems do is to permit the computer user a real-time interaction with a graphical image on screen, and provide some form of high quality, permanent, record of the end result of that interaction.

The PC user has several choices of graphics package in the general CAD field (AUTOCAD, DESIGNCAD II, IN*A*VISION, etc.), but these provide no generic facilities for the FORTRAN programmer. We will not pursue them further, except to recommend that you see and use as many as possible so that you develop a feel for desirable features which you can include in your own user interfaces. In contrast, the main 'desktop' interfaces are specifically designed to encourage the programmer to design applications using their particular features. At the time of writing, there are two of these in common use: the GEM system (from Digital Research) and Windows (from Microsoft). We will start by examining the properties of the computer terminal screens used for display.

13.2 MONITOR CHARACTERISTICS

The monitor for a personal computer is characterized by two main features: the resolution, and the colour capability. An early standard, almost the minimum acceptable, is provided on the IBM PC with 640 dots across, and 200 dots down, the screen. In some display modes, the horizontal dot array may be as little as 320. Other screen dot patterns for PCs of various manufacture are given in Table 13.1.

At the time this book was conceived, IBM PC computers were likely to sport the 640*200 resolution screens only. By the time this chapter came to be written, it was commonplace to find Hercules graphics (720*350) for monochrome, or the enhanced graphics adapter, EGA (640*350), for colour. No doubt, over the next few years the still higher resolution displays designed for IBM's PS/2 range of DOS and OS/2 computers will become the standard.

The sharpness of a display is a function of the total number of dots, the size of each dot, and (subjectively) the overall monitor size. The latter factor makes small monitors appear sharper, although they are less good at long range. A larger number of dots, or pixels (picture cells, or elements), makes it possible to display finer images, and to be more precise when picking coordinates off the screen. However, in principle, a finer pixel array makes screen redrawing slower.

Colour increases the information content of the displayed image and can partly overcome the resolution problems which one finds: colour monitors are usually of lower resolution, although of significantly higher cost, than monochrome ones. High resolution colour monitors are particularly expensive at the time of writing, although costs have decreased significantly (as indeed they have for all computer equipment) and this trend is expected to continue.

Table 13.1 Typical screen resolutions of PC monitors

Resolution (H) × (V)	Machine
640*200	IBM PC monochrome, Colour Graphics Adapter CGA, Amstrad PC1512, Data General 1 LCD and Apricot Portable LCD, (monochrome on the LCD screens, usually with a wider than normal aspect ratio, colour on the IBM CGA system, colour or colour or monochrome on late model Apricot F series machines)
640*256	Apricot F series, (European market, earlier models)
640*350	IBM Enhanced Graphics EGA, Apricot PC and XEN colour board (16 colours); Amstrad PC1640 colour; many AT-compatible computers use this as the colour standard
640*400	Olivetti M24/AT & T EGC (monochrome or colour), Toshiba 3100 gas plasma display
640*480	IBM PS/2 VGA; this is becoming the new colour standard
720*348	Hercules card (720*350 in text mode) monochrome commonly, but some colour capability with later cards; many AT-compatible computers use this as the monochrome standard
800*400	Apricot PC, Xi, Xen, Victor Sirius 9000, Vicki (monochrome)

Most, if not all, DOS microcomputer colour monitors are able to set the colour of individual pixels (earlier and cruder monitors often set the colour for blocks of pixels, sometimes corresponding to 'character cells' on the screen). The total number of colours displayed may be as low as four—scarcely better than the two of a monochrome monitor, particularly if the choice is limited—to 16, 256, or ultimately to many more. The number of shades which can be discerned in a line drawing on a screen is relatively limited, although shading (area fill) and patterns can effectively utilize the colour range of the latest hardware. A concept known as 'dithering' gives the appearance of a larger colour choice. This is basically a regular pattern of alternating pixels where the interval between repeat patterns is small. In combination with a small pixel size, even a limited colour choice can be significantly extended.

Many monitors have an aspect ratio of 4 horizontal to 3 vertical, although a few, notably on machines intended primarily for an assault on text formatting and desktop publishing, have the proportions of an A4 (or A3) page. Liquid crystal display (LCD) screens tend to be much wider than deep: this reflects a 'square' aspect ratio for the pixels, and is often incorporated in the machine's overall geometric design.

All the PC monitors of which we have knowledge display graphics as a pattern of dots on screen. Each screen dot corresponds to a bit somewhere in memory: more bits are required to maintain a map of a coloured screen. This means that the area allocated to the screen RAM may be quite large. In principle, all that is necessary is to set or unset bits in this screen RAM to cause images to appear or disappear. However, there are major problems associated with this approach. Firstly, the organization of the screen RAM is optimized for a particular display hardware. It may be far from obvious (to the FORTRAN programmer) why a particular array of bytes maps to a certain set of screen pixels, and the corresponding algorithms to draw a simple graphics primitive such as a single vector may therefore be complicated to code, and in any case, require access to functions (analogous to BASIC's PEEK and POKE) which are not normally provided with FORTRAN compilers and their support. Secondly, such programming is totally hardware specific and non-portable.

Extremely high resolution graphics display units can actually display vectors, rather than patterns of dots. While there is nothing in principle to prevent the connection of such a device to a PC, this combination will prove rare in the extreme. Many such VDUs manufactured for instance by Tektronix, support a serial communications protocol, and may easily be connected to the RS232 port of a PC. Indeed, using the DOS command CTTY, the CON device may be diverted to the graphics terminal, and the PC run from there.

However, a sort of 'halfway house' occurs with some add-on graphics facilities. An example of this is the PLUTO graphics system. It comprises driver hardware and its own RAM and processor, which may be fitted on a card for insertion into an expansion slot, or supplied in an external expansion unit. Graphics instructions are sent to such a device using a command language, and interpreted into a high resolution, multicoloured screen image for display on a second, dedicated, graphics display monitor.

With the enormous variety of screen types, resolutions, and colour capabilities, it is evident that considerable programmer effort could be expended in merely keeping pace with developments, and supporting a limited range of drawing primitives on a vast range of hardware. This effort has already been made by some software houses, and it seems a futile exercise to duplicate their work.

13.3 SCREEN DUMPS

Given that the screen image is a pattern of dots, and so is the final output of a dot matrix printer, one might ask 'Is it possible to copy the dot pattern from the former to the latter?' This is indeed possible, although with varying degrees of difficulty. On IBM PC compatibles, the operating system utilities feature a terminate and stay resident program named GRAPHICS. When this program is installed, pressing the PrtScrn key causes the bit pattern from a currently displayed graphics screen to be sent to the printer in the printers bit image graphics mode. This expects that the printer will be an Epson, or IBM personal computer printer (an Epson). (It is possible to obtain revised versions of the GRAPHICS program configured for different printers from the various public domain software groups.) The image printed is an exact copy of the pattern on the screen, and so must be expected to be relatively crude—it may only comprise 640 dots across the page, and 200 down it, for instance.

MS DOS computers incompatible with the IBM normally do not offer such a facility, although the production of screen dump programs for these is an oft-repeated game, and screen dump programs of relative degrees of sophistication and price may be obtained via user's groups or in the commercial software market.

Three main problems arise from screen dumps. Firstly, the lack of resolution may be compounded by printing in a small area or by spacing the dots out. This either gives tiny diagrams, or faint ones. Secondly, screen dumps under-use the graphics capability of the printer, even the cheapest model of which might easily achieve dot densities of in excess of 1000*1000 on a standard sheet of paper. Finally, unless printer, and computer hardware and software are perfectly matched, the 3*4 aspect ratio is lost. This may be fine for graphs and charts, but is undesirable for representational material, such as drawings.

The ideal solution is to use a proprietary system which permits high-level languages like FORTRAN to make calls on its facilities regardless of the hardware on which the eventual image will be produced. Such systems now exist, and ease the work of the FORTRAN graphics programmer—indeed, he is spoilt for choice. His primary requirements are divided between a number of considerations. Firstly, the system must be relatively easy to use, but it must not sacrifice too much, if any, power for this ease. Secondly, it must support a huge range of devices. These are predominantly in the area of screen type, although printer characteristics are important if the target system is intended to produce hard-copy via a dot matrix printer. Thirdly, the software developer must either secure a favourable licence to distribute the graphics system with his programs, or the system must be so cheap and readily available that the end-user can purchase his own copy.

There are a number of proprietary graphics systems which meet objectives one and two from this list. Most of these support the full range of graphics card options on the IBM PC and its compatibles, but not usually the 'incompatibles', and an adequate range of hard-copy devices. Such packages can successfully be interfaced to FORTRAN using the supplied bindings.

The third item (cost) is, of course, more important to the small developer than to a corporate one. It is worth bearing in mind the support given with a particular package when assessing the total cost. This support may be explicit, like a telephone hotline, or bulletin board, or may be implicit, in the form of top-class documentation, an error-free product, and the notification and supply of upgrades, particularly in respect of new devices.

13.4 CHARACTERISTICS OF A PC GRAPHICS SYSTEM

Since graphics lies outside of the FORTRAN standard, we need to rely on an external graphics system. The characteristics of a graphics system may be classified into several areas.

- General housekeeping functions
- Drawing operations
- Text operations

- Enquiry functions (in much software, the term 'inquiry' is used)
- Raster operations
- Graphical input

It is best to explain these by example.

13.5 GENERAL HOUSEKEEPING FUNCTIONS

Different PCs implement graphics in different ways. Some have separate graphics and text screen maps, and switch from one to the other as required. Others keep a bit image of the screen in RAM, with or without a corresponding ASCII equivalent map, the latter is needed if text screen dump facilities are to be kept simple.

Housekeeping functions exist to switch the screen between text and graphics modes and to clear it of images. These are normally extremely hardware specific, and are the responsibility of the authors of the graphics system.

Functions that need consideration at this stage include the selection of a coordinate system, and values for the coordinates, and whether or not it is possible to limit graphics to a window on the screen. Coordinate axis systems are of two main types: those that place the origin in the upper left-hand corner of the screen, numbering pixel columns left to right and pixel rows top to bottom; and those that put the coordinate origin in the bottom left-hand corner of the screen, such that rows are numbered bottom to top.

The 'upper left' system is a natural one for those programmers used to laying out text screens or text-only printouts, and indeed, since most computer displays refresh from top to bottom, this can be a sensible choice for the systems programmer. It is, however, an unnatural choice for the engineer or scientist used to graphical material, since charts, graphs and many diagrams implicitly assume the upper right-hand quadrant coordinate system that is implied by taking the origin at the lower left of the screen. We shall see in Chapter 14 that plotters normally assume this coordinate system. Plotters also have the advantage that they can produce a precisely dimensioned image. The choice of coordinate units is therefore immediately obvious: inches, millimetres, or some subdivision thereof. The choice for screens is by no means so obvious.

Screen coordinates are normally specified in pixels ('rasters'), or in an arbitrary system of units, NDC, or natural device coordinates. The problem with the former is that it is the applications programmer (i.e. you) who has to keep in mind the different target screen resolutions he is programming for. In contrast, a neutral system scaling the available screen area into a range of coordinates of 0 to 32 767 in each direction has the disadvantage that the conversion of this to pixel coordinates has to be done by the graphics system.

Neither system removes the need to remember the aspect ratio, both of the screen, and of the individual pixels, when programming the display of curves and text, although with new generations of screen display hardware, where the pixels have a 1 : 1 aspect ratio, this is simplified somewhat.

Limiting graphics to a part of the screen is known as 'windowing' or 'clipping'. It is easier to arrange this when dealing with pixel or raster coordinates than with NDC.

13.6 DRAWING OPERATIONS

Drawing operations at the simplest level consist of setting or resetting individual pixels on the screen. This is rarely useful in its own right, and the graphics system needs to provide higher level functions. The simplest of these is the function to draw a line between two points. Such a line is known as a 'vector'. Some graphics systems encompass the concept of 'polylines' or 'polyvectors'. These are a series of vectors which join end-to-end. An advantage of the polyline over many separate vectors is that the overhead of calling the graphics system is invoked only once, and as the graphics system steps through the elements one by one, it already has made part of the conversion from user coordinates to raster coordinates.

Lines or polylines may be solid, or made up from dot–dash patterns. This is usually implemented by means of a mask, normally comprising only one 16-bit word. This is mapped on to the line so that 'on' bits in the mask are lit with the line colour, and 'off' bits remain unaltered. Hence:

1111111111111111

will produce a solid line

1010101010101010

a fine dotted pattern, and

1111000011110000

will give rise to dashes of equal length. Many graphics systems will have at least one 'user definable' line style.

A useful graphics element in addition to the line is the marker symbol. It is possible to build such an entity from individual vectors or a polyline, but it is better if they are part of the graphics system. By analogy with the line and polyline, the concept of a 'polymarker', or set of markers, is similarly useful.

Many graphics systems include 'graphics primitives', such as rectangular boxes, boxes with rounded corners, circles, ellipses and both circular and elliptical arcs. In the simplest conceivable cases, these are all polyline operations, but the problems of screen and pixel aspect ratio are taken care of in the graphics system, which is of course especially useful in the case of curve drawing. At the lowest possible level, it may take hundreds of assembly language operations to do even the trivial thing of drawing a simple vector, the term 'primitive' is used here in a relative sense.

The drawing of alphanumeric characters in text mode is also a 'graphics primitive' operation, although a complicated one.

Some of the graphics primitives require an understanding of the concept of area fill. This involves the setting of all pixels to a given colour within an enclosing polyline. It is easy to imagine the algorithm for this if the polyline forms a rectangle, especially if the bounds of the rectangle are those of the whole screen, as indeed they are in a 'clear screen' operation. It is more difficult to visualize this for other shapes, although in principle, and at the machine code level, there may be little difference in the coding.

Area fills do not have to be single colour. Patterns of two colours are simply implemented by having a pattern mask in memory, and setting the pixel pattern on screen to the first colour when bits in the mask are on, and to another colour when they are off. The whole filled area is covered by repeating the mask. Quite striking patterns can be arranged with a 16-word vector, and the more comprehensive graphics systems will permit the user to define his own masks for custom design of area fills.

Some pattern masks are sketched in Figure 13.1 using a pattern of 0s and 1s. These correspond respectively to a 'dithered' pattern, diagonal lines, and a vertical/horizontal hatch. Note that the aspect ratio of a screen may make the latter into a rectangular, rather than a square, grid hatch, just as the difference between character pitch and line spacing in the figure below also renders the pattern rectangular.

```
1010101010101010    1000100010001000    1000100010001000
0101010101010101    0100010001000100    1000100010001000
1010101010101010    0010001000100010    1111111111111111
0101010101010101    0001000100010001    1000100010001000
1010101010101010    1000100010001000    1000100010001000
0101010101010101    0100010001000100    1000100010001000
1010101010101010    0010001000100010    1111111111111111
0101010101010101    0001000100010001    1000100010001000
1010101010101010    1000100010001000    1000100010001000
0101010101010101    0100010001000100    1000100010001000
1010101010101010    0010001000100010    1111111111111111
0101010101010101    0001000100010001    1000100010001000
1010101010101010    1000100010001000    1000100010001000
0101010101010101    0100010001000100    1000100010001000
1010101010101010    0010001000100010    1111111111111111
0101010101010101    0001000100010001    1000100010001000
```

Figure 13.1 Pattern masks for area fill.

Non-rectangular filled areas are often drawn using the 'flood fill' concept. In this, the polyline outline is drawn, then starting from some seed point, the filling pattern is mapped into the screen memory until pixels lit in the outline colour are encountered. This continues until no further avenue for 'flooding' lies open. On meeting the boundary, the fill may overwrite the boundary pixel, in which case the area fill is not outlined, or it may stop short, leaving the outline in place.

Sometimes, flood fill is available for the applications programmer. That then gives him the problem of finding a seed point: the efficiency of a flood fill operation is in part dependent on this choice.

To fully understand the whole business of area fills, and later on, raster operations, it is necessary to understand writing modes.

Imagine first drawing on white paper with a single black pen. Each line is overlaid on previous ones, but their detail is not removed. It may be obscured by a mess of black ink if too many lines are drawn close together, but it is not removed. This is equivalent to the first drawing mode, 'transparent'. When transparent drawing mode is chosen, each drawing operation sets pixels. Those that were already set, stay set, and those which were unset, become set. However, if the drawing colour is changed, in the analogy by using a pen filled with white correction fluid, and a line is overdrawn, it disappears from the drawing surface.

However, transparent drawing mode is really about area fills and text more than lines. This is because they are made up of foreground and background. In transparent mode, the existing colours show through the background in the overlaid image. Many graphics systems concern themselves only with the foreground image: if you want the background in a particular colour, it is essential to set the general background using a plain area fill, and then to draw over it with a transparent mode image in an alternative foreground colour.

Reverse transparent mode is where the pixels in the overlaid pattern which would have been in the new colour in transparent mode now allow the existing background to show through, and those which previously would have let the underlying image through now have the current foreground colour.

Opaque mode simply blots out everything underneath with the new image. In the case of text, the characters occupy a rectangular character cell, and the use of this mode unselectively may obscure much laboriously drawn image.

XOR mode is the final choice. This is the one to choose when drawing something you may wish to remove without leaving a trace. It is best visualized on a monochrome monitor. Black pixels in the original screen become white, and white ones become black as a solid line is drawn across them. The interesting property of this mode is that a second identical drawing operation (again in XOR mode) completely removes the lines, restoring the original image.

13.7 TEXT OPERATIONS

Text is a special case of the 'graphics primitive' type of operation. Individual characters may be created using a polyline approach, in a way that emulates a pen plotter. This makes it extremely easy to scale and rotate the text, to arbitrary sizes and orientations on the screen, and produces very readable text in the medium size range. It is also easy to arrange independent scaling in the text height and width directions, and to map the resulting characters to plotters. The effect is not pleasing, however, for very small or very large character sizes, or when the image is mapped to another, higher resolution, raster device, such as a printer.

Characters may also be implemented as filled areas. This demands that the typography of the characters be precisely defined in the form of straights and curves, and is much more difficult to do than 'plotter emulation'. Not only that, but characters will look odd at the smaller sizes because of the large screen pixel size. This method is probably the best of all, and has the advantage of allowing not only infinite scaling and rotation, but also the facility to do area fill operations on the characters including patterning and so on. (Laser printers supporting the Adobe PostScript language do it this way too.)

The final method is to keep the character as a pixel map. This is then moved as a 'bit image block' straight into the computer's screen graphics image RAM. Providing that the bit block move operation is efficiently coded, the method is fast. It does, however, have a number of drawbacks. The first of these is that if different character sizes are created as multiples of a basic character (i.e. by replacing single pixels by 2×2 or 3×3 etc), the range of character sizes is limited, and the larger ones have a definite 'blocky' appearance. Alternatively, complete fonts in different sizes may be created. They can take up large amounts of disk storage, or RAM. However, both very large and very small characters can be created which have a pleasant appearance. It is difficult to rotate these characters, except in 90 degree increments, and the pixel aspect ratio can determine the shape of a character to an unacceptable degree, requiring different vertical and horizontal fonts. (The HP LaserJet type laser printers use this method of keeping a bit map of every character in every size in every style.)

Where a graphics system has only a few fixed fonts, they will be embedded in the system, and automatically loaded into RAM with the system. Multiple fonts are usually kept in separate files and loaded as and when required.

A character occupies a rectangular cell (Figure 13.2). All cells may be the same size, leading to a monospaced font, or they may be of different widths, such that the letter 'i' is narrower than 'm'. This gives a proportional font. The relative widths of all the characters are an essential element of the 'font metrics', as are the basic proportions of the characters, and the distances above and below the character base line of such features as ascenders and descenders. For the highest quality work, all these features are available for each character, and a text string may be placed aligned to any one of its salient geometric characteristics. In simple graphics systems, every measurement is relative to the character cell base line.

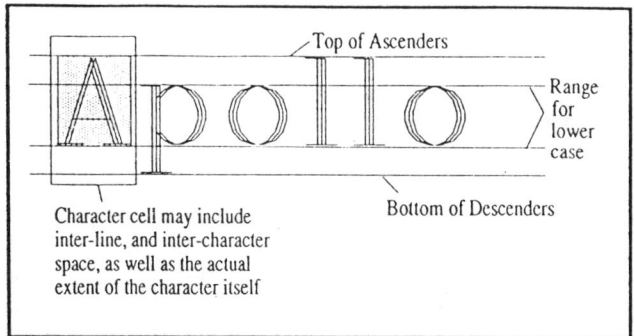

Figure 13.2 Character alignment

Typical functions in a screen graphics system will be to:

- load font(s) from disk
- specify the current font
- set text colour(s) and writing mode
- set text size
- set justification of proportionally spaced characters by interword or intercharacter spacing
- set text special effects such as underlining or emboldening
- specify text alignment
- release space occupied by fonts when they are no longer needed.

13.8 ENQUIRY FUNCTIONS

Most graphics systems contain 'Inquiry' (sic) functions. These enable the application to discover current settings for colours, writing mode, text size, and so on, as well as returning information of the overall capabilities of the target hardware.

Some of these functions appear to be redundant, since any careful programmer would keep a record of his choices in a few well-chosen variables. However, sometimes the graphics system is requested to select choices which are not implemented on a particular target hardware, and so substitutes a 'next best' choice. The applications programmer can be informed of this substitution via an inquiry function.

13.9 RASTER OPERATIONS AND 'BLITTING'

Small objects can be placed on a graphics screen in XOR mode, and moved about thereafter by redrawing them at the original position still in XOR mode, which has the effect of erasing the object and restoring the original screen contents, followed by a second redraw at the new position. This is simple and explicit to program, provided that the object is not complicated, so that it draws quickly, and screen refresh is similarly rapid. For complicated objects, especially with slow screens, the undrawing and redrawing operations can actually be seen, and can prove distracting. It does, however, have the advantage that the object can change size or shape between being removed, and being redrawn. The principle is used when drawing resizeable boxes, for instance.

Larger and more complicated graphical objects can be moved in this way by alternating between removal at the old site and redrawing at the new one, one vector at a time. Provided that there is no overlap, which confuses the operation, this can give a subjective impression of higher speed. In many instances, however, there is the requirement to obliterate a portion of the screen, say for the drawing of a temporarily displayed 'drop down' or 'pop up' menu or help prompt, and then to reinstate it when the menu is removed. Since the activity which created that part of the screen may not be easy to determine, the programmer has a number of choices. The first of these is to maintain a two screen system, with graphics on one, and all menus, help and so on, displayed on the other. Another choice is to blank the whole image before displaying a menu, and then redraw the whole graphics image when needed. A further choice is to reserve different areas of the screen for graphic images and interaction with the user, and to refresh each individually. Finally, we have the menu systems of GEM, Windows, and other Macintosh-like systems.

The way that these are implemented is to save an area of the screen which will be overwritten by the menu into another area of memory, display the menu, and restore the block on completion. This process of 'bit block moves' is sometimes known as 'blitting'. Modern screen hardware may well have blitting built in, but in older hardware it needs to be programmed. The ability to 'blit' may be accessible to the applications programmer, but it will normally be confined to rectangular areas of the screen, and these may be specified at the pixel boundary, or more economically to byte, word, or paragraph boundaries in the screen RAM. Blitting is also known as performing 'raster operations' or 'rasterops'.

Writing or 'blitting' to the screen RAM may be done in one of the four writing modes. Normally, this will be an opaque or replace mode operation, since the screen contents will have been saved in a preliminary, or simultaneous, 'blit'.

13.10 GRAPHICAL INPUT

Although digitizer tablets, lightpens, and joysticks have had vogues in the past, most modern PC computers expect input from the keyboard or from a combination of keyboard and 'mouse'. Ordinarily, a mouse consists of a movement sensor and buttons. As the mouse is moved over the desk surface alongside the PC, signals denoting its movement are transmitted to the computer, and these are translated into coordinates for the positioning of a cursor on the screen. We prefer to use a trackerball 'mouse'. This stays stationary, and a large ball in its upper surface is rolled with the tip of a finger, rather than moving the whole device (Figure 13.3). The mouse button is located on the side of the mouse, and operated with the thumb. It is certainly superior on a congested desk. Most normal mice need a clear area of about 500 mm square easily to hand. Their buttons are on the top surface, and are operated by the index finger. Mice are normally configurable for either left-handed or right-handed operation—unfortunately it is uniformly difficult to find the details whatever system is in operation.

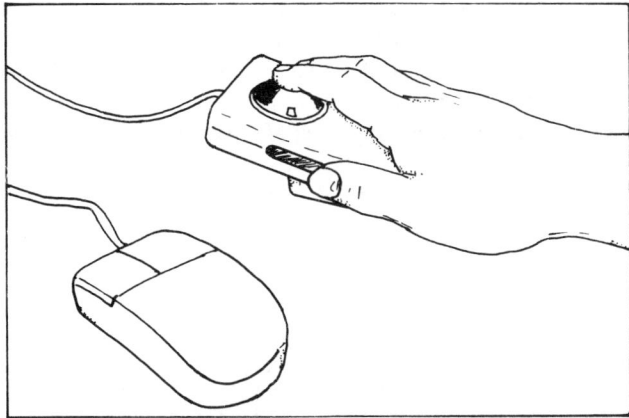

Figure 13.3

The device on the left is the familiar Microsoft mouse in its latest form, with buttons replaced by two pads. Other mice have one or three buttons, all designed to be pressed by the index finger. On the right is an example of a trackerball. The index finger is used to move the ball while the body of the device remains stationary. Buttons are provided on each side: on the left, to be actuated by the thumb, or on the right side, by the middle finger. Trackerballs with infra-red links are effective, because the mouse remains in one position. The trackerball also needs much less desk space, a positive advantage.

In order to use a mouse under DOS, suitable software must be loaded. This either comprises a loadable device driver, usually called MOUSE.SYS, which is loaded when the computer is booted, or a separate program called MOUSE.COM which can be run at any time. Many conventional and trackerball mice emulate the functionality of the Microsoft mouse: others are provided with their own drivers. Mice can be connected to a serial (RS232) port, direct to the bus using an expansion card, or to dedicated mouse ports.

Graphical input demands that the movement of the mouse be tracked on the screen continuously, and the position saved when a button is pressed. A system with graphical input will sense the mouse movement, and convert this into the movement of a pointer on the screen. Functions will exist to return screen coordinates.

More sophisticated software will permit the shape and size of the pointer displayed on the screen to be changed, and thus give a visual clue as to the current function of the pointer.

The way in which the pointer (usually, but not always, an arrow) is drawn on to the screen is interesting. It will not usually be possible to draw in XOR mode, then redraw to remove as outlined above, unless the pointer is an extremely simple object, like a one-pixel thickness crosshair. The reason why this is so is that unless the display is very fast, the pointer will flicker, or the retracing itself might be visible, and hence distracting. Also, the pointer must remain visible at all times, regardless of whatever objects it moves over.

Drawing the 'mouse pointer' is a two-stage operation. The first operation is to 'blit' a 'mask' on to the screen. All the pixels covered by 0s retain their original appearance, and those covered by 1s are turned to the 'mouse pointer background' colour. Then, the 'form' is placed on top of the mask. Once again, pixels covered by 0s show through, those covered by 1s adopt the 'mouse pointer foreground' colour. A typical mask and form, each a 16×16 array of pixels, are shown in Figure 13.4. It is convenient to have such an arrangement, made up of two 16-word blocks, because of the arrangement of RAM in a DOS computer.

```
0000000000000000        0000000000000000
1100000000000000        0000000000000000
1110000000000000        0100000000000000
1111100000000000        0111000000000000
1111111000000000        0111110000000000
1111111110000000        0111111100000000
1111111111110000        0111111111000000
1111111111111100        0111111111111000
1111111111111110        0111111100000000
1111111111100000        0110011110000000
1110011111110000        0100001111000000
1110001111111000        0000000111100000
0000000111111100        0000000011110000
0000000011111110        0000000001111000
0000000001111111        0000000000000000
0000000000000000        0000000000000000
0000000000000000        0000000000000000
  'Mask'                   'Form'
```

Figure 13.4 Elements required in the construction of a mouse pointer graphic

To see the general appearance of such a mouse pointer, run GEM or Windows!

Particularly with user-definable mouse pointers, it is important to define the 'hot spot' relative to the mouse form. The 'hot spot' is the point whose coordinates will be returned by an enquiry as to the position of the mouse pointer on screen.

13.11 INVOKING A GRAPHICS SYSTEM.

Graphics systems may be bound in with a FORTRAN program, or may be coresident in RAM with the program, and interfaced to it. The former technique normally creates hardware specific programs; in the latter, the system may be configured for the target hardware before the FORTRAN program is invoked. Normally, the first kind of graphics system will be accessed by subroutine calls, and may be made up of FORTRAN (or other high-level language) modules and assembler code. The second type may also be a mixture of source code types, but the interface between the two coresident programs will be via an interrupt. The graphics system will service the interrupt that the FORTRAN code makes via a short assembly language interface.

A stand-alone graphics system will have loadable programs called drivers that access machine specific features of the display hardware. It may also (probably will have!) other drivers for hard copy. The availability of these are just as important as the screen facilities offered.

The transfer of data from graphics system to FORTRAN program is a two-way process, and is made up of five basic types of data:

- Control parameters—deciding what functions to access
- Input only parameters—select between choices
- Input coordinates—where to place the image
- Output parameters—returned information relating to choice
- Output coordinates—returned information relating to position

Graphics systems either give separate FORTRAN subroutine calls for each function, to which the absolute minimum of parameters are sent, or they pass the five types of data to and fro between them explicitly. If the data is not explicitly interchanged, then it is still there, but is hidden.

13.12 A TYPICAL GRAPHICS SYSTEM: DIGITAL RESEARCH'S GSX AND GEM

The FORTRAN user has the choice of many graphics systems for DOS, especially if he confines his attention to IBM compatible hardware. Some software firms have attempted to launch highly portable graphics systems. These have been of the stand-alone type, and have had drivers for a range of display types. An early example of this was Digital Research's GSX (one of those concocted acronyms, this time standing for Graphic System eXtension!). This sported drivers for IBM graphics cards, and for a limited range of dot matrix printers and some plotters.

Variants of the system were produced for 8-bit CP/M microcomputers, such as the Amstrad PCW series of machines, and for CP/M86 and DOS computers.

When Digital Research produced their GEM user-friendly interface, they chose to implement it in two parts. The first was an enlarged and enhanced version of GSX, and the second was a much higher-level system which was called upon to manage the drop down menus, resizeable windows, icons, DOS functions such as file management, and so forth. The structure of GEM, being divided into these two parts, makes it highly suitable for our purposes, because we can take on board the underlying graphics, without all the WIMPs paraphernalia. This we do by using the virtual device interface (VDI), broadly the same as GSX, and not the application environment services (AES).

The advantages of doing this are that GEM screen and hard-copy drivers exist for a huge range of hardware. The GEM system is in widespread use, or can be obtained cheaply: it is often bundled with computer hardware, or with software which uses the GEM environment as a standard method of accessing a WIMPs system. A large number of computers originally supplied with GSX still remain in widespread use, and much of what we have to say applies equally to the earlier system.

We show you a simple method of accessing GEM VDI in Chapter 15, and include a FORTRAN-GEM VDI interface library on the disk set which can be purchased to complement the book.

CHAPTER 14

PRINTING AND PLOT-TING — THE HARD-COPY JUNGLE

14.1 INTRODUCTION

In this chapter we look at the printing and plotting of text and graphics from FORTRAN programs. If you are yet to buy a printer and plotter then you are faced with some important decisions. One of the advantages of the popularity of the IBM PC and compatibles is that there are a vast range of compatible printers and plotters to choose from, the disadvantage, particularly when buying a printer, is that the manufacturers seem reluctant to standardize on a particular programming interface. There is nothing more frustrating than buying a printer that is capable of near letter quality (NLQ) printing and fancy graphics only to find that the software that you have just purchased will not make use of these facilities. It is instructive to play with a word processing package which purports to support a vast range of printers. Set up ('install') the word processor to output to different printers in turn. You will find that the vaunted facilities for which you bought the word processor in the first place are only available on certain types of printer. For some printers such indispensable facilities as superscript and subscript may not be implemented.

Fortunately the situation is slowly improving. If you are buying a printer then make sure that it is Epson compatible; if it is also IBM compatible then so much the better. For plotters the situation is better still with the Hewlett Packard Graphics language (HPGL) being the preferred standard on most plotters.

Other considerations when buying printers and plotters are quality, speed, noise (for printers), and paper size (for plotters). Competition in the peripherals market is fierce, and it is worth taking a look at some of the micro magazines. Most of the space in these magazines is devoted to reviews of software and hardware. You can very often find articles which compare leading printers and plotters, or which review the latest models.

14.2 PRINTING TEXT

All FORTRAN programmers are called upon to master the FORMAT statement at some time

---

during their programming careers. This may have been sooner (especially for those who learnt FORTRAN in the past with card based input systems) or later, for those who acquired their FORTRAN skills on a tolerant terminal based system, using list directed (or similarly 'free format') I/O procedures. This latter group may only recognize FORMATs on output statements, being unaware that FORTRAN utilized fixed formats for input as well as output originally.

A number of features require some thought, for example, the use of the FORTRAN carriage control conventions. The earliest FORTRAN expected each WRITE statement to begin a 'new line', (so did each READ). The only formatting possible was a control at a line-by-line level. Later, a convention demanding an interpretation of the first character output to the printer became the standard. A number of possibilities exist as shown in Table 14.1.

Table 14.1 FORTRAN carriage control conventions

Character		Meaning
The digit	1	Skip to the start of a new page
	0 (zero)	Leave a blank line, then print
	(blank)	Just go to the next line
	+	Overprint on the last line of the previous statement

Tragically, FORMATs whose numerical data is misinterpreted as carriage control are still generated. Confusion is added to by the tendency of systems to distinguish between physical output devices, where the carriage control is **obeyed**, and files, in which it is **inserted** as data. The VAX minicomputer system running VMS makes this distinction, but is sufficiently intelligent to associate a 'generated by FORTRAN' attribute with each affected file, so that the carriage control information is acted upon when the file is TYPEd or PRINTed: all DOS FORTRANs are very dumb in comparison.

PC FORTRANs do recognize some devices as needing to action carriage control instructions. These are normally the CON and PRN devices, although the treatment of pre-connected devices varies—between compilers, and also between different versions of the same compiler! One might think that the 1, 0, and space options would cause the emitting of the FF (ASCII 12 or form feed), CR LF CR LF or CR LF (ASCII 13 and 10 respectively) sequences into a file which did not action the carriage control sequences. This sensible response is not taken. Instead, the carriage control is included literally. This makes the printing of a FORTRAN file occasionally quite an interesting event, if sometimes untidy.

It is often far tidier to use the '/' symbol in FORMATs to control vertical alignment (even after recognizing that the number of new lines generated following a sequence of such characters might be somewhat varied, but normally by one line only). All DOS FORTRANs interpret this by emitting CR LF (or an equivalent) to the destination file or device.

An associated problem is the need to inhibit carriage control after the sending of a line of data to the print device. In some FORTRANs, the backslash '\' or dollar symbol '$' may be used for this, although it is a non-standard feature. How this is treated depends not only on the intent of the programmer and the compiler, but also on the set-up of the printer in use. With many printers, the CR code performs the actions normally undertaken by CR LF, and if it is genuinely wished to overprint a line, it is necessary to send the escape sequences (see below) to enter reverse line feed code, do a line feed, and then print. Moreover, it is probably also necessary to return to the normal line feed direction *before* printing, since the end of print is usually signalled by the sending of CR, which the printer interprets as CR LF...The results of failure to change the feed direction, or of sending these escape codes to a different type of printer, or for that matter to a similar printer which has DIP switches set so that the LF is required, can be far from the programmer's intent.

Modern dot matrix printers have an extended range of characters relative to the restricted character sets of old-fashioned, card based, FORTRAN. A full 256 character ASCII set is recognized (some FORTRANs will accept characters with ASCII codes above 127 in CHARACTER constants, but forbid the use of CHAR(N) where N > 127, others refuse anything to do with such characters; Microsoft FORTRAN permits the use of both types). At the risk of becoming slightly printer specific, programs can make use of the ASCII characters numbered 128 to 255 inclusive for special effects. On C Itoh printers, this includes a near complete range of Greek letters and mathematical symbols; Epson printers have italic letters and numerals, box drawing characters, or other exotica (depending on the model).

Escape sequences to select optional printer functions are much more useful, although they tend to be equally printer specific. An escape sequence is a set of characters beginning with ASCII 27, or ESC (ESCape sequences). The ESCape character tells the printer: 'the following characters are part of an instruction to change a printer characteristic, not characters to print literally'. For example, the sequence ESC P (CHAR(27)//'P' in FORTRAN 77) selects 10 characters per inch spacing on an Epson printer. As well as ESCape sequences, some single 'characters' low down in the ASCII set also control printer functions. The most obvious of these is FF or 'form feed' which causes the printer to roll to the start of a new page (or load a new sheet of paper in a sheet feed printer), LF or 'line feed', and CR - 'carriage return'. The last of these certainly betrays its Teletype origins. (Beware of confusing FF 'form feed' with FF the hexadecimal value for the very highest possible byte value.)

ESCape sequences permit access to extremely sophisticated print functions.

- Print pitch, or the horizontal spacing in characters per inch
- Vertical spacing
- Type font, and or boldness (by overprinting)
- Superscript and subscript print modes
- Block graphics, or border characters
- Bit image graphics

Taking first the character pitch. Typewriters and daisywheel printers have traditionally produced text at 10 or 12 characters per inch. Modern machines can usually accommodate both of these spacings: so can dot matrix printers. This means that the commonest printers which have 8 inch wide platens can accommodate 80 and 96 character lines. Most dot matrix printers have a condensed print mode, somewhere between 15 and 17 characters per inch, which can be turned on and off via ESCape sequences. This enables them to emulate the 15 inch platen printers which are significantly more expensive, and to produce the 130+ character lines the programmer might be familiar with from his mainframe line printer. Of course, the wide platen printers also have a condensed print mode.

The effect of a new ribbon is striking, but more from idleness than penny pinching most computer users permit ribbons to stay on printers far past the end of their useful lives. Double striking can improve apparent print quality (compared to a single pass with a new ribbon, it is likely to be fuzzier), and can be invoked with an ESCape sequence, although at a cost in reduced printer throughput. Some printer operations may need double striking anyway, such as NLQ typeface selection on eight- and nine- pin printers, and the use of subscript and superscript print mode on Epson printers.

14.3   BIT IMAGE GRAPHICS ON A DOT MATRIX PRINTER, AND THE 'SCREEN DUMP'

Virtually all dot matrix printers are capable of 'bit image graphics'. In normal print mode, a series of bytes sent to the printer are interpreted as the corresponding ASCII characters. The pattern of dots to make up the character are held in ROM in the printer, and as the print head moves over the paper, the pins are fired in sequence to press the printer ribbon onto the paper and form the dots. Ink jet printers do a similar job by projecting droplets of ink, and laser printers by scanning a sensitized drum, but essentially the same principle is involved.

Imagine an eight-pin printer. (Many dot matrix printers have nine pins. One is reserved for underlining, and the other eight form the characters, or are available for bit-image graphics. To all programmable intents and purposes, they are eight- pin printers.) This can interpret a byte as the instructions to fire its pins - the pins which correspond to set bits in the byte fire, and the pins corresponding to unset bits do not. Suppose the character cell is in the form of an 8×8 matrix. It needs eight consecutive bytes to form the character, and so for every character in the printer's ROM (read only memory), there must be 8 bytes of pin instructions.

For more complicated arrangements, notably those of the 24-pin printers, several bytes may be needed to form each column of the character. Accordingly, more space is reserved for these bit maps in the ROM.

Normally, this whole process is transparent to the user, as he just sends the characters he wants to print, and the printer does the rest. However, it becomes necessary to understand the procedure if the programmer wishes to create his own bit maps (large or small) to create effects not in the printer's standard repertoire. Such effects fall into a number of categories, listed in order of complexity:

- Describing single characters not available in the printer as a special effect (e.g. the odd Greek letter, or specialist mathematical symbol)
- Downloading characters to the printer
- Making fancy rules and tabulations
- Generating complete graphics images

14.4 SENDING SINGLE 'SPECIALS'

The principle involved in generating single characters is essentially similar to that which the printer does automatically. First of all, however, a sketch of the required dot pattern should be drawn on squared graph paper. Note that some printers do not like horizontally adjacent dots, because this makes the same pin fire at consecutive positions as the print head moves, which leads to overheating where the pin spacing is small (24-pin printers) or the printer has a fast rate of movement. Having drawn the required dot pattern on graph paper instructions can be built up for sending it to the printer. They normally adopt the following protocol:

- Announce that the printer is to shift into bit image mode
- Declare the number of bytes of bit image data
- Follow with the bit image data
- Possibly reset the desired normal text characteristics

As can be imagined, this leads to extremely printer dependent code. For a start, the ESCape sequences to switch modes may vary, the method of sending the length of bit image data varies, and some printers expect the bit image data to have the most significant bit (MSB) at the top of the character, and others expect it the other way round. As if this were not enough, most PC FORTRANs impose their own obstacles when attempting to create the bit image data—in not letting you use bytes with the MSB set, for instance.

Perhaps the most obvious way of getting the bit image data into a program would be to specify it as an unsigned, INTEGER*1, variable, and setting this byte as a radix 2 constant. Some mainframe FORTRANs extend the standard to include such a data type, sometimes termed BYTE, and permit it to be operated on as INTEGER*1 or CHARACTER*1. Unfortunately, even the compilers which permit INTEGER*1 expect it to be signed, and this gives problems in specifying a bit pattern, since signed numbers are interpreted in twos complement. Simplest, if possible, is to specify the number as an INTEGER*2 type, again using radix 2 constant forms, and then convert it to its byte form by use of the CHAR character function. This is easy to do with Microsoft FORTRAN, which permits the parameter of CHAR to lie between 0 and 255; but not with Ryan MacFarland FORTRAN or Digital Research FORTRAN 77, which forbid the parameter to exceed 127. With only the parameters 0 to 127, the high bit cannot be set, and these FORTRANs are difficult to use for bit image work.

It might be thought that 24-pin printers would use 3 bytes to define each vertical line of a character. In practice, they normally use the six least significant bits of 4 bytes, thus building the line up from 4×6 bits rather than 3×8 bits. This enables all FORTRANs to be used quite successfully.

When doing 'specials' it is worth making the total number of bytes sent a perfect multiple of the number of vertical columns of dots per normal character. Thus when normal print mode is restored, the character positions are properly aligned.

14.5 DOWNLOADABLE CHARACTERS

In Section 14.4, the procedure was for single characters. Although fiddly at first this is not impracticable for the odd symbol in a table, but is not cost effective if any quantity of repeats of the dot pattern are required. Increasingly, printers are manufactured to take account of this requirement, and they have an area of RAM into which the bit images of a number of characters can be 'downloaded' from the computer. They are then accessed in the text to be printed by ESCape sequences. Downloadable character capabilities vary from none, to small numbers (say 4), to complete alternative character sets. Where a small number of characters is all that can be downloaded, they are probably accessed with a different ESCape sequence for each character, but where a whole alternative set is available, the ESCape sequence is likely to be of the sort which changes from the default character set to a particular downloaded font, and back again—perhaps pages later.

It would be unusual to send the dot pattern for a single inserted character within near letter quality (NLQ) text, complete with the data for both passes of the print head (assuming an eight-pin head—24-pin heads produce NLQ in a single pass). This may mean supplying a large amount of bit image data. It is sometimes possible to obtain data files for whole new typefaces from printer manufacturers or retailers, and this would be preferable to coding it oneself.

Commercially available downloadable fonts are the rule rather than the exception when it comes to Hewlett Packard compatible laser printers. At 300 dots per inch in both directions, the effort of coding a single character of any size, let alone a whole character set, is too horrific for the FORTRAN programmer to contemplate.

14.6 MAKING FANCY RULES AND TABULATION

Many printers have a set of border characters in their basic character set. One can often find a double rule character, which makes a better, neater, divider for tabulated data than repeatedly printing the equals sign, because that comes out with gaps, and which is more prominent than the single underscore repeated (which also forms a continuous line). If a degree of printer specificity is not of too much concern, ESCape sequences which imply 'repeat the following character so many times' may be used when they exist. As a further refinement, a bit image pattern may be repeated across the page. It may not be necessary to generate too complex an output format, since ESCape sequences of the form 'repeat the following byte, assuming that it is bit image data, so many times', are often provided. Naturally, repeating a single-bit image byte in this way is only permissible on printers where the pins do not overheat when the same pin is repeatedly fired.

The sparing use of vertical rules makes tabulated data sometimes easier to read. This is well known, for instance, by the compilers of mathematical tables. In just the same way as the printers offer ruling characters for horizontal rules, vertical line characters are often provided too. These will not normally join up vertically because the character height is, for obvious reasons, less than the normal line spacing. For joined up vertical rules you will need twice the number of passes, at, say, half the normal line spacing. Not only could block graphics (another way of saying crude ruling characters) be used in this, but so could one or more lines of bit image data. A sequence in a format might be something like:

- initialize by setting line spacing to $^1/_{12}$ th inch

then for each output line:

- carriage control
- jump to character position for first vertical rule and print
- jump to character position for last vertical rule and print
- newline (i.e. by using '/')
- repeat the above, but with the tabular data inserted between the vertical rules

and finally

- reset the line spacing to normal

Some printers might include ESCape sequences for 'jump to horizontal character position n' or even 'jump to horizontal dot position n'.

The documentation for the setting of horizontal and vertical tab stops is most often the least penetrable part of printer documentation, so beware. Both of us own C Itoh printers (bought before Epson set the *de facto* standard), which set and reset tab stops with the sequences 'ESC (' and 'ESC)' respectively. The poor old typesetter who set the manual got terribly upset by the apparent unmatched parentheses, and tried to inject a little order of his own. As a consequence, this section of the manual is incredibly confused! In contrast, Epson printer manuals are normally models of clarity.

14.7 DRAWING WITH BIT IMAGE GRAPHICS

A typical eight-pin dot matrix printer can usually produce 130 characters or so in compressed print on an 8 inch (200 mm) wide sheet of paper. If each character is eight dots wide, and some are ten, then about 1040 to 1300 dots are printable across the page. This is roughly 130 to 160 dots per inch. Similarly, with eight dots height for a $^1/_{10}$th inch high character, the basic vertical scaling is about 80 dots per inch. This can be improved by overprinting with half a dot space vertical movement between passes to about the same as the horizontal spacing.

Twenty-four-pin printers can be up to half as good again, and perform to this accuracy in a single pass. (They are often slightly better horizontally too.)

One should note that dot matrix printer resolution is about half to three-quarters as good as a laser printer. Stunning graphics can be produced, but at the cost of much processor and printer time, and extremely short-lived printer ribbons. Driving a dot matrix printer to its limits in this way needs huge amounts of data: a 10×10 inch sheet, printed with two passes of an eight pin printer to cover the whole surface needs about 2.5 megabytes, not including all the overhead of escape sequences. It also requires high quality paper!

The processor overhead of setting the 20 million different bits is also enormous, and the programmer's task to optimize this extremely arduous. Not only that, but it is a waste of time, since cheap, readily available graphics interfaces exist to do this job. One such is GEM VDI, introduced in Chapter 13 in the context of screen graphics. The application of this to printer graphics is described in Section 14.8.

It is only in the area of screen dumps that the FORTRAN programmer should even want to concern himself with details, and there only under protest. IBM compatible, and many other incompatible, DOS machines have the GRAPHICS command which permits a screen dump to be produced when a key is pressed (PrtSc on the IBM PC). The standard program assumes that the printer is an Epson compatible, but various modified programs are available. For those machines which do not offer this facility, memory resident programs which do the same thing are available cheaply either commercially, or through user's groups. Writing such a routine demands detailed knowledge of how the pixels on the screen map to memory, and precisely what printer is to be used.

Screen dumps are an exact copy of the bit pattern that appears on the screen. It is difficult to get the same aspect ratio on the printer as on the screen, so precise scaling is not possible. What is more, the screen dot pattern is many times cruder than can be achieved by the printer, so that one either gets a small, dense image, or a faint image on a full sheet. However, if you have produced your screen graphics using Microsoft Windows or Digital Research's GEM VDI then you need not worry about screen dumps since these graphics systems have drivers for most printers, and so the same software that gave you your screen graphics will give you the printer graphics as well.

14.8 PRODUCING GRAPHICS ON A DOT MATRIX PRINTER

In Chapter 13, the use of the GSX and GEM VDI system was recommended for providing an inexpensive, high quality screen graphics interface between FORTRAN programs and a huge variety of hardware, and, in Chapter 15, advice is given on how to access these systems from Microsoft FORTRAN programs. The reasons for this choice were that the extremely hardware dependent, and low-level, coding required for screen graphics was difficult, and had already been done in a highly optimized fashion in graphics systems such as GEM VDI. The same argument applies to hard copy via a raster device, and indeed, to hard copy using a vector device like a plotter, if area fill is required.

GEM VDI is distributed complete with a selection of drivers for popular printers. Drivers for common printers, and many others, are available. Of increasing importance is support for laser printers: this too is available.

When programming hard-copy devices under GSX or GEM VDI, all that is necessary is to open the appropriate graphics hard-copy device driver, and generate the necessary graphics calls. The added flexibility of the GEM VDI system makes it preferable to GSX, especially in the area of **metafiles**.

A metafile is a file of graphics commands that can be interpreted by certain GEM applications, notably paint and draw, in such a way that it may be enhanced by the particular capabilities of those packages. It may be, for instance, that a FORTRAN program generates a graph with a number of headings. To rerun the program merely to delete, relocate, or amend one of these could be tedious in the extreme, especially when it could be retouched by a specialist program before printing. Furthermore, the output application under GEM allows the picture to be sized (by choosing to output at full scale, or in 'best fit' mode), or only part of the picture to be printed using the snapshot accessory. Also, the graphics is hardware independent, the choice of output device is left to the last moment when the picture is to be printed. Additionally, metafiles can be created quickly, for unattended spooling later. This leads to an increase in productivity, and a decrease in fatigue where noisy dot matrix printers are the primary graphics output device.

There are a number of caveats to the use of GSX and GEM VDI for hard copy. Readers should be first familiar with the concepts of screen handling in graphics mode dealt with in Chapter 13.

GSX and GEM VDI have INQUIRY functions which return information on the physical characteristics of the 'workstation'. For a dot matrix printer, this might include the size of a dot or pixel in microns (0.001 mm), as an integer number. Scaling from the screen to a printer is approximate for a number of reasons. A worn mechanism or a different tension will cause variations, and there may be other small differences between otherwise identical printers. There almost certainly will be minor differences between compatible printers. For accurate work you are advised to carefully scale off the dimensions of the printed area, and keep them in a file that your FORTRAN program interrogates before deciding on the precise scaling. This applies not only to GSX and GEM VDI graphics systems, but to all which use raster devices for graphical output.

The second problem also relates to size. If output is directed to a metafile (under GEM VDI), then the 'real coordinate' units are tenths of a millimetre. If this system is chosen for a printer, then the units become pixels, which have a finite size and aspect ratio. The comments above relating to working with the NDC system apply here equally. Precise scaling, and the subdivision into a number of diagrams printed separately, is the responsibility of the OUTPUT application under GEM if one chooses a metafile, but of the FORTRAN programmer, if he chooses to print direct.

Thirdly, although this applies particularly to the earlier GSX system rather than to GEM, text may be crude in appearance at certain sizes, and indeed, may have a limited range of sizes available. Text may not be clipped at the edge of the 0 to 32 767 NDC space, but if across the printer page may 'wrap'. In contrast, the full extent of overspill text in the other direction may be printed in its entirety, with the result that the main figure is displaced, and inevitably spans a paper perforation line. Also, since the text fonts native to the drivers were defined via a pixel pattern, the text appears differently on different manufacturer's printers. GEM VDI has much improved methods of defining text and its location on the printed page. This includes being able to define a 'window' into which the text fits, rather than a start point, and a character size. The latter is fine if the range of character sizes is infinite, but is poor when a finite, and small, range is available.

There is one final solution to the problem of producing high resolution dot matrix printer graphics from a FORTRAN program. That is to imagine that you are producing output for a plotter, and a particular type of plotter: one which accepts Hewlett Packard Graphics Language commands. The rules for doing this are given in Section 14.9. Instead of sending the commands direct to a printer, save them to a file. Many computer aided design programs for PCs can accept HPGL commands as input. A typical example program that can do this is DesignCAD II (formerly ProDesign II). Then you can perform some manipulation of the diagram before dumping it to a dot matrix printer. Not only that, but some desktop publishing programs (e.g. PageMaker, Ventura Publisher) can also accept HPGL files as graphics objects. The amount of further enhancement outside of scaling and cropping is small, and high quality output may be restricted to laser printers, but the general principle works.

14.9 PRODUCING GRAPHICS ON A PLOTTER

As PC computers have become commoner and cheaper, so too have pen plotters. Small plotters are now obtainable for the same sort of price as printers, and are essential where high quality line drawings have to be produced.

The instructions to drive modern pen plotters are fairly simple, and the codes used to drive them fall into two quite well-defined groups. Typical of the former are the commands to drive Roland and Western Graphtec (Watanabe) plotters, and the latter are best seen in the Hewlett Packard plotters, and their compatibles. Hewlett Packard Graphics Language (HPGL) is so widely used (or emulated) in plotters, that has become the effective standard, and is even supported as a command language on some laser printers.

We will develop the basic principles for programming plotters from FORTRAN in Section 14.11 with reference to the Graphtec/Roland type of command language, which is simpler than HPGL. Once the principles are established, we can treat HPGL in depth. The description of HPGL commands occupies Sections 14.12 to 14.16 inclusive.

14.10 PLOTTER AND PEN TYPES

The user normally has a choice between a variety of types of plotter, and of using different types of pen. For large plots, the commonest principle is of a roller over which the paper travels. It may be friction fed or have sprocket holes, and whereas the former enables standard preprinted sheets to be used, the latter has the advantage of using continuous paper, and of handling a series of large plots without operator intervention. Pen movement is confined to one axis, which is along the axis of the roller, and roller rotation permits the pen to move to any point on the paper surface.

Flat-bed plotters, where the paper is held flat against a very precise plane surface and the pen is moved across it in both axes on an arm, have begun to become common even in large sizes, A1 and A0, whereas a few years ago this type of plotter was prohibitively expensive. However, they are still commonest at A3 size and below. A variant has paper on a roll, which is advanced by a 'change paper' command, although plotting is still only done over the flat-bed area.

In a third type of plotter, the paper is pinched between rollers on each side. These move the paper backwards and forwards to get the motion in one axis, as the pen(s) move in the other. A drawback of this type of plotter is that it demands a clear area both in front and behind if the paper is not to get caught up and crumpled. Plot sizes up to A3 use this principle, which is commonest for A4 paper and below.

The choice of pen type is somewhat limited by the medium on which the plot is to be prepared. This can be acetate sheet, for overhead projection or other specialist purposes, or coated paper. The pens for use on acetate sheet are felt or fibre tipped, and use both spirit and water based inks. Coated paper is the best for detailed work, as it has less friction and so is less abrasive to the pens, and inks do not spread as they are absorbed. One must always be careful not to smudge these when removing the finished drawing from the plotter. On nearly non-absorbent coated papers the same sorts of pens as are used on acetate may also be used, together with varieties of ball-point and tubular nib drafting pens.

Ball-point pens may be of the wet ink type, commonly known as 'rollerball', or of the more conventional 'Biro' type. Both tend not to start immediately, and are at their best when drawing long vectors at low to moderate speeds. The wet ink rollerballs are particularly prone to take some time to start, although the Biro type have the habit of producing spotty lines from time to time. In addition, the Biro pens gather paper fibres, dust, and superfluous ink which builds up on the pen tip and eventually drops off on to the paper surface. Care has to be taken in removing this ink-laden detritus from the paper surface without smearing it.

Wet ink rollerball and fibre tip pens tend to 'bleed' if left in contact with the paper surface. This is avoided by issuing 'pen up' at the temporary end of plotting. Many plotters do this automatically, but the 5 second delay is usually too long. Fibre tip pens are particularly susceptible to wear, and their lines get progressively thicker. It is most obvious after a series of dotted or dashed lines have been drawn, as the pen tip is repeatedly impacted on the paper surface.

Tubular nib pens ('Rotring') are used for high quality output. Varieties of pen are compatible with all types of ink, even acid etching inks for use on acetate. They are especially prone to drying up, and the pens need constant attention to prevent the tubular nibs from becoming blocked. However, they can be supplied in a large range of line widths, and the choice of ink shade is unlimited. The line width is kept very constant almost until the pen is worn out. Usually, the pen needs to get started, but thereafter starts instantly even on tiny line segments. Not all plotters have the necessary mechanism to 'soft land' these pens so as to get the most out of them.

Perhaps the best pen type for the PC user is the ceramic tip pen. In this pen, ink is drawn through a hard-wearing ceramic 'fibre' from the reservoir to the paper, by capillary action. They are more resistant to drying out than other types, but still suffer to some degree. They also start well, and are particularly useful for fine text or figures. Since the ceramic is hard, it is wear resistant, and the line thickness maintains well.

14.11 PRINCIPLES OF PROGRAMMING PLOTTER COMMANDS

The available plot area on an A3 size plotter will be approximately 360 mm across and 270 mm down the A3 page, located on the plotter in landscape format. These dimensions vary slightly from device to device, but within a small enough range that the plot area has the 3 (V) to 4 (H) aspect ratio of a video monitor. An arm sweeps across the page, and a pen carrier moves up and down the arm, such that the point of the pen may be positioned anywhere within the plot space. Positioning is to a notional accuracy of 0.1 mm, and this unit is known as the 'plotter step'. In old-fashioned units, only one motion took place at a time, so that the line was actually formed of tiny steps, but in modern plotters, both motions take place simultaneously, and a much smoother line is generated. In cheap plotters, an initially wavy portion might occur as the plotting gets under way. This is the result of a flimsy, or worn, mechanism.

Movements of the pen are commanded by sending a command letter, followed by a pair of coordinates. The command letter for a movement with the pen raised is usually 'M', and to draw a line with the pen lowered is usually 'D'. This command letter is followed by a pair of coordinates in plotter steps relative to an origin at the bottom left-hand corner of the sheet. The x coordinate is given first.

A typical sequence to draw a 10 mm square would be as follows:

```
M 100 100
D 200 100
D 200 200
D 100 200
D 100 100
```

This appears to be straightforward. However, some plotters have peculiar foibles about the format of the information on each line. The command letter may need to be the first letter on the line, or space characters might be ignored. The separator between the coordinates might be satisfactory as a space character, or a comma might be needed. It may indeed be the case that, with another command, one can specify what the separator will be. The line may need to finish with CR LF, just CR, or with some special character like ';', or with an ASCII control code. It might be possible to string all the commands together on one line, for example:

```
M 100 100;D 200 100 200 200 100 200 100 100
```

Maximum and minimum values of these coordinates vary in a way which depends on model and manufacturer. At the cheap end of the scale, plot coordinates (which are in tenths of a millimetre remember) may not attempt to position the pen outside the available plot area. This might be from 0 to 3600 in x, and 0 to 2700 in y or thereabouts. In contrast, other plotters may intelligently clip lines which attempt to cross the borders of the plot area, and allow coordinates to range from say -16 383 to +16 383, or -32 767 to +32 767. The latter are using a full sixteen bits to store the coordinate, the former possibly uses bit for parity checking internally. The limitations on the allowable range of input coordinates should not prove a problem if one has a reasonable scale range and some clipping. The very best plotters permit the clipping window to be set by a command, followed by the two pairs of coordinates for diagonally opposite corners of the window. The command letter for this, where available, tends to be machine specific.

Only one other command letter is required, and that is the command to change pens. This is usually the letter J, followed by the pen number which should be picked up. Again, plotters differ in their intelligence: at the low end of the scale, often crashing a pen into a full stocker, or picking up nothing. The better ones are able to remember where they have temporarily left a pen.

Really portable software will perform all clipping in the FORTRAN code. This means that windows can be set regardless of the firmware in the plotter. Benefit is also found if only the three fundamental operations 'move', 'draw', and 'pen select' are used. With only these three commands, it is possible to do all graphics primitives (circles, arcs, boxes) and drawing text by instructing the plotter to draw the appropriate series of individual vectors. The overhead of this is surprisingly small.

Where a plotter is directly connected to a PC, even repetitive calls to inefficient routines to generate the many 'move' and 'draw' commands needed to plot text and graphics primitives will still leave the PC able to far outstrip the plotter. Additional speed is obtained where the plot commands are saved to a file. They may be plotted subsequently by sending the contents of this file to the plotter with a print spooler program. However, where the plot instructions are saved to a file, generating all the vectors for each plot primitive will lead to long and overly complex files. Economies of file size are obtained by using the plot primitives built into the plotter. For example, all the plotters of the Graphtec/Roland type will output a string of text with the current size, spacing and pen/type when commanded with a leading 'P'. For example:

```
FORMAT(' PThis is the Job Title: ')
```

To generate the individual plot vectors for this simple line of text may need a hundred or so move and draw commands. As a corollary to this, the plotter may take a considerable length of time in drawing text. Most modern devices have a large buffer in which the commands are stored. It would be desirable to hold the entire plot, so that the PC was returned to service as quickly as possible. However, when the plotter's buffer is filled with multi-vector commands, such as character generation and shading, it may take so long executing them that the PC 'times out' the serial port, terminates data transfer, and returns control to the application program with an incomplete diagram. Rectification of this common situation is to set a long delay by one of the uses of the DOS 'MODE' command.

Text drawn with the explicit P command may be sized by the use of the S command. Ordinarily, each character is plotted in a square box whose size is an exact multiple of 0.7 mm in each coordinate direction. Characters (including descenders, or the 'below the line' part of letters such as 'g', 'j', 'p', 'q' and 'y') fill the y extent of this box, and most often $^5/_7$ of the width, leaving a space of $^2/_7$ the width as an intercharacter gap. The spacing of characters is adjustable on most plotters, essentially making the individual character cells non-contiguous. The parameter for the S command confusingly starts from 0, not 1, so that the width of the character is 0.7*(n+1) where an 'S n ' command is given. There may be a limited range of character sizes.

Text may also be rotated: in some cases to arbitrary orientations; in others, only to four positions corresponding to the cardinal points.

Important primitives are the circle and arc. These tend to require an implementation specific command letter, and need, as parameters, the origin or centre coordinates, radius, and, in the case of an arc, some data on the start and end points. Some plotters can produce spirals too. All of them have a marker symbol facility.

Line types, including solid and various dot—dash patterns, may be generated. The facility to change the repeat period of a patterned line is usually available. Experience shows that dot–dash patterns are often disappointing even on good plotters. This is because the numerous impacts destroy the fineness of the point of a fibre tip pen, and ball-point types have a poor flow of ink initially, leading to a faint start to each dash, and an overall poor quality. A defect which may also prove unacceptable is that the dot–dash algorithm does not correct for the length of a vector such that it always starts and ends with a dash, as a human draughtsman would, but they often start and end with the 'gaps'. One may need to supplement the dashed drawing with a set of symbols to mark the endpoints of each vector.

A further facility which all of plotters boast is the facility to move, not to absolute coordinates, but to a position relative to the last pen position. The use of relative move and draw commands, especially following text operations, makes it difficult to refine the appearance of diagrams: a small adjustment of the size of the text leads to a dislocation of plot details before and after. This is worsened by the fact that plotters fall into two camps, those that consider a 'plot relative' command given after a text string instruction to relate to the coordinates given for the start of the string, and those that consider that it should be relative to the final pen position at the end of the string. Ostensibly identical plotters can differ in this important respect.

Furthermore, many relative moves one after another give rise to a problem of 'round-off'. Suppose a graph axis is to be marked with 40 ticks. The gap should be 6.25 mm, so that the overall length is 250 mm. However, the nearest increment is, say, 62 plotter steps, and the overall distance is short by 2 mm. This may be glaringly evident in the finished product. In this case, it could of course be corrected with the use of alternate 62 and 63 step intervals, but the general case is usually more intractable. Most plotters have commands for drawing axes with evenly spaced tick marks.

Plotters may have a serial (RS232) interface, a parallel (Centronics) interface, or increasingly they are supplied with both. As with printers, connecting to the parallel interface gives fewest problems, since there are few or no system configuration parameters at either computer or plotter ends. This is not the case with serial interfaces. In case of doubt, it is best to set both devices to the slowest possible data transmission rates, and to gradually increase them until a communications problem occurs. At that point, it should be obvious what is the source of the trouble. Taking it slowly allows one to finally arrive at a situation where communications proceed at 9600 baud with no loss of data.

A more serious problem with FORTRAN programs potentially arises when one considers the DOS devices to which a plotter might be connected. Typically, the parallel port will be known to DOS as PRN, LPT, LPT1, etc. The serial port may be known as AUX, AUX1, COM, COM1 etc, or if the serial port has been assigned to be the printer port, it may assume the names PRN or LPT. Where the serial port is assigned the role of primary print device, it may not be possible to access the parallel port.

Most FORTRANs assume that the carriage control characters that appear in column 1 of formatted output should be obeyed for the CON and PRN/LPT devices, but not for AUX/COM, etc. Any attempt to produce output on a range of possible connections can cause problems. The following is an example of what can occur, in this case a Roland DXY 101 plotter was used. When connected to a serial port it reacted well to commands of the form

```
FORMAT('D 100 100')
```

but since the 'D' was snatched to act as carriage control when output was directed to the parallel port, the plotter could not interpret the command. Changing the format to

```
FORMAT(' D 100 100')
```

led to the plotter working fine when connected to the parallel port, but it needed the stricter format, without the leading blank, when connected to the serial port. To be perverse, when the serial port was known as the PRN device, the latter format worked again.

It is well worth trying some simple permutations of this on a particular plotter, to see if it is sensitive to the strictness of the format of the data it is sent. Later Roland plotters appear not to be so fussy.

Table 14.2 gives a list of the commands for the Graphtec/Roland type of plotters it will be noticed that the differences are often subtle, but enough to crash an unsuspecting program. It is therefore reassuring to see that the HPGL standard is becoming more widely accepted—any standard makes life easier, and where it is better, or as good, as the alternatives, that must be a good thing. Even when a standard is just slightly poorer than the alternatives, it is acceptable. Fortunately, HPGL offers all that the others do, and more. This has been recognized even by manufacturers who produced plotters with the Graphtec/Roland plotter command language: their later machines support HPGL as an option.

Table 14.2 Commands for some Graphtec and Roland plotters

Command	Command letter	Comments
Move to absolute coords	M	Follow with coordinates in 0.1 mm steps
Draw to absolute coords	D	(As the move command)
Move to relative words	R	Similar to M/D commands, but relative to last pen position
Draw to relative words	I	(As the move command)
Pen change	J	Follow with pen number
Home (go to standby position)	H	No parameter
Print text	P	Follow with text string
Size text	S	Follow by size number (limited on some plotters
Set text spacing	O	Not on all plotters: where available complements S command
Set character rotation	Q	Follow by 1, 2, 3, 4 to denote 90 degree rotations. Some plotters interpret parameter >4 to be rotation in 0.1 degrees...up to 3604!

Table 14.2 Commands for some Graphtec and Roland plotters (continued)

Command	Command letter	Comments
Set line type	L	Give line pattern number
Set line type repeat length	B	This may be specified in mm or tenths
Place a marker	N	Follow with marker number (may be 0...4, or 0...15)
Draw a circle		} These commands are quite machine } specific
Draw an arc		}
Hatch a rectangle		}
Set plot window		} These aren't implemented on all } plotters
Draw axes, with or without tick marks		}

14.12   HEWLETT PACKARD GRAPHICS LANGUAGE (HPGL)

Many plotters use a command language which emulates that designed originally for Hewlett Packard plotters. The Hewlett Packard devices are usually of a very high standard of design, construction and performance, but may cost several times as much as similar (and compatible) equipment sourced from elsewhere.

The essence of the HPGL is that each command starts with a two-letter code, in capitals, rather than the single letter of the other effective 'standard' described above. There are fewer variations on the HPGL standard than on the single command letter type of control: anything which is compatible is usually identical. Occasionally, an otherwise compatible plotter does not respond to the HPGL command to 'show thyself', whereby the plotter replies with its (HP equivalent) model number. This is understandable, if annoying, since some software uses the reply to decide how large a plot area there is. HP plotters usually only have a serial interface. Many compatible plotters have parallel interfaces, and those tend to support unidirectional communications, so cannot respond to any enquiry function.

We only know of one non-HPGL plotter language with a two-letter command set, although no doubt there are others. The one we know is the Epson HI-80 plotter in mode 0. On the other hand, that plotter also has a mode 1, which follows the Graphtec/Roland format, and mode 2 (with an optional ROM fitted), which is essentially HPGL. Instead of separate move and draw commands, the HPGL has commands for pen up, and pen down, but only a pen move command. Whether or not a line is drawn depends on whether the pen is up or down. Since there are relative and absolute move commands, this approach is neither better nor worse than that described above.

The command for 'pen up' is PU, and for 'pen down' is PD. Movement is in terms of coordinates, which may be specified in thousandths of an inch, or in some plotters, 0.025 mm units. Since 0.001 inch is 0.0254 mm, error can accumulate if the constant is wrongly assumed. For non-representational diagrams, however, the error may be neglected.

To make the pen carriage move to absolute coordinates, the PA command is given, and for relative coordinates, PR. Following the coordinates, and several pairs of coordinates may be given which will be moved to consecutively, the HPGL expects a ';' (semicolon) to terminate the command. Commands may be strung together on the same line, but must be separated by semicolons. For example, the square box is produced by

```
PU;PA 400 400;PD;PA 800 200 400 400 200 400 200 200;
```

If the 'select pen' command SP (followed by the pen number) is included, all graphics operations may be programmed with the four commands:

```
PU          PD
PA          SP
```

Table 14.3 lists the primary HPGL commands with some brief notes. More detailed explanations of most of the commands follow in the text.

Table 14.3 HPGL commands

Command	Command letters	Notes
Initialize plotter settings	IN	} The IN and DF commands } are fundamentally quite } similar, and differ in
Set defaults	DF	} detail only
Set a rectangular clipping window	IW	Follow with coords of two opposite corners
Input control points	IP	Give the coordinates of the control points

Table 14.3 HPGL commands (continued)

Command	Command letters	Notes
User scaling	SC	Give the user coords which map to P1 and P2
Move to absolute coords	PA	Follow these commands with pairs of coords
Move to relative coords	PR	Follow these commands with pairs of coords
Pen up	PU	Follow these commands with pairs of words (optional)
Pen down	PU	Follow these commands with pairs of words (optional)
Set line type	LT	Line type number
Pen change	SP	Pen number
Home (go to standby position)	SP 0	
Print text	LB	Follow with text, and terminate with ASCII 03
Skip char spaces	CP	Say how many
Size text (relative)	SR n m	Horiz. and vert. sizes relative to P1 and P2
Size text (absolute)	SI n m	Horiz. and vert. sizes
Character slant	SL n	Meaning of n is given in the text
Direction of text (relative)	DR	Give two parameters relative to P1 and P2
Direction of text (absolute)	DI	Give two parameters for components in page x and y

Table 14.3 HPGL commands (continued)

Command	Command letters	Notes
Designate and select primary and alternate character sets	CS, CA, SS, SA	May use with SM command
Set line type repeat length	LT	Uses second parameter to LT
Draw a circle	CI	Circle and arc commands: see text
Draw an arc	AA, AR	
Area fills	FT PT RA EA RR ER WG EW	See text
Set up axes	YT XT TL	See text

14.13 PLOTTER INITIALIZATION IN HPGL

There are basically two commands which return the plotter to its power on status, cancelling instructions sent for the previous plot. These are the IN and DF commands. Of these, the DF command tends to be a subset of the IN command. the IN command should be used in preference to the DF command, even if this means resetting the options, because it gives more complete control and total portability.

Following the IN command, it is desirable to set up a plot window, and plot scaling. We personally favour doing all the scaling in the FORTRAN program, and issuing raw commands to the plotter. This means ignoring the SC (scale) command, although it will be described a little later for completeness. The command to set up a plot window is the IW ('input window') command. This may be given without parameters, in which case the available plot window is the whole accessible paper surface. The size of this is set on the plotter using DIP switches or panel switches depending on model, and the available plot area varies slightly. As a preference, we select 360 mm by 270 mm on ISO A3 paper. This partly reflects a prejudice for an early plotter which had those limits as its maxima, but also reflects the fact that these are the largest round numbers that will fit and yet retain the 4 : 3 aspect ratio of a typical video monitor screen. This eases the mapping between screen and plotter images.

Basically, the `IW` command with parameters needs to be given the coordinates of the lower left and upper right points of the plot window. To set the preferred area, and remembering that each plotter step is 0.025 mm, send

```
IW 0,0,14400,10800;
```

HPGL plotters will crop the individual pen vectors when they come up against the limits of the window. This applies whether or not the vector is one sent directly from the program, or one which the plotter generates itself from one of the more complicated functions (plot text, arcs, etc.).

The `IP` ('input points') command is easy to confuse with `IW`. It has a completely different role, however. By sending the `IP` command, it is possible to set a standard length on the plot for use in some sizing operations, and in combination with the `SC` ('scale') command, it enables one set of user coordinates to be mapped to a particular area on the plotter surface. The format of the `IP` command is

```
IP xp1,yp1,xp2,yp2;
```

where (xp1,yp1) are the coordinates of the lower left-hand point termed P1 in the documentation, and (xp2,yp2) are the coordinates of the upper right point P2. The allowable range for these coordinates is a function of plotter size and paper size, and they are given in plotter steps. Giving no parameters is the same as giving them the maximum allowable values for that paper size. This setting can affect such things as character height.

The `SC` command associates user coordinates with P1 and P2. It has a similar format to the `IP` command, in that it has the two letters of the command followed by two pairs of coordinates and a terminator, as in

```
SC xq1,yq1,xq2,yq2;
```

The locations of the points (xq1,yq1) and (xq2,yq2), which may be in metres, miles, gallons or whatever, are mapped to points P1 and P2, and intermediate points are scaled to lie on the plot at the appropriate position between them. This then means that after setting the scaling factors, raw coordinate information can be sent to the plotter.

Suppose we call these two points Q1 and Q2 so that they are easy to refer to. What happens if a point is specified in raw or unscaled coordinates which lie outside the rectangle defined with Q1 as its lower left and Q2 as its upper right corner? Provided that when mapped with the scaling factors that result from the application of `IP` and `SC` commands it still lies within the physical plot window set by means of the `IW` command, then it will be plotted correctly. There is therefore some merit in setting `IP` and `IW` parameters in a connected way, i.e. unless there is good reason to the contrary, set both to the same values each time.

Using SC on its own, with no parameters, resets a 1 : 1 scaling, that is, the coordinates sent to the plotter are assumed to be in plotter steps. One use of the IP, SC pair is to set the available plot area to accept the NDC coordinate system of 0 to 32 767 in x and y, just like the GSX and GEM VDI screen and printer drivers do.

Some HPGL plotters have a choice of interfaces. Those that are connected to a parallel (Centronics) port cannot send information back to the computer, those connected to the serial port can. This gives rise to the OP and OW commands, which are similar to IP and IW, except that the command is sent to the plotter without parameters, and the plotter returns the current settings. Hence a program could interrogate the plotter to find the paper size, or cropping window size. For a given plotter there may be a range of enquiry or output functions. These normally start with the letter 'O', and have a direct analogue in a function to set a characteristic. The details of each of these are left to the reader to discover from his manuals. The most important function is to determine the 'power on' settings of a given device: after that, the application should keep track of changes in commands via software.

14.14 LINE TYPES IN HPGL

Line types are governed by the LT command. This has one or two parameters, the first of which is the line type number. What is selected here governs the dot–dash pattern obtained. Within the range of options permitted by the particular plotter, the smaller the number, the more open the pattern. Hence setting the first parameter to zero makes the plotter merely put a dot at the consecutive coordinates it is instructed to move to, even with the pen down, and setting the first parameter to 1 or more gives a dotted or dashed line. A Roland DXY880A, which has an HPGL- compatible software interface, allows negative pattern numbers: selecting one of these is an instruction to the plotter to select the corresponding positive numbered pattern, but to automatically adjust it so that the line starts and ends with a dash. This is useful where a neat finish is required, or where one might wish to clearly delineate the points where line sections meet.

The second parameter gives the pitch over which the pattern repeats. This is specified as a percentage of the distance between input points P1 and P2. If the second parameter is not given, the plotter assumes a value, normally around 1.5 per cent of the diagonal distance between P1 and P2. Solid line drawing is restored by giving the LT command with no parameters.

Drawing dot–dash patterns is noisy, and shortens pen life as the point is repeatedly impacted on to the paper surface. This is particularly noticeable when a dot only pattern is selected: to be clearly visible this needs to have a repeat pitch smaller than for the other line types, and very many impacts can be required in even a short section of line. Where the total number of pens permits, it is better to switch to an alternate colour rather than use this line type. Where more line types are required than are avilable, consider the possibility of drawing the line twice, first in a solid light colour, and then with a straightforward dash pattern in a second colour. This works best with longer line segments. Note too that there will probably be a colour interaction between the underneath and overlaid pen colours: for obvious reasons if the underneath colour is black, this method is useless.

A VS or pen velocity command is provided to set pen speed. This should be slow if the pen needs 'starting'. Special spirit based fibre tips for use on overhead projector (OHP) transparency film normally start well, and have low friction, so may be run at the highest speed. The VS command is followed by a speed parameter with a machine dependent range.

14.15 GRAPHICS PRIMITIVES IN HPGL

HPGL plotters have a range of graphics primitives and related commands. The following are among the functions which can be produced by one or two commands:

- Plot axes with ticks (XT, YT, and TL)
- Mark points with symbols (SM)
- Draw rectangles which are empty or filled with pattern (RA, EA, RR, or ER)
- Draw pie slices which are empty or filled (WG or EW)
- Set the fill pattern, and 'pen thickness' for solid fill (FT and PT)
- Draw arcs (AA and AR)
- Draw circles (CI)

Space precludes a detailed treatment of all of these commands.

Pen plotters are inefficient at area fill, and it is suggested that for complex filled areas one has immediate recourse to a standard graphics system: HPGL on its own is not enough, except for bars, pie slices, and triangles, and the labour of coding the area fill subroutines is unrewarding. Both GEM VDI and Windows have HPGL plotter drivers. We will concentrate on the marker (SM) command, and the arc/circle commands (AA, AR and CI).

Taking first the SM command. This command is followed by a single character. That character is then plotted centred on the current pen position. It is affected by 'size' and 'direction'. One could use this to mark the data points on a line with strings of a or b. To invoke the proper marker symbols, it is necessary to designate the special character set. This substitutes the marker symbols for the upper case letters in the currently active character set before commanding the appropriate letter.

The arc and circle commands differ in one important particular. Whereas the start point of an arc is the current pen position, the circle is centred on the current pen position. In neither case is both the start point *and* the centre given in the command, so each must be preceded by an appropriate pen move or draw command. In both cases, the curve is made up from straight line segments. The default is to build it up from 5 degree segments, although as little as 1 degree may be selected. 1 degree segments make for a very smooth curve. Coarser selections may be made: 60 degree segments turn the circle into a hexagon. All polygons from triangles upwards may therefore be produced. The circle (CI) command must be followed by the radius in plotter steps, and then optionally by the resolution in degrees. The arc commands may either be in absolute (AA) or relative (AR) modes. The two-letter code is followed by the coordinates *x*, *y* (absolute or relative to the current pen position), the central angle, and optionally, the resolution as for the circle. The central angle for the arc command is taken as positive *ANTI*-clockwise from the current pen position, and may be positive or negative. A full circle can be drawn with the arc command.

14.16 TEXT IN HPGL

The fundamental command in HPGL for text is the LB or 'label' command. This should be followed by a text string, which will be plotted with the current pen and character size, rotation and other settings, up to an ASCII 03 character. This is a non- printable character which is reserved for terminating text strings in HPGL. An example of the use of this command is given by the following:

```
      CHARACTER*21 STRING
      STRING = 'H-P GRAPHICS LANGUAGE'
      WRITE ( 8, 100 ) STRING, CHAR(3)
100   FORMAT (' LB',A21,A1,';')
```

It is possible to exchange the ASCII 03 (CTRL-C) character as a data terminator with another one, but almost all FORTRANs permit this character to be output, so there is little merit in so doing. The procedure for altering the terminator is to use the DT command followed by the new terminator and completed with the obligatory semicolon. A command CP permits the pen to be moved in multiples of the character cell size. The key phrase CP is followed by two parameters, which give the number of character cells to move in the *x* and *y* directions respectively. Either or both may be zero, and giving the command with no parameters can be visualized as if a CR LF sequence had been given. Using this mode is more convenient than using PA or PR commands in many instances.

The size of the character which is plotted can be set using the SI and SR commands. The SI command is the easiest to understand. This needs to be followed by two numeric parameters which are the width of the character cell in centimetres and its height in centimetres. It is possible to scale these two independently: in contrast, most of the single letter (Graphtec/Roland plotters) commands permit only one scaling, although it is usually possible to modify the gap between characters too. It is, however, somewhat confusing that the units for the SI command should be different to those for other commands. A minimum and maximum character size exists for a given plotter. The command needs to be terminated as usual with a semicolon.

The SR or 'size relative' command designates the character cell size with parameters which are percentages of the distance defined by the 'input points' command. For example, giving

```
SR  0.5 2.5;
```

would set the width of the character to 0.5 per cent of the distance between the x coordinates of P1 and P2, and the height to 2.5 per cent of the difference in y coordinates.

Both the SI and SR commands accept integer or real parameters, and if given without parameters will restore character size to its machine default value. The appearance of the SR and SI commands are similar, but their effect may be quite different. Using the SR command exclusively will enable both plot vectors and text to be scaled using the method outlined above under the IP and SC commands.

A modification to the character appearance may be made simply by slanting the letters to produce a crude italicization. This is done with the aid of the SL command. The single parameter which follows the SL is the tangent of the angle of inclination. A negative parameter slants the letters backwards. Optimum effects are gained with small degrees of forward slant. Slanting is turned off by the DF command, or by using SL with a zero value, or no parameter at all.

In the same way that there are absolute and relative size commands, there are absolute and relative direction commands. These two have the DI and DR codes. Each is followed by two parameters called 'run' and 'rise'. In the case of the DR command, they are percentages of the differences in x and y coordinates between P1 and P2, and in the case of the DI command, they can be specified in any units. The base line of the text is rotated by an angle theta, such that tan (theta) is given by the formula:

$$\tan (\theta) = \text{rise/run}$$

In the case of the relative (DR) command, run and rise are scaled before this evaluation is made. Either or both of rise and run may be zero or negative, as text may be drawn at any inclination. The CP command (above) reacts to the DI and DR commands by moving relative to the inclined character baseline.

There is a sequence of commands for designating and selecting character sets. However, what might seem at first glance to be a means of selecting a set of alternate fonts turns out to be nothing of the sort. Basically, in the ASCII code table there are a number of characters which have special national designations. For example, the currency symbols change. The ASCII code table with this small number of symbols changed to accommodate a particular national preference is referred to as a character set. It is possible to designate one of these as the standard set, and another as the alternate set, and to switch the standard or alternate sets into play as the current set. This would hardly be worth bothering with, since it is normally possible to select a character set via DIP switches, were it not for the fact that HPGL does not have a 'produce mark symbols' command. The method for obtaining marker symbols is to select as the primary character set one national set, and, as the alternate one, a set in which upper case letters (usually) from A to O inclusive are replaced by a marker symbol. Then when the letter is commanded, and the alternate set is selected, a marker symbol is plotted. The printing of marker symbols is probably the main area in which the HPGL language is inferior to the Graphtec/Roland standard described earlier in this chapter. HPGL commands also tend to be slightly more long-winded.

The Roland DXY880A has Greek letters and Japanese symbols in ASCII codes 128–255, and these may be plotted by sending the appropriate ASCII codes in the LB command. A single special character may be formed by use of the UC ('user defined character') command. The reader is referred to the plotter documentation for details of this facility for which we find little use.

The two commands which select the standard and alternate character sets are the CS and CA commands respectively. Each of these is followed by the set number to be selected: this is machine dependent. Subsequently, the standard and alternate character sets may be selected using the SS and SA commands, neither of which has a parameter. To change sets 'on the fly', the 'shift in' and 'shift out' characters 14 and 15 in the ASCII set may be slipped into an LB command.

14.17 CHOICE OF GRAPHICS OUTPUT DEVICE

Some of the characteristics of hard-copy devices may be seen in Figure 14.1.

Plotters are fast, and can produce coloured illustrations at sizes larger than ISO A4. Printers offer somewhat improved resolution for graphics. Colour printers are available, but are substantially more expensive than black on white printers. They may be of equivalent cost to plotters. The maximum size of paper is similar to ISO A3.

Maximum resolution is obtained with laser printer technology, although adding colour and/or large paper sizes (i.e. bigger than A4) is prohibitively expensive. Speed, however, may rival or exceed that of plotters.

For areas of solid colour 'fill' in simple geometric shapes, plotters excel. Where more complex shapes are to be filled, the outline needs to be traced afterwards to finish off the ragged edge. Plotters can do hatch fills easily, but patterns only with difficulty.

Printers, even laser printers, are poor at large areas of solid fill. They excel at pattern fill, and at some hatching–particularly horizontal lines, and horizontal grids. Diagonal hatching is usually disappointing on a dot matrix printer.

Plotters are best for vector graphics, and an inexpensive plotter will give excellent vectors in all directions. Raster devices, like printers, can give a staircase effect on diagonals, or erratic verticals when the printer is not in adjustment or is printing bidirectionally.

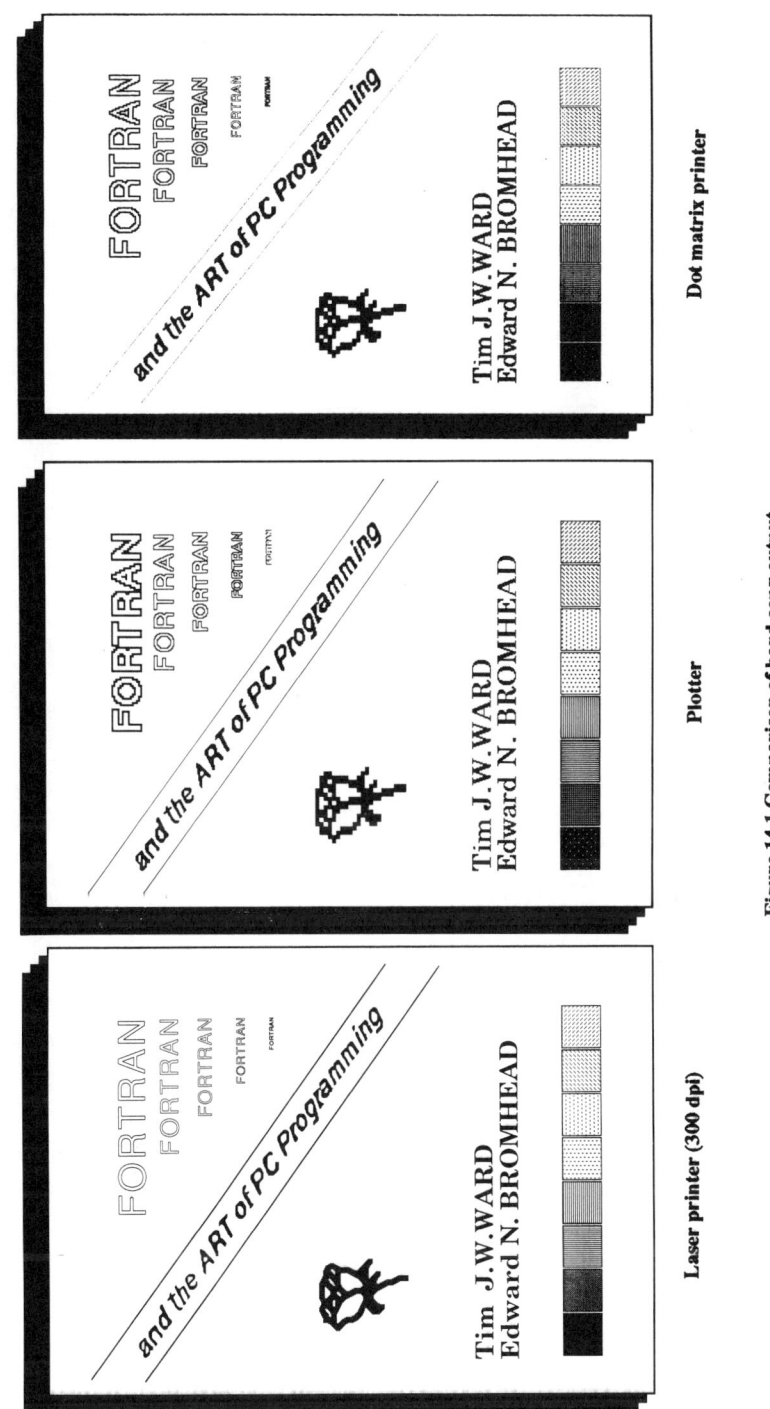

Figure 14.1 Comparison of hard copy output

CHAPTER 15

FORTRAN LIBRARIES
AND UTILITIES

15.1 INTRODUCTION

In this chapter we look at FORTRAN libraries. A library file will typically consist of object code from a number of subroutines and functions (notice that the origin of the object code is not specified, it could be FORTRAN, PASCAL, C, or assembler, however, it is only of interest in the current context if it is callable from FORTRAN). An experienced FORTRAN programmer, who has adopted a modular programming style, will have written a great many useful little subroutines and functions which he will use over and over again. He will keep these program units in one or more utility libraries. Indeed many such utilities have become commercially available, and in recognition of their value both Microsoft and Ryan Mac-Farland publish a list of third party utilities which is distributed with their compilers.

In the same way, we have developed utility libraries to give us control over DOS and our microcomputers from FORTRAN. These include two libraries which make available almost all of the DOS (interrupt 21 hex) functions, certainly all the useful ones. We also have a library of screen handlers, using ANSI escape sequences and DOS functions. A fourth library provides an interface between FORTRAN and the Digital Research graphics packages GEM and its predecessor GSX. Examples of the assembler source code from some of the subroutines which make up these utility libraries appear throughout the text of the book. The complete set of utilities are included on the disk set which can be purchased to complement the book, and a brief description of the contents of these libraries is given in Section 5.4.

Although the routines are coded to interface with Microsoft FORTRAN, they can be called from Ryan MacFarland FORTRAN using the interface routines which they supply in their compiler package. It should prove fairly simple to modify these utilities to suit any FORTRAN compiler, as assembler source code is provided.

In the remaining sections of the chapter we look again at graphics and graphics systems using routines from the GEM/FORTRAN interface library, with source code examples of some of the assembler routines involved. To get the most out of these sections you will need access to the graphics primitives and drivers in GEM or GSX. Any one of the useful GEM applications contains these primitives and drivers so you don't need to purchase the more expensive GEM programmers toolkit. If you have some other graphics system then you may still find that the information contained in these sections is helpful—most systems contain a similar kernel of graphics primitives and functions.

15.2 WHAT ARE FORTRAN LIBRARIES?

When you compile a FORTRAN source file which contains one or more program units (such as subroutines and functions), you obtain an object file (provided there are no syntax errors) of relocatable machine code. This object file can then be bound together with other object files to obtain an executable file. This process is called 'linking'. When you run the link program you have to provide a list of object files which contain all the program units that you reference (subroutines that you call, functions that you use). The linker then searches through the list of object files making the links between the 'calls' to the program units and the particular subroutines and functions. If you forget to include an object file containing a program unit referenced by your program you will obtain an error message 'unsatisfied external references' followed by a list of subroutines and functions that the linker cannot find.

As an alternative to providing a list of object files for your linker you can put all the object files (except the one containing the main program unit) into a library file (.LIB) and then provide only the library file name in the link list (following the object file name containing the main program unit). More generally a link list will contain the object file of the main program unit, a number of other object files and then a number of library files.

The linker will always reference at least one library file, this is the library file (or files) provided with the FORTRAN compiler. This file will contain, amongst other things, the machine code for all the FORTRAN statements, symbols, and intrinsic functions that are provided by the compiler, as well as all the run-time error messages. You may not need to specify the name of this library file in your link list, but you will have to provide a search path in your CONFIG.SYS file to the directory where the library is stored or you will need to have this in a specific directory so that the linker knows where to find it.

Some linkers are one pass linkers, they search through the link list once only in the order in which the object files and libraries are listed, looking to satisfy all 'external references'. This means that a routine in a file at the start of the list will not be found if called from a subroutine in a file later in the list. Even if your linker is not a one-pass linker, it is more efficient to put the files in the link list in a logical order. Indeed most linkers require library files to come last in the link list with the FORTRAN library or libraries provided with the compiler coming last of all (if they need to be referenced explicitly). This is because program units that are kept in libraries are generally utility routines which may be called from a number of different program units and so, by putting them at the end of the list, all external references to these utility routines will be resolved on the first pass of the linker.

For more information about compiling and linking, the reader is referred to Chapter 5.

A library file contains the relocatable machine code of one or more object files. It is not, however, simply a collection of object files under one name. The library file is a single file with header information which contains information about all the program units in the library. There are two common forms in which FORTRAN libraries are built. The first is the more standard Microsoft form, and the second is the Intel form. Usually, linkers and library managers have a 'native mode'. Exceptionally, the Phoenix PLINK86 and its associated library manager PLIB86 can handle either form. The precise details of how the object files are stored in a library is something the FORTRAN programmer is unlikely to need to understand.

A library of object files is different from a single object file containing a collection of program units. For one thing if a call is made to a program unit in an object file then the complete object file is linked into the executable code with all the other program units whether they're required or not. This could make for an extremely inefficient and cumbersome executable file, with 'dead code' or instructions that are unreachable. Also, each time a program unit in the source file is changed, the complete file will need to be recompiled, this could become very tedious if a large number of program units are gathered in one file—particularly during the testing and debugging stages of a new section of code. With a library only those units that are called are bound into the executable code, and each unit in a library can be modified in isolation. In addition most library managers provide a number of useful functions for the maintenance of the code they contain.

15.3 WHY USE LIBRARIES?

If you exploit one of the most powerful features of the FORTRAN programming language—modularity—then you will very quickly accumulate a collection of utility program units which will be useful in the development of programs beyond the one that you are currently developing. Or if you are writing a particularly large and complex program you may have a collection of routines that serve a specific purpose within that program and which will be accessed by a number of different program units. In these circumstances it makes sense to gather all this code into one library file.

Another common use for object libraries is to collect all program units that use non-standard FORTRAN statements or structures. Then when the code is ported to a new machine or compiler it is only the program units in this library that will need to be amended. This makes the support of code over a number of different machines a well-defined and manageable task.

As we have seen in examples throughout the book, it is also possible to link assembler subroutines with FORTRAN code. You would use assembler subroutines to access operating system functions not provided by your FORTRAN compiler or to speed up inefficient FORTRAN subroutines, or indeed if you wanted, for accuracy, to store and manipulate numbers to a precision not supported by your compiler. It would be natural to keep all assembler object code in a separate library or libraries.

15.4 THE LIBRARY MANAGER

The library manager, or librarian, usually comes with the compiler (as does the linker, utilities to produce cross- reference maps, etc., and a debugging system—if there is one). The library manager should provide facilities for creating, naming, and maintaining your libraries. Microsoft FORTRAN comes complete with a fairly effective library utility called, appropriately enough, LIB.

When creating an object library for the first time you will give the library a unique name with the extension 'LIB'. Some library managers may allow you to choose an extension as well as the name of the library file. However, it is generally better to use the default extension. In this way library files are always instantly recognizable in a directory listing. In addition, if you do not use the default extension for your object libraries, the linker will not recognize your file automatically as a library file and you will be forced to give the complete file name and extension in the link list. Since you are creating a new library you will want to *add* object files. You will add files by giving a list of object file names—this is typically allowed to extend over a number of lines.

In addition to being able to add files to a new or existing object library, you should also be able to replace modules with new versions, delete modules no longer required, and get a complete description of the library's contents. You may also be able to combine two or more existing object libraries to form a single library.

15.5 THE UTILITY LIBRARIES

On the available disk set there are three utility libraries. Two of these libraries make all the useful DOS functions available to the FORTRAN programmer. The third library uses DOS functions and ANSI escape sequences to provide a comprehensive set of screen handling facilities. We provide all the FORTRAN and assembler source code, and demonstration programs using each utility.

The first library allows you to do many of the things you might want in your FORTRAN program but which aren't supported as standard library functions. You can set the system date and time, or read the current date or time into your program. You can interrogate the operating system to see which version of DOS it runs, see if a named file is on a disk, get or set the default directory, find the amount of disk free space, and so on. The complete contents are given in Table 15.1.The second library is more esoteric, and allows you access to some of the fancier facilities in DOS 2 and 3. Just about all the system functions are implemented, all through subroutine calls. If you want to create or delete subdirectories, use file 'handles', tinker with file attributes, 'lock' and 'unlock' parts of files, send and receive data from 'block' devices, then this is the library for you. For a list of contents see Table 15.2.

The library of screen handling routines discussed in Chapter 12 forms the third library. Functions are included to handle generalized INTEGER, REAL, and CHARACTER input, and to program

---

a cursor-selectable menu. The assembler and FORTRAN code is given (see Table 15.3).

Table 15.1 Contents of the first utility library –the UTIL1 library

Routine name	Description
DATER	Return the current date
DLFILE	Delete named file from disc
IDDOS	Determine the version of the MS DOS operating system
IDFS	Return the amount of free space on the disc, and also the amount of total space on the disc
IDRN	Return the default drive number
INK	Read one character from the keyboard buffer
IRENAM	Rename a file
ISCHAR	Look to see if there is a character in the keyboard buffer; if there is it is read
ISETDR	Change default drive number
ISETDT	Set the date
ISETIM	Set the time
ISFILE	See if the file is on the disc
JOINST	Concatenate two strings of known length
PRCHRS	Send a character to the printer
TIMER	Read the current time

Table 15.2 Contents of the second utility library–the UTIL2 library

Routine name	Description
CHCDIR	Change the current directory
CHDIRE	Change a directory entry
CLHAND	Close a file using a file 'handle'
CNTDAT	Get/set country dependent data
CONDAT	Get/set control data relevant to character or block device
CRENEW	Create new file for use with with a handle
CRHAND	Create a file for access with a handle
CRSDIR	Create a subdirectory
CRTEMP	Create a temporary ('scratch') file for use with a handle
CURDIR	Return the current directory path
DEVDAT	Get/set device data
DEVRDY	Check if a device with a specified handle is ready for I/O
DLDIRE	Delete directory entry
DRTYPE	Is named drive a local or remote (MS-NET) drive?
DSKTYP	Disc type–hard or floppy disc
DTDIRE	Get/set date and time of directory entry
DUPHND	Obtain a duplicate handle for a device
FDUPHD	Force a duplicate handle of your choice for a device
FILPTR	Position file pointer
HDTYPE	Is file with specified handle on a local or remote device
LOCKFL	Lock part of file

Table 15.2 Contents of the second utility library—the UTIL2 library (continued)

Routine name	Description
NUMTRY	Number of retries if a disc operation fails because file is shared
OPHAND	Open file for use with a handle
RDHAND	Read from a file with a specified handle
RMSDIR	Remove a subdirectory
WRTHND	Write to a file with a specified handle
UNLKFL	Unlock part of a file

Table 15.3 The screen handling library—the SCREEN library

Routine name	Description
CLS	Clear the screen using ANSI ESCapes
GOTOXY	Position the cursor
REVID	Reverse video
NORMAL	Normal video
BEEP	Sound the bell/buzzer
CURSON	Show the cursor
CURSOFF	Remove the cursor
GETCHR	Sample a character from the keyboard buffer
PUTCHR	General character and string output routines
PUTTXT	
SHWBYT	
SHWTXT	
MENU	Operate the cursor selectable menu
GETINT	General input/editing routines
GETFLO	
GETTXT	

15.6 The GSX system

GSX consists of three elements: a loader, an assignment file, and the device drivers. When the loader, which is a 'terminate- and-stay, resident' utility, is invoked, it opens the assignment file, and taking the first device driver listed therein, it loads this into memory. It then modifies the addresses in the 8086 interrupt table for interrupt EFh in the base page of memory to point to the entry point of the device driver.

An application needing to access GSX merely has to reach this entry point each time, and that is achieved by having a subroutine, written in assembler that calls the appropriate interrupt. Communication between the programmer and GSX is provided by setting and reading values in five arrays. This allows the programmer to choose between the different facilities in the graphics system and also allows the graphics system to return values describing the current status of the workstation (e.g. the screen, the plotter, etc.). To enable this communication, GSX has to know the start addresses of the five arrays. This is achieved by placing the addresses in a parameter block, the address of the parameter block is then placed on the stack immediately prior to invoking the GSX system.

GSX functions include the unloading of a particular device driver and reuse of the memory it occupies by a different driver. This is an economic procedure when RAM is in short supply. However, it demands that the first driver loaded is the biggest driver, this ensures that there is sufficient room for all the other drivers to load when required. Only one device driver is allowed in RAM at one time.

The GSX system device driver loader is called GSX.EXE. The look-up table, which *MUST* be named ASSIGN.SYS, lists the individual loadable device drivers. Finally, there are the individual drivers themselves.

In the look-up table ASSIGN.SYS appear the names of the loadable graphics device drivers alongside a number which indicates how the device is to be known by GSX. The driver which is physically the largest appears first in the list, regardless of its identification number. This is because, on the invocation of GSX, the first-named driver will be loaded into memory. All changes of graphics device thereafter will cause another driver to be overlaid in the same area of RAM. This may mean a slight inefficiency in processing speed, especially if a hard-copy (say printer) driver is the biggest and has to be loaded into RAM, only to be overlaid by a screen driver read from floppy disk as the first operation of an application. The inefficiency would be compounded each time there is a swap from screen to hard copy and back again, and necessitates the loss of the graphics image from the screen while the hard copy is in progress. However, memory *IS* used efficiently.

Invoking GSX merely demands:

```
A>GSX
```

and removal of the system, with a consequent increase in available RAM, is by

```
A>GSX N        (or NO instead of N)
```

For an IBM PC with colour graphics, and an Epson printer driven in 8-bit mode, the ASSIGN.SYS file might be:

```
21 DDFXHR8.SYS ; Epson FX/MX/RX 80 printer  - 16 kbytes
01 IBMCGA.SYS ; PC 640*200 driver      - 12 kbytes
```

The file name extension 'SYS' is preferred, and if used, may be dropped from the assignment table. The text following ';' is ignored as a comment.

Device driver numbers exist in ranges: 1–10 for screens, 11–20 for plotters, 21–30 for printers, 31–40 for metafiles, and so on.

15.7 THE GEM VDI SYSTEM

A nearly identical system to GSX is found in GEM VDI, except that the equivalent program to GSX.EXE is named, unsurprisingly, GEMVDI.EXE. GEMVDI.EXE is about 10 per cent shorter than GSX.EXE, but the device drivers are at least double the length for GEM than GSX. This reflects the more generous allowance of RAM in modern computers compared to the mean supply provided *circa* 1983 when GSX was a current product, as well as the substantially enhanced capabilities of the GEM VDI.

GEM VDI, however, expects the screen driver to remain resident at all times. This is revealed by the use of the symbol 'r' against the first driver in ASSIGN.SYS (under GEM version 1; it is not required under GEM version 2). Hard-copy drivers are loaded in addition to the screen driver, and not necessarily in the same area: they are loaded and unloaded as necessary by GEM VDI. GEM VDI may be invoked from the command line of DOS in exactly the same way as GSX, but, if this is done, it expects the GEM desktop (another of the fancy names for DOS 'shells' or user interfaces) to be loaded. GEM VDI then stays resident until GEM is abandoned. It may, however, be invoked as graphics support for a single application, and will unload itself on completion. This is done by giving the application name following a '/' symbol, e.g.

```
A>GEMVDI /myappl
```

Although a path can be specified for GEMVDI.EXE (GEM expects to find it in the \GEMSYS subdirectory), this may make the finding of ASSSIGN.SYS and the drivers unnecessarily complicated. A path is better given to the application, for example

```
A>GEMVDI /\NEXT\FINAL\myappl
```

and so on.

GEM VDI has the same ASSIGN.SYS look-up table method of linking device drivers to unit numbers as does GSX, but the table is made more complicated in that each driver now has loadable fonts. A font is the pattern of dots needed to build characters on the screen. These patterns need to be different for different sizes of character, and so there may be many font files. A list of the filenames for these follows each driver in ASSIGN.SYS. Of course this can become complicated: on an AMSTRAD PC1640 (IBM PC compatible) with an Epson printer, the assignment table is shown in Figure 15.1.

The differences between GSX and GEM lie in a few areas only. GEM VDI supports the majority of the graphics DISPLAY options of GSX, and indeed, generally extends and enhances these. For example, the GEM driver for the IBM colour graphics adapter (CGA) has a number of enhancements and additions over the GSX driver.

It is in the area of graphical input that GEM departs most from its GSX roots. This is principally to give the application more control over cursor appearance, and a better real-time interaction with the mouse and cursor. However, the GEM system makes demands on the movement of bit maps from screen RAM to other areas of memory to support the application interface. Since this might include fundamentally text based applications (e.g. GEM Write word processing software running in the graphical environment of GEM), the treatment of text fonts is much more sophisticated too–there are a whole range of functions to load fonts, and to handle their attributes, which do not exist in the more primitive GSX.

```
01 AMSTRAD; Amstrad PC1640 Hercules 720x348 resolution
;
 IBMHSS07.FNT; Hercules Swiss 7 Point
 IBMHSS10.FNT; Hercules Swiss 10 Point
 IBMHSS14.FNT; Hercules Swiss 14 Point
 IBMHSS18.FNT; Hercules Swiss 18 Point
 IBMHSS36.FNT; Hercules Swiss 36 Point
 IBMHTR07.FNT; Hercules Dutch 7 Point
 IBMHTR10.FNT; Hercules Dutch 10 Point
 IBMHTR14.FNT; Hercules Dutch 14 Point
 IBMHTR18.FNT; Hercules Dutch 18 Point
 IBMHTR36.FNT; Hercules Dutch 36 Point
11 IBMHP744; HP Plotter
;
21 EPSONHI4; Epson FX80 High resolution mode
; LPT1:
 EPSHSS07.FNT; EPSON Hi Res (120x144 dots/inch) Swiss 07
;                                                Point
 EPSHSS10.FNT; EPSON Hi Res (120x144 dots/inch) Swiss 10
;                                                Point
 EPSHSS14.FNT; EPSON Hi Res (120x144 dots/inch) Swiss 14
;                                                Point
 EPSHSS20.FNT; EPSON Hi Res (120x144 dots/inch) Swiss 20
;                                                Point
 EPSHSS28.FNT; EPSON Hi Res (120x144 dots/inch) Swiss 28
;                                                Point
 EPSHSS36.FNT; EPSON Hi Res (120x144 dots/inch) Swiss 36
;                                                Point
 EPSHTR07.FNT; EPSON Hi Res (120x144 dots/inch) Dutch 07
;                                                Point
 EPSHTR10.FNT; EPSON Hi Res (120x144 dots/inch) Dutch 10
;                                                Point
 EPSHTR14.FNT; EPSON Hi Res (120x144 dots/inch) Dutch 14
;                                                Point
 EPSHTR20.FNT; EPSON Hi Res (120x144 dots/inch) Dutch 20
;                                                Point
```

```
EPSHTR28.FNT; EPSON Hi Res (120x144 dots/inch) Dutch 28
;                                                   Point
EPSHTR36.FNT; EPSON Hi Res (120x144 dots/inch) Dutch 36
;                                                   Point
 31 METAFIL4 ; GEM File
```

Figure 15.1 Assignment table for AMSTRAD 1640 with an Epson printer

It is emphasized that it is not necessary to use the full facilities of GEM in applications to benefit from the portable graphics interface of the GEM VDI. Furthermore, it is not necessary to obtain expensive bindings: all GEM applications contain the screen and hard-copy drivers, if you do not already have a GEM application installed on your microcomputer then you will need to purchase one of these useful applications–or the least expensive. The FORTRAN programmer can produce his own bindings on the basis of the skeleton assembly language interface shown below or he could, for example use the more sophisticated bindings on the disk set which can be purchased to complement this book. It is undoubtedly the most cost effective and simplest means of obtaining high portability from graphics applications software, and is to be recommended.

15.8 PROGRAMMING DETAILS FOR GSX AND GEM

The data structures consist basically of five separate INTEGER*2 arrays. One of these is filled with data which sets up various graphics options, and two each are for data passed to, and returned from, the graphics system. In the Digital Research documentation these are termed the CONTRL, INTIN, PTSIN, INTOUT, and PTSOUT arrays. These names do not reflect the implicit typing of FORTRAN, but experience has shown that it is more important to recognize the names, and be able to reconcile them with the documentation than it is (in this case) to save the effort of explicit typing, and the consequent danger that the INTEGER characteristics of these variables will not be self-evident to the programmer. One further problem is that the documentation uses both base 0 and base 1 for the array dimensions. This needs to be standardized somewhere, and in this chapter an array index base of 1 will be used.

The CONTRL array is used for the fundamental choice parameters which can be made in a call to GSX or GEM: it is used both for transmitting these selections to the graphics system, and returning data from it. In contrast, the other four arrays are used for one way communications only. INTIN and PTSIN passing data to the graphics system, and INTOUT and PTSOUT being used to receive information from the graphics system. INTIN and INTOUT essentially relate to parameters which more completely specify the choices made by the settings of CONTRL, and the two arrays PTSIN and PTSOUT are used primarily for coordinate information.

The method of invoking the graphics system may be at one of two levels: making a simple subroutine call, specifying the five arrays as parameters, or by using the more sophisticated bindings in the GEM/GSX library. In effect, the latter merely obscure the detail of the call, but make its purpose clearer by needing fewer parameters.

In the following section the simple subroutine call is described. Use of the GEM/GSX library is left to Section 15.10.

15.9 ACCESSING GEM VDI AND GSX USING A SIMPLE SUBROUTINE CALL

The interface subroutine (called GEM or GSX in the following) places the addresses of the five parameter arrays on to the stack and then invokes the graphics system. Suppose we are programming in Microsoft FORTRAN, and intend to call the subroutine GEM. Both GEM VDI and GSX expect a 4-byte address to be given in the DS:DX data registers which points to a parameter block, giving, in order, the addresses of the start of CONTRL, INTIN, PTSIN, INTOUT, and PTSOUT. Since the call to the subroutine will have already placed the addresses of these five parameter arrays on to the stack, all that is needed is to preload DS:DX and then to transfer program control to the relevant graphics system with an interrupt. This should be E0h for GSX and EFh for GEM, although the GSX interrupt works fine in the majority of GEM installations too. The following assembler routine, assembled using the Microsoft MACRO Assembler, and linked with the FORTRAN code will provide the GEM interface:

```
        PUBLIC  GEM
        NAME    GEMFOR
        ASSUME  CS:CODE,DS:DATA
DATA    SEGMENT PUBLIC
DATA    ENDS
CODE    SEGMENT PUBLIC
;
GEM     PROC    FAR
        PUSH    DS          ;save previous data segment register
        PUSH    ES          ;save previous extra segment register
        MOV     AX,SS       ;move stack segment into AX
        MOV     DS,AX       ;to set DS = SS
        MOV     AX,SP       ;move stack pointer into AX
        ADD     AX,8        ;add 8 to point past DS,ES
                            ;and ret address
        MOV     DX,AX       ;move into DX for GEM
        MOV     CX,0473h    ;GEM function number into CX
        INT     0EFh        ;call GEM. int E0h for GSX
        POP     ES          ;get previous extra segment
        POP     DS          ;get previous data segment
```

```
        RET     20          ;return and pop 5 array addresses
                            ;off stack
GEM     ENDP
;
CODE    ENDS
        END
```

The method of calling the GEM VDI (using subroutine GEM above) is to give the five arrays in 'reverse order' as parameters to a conventional subroutine call as follows:

```
CALL GEM (PTSOUT, INTOUT, PTSIN, INTIN, CONTRL)
```

The reason that the array names are listed in what appears to be a backwards order is that the Microsoft FORTRAN convention is to push the addresses of these variables on to the stack from left to right. Given that the stack grows *downwards*, the address of the array CONTRL occupies the lowest stack segment address, or the start of the parameter block. We have assumed here that the arrays CONTRL, INTIN, and PTSIN have been set in the preceding lines of FORTRAN code.

All of the GEM and GEM VDI functions, from the simplest and most primitive, to the most complex, are accessed by setting codes in the CONTRL, INTIN, and PTSIN arrays, and calling the graphics system in this way. Some of the operations will return values in the INTOUT and PTSOUT arrays.

In the GSX system, there are a large number of operations possible, and there are even more under GEM VDI. These broadly fall into the categories listed in Chapter 13. At the inception of the book, we felt it might be sensible to list and describe at least the most useful subset of these functions, but the passage of time, and the publication of complete books on the subject, has made it desirable to save the room for something else. The GSX user will find the complete GSX system described in *GSX Handbook* published by Glentop. This is basically a reprint of the GSX manual produced by Digital Research. Users of some CP/M systems too will find this of use. Somewhat surprisingly, the best book on the GEM VDI system, for the FORTRAN programmer at least, was not directed at the PC market at all. It is *GEM on the Atari ST* by Szczepanowski and Gunther. The book lists all of the function codes and parameters for the GEM VDI system in considerable detail, and although based on the Digital Research documentation, it contains additional material.

If you wish to invoke GEM VDI or GSX using the simple subroutine call to GEM (or GSX) we suggest you create a library of subroutines, each of which performs just one of the graphics functions, and which is passed only the required subset of parameters.

For instance, a program to initialize the GSX system for screen graphics could be written (using the call to the assembler routine above, with 'INT 0E0h' instead of 'INT 0EFh' as follows:

```
        SUBROUTINE GSXOPN ( IDEV )
C-------------------------
C
C       Open a GSX workstation, number IDEV.
C
C------------------------------------------------------------
        INTEGER*2    CONTRL, INTIN, PTSIN,    INTOUT,  PTSOUT
        COMMON/GSXINF/CONTRL(12),  INTIN(80), PTSIN(150),
       1                           INTOUT(45), PTSOUT(100)
C
C       ----preload CONTRL with parameters
        CONTRL(1) = 1
        CONTRL(2) = 0
        CONTRL(4) = 11
        INTIN(1) =  IDEV
C
C       ----should set defaults for INTIN here
        DO 30 I=2,10
30      INTIN(I) = 1
        INTIN(11)= 0
C
C       ----call the function (the assembler routine called
C           here GSX not GEM because of the change to the
C           interrupt!)
        CALL GSX (PTSOUT, INTOUT, PTSIN, INTIN, CONTRL)
C
C       ----if required, save the responses before returning
        RETURN
        END
```

This would need to be enhanced in GEM VDI in a number of ways. Firstly, the 'open workstation' call returns a number termed the 'device handle'. This must be given back to GEM VDI each time the workstation is accessed—just so that GEM VDI goes to the correct driver. Hence, the device handle must be saved before continuing. Next, the soft fonts must be loaded. This is vital for text operations on hard-copy devices, and pretty important on screens too, despite some of the misinformation in official documentation.

Since GEM VDI has more to do—opening a 'workstation' takes longer—hence we should certainly load the screen workstation at the start of the program, and switch it into text mode. This option is also available in GSX.

```fortran
      SUBROUTINE GEMOPN ( IDEV, IHANDL )
C-----------------------
C
C     Open a GEMVDI workstation, number IDEV.
C
C-------------------------------------------------------------
      INTEGER*2    CONTRL, INTIN, PTSIN,    INTOUT, PTSOUT
      COMMON/GEMINF/CONTRL(12),  INTIN(80),  PTSIN(150),
     1                           INTOUT(45), PTSOUT(100)
C
C     ----preload CONTRL with parameters
      CONTRL(1) = 1
      CONTRL(2) = 0
      CONTRL(4) = 11
      INTIN(1) =  IDEV
C
C     ----should set defaults for INTIN here
      DO 30 I=2,10
30    INTIN(I) = 1
      INTIN(11)= 0
C
C     ----call the function
      CALL GEM (PTSOUT, INTOUT, PTSIN, INTIN, CONTRL)
C
C     ----if required, save the responses before return-
C        ing, save the device handle
      IHANDL =  CONTRL(7)
C      ----now load fonts...
      CONTRL(1) = 119
      CONTRL(2) = 0
      CONTRL(4) = 1
      CALL GEM (PTSOUT, INTOUT, PTSIN, INTIN, CONTRL)
C
C     -------now set alpha screen
      CONTRL(1) = 5
      CONTRL(2) = 0
      CONTRL(4) = 0
      CONTRL(6) = 3
      CALL GEM (PTSOUT, INTOUT, PTSIN, INTIN, CONTRL)
C
      RETURN
      END
```

The Programmers Toolkit for GEM includes a library of such subroutines, not only for calling GEM VDI, but also for executing the AES operations. These include drop down menus and the overlaid, dynamically sized, windows that are generated via multiple GEM VDI graphics calls. Indeed, the formal GEM Toolkit documentation is only comprehensible if one realizes that each function has its own procedural name, corresponding to the name of the 'subroutine' in the Toolkit library. Unfortunately for the FORTRAN programmer, these are in the C language.

Prospero Software market a set of subroutines, in a library called Prospect, to interface Prospero FORTRAN to GSX. A library of GEM VDI and AES bindings is marketed by the same company in a package that includes an editor, debugger, compiler, linker, and librarian which all operate under the GEM desktop environment. It is known as 'Prospero FORTRAN for GEM' and was launched in mid 1987. Obviously, the routines correspond to the Prospero FORTRAN calling conventions, and for simplicity, have the same procedural names as those in the C language bindings supplied by Digital Research (or as near as FORTRAN will allow).

In the disk set which can be purchased to complement this book will be found a library of routines to access the GSX and GEM functions.

We had to make a choice of what to include, and chose the minimum useful level. Later on in this chapter, you will find out how to add extra functions and functionality to our bare library.

15.10 USING THE UTILITY DISK GRAPHICS LIBRARY

The first routine to call is GEMDAT. This has as its five parameters the five arrays mentioned above. In effect, it tells the graphics system where they are. We advise keeping them in a named COMMON block. At this point, and for many GSX programs, you can forget that they exist. For GEM VDI, and fancy GSX programs, you need to preset one or two of the array values, notably in CONTRL, but also in INTIN and PTSIN. You may also wish to examine the values returned in INTOUT and PTSOUT.

After that, the basic graphics functions can be accessed by calling the routines in the library. Each subroutine in the library is designed to require the minimum of parameters necessary to define completely and unambiguously what is required.

The contents of the graphics library are listed below. It includes a general graphics call subroutine named GEMCAL which is useful when a function does not appear in the library. The general opening protocols are therefore (GEM VDI example):

```
        INTEGER*2     CONTRL, INTIN, PTSIN,     INTOUT,    PTSOUT
        COMMON/GEMINF/CONTRL(12),   INTIN(80),  PTSIN(150),
     1                              INTOUT(45), PTSOUT(100)
C
        CALL GEMDAT (CONTRL, INTIN, PTSIN, INTOUT, PTSOUT)
C
C       --------open a device for graphics use,
C               IDEV set in the calling program
        CALL GEMOPE (IDEV,IHANDL)
C
C       --------now load fonts...not a special library
C               function...
        CONTRL(1) = 119
        CONTRL(2) = 0
        CONTRL(4) = 1
        CALL GEMCAL
C
C       --------now set alpha screen...again, not in library...
        CONTRL(1) = 5
        CONTRL(2) = 0
        CONTRL(4) = 0
        CONTRL(6) = 3
        CALL GEMCAL
C
```

You will find two libraries: one contains INT E0h for GSX, and the other EFh for GEM
VDI.

15.11 CONTENTS OF THE GRAPHICS LIBRARY

The functions that you will find in the graphics library are given in Table 15.4, referred to by
their FORTRAN subroutine name.

Table 15.4 The GEM/GSX library

Routine name	Description
GEMCAL	Call the GEM system (GSXCAL)
GEMOPE	Open a device for graphics use (GSXOPE)
GEMCLO	Close a device (GSXCLO)
GEMCLR	Clear a graphics device (GSXCLR)
GEMLIN	Draw a line between end points–a vector, or two point polyline (GSXLIN)
GEMTXT	Write a string of text (GSXTXT)
GEMUPD	Update a device (GSXUPD)

Table 15.4 The GEM/GSX library (continued)

Routine name	Description
POLYLN	Join a series of points by lines–the polyline
POLYMK	Put a marker at a series of points–the polymarker
POLYFL	Draw a filled area
GEMBAR	Draw a filled bar (GSXBAR)
TXTHT	Set height of text characters
TXTDIR	Set the direction of the text
LINTYP	Set the line type
LINWID	Set the line width
FILTYP	Set type of interior style for a filled area
FILIND	Set type of pattern or hatch to be used for a filled area
GSXLOC	Move a location indicator and return the final coordinates (not GEM VDI)
FINVAL	Change a value (cursor appears on the screen)
GEMCHO	Return an entered choice (GSXCHO)
GEMGET	Get a string from the keyboard (GSXGET)
GEMMOD	Set mode for screen display drawing (GSXMOD)

15.12 ADDING NEW FACILITIES

Inevitably, you will find that the routines in this library allow you to access only a subset of the functions available in GSX or GEM VDI. You will want to add extra facilities. Perhaps these will encompass more than one graphics function at a time. We have provided an example below. This sets the colours in which lines, area fills, text and marker symbols are drawn. The routine, named COLOR3, has four parameters: the colour indices for each of the drawing modes.

We have used the graphics library routine GEMCAL, and this assumes that the locations of the data arrays have been sent to the graphics system by GEMDAT already. Alternatively, you can code *all* the calls using the method described in Section 15.9, the only difference in subroutine COLORS would be a call to GEM with the five parameter arrays instead of the call to GEMCAL.

You will find a number of such composite routines in source FORTRAN on the utility disk.

```
      SUBROUTINE COLORS (ILINE, IMARK, IFILL, ITEXT)
C-----------------------
C
C     Subroutine to set GEM/GSX line, marker, fill, and
C     text colour indices
C
C-----------------------------------------------------------
```

```
          INTEGER*2    CONTRL,  INTIN,   PTSIN,   INTOUT,   PTSOUT
          COMMON/GEMINF/CONTRL(12),   INTIN(80),   PTSIN(150),
     1                                INTOUT(45), PTSOUT(100)
C
C         -------set text colour
          CONTRL(1) = 22
          CONTRL(2) = 0
          CONTRL(4) = 1
          INTIN(1)  = ITEXT
          CALL GEMCAL
C
C         -------set fill colour
          CONTRL(1) = 25
          CONTRL(2) = 0
          CONTRL(4) = 1
          INTIN(1)  = IFILL
          CALL GEMCAL
C
C         -------set marker colour
          CONTRL(1) = 20
          CONTRL(2) = 0
          CONTRL(4) = 1
          INTIN(1)  = IMARK
          CALL GEMCAL
C
C         -------set line colour
          CONTRL(1) = 17
          CONTRL(2) = 0
          CONTRL(4) = 1
          INTIN(1)  = ILINE
          CALL GEMCAL
C
          RETURN
          END
```

It is important to note, from this routine, some of the important factors. First of all, the data which GSX/GEM VDI needs is very limited: there is the function opcode, which goes into CONTRL(1), and the actual colour index, which goes into INTIN(1). For many purposes that is all that needs to be set. However, the lengths of PTSIN and INTIN should be set in CONTRL(2) and CONTRL(4) respectively. This is particularly important when using a metafile device (GEM VDI). The reason for this is that the metafile is made up of variable length records, each of which comprises, in effect, the entire useful contents of the CONTRL, INTIN, and PTSIN arrays. It is important to know a priori just how much of INTIN and PTSIN are in fact relevant.

Secondly, this routine assumes that the device handle (the value of which is passed via CONTRL(6)) has been set outside the routine, and indicates the device on which the colours are to be set. This makes the routine applicable to both GSX and GEM VDI. GSX does not need a device handle, because it can only have one graphics device driver loaded at any time. GEM VDI can have many, and needs the device handle to determine which is 'current'. GEM VDI uses CONTRL(6-12) differently to GSX in any case.

Other useful routines of this sort that we regularly use include one to check whether the circle drawing primitive is supported before requesting it. If it isn't, a circle needs to be generated by a polyline instruction.

15.13 GRAPHIC INPUT

Graphic input is much simpler in GSX than in GEM VDI. The functions in the library relate to the earlier GSX system: one function call put a cross-hair cursor on the screen at given coordinates, tracked it, allowing it to be moved by mouse or numeric keypad and cursor keys, and returned the screen coordinates when a 'terminating event' occurred. Such an 'event' would be pressing the return key, or a mouse button.

In the GEM system, such simple functions have been disabled and graphical input transferred to the AES part of the system. To use that, you must write a proper GEM application. Otherwise, you have to explicitly build the mouse form, show it, track it, and continuously sample the mouse button state. Functions are, of course, provided within GEM VDI for all of these operations. When a terminating event occurs (and you have to catch the button being down and then up!), it is up to you to remove the mouse pointer from the screen.

Sadly, the amount of FORTRAN code to do all this is too great for the book. You will find the appropriate routines in FORTRAN source on the available disk set.

15.14 WRITING APPLICATIONS FOR GEM ITSELF, OR FOR WINDOWS

In the bulk of this chapter, we have made a great play on using GEM VDI as the main graphics system for your PC. This is because the VDI (Visual Display Interface) can be separated from the full GEM system, and used simply and easily from a FORTRAN application program. We believe that using the GEM VDI in this way permits the FORTRAN programmer access to superb graphics not only easily and cheaply, but in a way that permits portability of the application from screen device to screen device. No expensive bindings are required, only the simple codes outlined in this Chapter, and found on the available disk set.

However, the reader should not imagine that his graphics program will run under GEM itself: that is an entirely different proposition! It is a simple matter to write a program that is well behaved within the DOS environment, and GEM VDI only opens up one small chink in DOS's armour. GEM applications proper must continually keep the system informed of what they are up to, and do operations strictly in accordance with the GEM protocols. It would take a complete book to begin to explain these.

Similarly, applications which run under Windows need to obey the protocols properly. In contrast to GEM, it is not possible to extract the graphics system and use it 'stand-alone'. For this reason, the GEM system graphics kernel is easier to use. Finally, and not least, the GEM VDI printer drivers drive their hard-copy devices to the maximum resolution of which they are capable. Output is therefore denser, and more finely detailed, although slower than from a Windows application.

15.15 DEMONSTRATION GRAPHICS PROGRAM

The program GEMDEM is a demonstration of GEM VDI graphics capabilities (it will run with slight modifications under GSX). It produces the illustration shown in Figure 15.2.

Those routines in GEMDEM which are not part of our GEM library are shown in full below. It would be a simple matter to substitute equivalent FORTRAN routines for those in the GEM library using the GEM interface described in Section 15.9. The details are left to the reader.

Figure 15.2 Screen dump of image generated by GEMDEM

```
      PROGRAM GEMDEM
C-----------------------
C
C     This is a demonstration of some of the facilities in
C     GEM VDI, using some of the graphics library functions,
C     and some custom functions.
C
C-----------------------------------------------------------
      INTEGER IX(10), IY(10)
      LOGICAL HARD
      INTEGER*2      CONTRL, INTIN,  PTSIN,    INTOUT,
     *               PTSOUT
      COMMON/GEMINF/CONTRL(12),   INTIN(80),   PTSIN(150),
     1                            INTOUT(45),  PTSOUT(100)
      DATA IBACK,ILINE,IMARK,IFILL,ITEXT/0,1,2,3,4
      DATA IX,IY/2000,20000,22000,31000,2000,31000,
     1     2000,11000,13000,31000,
     2     22000,30000,22000,30000,13000,19000,
     3     2000,10000,2000,10000/
     3     IJ, IK, IL, IM / 0, 0, 32767, 32767/
C
C             open screen as graphics device
C             IDEV =  1 - screen
C                  = 11 - plotter
C                  = 21 - printer, etc.
C
      CALL GEMOPN (1, IHANDL)
      HARD = .FALSE.
C
1     CONTINUE
      IF (HARD) THEN
            CALL FILTYP (2)
            CALL FILIND (2)
            IFILL = 1
            ELSE
            CALL FILTYP (3)
            CALL FILIND (3)
            ENDIF
      CALL COLORS (ILINE, IMARK, IFILL, ITEXT)
      CALL GEMBAR (IJ,IK,  IL,IM)
      CALL COLORS (ILINE, IMARK, IBACK, ITEXT)
      CALL FILTYP (1)
C
C                without the CALL FILIND (or something) in
C                the loop, the Microsoft FORTRAN optimizer
```

```
C                     will not compile the loop properly!
C

      DO 10 I=1,5
      CALL FILIND (1)
      IJ = IX(2*I-1)
      IL = IX(2*I)
      IK = IY(2*I-1)
      IM = IY(2*I)
      CALL GEMBAR (IJ,IK,IL,IM)
      CALL BOX     (IJ,IK,IL,IM)
   10 CONTINUE
C
      CALL PYRAM (IX(3),IY(3),IX(4),IY(4))
      CALL PYRAM (IX(7),IY(7),IX(8),IY(8))
      CALL ADDTXT (HARD)
C
C                     Is this the pass for HARD COPY?  If so,
C                     close printer, then screen, and stop.
C
      IF (HARD) THEN
              CALL GEMCLO
              CONTRL(7)=IHANDL
              CALL GEMCLO
              STOP
      ENDIF
C
C                     It must have been the pass for screen
C                     display, ask if hard copy required?
C
      CALL TXTSCR (HARD)
      IF ( .NOT. HARD) THEN
              CALL GEMCLO
              STOP
      ELSE
              CALL GRFSCR (IHANDL)
              CALL GEMOPN (21, JHANDL)
              GO TO 1
      ENDIF
      END


      SUBROUTINE GEMOPN ( IDEV, IHANDL )
C-----------------------------
C
C       Open a GEMVDI workstation, number IDEV.
```

```
C
C---------------------------------------------------------------
C
        INTEGER*2       CONTRL, INTIN,  PTSIN,    INTOUT,
                        PTSOUT
        COMMON/GEMINF/CONTRL(12),   INTIN(80),  PTSIN(150),
     1                              INTOUT(45), PTSOUT(100)
C
        CALL GEMDAT (CONTRL, INTIN, PTSIN, INTOUT, PTSOUT)
        INTIN(11) = 0
        CALL GEMOPE (IDEV,IHANDL)
C
C       -------now load fonts...not a special library
              function....
        CONTRL(1) = 119
        CONTRL(2) = 0
        CONTRL(4) = 1
        INTIN (1) = 1
        CALL GEMCAL
C
        RETURN
        END
```

```
        SUBROUTINE COLORS (ILINE, IMARK, IFILL, ITEXT)
C---------------------------
C
C       Subroutine to set GEM/GEM line,  marker,   fill,
C       and text colour, indices.
C
C---------------------------------------------------------------
        INTEGER*2 CONTRL,  INTIN,  PTSIN,  INTOUT,  PTSOUT
        COMMON/GEMINF/CONTRL(12),    INTIN(80),  PTSIN(150),
     1                               INTOUT(45), PTSOUT(100)
C
C       -------set text colour
        CONTRL(1) = 22
        CONTRL(2) = 0
        CONTRL(4) = 1
        INTIN(1)  = ITEXT
        CALL GEMCAL
C
C       -------set fill colour
        CONTRL(1) = 25
        CONTRL(2) = 0
```

```
        CONTRL(4) = 1
        INTIN(1)  = IFILL
        CALL GEMCAL
C
C       -------set marker colour
        CONTRL(1) = 20
        CONTRL(2) = 0
        CONTRL(4) = 1
        INTIN(1)  = IMARK
        CALL GEMCAL
C
C       -------set line colour
        CONTRL(1) = 17
        CONTRL(2) = 0
        CONTRL(4) = 1
        INTIN(1)  = ILINE
        CALL GEMCAL
C
        RETURN
        END
```

```
        SUBROUTINE ADDTXT (HARD)
C----------------------------
C
C       Subroutine adds the text FORTRAN and the Art of PC
C       Programming, together with the authors names.
C
C-----------------------------------------------------------
        INTEGER*2 IX(3), IY(3), IJ, IK, IL, IM
        INTEGER*2 ISIZE(3), JSIZE(3)
        LOGICAL HARD
        DATA IX, IY / 2700, 3500,  13800,
     1               24200,15300, 7000/
        DATA ISIZE, JSIZE / 8000,2500,2500,10000,1800,1800/
C
        IF (HARD) THEN
                L = JSIZE(1)
                M = JSIZE(2)
                N = JSIZE(3)
        ELSE
                L = ISIZE(1)
                M = ISIZE(2)
                N = ISIZE(3)
        ENDIF
```

```
C
      JJ = IX(1)
      JK = IY(1)
      CALL FONT (2)
      CALL TXTHT (L)
      CALL GEMMOD (2)
      CALL GEMTXT ('FORTRAN',7,JJ,JK)
C
      JJ = IX(2)
      JK = IY(2)
      CALL FONT (14)
      CALL TXTHT (M)
      CALL GEMTXT ('and the Art of PC Programming'
                   ,29,JJ,JK)
C
      JJ=IX(3)
      JK=IY(3)
      CALL FONT (2)
      CALL TXTHT (N)
      CALL GEMTXT ('Tim Ward',8,JJ,JK)
      JK = JK - 4000
      CALL GEMTXT ('Eddie Bromhead',14,JJ,JK)
C
      DO 10 J=1,100000
      X=X+J
 10   CONTINUE

      RETURN
      END

      SUBROUTINE FONT (N)
C----------------------
C
C     Makes the named font the current one.
C
C-------------------------------------------------------------
C
      INTEGER*2   CONTRL, INTIN,  PTSIN,   INTOUT,  PTSOUT
      COMMON/GEMINF/CONTRL(12),  INTIN(80),  PTSIN(150),
     1                               INTOUT(45), PTSOUT(100)
C
C     -------now select font 2= HELVETICA, 14= TIMES ROMAN
      CONTRL(1) = 21
      CONTRL(2) = 0
      CONTRL(4) = 1
```

```
        INTIN (1) = N
        CALL GEMCAL
C

        RETURN
        END


        SUBROUTINE TXTSCR (HARD)
C-------------------------
C
C
C       Switch into text screen, ask if hard copy is
C       required.
C
C----------------------------------------------------------------
        LOGICAL HARD
        CHARACTER*1 A
        INTEGER*2   CONTRL, INTIN, PTSIN,   INTOUT,  PTSOUT
        COMMON/GEMINF/CONTRL(12),   INTIN(80),  PTSIN(150),
     1                               INTOUT(45), PTSOUT(100)
C
C       -------set text screen
        CONTRL(1) = 5
        CONTRL(2) = 0
        CONTRL(4) = 0
        CONTRL(6) = 3
        CALL GEMCAL
C
        WRITE(*,*) ' DO YOU WANT A HARD COPY ? (Y/N)'
        READ(*,100) A
        IF (A .EQ. 'Y'   .OR.  A .EQ. 'y') THEN
              HARD = .TRUE.
        ELSE
              HARD = .FALSE.
        ENDIF
        RETURN
 100    FORMAT (A1)
        END


        SUBROUTINE GRFSCR (IHAND)
C-------------------------
C
C
C       Switch into graphics screen.
C
C----------------------------------------------------------------
        INTEGER*2   CONTRL, INTIN,  PTSIN,   INTOUT,  PTSOUT
        COMMON/GEMINF/CONTRL(12),   INTIN(80),  PTSIN(150),
```

```
      1                                 INTOUT(45), PTSOUT(100)
C
C            -------set text screen
             CONTRL(1) = 5
             CONTRL(2) = 0
             CONTRL(4) = 0
             CONTRL(6) = 2
             CONTRL(7) = IHAND
             CALL GEMCAL
C
             CALL GEMCLR
             CALL TXTHT(6000)
             CALL GEMTXT('Printing....',12,9000,15000)
             RETURN
             END

             SUBROUTINE BOX (I,J,K,L)
C---------------------------
C
C
C     Draws a box.
C
C------------------------------------------------------------
             INTEGER*2   CONTRL, INTIN,  PTSIN,   INTOUT,  PTSOUT
             COMMON/GEMINF/CONTRL(12),   INTIN(80),  PTSIN(150),
      1                                 INTOUT(45), PTSOUT(100)
C
             PTSIN (1) = I
             PTSIN (2) = J
             PTSIN (3) = K
             PTSIN (4) = J
             PTSIN (5) = K
             PTSIN (6) = L
             PTSIN (7) = I
             PTSIN (8) = L
             PTSIN (9) = I
             PTSIN (10) = J
             CALL POLYLN (5)
             RETURN
             END

             SUBROUTINE PYRAM (I, J, K, L)
C---------------------------
C
```

```
C       Draws NESTED boxes.
C
C---------------------------------------------------------------
C
        IDX = (K-I)/10
        IDY = (L-J)/10
        DO 10 IQ=1,5
        II = I + IDX*IQ
        JJ = J + IDY*IQ
        KK = K - IDX*IQ
        LL = L - IDY*IQ
        CALL BOX (II,JJ,KK,LL)
10      CONTINUE
        RETURN
        END
```

CHAPTER 16

CHOOSING A FORTRAN COMPILER

16.1 INTRODUCTION

When this book was first conceived, there were already a multiplicity of compilers on the market. It would have been difficult, but not impossible, to make a comparative review. Two things have rendered that objective impractical. Firstly, it has become apparent that the development of these products is far from static: anything written here will be out of date before publication. Similarly, FORTRAN *is* alive and well in the PC world, and new products are being launched all the time.

It is all too soon to consider MS DOS and PC DOS to be 'washed up' and ready to be entirely superseded by OS/2. For a start, that operating system needs so much memory, and at least an 80286 chip in the computer, that it will never address the needs of millions of 8088 and 8086 machine owners, or indeed those whose (rarer) machines are driven with 80186/80188 chips. Not only that, but many compatible 80286 computers will not be able to run OS/2. For the foreseeable future MS DOS must remain the predominant single-user PC operating system. And for that matter, FORTRAN compilers for the PC world are still being launched.

In the beginning, one had a choice between FORTRAN 66, subset FORTRAN 77, and full FORTRAN 77 compilers. The initial category were usually restricted in the memory models they supported, but generated physically short EXE files. Also producing compact code were the subset FORTRAN 77s, but these often had annoying shortcomings. Finally, there were professional compilers offering the full standard and virtually no limit on memory model: but these produced huge executable files. Most compiler implementations for FORTRAN 77 (full or subset) gestured in the direction of FORTRAN 66 compatibility in a few respects: many users would have to grapple with the subtleties of the changed standard as well as gaining experience on their PC.

Between 1983 and 1987, the FORTRAN 66 compilers outran their usefulness as more and more users demanded block IFs and CHARACTER variables. Similarly, the primary subset FORTRAN 77 compilers (principally the Microsoft compiler) were developed into full standard products. This led inevitably to increases in executable file size. Utilities for packing (i.e. removing repeated byte patterns from the EXE file) the code appeared, and removed many of the differences between FORTRAN 77 compilers in respect of EXE file size. The other innovation was the launch of very low-priced compilers, at less than £50 or ($50); software often better than the early releases of more mainstream products.

When buying a FORTRAN compiler, you must decide what you want it for, and how much you are prepared to pay.

The rest of this chapter is a sort of bibliography of software mentioned in the text, or which the authors know is available on the PC.

16.2 FORTRAN COMPILER PACKAGES

MICROSOFT FORTRAN

Early versions of the Microsoft FORTRAN compiler were genuinely awful. They supported a subset of a subset of the FORTRAN 77 standard. In its latest versions, Microsoft FORTRAN is a full standard compiler. Versions below 3.20 are comparatively limited, and often bug-ridden, but it is possible to use all version 3 and 4 releases for serious programming.

Of all the compilers of which we have experience, this one has shown the biggest improvements—but then they were needed! All the examples in this book (except where noted) assume Microsoft FORTRAN. It is essentially the market leader.

Versions up to 3.20 use file control blocks to handle files, and so can be used even with DOS 1. Version 3.20 is somewhat different from preceding versions, in that it handles bigger-than-a-segment data structures, whereas none of the others does so.

File operations using handles were introduced in v. 3.30, and so enable paths to be used in file specifications, and as a result, the use of DOS 2 or later is essential, and DOS 1 support was dropped. Version 3.31 fixed a number of minor bugs in v. 3.30. The biggest improvements of 3.3x over the preceding versions were:

- implementation of substrings
- implementation of interfaces to other languages
- implementation of BLOCK DATA and COMPLEX
- proper handling of huge data structures
- a revised memory map which would lead to better behaved programs in a multiprogramming environment (principally, less likely to damage DOS)

Up to v. 3.31 (which immediately preceded 4.0) the compiler was suitable for running on a twin floppy PC. A hard disk will definitely be preferred if v. 4.0 is used, or at the very least, the higher capacity 1.2 megabyte or 720 kbyte floppy disks which are becoming more prevalent.

Compiler options were selected on the basis of metacommands embedded in the source code, or by linking with an appropriate library: from v. 4.0, command line arguments may be used in addition to control compilation and linking options.

Version 4.0 introduced a number of additional features, notably in the area of character handling, where the full range of FORTRAN 77 operations is now supported, and in file operations where there are more options in the OPEN statement, and extensions to the INQUIRE statement. Starting from v. 4.0, Microsoft FORTRAN is supplied with Microsoft's CodeView debugging program.

Users of early versions are advised to upgrade: prior to v. 3.20 no data structure (e.g. COMMON block) could exceed 64 kbytes, and since then the INDEX and LEN character functions, substrings, CHARACTER* (*) declarations, concatenation, and such like have been progressively introduced. Later versions support Hollerith data in a limited way. The memory models supported range from medium to large.

The package must be considered seriously because of the wealth of 'add-on' libraries available. It comes complete with linker and librarian programs, a number of utilities, and a debugger. Microsoft LINK supports a limited depth of overlays. An overlaid program is generated in a single EXE file: this may be of significant size.

Version 4.1, released as we write, permits the binding of executable code to DOS or OS/2.

DIGITAL RESEARCH FORTRAN 77

Another company well known in the software field, Digital Research, were a late entrant to the FORTRAN market. Their compiler is a full FORTRAN 77, with many concessions to FORTRAN 66, including ENCODE and DECODE (also with a pseudo FORTRAN 77 syntax), and Holleriths.

The package is released with overlay linker and librarian, and supports small or large memory models. The link program supports nested overlays to a considerable depth. Each overlay is written to a separate file.

One major disadvantage is that only the first seven bits in CHARACTER entities are significant: hence special characters and bit image data cannot be processed.

Digital Research FORTRAN 77 generates relatively slow code, and large executable files. Why use it? The answer to this is two fold. Firstly, it does a thorough job of syntax checking during compilation (although it isn't perfect!), and, in containing pretty much all of the FORTRAN 66 extensions, makes it singularly easy to compile hybrid FORTRAN code.

RYAN MACFARLAND RM FORTRAN

RM FORTRAN is one of the two original full standard FORTRAN 77 compilers. It generates lengthy, but efficient, code in large memory model format. It is second only to Microsoft FORTRAN in the number of third party libraries, and in recognition of the prevalence of MS

FORTRAN add-ons, interfaces are supplied to enable MS FORTRAN-conforming assembler routines to be used in RM FORTRAN programs.

The package comes complete with a linker, which supports minimal overlaying, and a few utilities. Early versions of RM FORTRAN were supplied with Microsoft LINK, later versions with a specially customized version of PLINK86. Where disk storage is tight, try linking with LINK, because this is only two-thirds of the size of the supplied linker. On the other hand, the full version of PLINK86 is so fully featured that it is worth learning the syntax with the cut-down version, and then investing in its big brother which you have to buy separately. The RM FORTRAN package has a powerful debugger, and in the latest version of the compiler this operates in a windowed fashion.

Early versions of the math library demanded the presence of a numeric coprocessor in the target system. Later versions include software emulation of the functions of this extra chip.

RM FORTRAN compiles slowly, but code optimization is thorough, and the resulting executable code is fast (although at the time of writing, Microsoft FORTRAN version 4 was slightly faster).

Like Digital Research FORTRAN, this compiler limits the user to the first 128 characters of the ASCII sequence, and is thus useless for bit image processing, or sending special characters to the screen.

LAHEY F77L

This is the second original full FORTRAN 77 standard compiler. Like early versions of the Ryan MacFarland compiler, early Lahey F77L versions needed the presence of a numeric coprocessor. The large memory model is supported. In contrast to Ryan MacFarland and Microsoft FORTRANs, compilation is fast, but execution slower. In fact, compilation is not just fast, but exceptionally so in comparison to most other PC FORTRAN implementations. We know of a 250 000 statement FORTRAN program compiled using Lahey F77L, and linked to form a 4.5 megabyte (overlayed) executable file. The whole process only took 2 hours on an 80386 DOS machine, which compares favourably with many minicomputers. Indeed, the whole system runs in 640 kbytes of RAM.

The strength of Lahey FORTRAN is the way it is less restrictive about subroutine parameters than are the other very strong professional compilers from the US.

Responding to market pressures, Lahey have introduced new maths libraries which no longer demand a numeric coprocessor, and also cut-down 'personal' versions of the compiler.

PROSPERO FORTRAN 66 AND FORTRAN 77

Prospero's original FORTRAN 66 compiler is fast and efficient, supporting small and medium memory models. The newer FORTRAN 77 compiler adds the large memory model, but initially made fewer concessions to FORTRAN 66 compatibility than one would like or expect. This has been progressively relaxed as later versions come out. The package has an overlay linker, librarian, and symbolic debugger. It also has perhaps the shortest documentation of any of the compilers: this is an asset, not a disadvantage!

Prospero's code is somewhat different to that generated by the other compilers in two respects, memory allocation and overlaying. In the small and medium memory models, memory allocation for data areas is static, and similar to Microsoft FORTRAN. It differs in the large (Prospero's 'Jumbo' model) memory model, which is available in the 77 compiler. Each COMMON block is allocated out of free memory as required. The techniques for doing this are outlined in Chapter 11, but they are automatic here. In effect, memory allocation is dynamic, and the SAVE statement of FORTRAN 77 may need to be used to override this in programs which rely on a static allocation of memory. Arrays may transcend the 64 kbyte limit even in the medium model, provided that they reside in blank COMMON.

Prospero's overlay linker also operates in a different way. Essentially, overlay units and areas are *not* defined in the way that static structures need, rather the modules are grouped into overlays which are handled as a 'last in first out' (LIFO) stack. This leads to efficient use of memory, especially when taken into consideration with the data allocation.

The Prospero FORTRAN libraries include standard routines for calling DOS interrupts, EXECing other programs, getting command line arguments back into the program as text strings, and so on. These make the package very powerful. Executable code is not as fast, however, as Microsoft or Ryan MacFarland FORTRAN, when used in numerically intensive applications.

There are many applications where small executable program files are at a premium. Typically these applications include print formatting and other utilities. Prospero FORTRAN with its small memory model ideally suited to this work because of its economic EXE file sizes.

Prospero's libraries are in the less-common Intel form, rather than in Microsoft format. They appear as OBJ files, and any generated OBJ file, as well as a library, can be selectively searched to only include referenced modules.

PROSPERO FORTRAN FOR GEM

In this package, library options have been stripped away, leaving only the no-coprocessor and the medium memory model (data structures may not exceed 64K unless in blank COMMON). However, the package includes a compiler, linker, librarian, and editor tailored to work under GEM, and a library of GEM VDI and GEM AES bindings so that the programmer can write applications that run under GEM, or just use the VDI graphics as a stand alone system.

The compiler is full FORTRAN 77 standard, and the normal library incorporates a number of utility subprograms.

The documentation runs to 600 pages, of which 500 are a description of the GEM VDI and AES systems.

The difference between calling the VDI in GEM and GSX is small, and revolves around a single interrupt. This is INT EFh for GEM, INT E0h for GSX. One gains all the benefits of having a single function or subroutine for every single operation even when using GSX by making the following simple alteration to the GEM VDI library.

Use DEBUG on the GEM library F77GEMLIB.OBJ. Search for the sequence CD EF (in hexadecimal). This occurs twice, once is the VDI call, the other is the AES call. Now you can either look around to see which is which, or change them both to CD E0. Remember that not all operations are available in GSX, and none of the AES services. Otherwise, the system runs fine. Do not do this if you want the programs to run under GEM VDI.

OTHER PROSPERO UTILITIES FOR THE FORTRAN PROGRAMMER

Prospero have a number of packages which interface with their compilers. The first of these, Prospect, is a library of graphics functions which interface with the GSX graphics system from Digital Research (a copy of the GSX system is also provided). There is a database package called Shark and an integrated programming environment similar to that supplied in the 'FORTRAN for GEM' package, but not requiring the GEM system installed.

The Prospero FORTRAN compilers include a cross-referencing system which lists all symbolic names and the locations in which they occur in the FORTRAN source.

SUPERSOFT FORTRAN

Bearing a generic similarity to WATFOR (the University of Waterloo's FORTRAN, familiar to readers of McCracken's elementary book on FORTRAN programming), the compiler has a number of hybrid and non-standard features. These include CHARACTER type constants. It supports a medium memory model.

The structured programming facilities now obtainable in FORTRAN 77 can be obtained through use of the RATFOR preprocessor. This program is supplied in source form, and can be compiled using the Supersoft compiler. It is then possible to convert programs written using the special quasi-FORTRAN constructs into Supersoft FORTRAN compatible source code.

The package is fairly basic, without linker, librarian, or debugger, and it is not widely advertised nowadays. The instructions on interfacing assembler, and the utilities offered in its libraries, are much better than in later and more advanced products.

UTAH FORTRAN

At about a tenth of the price of other software, this FORTRAN 66 package must be sampled. It offers FORTRAN 66 with some extensions.

FORTRANSOFT FORTRAN

Britain's answer to Utah FORTRAN, this 77 standard compiler is Microsoft FORTRAN compatible. The manufacturers offer several libraries for graphics and database applications. What limited experience we have suggests that the calling protocols for these are a little long-winded.

UCSD P_SYSTEM FORTRAN AND PECAN

The subset FORTRAN 77 available under the p_system has been developed and refined so that it operates under DOS (PECAN). p_system FORTRAN was slow, and relatively poor in features. It did, however, operate within a complete programming environment, so that the user could, if requested, jump straight from a run- time or compilation error to the offending place in the source code.

IBM FORTRAN

Early versions of the IBM FORTRAN compiler were the Microsoft FORTRAN compiler with a slightly changed title. They were truly awful. Later on, IBM used Ryan MacFarland FORTRAN instead, and termed this 'Professional FORTRAN'. The version marketed by IBM may be several releases behind that offered by the vendor direct.

16.3 OTHER SYSTEM SOFTWARE

You will need a text editor and possibly an assembler. The choice in the former is enormous, in the latter, quite small. Almost any word-processing program will have the requisite 'non-document' mode for program and data file creation. WordStar is usable (although you will need one of the small utilities for stripping the high bit from every byte in the source code, for use after you have inadvertently edited FORTRAN source in document mode!), if a little slow in operation on an 8086/8088 machine. For reasons that will become obvious pretty quickly, if you try to use EDLIN (DOS, own line editor), the full screen editing facilities of the cheapest and nastiest wordprocessor will be far superior to those of any line editor. If you are choosing a screen editor, pick one that loads quickly, rather than one which has fancy formatting capabilities.

For an assembler, choose the Microsoft Macro Assembler, Digital Research, or Phoenix products, or if you are really impecunious, obtain a copy of CHASM—the 'CHeap ASseMbler' from any public domain software group. CHASM is broadly compatible with the early versions of the Microsoft Assembler MASM. As we write, Borland International, famous for their inexpensive Turbo range of products, have just announced TASM their Turbo Assembler. This comes with a debugger, is Microsoft compatible, and is sure to be worth considering.

Everything after that is more or less a luxury. It is possible to buy more advanced link and librarian programs than you may get supplied with your FORTRAN package. Phoenix

PLink86 and PLib86 are examples that spring readily to mind. They may not be so much of a luxury if you are stretching DOS to its limits.

Other software that the FORTRAN programmer can buy includes add- on libraries of the sort we have already discussed, and tools to reformat or rewrite your code into more efficient, or more maintainable forms. Such software tends to be expensive in comparison to the compiler.

APPENDIX 1

THE ASCII CODE TABLE

The ASCII Code Table is shown in Figure A1.1. The meanings of the first 33 ASCII codes and code no. 127 are as follows:

NUL	A means of causing a delay
SOH	Start of heading, indicating that the following text is a title
STX	Start of text, i.e. of the body of the message
ETX	Corresponding end of text
EOT	End of transmission—over and out!
ENQ, ACK	Enquiry and acknowledgement; used as part of a software handshaking or communications protocol
BEL	Rings the bell—often a buzzer
BS, HT, LF	Backspace, horizontal TAB (the normal sort); and line feed
VT, FF, CR	Vertical TAB (more than a line, less than a page), formfeed (a page), carriage return (back to start of line)
SO, SI	Shift out is the start of a control sequence, shift in is its end.
DLE	Data link escape–similar to ESC
DC1-4	Device controls 1 to 4; spare, so may be used as desired.
NAK	Negative acknowledgement; transmission was not received correctly, for example, parity failure, or cyclic redundancy check failed
SYN	Synchronous idle; similar to NUL
ETB	End of transmission block—now checks can be made on what has been transmitted
CAN	Cancel transmission—disregard the data that was sent
EM	End of medium—the tape is about to run out...
SUB	Start of an error correction substitution message
ESC	Lead in to an ESCape sequence
FS, GS, RS, US	File, group, record, and unit separators; have the effect of punctuation and layout in a book
SP	Space
DEL	Delete

Printers commonly support only a subset of the ASCII control codes. Typically, BEL, BS, CR, FF, LF, and ESC are the only ones, although VT may be used on some printers and the vertical spacing is set with an ESCape sequence. SO and SI are sometimes used to switch into and out of double-width character spacing.

Figure A1.1 The ASCII code table

0x	1x	2x	3x	4x	5x	6x	7x	8x	9x	Ax	Bx	Cx	Dx	Ex	Fx
00 NUL 0	10 DLE 16	20 SP 32	30 0 48	40 @ 64	50 P 80	60 ` 96	70 p 112	80 128	90 144	A0 160	B0 176	C0 192	D0 208	E0 224	F0 240
01 SOH 1	11 DC1 17	21 ! 33	31 1 49	41 A 65	51 Q 81	61 a 97	71 q 113	81 129	91 145	A1 161	B1 177	C1 193	D1 209	E1 225	F1 241
02 STX 2	12 DC2 18	22 " 34	32 2 50	42 B 66	52 R 82	62 b 98	72 r 114	82 130	92 146	A2 162	B2 178	C2 194	D2 210	E2 226	F2 242
03 ETX 3	13 DC3 19	23 # 35	33 3 51	43 C 67	53 S 83	63 c 99	73 s 115	83 131	93 147	A3 163	B3 179	C3 195	D3 211	E3 227	F3 243
04 EOT 4	14 DC4 20	24 $ 36	34 4 52	44 D 68	54 T 84	64 d 100	74 t 116	84 132	94 148	A4 164	B4 180	C4 196	D4 212	E4 228	F4 244
05 ENQ 5	15 NAK 21	25 % 37	35 5 53	45 E 69	55 U 85	65 e 101	75 u 117	85 133	95 149	A5 165	B5 181	C5 197	D5 213	E5 229	F5 245
06 ACK 6	16 SYN 22	26 & 38	36 6 54	46 F 70	56 V 86	66 f 102	76 v 118	86 134	96 150	A6 166	B6 182	C6 198	D6 214	E6 230	F6 246
07 BEL 7	17 ETB 23	27 ' 39	37 7 55	47 G 71	57 W 87	67 g 103	77 w 119	87 135	97 151	A7 167	B7 183	C7 199	D7 215	E7 231	F7 247
08 BS 8	18 CAN 24	28 (40	38 8 56	48 H 72	58 X 88	68 h 104	78 x 120	88 136	98 152	A8 168	B8 184	C8 200	D8 216	E8 232	F8 248
09 HT 9	19 EM 25	29) 41	39 9 57	49 I 73	59 Y 89	69 i 105	79 y 121	89 137	99 153	A9 169	B9 185	C9 201	D9 217	E9 233	F9 249
0A LF 10	1A 26	2A * 42	3A : 58	4A J 74	5A Z 90	6A j 106	7A z 122	8A 138	9A 154	AA 170	BA 186	CA 202	DA 218	EA 234	FA 250
0B VT 11	1B ESC 27	2B + 43	3B ; 59	4B K 75	5B [91	6B k 107	7B { 123	8B 139	9B 155	AB 171	BB 187	CB 203	DB 219	EB 235	FB 251
0C FF 12	1C FS 28	2C , 44	3C < 60	4C L 76	5C \ 92	6C l 108	7C	124	8C 140	9C 156	AC 172	BC 188	CC 204	DC 220	EC 236	FC 252
0D CR 13	1D GS 29	2D - 45	3D = 61	4D M 77	5D] 93	6D m 109	7D } 125	8D 141	9D 157	AD 173	BD 189	CD 205	DD 221	ED 237	FD 253
0E SO 14	1E RS 30	2E . 46	3E > 62	4E N 78	5E ^ 94	6E n 110	7E ~ 126	8E 142	9E 158	AE 174	BE 190	CE 206	DE 222	EE 238	FE 254
0F SI 15	1F US 31	2F / 47	3F ? 63	4F O 79	5F _ 95	6F o 111	7F DEL 127	8F 143	9F 159	AF 175	BF 191	CF 207	DF 223	EF 239	FF 255

Screens, printers, and plotters use the characters with numbers greater than 127 for their own special purposes. They include Greek letters, mathematical symbols, or italic versions of their analogues in the lower half of the table. Sometimes Japanese characters are held here. The upper half-table control character positions may be interpreted as control characters, or optionally on some printers as block graphics characters. Screens and plotters tend to interpret these characters (128 to 159 decimal) as valid displayable characters (i.e. not control characters) anyway.

Punctuation symbols, particularly 123 to 126, but also between Z and a or between 9 and A, are varied to build up different 'National Character Sets'. These normally shouldn't confuse, but beware of 'grey imports', which may come set with the wrong national symbols, so that the printer doesn't match the screen.

In the UK, the £ symbol is often mapped to the # character 35 decimal. Sometimes, however, it is mapped to $, or the 'money symbol'.

APPENDIX 2

Differences between FORTRAN standards

FORTRAN 66	FORTRAN 77
Blanks in columns 1–72 did not imply a comment line, and could imply the initial line of a statement.	Blanks in columns 1–72 imply a comment.
Columns 1–5 of a continuation line could contain any characters, except C in column 1.	Columns 1–5 of continuation lines *must* be blanks.
Hollerith constants allowed in DATA statements and subroutine CALLs, numeric variables can (must!) appear as list elements in formatted I/O with A edit descriptors, and referencing of non-character arrays as subscripts allowed.	Hollerith constants and data are not supported. H edit descriptors allowed in FORMATs because strictly they are not Hollerith constants. (This is often relaxed as an extension)
A subscript expression can exceed the value of its corresponding upper bound in the DIMENSION statement, so long as it does not exceed the maximum total value of the array subscripts.	Individual subscript expressions within an array subscript cannot exceed the value of their upper bounds as declared in the DIMENSION statement.

Example:

```
DIMENSION X(5, 4)
Z = X(1, 6)
```

is legal in FORTRAN 66

(Bounds checking is time consuming, and where carried out, is normally only done as an option)

Two- and three-dimensional arrays can appear in an EQUIVALENCE statement with a one-dimensional subscript.	Arrays must always have the correct number of subscripts.

FORTRAN 66	FORTRAN 77

Example:

```
DIMENSION X(5,4,1),C(3,3)
EQUIVALENCE (X(7),C(1,1))
```

would be illegal in FORTRAN 77

No explicit prohibition.	The type of a name cannot be specified more than once in a program unit.
Allows extended range of a DO loop, and transfer of control into a DO loop under certain conditions.	Transfer of control into the range of a DO loop from outside is not permitted. Only DO statements can enter a DO-loop range.
Labelled END statements can conflict with the initial line of a statement.	Labelled END statements cannot so conflict.
Reading of ENDFILE records is undefined.	Records cannot be written after ENDFILE records in sequential files.
Sequential files can contain both formatted and unformatted records.	Sequential files cannot contain both formatted and unformatted records.
Negative values are allowed for variable I/O unit identifiers	Negative values for variable I/O unit identifiers are prohibited.
Allows simple I/O lists in parentheses, thereby allowing syntactic ambiguity due to complex constants in list-directed output lists.	Simple I/O lists in parentheses are not allowed. Parentheses around more than one I/O item signify an implied DO loop.
Associated entities are defined at the end of input statement execution.	Entities associated with entities in input lists are defined at the same time as the list entity.
Allows reading into H edit descriptors in FORMAT statements.	H edit (field) descriptors in a FORMAT statement cannot be read into.
Does not restrict ranges or define reasonable values.	Scale factor ranges for E, D, and G output fields are limited to defined reasonable values.

FORTRAN 66	FORTRAN 77
Requires negative zero if the internal value of a REAL or DOUBLE PRECISION value is negative.	Does not allow numeric output fields with negative zero.
Allows leading zeros.	The I edit descriptor must not produce needless leading zeroes on output.
Allows leading zeros.	The F edit descriptor must not produce needless leading zeroes on output; it can produce a leading zero for values less than one
Permits a blank instead of a + on an exponent in a D or E field to denote its sign.	Requires the + or - sign to explicitly denote the sign of an exponent in a D or E output field.
INTRINSIC function names may appear in an EXTERNAL statement.	Intrinsic function names that act as actual arguments must appear in an INTRINSIC rather than an EXTERNAL statement. The intrinsic function class includes the basic external functions of FORTRAN 66.
This condition is sufficient to remove an intrinsic function name from the intrinsic function class.	Intrinsic function names in type statements whose names conflict with those specified as standard functions are not removed from the intrinsic function class.
Has a smaller set of intrinsic functions, not including those defined opposite.	Adds the following intrinsic function names, which pose a potential conflict with subprograms: ACOS ANINT ASIN CHAR CDSH DACOS DASIN DCOSH DDIM DINT DNINT DPROD DSINH DTAN DTANH ICHAR IDNINT INDEX LEN LGE LGT LLE LLT LOG LOG10 MAX MIN NINT SINH TAN
The units of intrinsic and basic external functions' results and arguments, and their ranges, are undefined.	The units and ranges of intrinsic and basic external functions' results and arguments are specified. The specifications can differ from those used under FORTRAN 66.

FORTRAN 66	FORTRAN 77
Can be interpreted to permit more than one unnamed BLOCK DATA subprogram.	Executable program can contain only one unnamed BLOCK DATA subprogram.

The following factors can affect portability between FORTRAN 77 and FORTRAN 66 programs:

- The collating sequence is not completely specified, therefore, character relational expressions (apart from tests for equality) do not necessarily have the same value; the intrinsic functions LGE, LGT, LLE, and LLT improve this
- Certain characters in CHARACTER data, H edit descriptors, apostrophe edit descriptors, and comment lines might be acceptable to one system and not another; the use of $ as a valid character is suspect
- Procedures in languages other than FORTRAN might not (almost certainly will not!) prove portable
- Loss of ENCODE/DECODE, introduction of zero-trip DO loop
- Cannot replace Hollerith data with CHARACTER since location of storage may need changing too

Factors impairing portability across FORTRAN 77 compilers are as follows:

- Failure to implement the full FORTRAN 77 standard
- Extensions to the standard, particularly those introduced to assist mixed language programming
- Values returned via IOSTAT, or from INQUIRE options generally
- Valid options for CHARACTER variables used in OPEN statements, including file naming conventions.

APPENDIX 3

ENHANCED VT 52
ESCAPE SEQUENCES

Some MS DOS computers support an enhanced VT52-style ESCape sequence handler in their BIOS. These include early Zenith models, the Sirius 1/Victor 9000, and the Apricot family. The Sirius and Apricot support more than twice the total number of ESCape sequences shown in Table A3.1, which is a subset of the most useful and widely supported of these.

Table A3.1

ESCape sequence following the ESC character	Function
(	High intensity set
)	High intensity cancelled
0	Underlining set
1	Underlining cancelled
2	Cursor on (blink on, on Apricot)
3	Cursor off (blink off)
A	Cursor up } by one line
B	down }
C	right } by one char
D	left }
E	Clear screen
H	Home cursor to top left
J	Erase from cursor to end of screen
K	to end of line
L	Insert a line
M	Delete a line

Table A3.1 (continued)

ESCape sequence following the ESC character	Function
Y	Direct cursor addressing. Follow the ESC 'Y' with a 2-byte sequence: CHAR (31+ROW) CHAR (31+COL) to set cursor to ROW and COLumn
b	Erase from top of screen to cursor
j	Save current cursor position
k	Restore cursor to saved position
l	Erase current line
o	Erase from start of line to cursor
p	Reverse video on
q	off
v	Set 'wrap at end of line' on
w	Set to discard characters at end of line, i.e. characters at column no. greater than 80 are 'lost'
z	Reset all the terminal's functions

In addition, the following functions are likely to be supported (see Appendix 1 for the meaning of the symbols):

BEL	
BS	
HT	(8 characters)
LF	VT and FF *may* function as LF
CR	

The functions are supported by VT52.SYS, a DOS loadable device driver on the accompanying disk set.

INDEX